MOLLISON
The Flying Scotsman

HEASLIP
1/32
NEW YORK
15 min-Sketch

MOLLISON
The Flying Scotsman

Foreword by Raymond Baxter

David Luff

Lidun Publishing

'Your righteousness reaches to the skies, O God, you who have done great things. Who, O God, is like you?'

Psalm 71 v 19 (N.I.V.)

ISBN   0   9521839   0   0

First published in 1993 by:
Lidun Publishing., 63 Hall Park Drive,
West Park, Lytham St. Annes,
Lancashire, FY8 4QZ.
(Tel: 0253 733349)

Typeset by: The Wordfactory, Falmouth, Cornwall. Tel: 0326 313211

Printed by: Biddles Limited., Guildford, Surrey, England.

Contents

Foreword

The influence of childhood heroes in our adult life is a matter for psychiatrists to analyse. Doubtless it varies between individuals, but many recollections of my own childhood have survived more than sixty years with startling clarity. And writ large amongst those memories are names which have become legendary. Malcolm Campbell, George Eyston, Sir Henry Seagrave - our toy models of their successive record-breaking cars were the pride and joy of lucky little boys of my generation.

Names as much revered by many, including myself, were those of the Great Aviators. Alcock and Brown, Lindbergh, Scott and Black, Amelia Earhart and Amy Johnson (was it possible that ladies could be so brave?). And, of course, Jim Mollison.

Breathless with anxiety, I followed the progress of the epic flights of the late Twenties and early Thirties on the wireless - an excitement in itself.

Can it be mere coincidence that aviation and motor racing - not to mention radio and television - have occupied so prominent a part of my adult life?

Be that as it may, Jim Mollison had every qualification to be amongst my boyhood heroes. Even to a ten year old (when Mollison was on his way to the Cape) and certainly later as a teenager, his swashbuckling style on the ground was as enviable as his achievements in the air. Here was Biggles and Bulldog Drummond combined in a single "real-live" person. As an RAF pilot, he had flown "in action" on the fabulous NW Frontier. He broke record after record - crashed quite a lot. He was given a ticker-tape reception on Broadway. He dressed the way we would all have liked to dress. My father growled a bit about his private life, but I was too innocent to understand or care.

Later during the War, when I was less innocent and flying myself, I heard, at second hand, of some of his remarkable ATA exploits. And later still, I learned of the sorry circumstances into which he had fallen.

I am sad that I never met the man. But to everyone like me, and anyone who cares about the history of Flight, this book is the next best thing.

Raymond Baxter

Preface

This is the story of one extraordinary man. The pioneer solo aviator James Allan Mollison. A man whose ephemeral star burned brightly across the pages of aviation history in the 1930s, only to be extinguished seemingly almost without trace.

Jim Mollison's record-breaking flights made front page news during a period considered by many to be the Golden Age of aviation. The public were not only intrigued by his flying exploits but equally so by the roistering of his not-so-private life. Here was the archetypal swashbuckler. The hard-drinking womanising playboy. One who could rival even the most publicised of Hollywood's screen Lotharios. His toughness and charm vied with that of a Cagney or Bogart long before they had become cult figures. Where women were concerned the throwaway lines of Margaret Mitchell's fictional hero Rhett Butler to a tearful Scarlett O'Hara of, 'Frankly my dear, I don't give a damn', might well have been scripted just for him. The Hollywood stars acted it, whereas Mollison lived it out. Moreover, he didn't need a stuntman when the going really became tough.

Mollison also had a finely tuned talent for the *mot juste* and when interviewed by the press his pawky humour usually provided an entertaining story. The world has always admired the risk-taker and it seemed that the young Scot was purposely there at that time to satisfy the public's craving for excitement and vicarious adventure. Whether he was about to climb into the cockpit before setting out on some highly dangerous ocean flight, or when chatting at the bar of a nightclub, they knew that his dry laconic wit would go down well with their readers.

For most, his name is inextricably linked in folk-memory with the legendary aviatrix Amy Johnson. Unfortunately, their brief but turbulent marriage partnership has meant that he has always languished under the shadow of his former wife's fame. Even today when his name is mentioned, invariably will come the unintended disparagement of, 'Oh yes, I remember. Wasn't he the man who married Amy?'

This authorised biography sets out to show that Mollison was equally famous in his own right as a pioneering aviator. He was the first to make a successful trans-Sahara flight to South Africa when he set a new Cape record in 1932, and his audacious westward crossing of the North Atlantic ocean in the same year has been acknowledged by many as being one of the greatest solo flights in the history of aviation. The world had to wait another five years after Charles Lindbergh's magnificent easterly crossing of that ocean in the *Spirit of St Louis*, before anyone dared to fly it solo in the more difficult and dangerous direction.

Preface

On a westerly crossing of the North Atlantic one not only had to overcome the fuel-sapping prevailing headwinds that could bring disaster, but also to combat the notorious Newfoundland fog-banks at the end of the flight and at a time when the pilot's physical reserves were at their lowest ebb. Charles Lindbergh, never one to be taken in by the ballyhoo and hype of his age, recognised the difficulty of Mollison's flight and paid homage to the Scotsman when he visited him in New York shortly after his crossing. The American knew and acknowledged raw courage when he saw it.

Not content with a North Atlantic solo crossing, Mollison went on within six months to conquer the South Atlantic, and thereby become the only man to solo both oceans. No other pioneer aviator of his time ever made a second solo attempt on either ocean after having flown it once. It stands as a tribute to the man's bravery and sheer determination that out of the seventeen non-stop, solo crossings made between Lindbergh's 'first' in May 1927, and that of 'Crazy' Corrigan's in July 1938, Mollison made no less than *three* of them! Moreover, he risked it again in a single-engined aircraft in 1946, when he made a solo flight across the South Atlantic to deliver one of Britain's first export orders to Brazil.

Today's modern jet-passenger, sitting comfortably in the encapsulated world of a Boeing 747 as it thrusts its way across these vast oceans, has little idea of the immensity of the task that the pioneers had to face. Not for Mollison the luxury of the modern airliner with its pressurised-cabin and powerful turbo-fans enabling it to fly high above the weather hazards. He would never have dreamed of inertial navigation systems measuring velocity and distance to give him his exact position at any one time. Not for him the safety of weather-radar, ground-mapping devices and automatic landing systems that can guide an aircraft through fog-laden skies onto airport runways. Armed with but the most primitive of instrumentation, comprising of one or two compasses, a turn-and-bank indicator, altimeter, airspeed indicator and aided by a strip-map and a dubious weather-report, he, like other pioneers of that era, relied on a crude 'dead-reckoning' method of navigation. For many it often meant a heavy emphasis on the word *dead*.

As 'The Mollisons', Jim and Amy were unique in the history of aviation. No other husband and wife team, with each partner holding records in their own right, was ever more widely acclaimed by the media. Their fame and sybaritic lifestyles entranced their admiring fans and enabled them to command a public interest in Britain rivalled only by members of the royal family. They had only to appear in the royal box of the London Palladium in the early Thirties for the spotlight to beam on them, whereupon the whole auditorium would stand to applaud them. In fact their newsworthinesss was only finally eclipsed in that period when Edward, Prince of Wales, and his paramour Wallis Simpson took centre stage.

Abroad, Jim and Amy were no less popular. In 1933, after crash-landing in a Connecticut swamp at the termination of an incredible thirty-nine hour flight from Pendine to Bridgeport - the first direct flight by aeroplane from the UK to the USA - they were both awarded the Freedom of the City of New York after being given a rapturous ticker-tape welcome down its skyscraper canyons. No doubt much of their celebrity-value was due to the coincidence of their time with that of Hollywood's own Golden Age. They not only rubbed shoulders with the *glitterati* of the silver-screen, but were accepted as Britain's equivalent. As the 'Flying Sweethearts' their exploits would be sandwiched between the 'A' and 'B' movies at the local picture-palaces of the period, with the rich, mellifluous tones of Pathe Newsreels' commentator Bob Danvers-Walker detailing their arrivals and departures. This all came at the time of the Great Depression, when folk conveniently sought refuge from the drabness of their own lives in their weekly dose of escapism at the local cinema.

Jim Mollison's private life was never as successful as his professional one as an aviator. Success and his subsequent acclaim by the press spoilt him. He not only found it hard to handle fame but more tragically, relationships too. The derisive ephitets levelled at him were legion; egotist, braggart, hedonist, drunkard, alcoholic, womaniser, charmer, cad, bounder, sociopath, icono-clast, are some of them. It is true that he made a fool of himself where women were concerned - all three of his marriages ended in divorce or separation - but it seems from the accounts of those who knew him best, that there was never a willing intention on his part to inflict hurt upon others. He just marched to a different drumbeat from those around him. Decisions, agreements, appointments, even marriages, were there to be broken.

It might sound trite but there is no doubt his destructive philosophy of life was forged on the anvil of a deep-seated insecurity inherited from his early years. Winston Churchill once said that famous men are usually the product of an unhappy childhood. It was most certainly true in the case of Mollison. Having had a father who was an alcoholic, perhaps it was inevitable that he sought to suppress his fears in the same way. Paradoxically, the unsettled years of his childhood ultimately became the driving force and strength which gave him the will to succeed and to make his mark in history.

It has been said with some justification that there was a mutual exploitation between the press and Jim Mollison. Whereas on the other side of the Atlantic Charles Lindbergh shunned publicity, especially after the kidnapping of his baby son in 1932, Mollison on the other hand courted and used it. Hiding his insecurities under the persona of the hard-drinking and macho playboy, he pursued the role for all he was worth. The sharp suits, suede-shoes, perfumed toiletry and Oxford drawl were to become his stock in trade. All of this was aided by his good looks and a natural Gaelic charm, a combination to which many women succumbed. Even Warner Brothers' studios were impressed enough to offer him a role not only as a technical director to their latest flying film, but also an acting part in it. The film's leading man, Douglas Fairbanks, Jnr., was sent to New York to meet Mollison in order to cajole him into acceptance. The Scot not only knew his limitations but was unwilling to forsake the freedom he enjoyed in his flying career and therefore declined. One wonders if he ever had misgivings later in life when he realised that he had not only turned down a part with Fairbanks Jnr., but also with the actor's relatively unknown leading lady - Miss Bette Davis!

By 1936 the era of the record-breaking aviators was coming to a close, but not before Jim Mollison had established the fastest time for a crossing from New York to Croydon. War clouds were looming on the horizon and the Battle of Britain's 'few' were soon to become the ones in the limelight. The divorce between him and Amy became absolute in 1938 and he again married, this time to the wealthy socialite Phyllis Hussey. Their marriage was however a short-lived affair, his heavy drinking causing them to separate within a few months.

Strangely enough WW2 was to have a salutary effect upon Mollison. Always the patriot, he soon found in it a purpose and recognition that for the past three years had eluded him. At the outbreak of hostilities he attempted to rejoin the RAF but was rejected as being too old for flying duties. He subsequently joined the Air Transport Auxiliary as a ferry pilot, where his consummate skills as a pilot and navigator were highly valued. Amy too had joined the ATA only a few months earlier, and it was whilst delivering a twin-engined Airspeed Oxford trainer from the north of England that she perished in the Thames estuary during the early months of the war. On the day she died, Jim was ferrying a Hurricane on a short delivery flight from the Hawker factory at Langley to Aston Down. Uncannily, Amy had gone the same way as her American counterpart, Amelia Earhart. An untimely death by drowning under similarly mystifying circumstances.

During the postwar period the once famous aviator again achieved some low-key publicity by risking his neck ferrying demonstration aircraft from the UK to South America and India. Desperate for work, he convinced the manufacturer that it was cheaper to fly aircraft to their destinations rather than by shipping them there. However, the prosperous days of the Thirties were never to return for Mollison.

A further disastrous marriage to the wealthy Dutch widow Maria Kamphuis in 1948, left him living in relative poverty in a Surbiton hotel. There is no doubt that he had fully expected to die with his feet firmly on the rudder bar and by this time the ravages of alcohol had begun to take their toll and his health was rapidly deteriorating. Unable to come to terms with obscurity, and bored with his enforced idleness, he drifted deeper into the lonely world of the alcoholic. In spite of the love and unyielding devotion of his mistress, he had lost the will to live. Tragically, his death could almost be described as a lingering suicide. He died in a coma on 30 October 1959 in a Surrey nursing home at the comparatively young age of fifty-four, and the press, as if in one last gesture of a loyalty owed, gave him a brief column on their inner pages.

Amy Johnson has been embalmed in history as a legend by dying young and dying mysteriously in a wartime tragedy, whilst her erstwhile partner is remembered by few today. Hopefully, this first complete biography will help to remedy that injustice.

Chapter 1

'The Girton Excursion'

The early morning fog had lifted from the aerodrome and visibility was now good enough for the flying to start. Impeded by their heavy winter flying-suits the eager, excited pupils and their bored looking instructors made their way across the field towards the line of waiting aircraft. Recalcitrant rotary engines, damp from the chill December afternoon, coughed puffs of blue smoke as their busy mechanics coaxed and swore them into life. The day's work at RAF Duxford's Flying Training School was about to commence.

One young baby-faced novitiate was soon being briefed by his veteran instructor before he took off for his second solo flight. 'Remember, laddie you are on your own. Don't do anything stupid, and keep to the precincts of the aerodrome. Circuits only. And be back in the hour.' The eighteen year old nodded his understanding as he buttoned his helmet and stepped lively onto the footstep of the Avro's lower wing. Left foot into the toe-hold of the boarding step's cavity and he heaved himself into the rear pilot's seat, ready for the control check. Flying Officer Pearce stood clear as the square-winged biplane taxied slowly out to the misty perimeter of the aerodrome. His keen eyes noting every critical detail of the manoeuvre as the trainer turned into wind and made its take-off run. 'Not bad,' he mused, 'A bit headstrong that one. Scottish. Needs watching, but a born flier if ever there was one.' He turned to make his way towards the next Avro 504K, where there was an even greener pupil waiting to try his patience.

After one or two circuits, impeccably performed just in case he was still under the surveillance of his instructor, the sprog pilot headed north towards Cambridge. He felt sure that no one would notice if just one aircraft went missing from the procession of those doing the usual circuits and bumps in their first term. It was breaking the rules he knew, but who would find out if he made a mere twenty mile detour – just a simple cross-country flight. The magnet that drew him on was the attractive girl from Girton College, whom he had met once or twice during clandestine meetings in

Cambridge. On their last meeting he had told her to make a special note in her diary for December 11th when he would buzz the College, just two miles north west of the city.

Life could not have been sweeter as the young Acting Pilot Officer surveyed the flat Cambridgeshire countryside through the blur of the spinning propeller. The familiar patchwork quilt of green and snuff-coloured fields, separated by their neat, black hedges and winding lanes, stretched as far as his eye could see until they merged with the misty horizon. He could pick out the railway line from London, running north to the east of Cambridge, and snaking alongside it like a silver thread, the river Cam. And then to the north-east, the Gog and Magog hills stood out as a landmark, framed in the landing wires of the biplane's starboard wing.

From 200 feet he viewed the city centre, looking for the old Roman road, the Via Devana, branching out like the spoke from a wheel and running as straight as an arrow towards Huntingdon. He knew that if he followed it for only a few miles it would lead him to his quarry. The College was an easy landmark from the air, and as he craned his neck over the side of the coaming he could see the tiny figure of his friend quite clearly. She stood on the lawn waving her scarf enthusiastically as he swooped overhead. Whow! the lads back in the Mess would never believe him when he told them this one!

The thought ran through his mind to perform a couple of loops for her benefit. After all, he had performed one over the aerodrome during his first solo only six weeks previously. However, discretion became the better part of valour and he settled for a few steep turns, sufficient to impress her. And then with a slow nonchalant salute of the hand, much as he imagined Richthofen would have given after shooting down his sixth victim of the day, he headed back towards Duxford.

Unlearned in the mysteries of compass bearings and cross-country navigation, he relied purely upon his limited skill at map-reading. It was a skill that was soon to be tested, for on the return journey the landscape took on an unfamiliar pattern. One that caused him to sweat, even in the chill air of a winter's afternoon. To make matters worse, the fog seemed to have thickened and this only added to his panic. 'Where are those damned hills, and the river Cam?' 'Am I flying towards the Fen country and Scotland, or to the south coast of England?' 'If I can only pick up the railway junction at Trumpington where the line diverges for London, then it will be easy.' What would the C.O. back at Duxford have to say if he didn't manage to find his way home? What was he going to tell his peers when he got back, if he ever did get back alive? Engine failure? They were not likely to buy that one. It could be too easily checked out by the ground staff. No doubt all of these thoughts spun around in his confused mind as he circled the fog-laden countryside for more than an hour, hopelessly lost.

What were those things he had been taught by his instructors when confronted by the necessity of a forced-landing? Establish the correct direction of the wind. Look out for smoke coming from household or factory chimneys. Look for washing on the line and note the way it was blowing. Note the position in which cows in the field were facing. Pick out a grass field which looked smooth and firm, and if it had to be a ploughed field make sure not to land across the furrows. All these pearls of wisdom were forgotten in the panic, as he closed the air and fuel-levers and made his approach towards the soft ploughed field. The even note from the nine rotating cylinders of the Le Rhone engine subsided into a gentle whine as it surrendered to the sound of the wind singing in the wires. He leaned forward in the cockpit and with his gloved hand hastily rubbed some offending oil-spots from the windscreen.

The Avro trainer flared out and its wheels touched the dirt, testing the elastic cord shock absorbers to their limit, whilst the undercarriage's wooden central landing skid began to slice through the soft, brown earth like a knife in butter. Wing tip skids squealed their protest to the accompanying tune of splintering wood and tearing fabric as the young pilot cut the ignition switches. The yellow underside of wings and fuselage rose slowly to meet the sky, as £650's worth of His Majesty's aeroplane came to rest upside down.

The perspiring youngster hung from the straps of his Sutton harness, breathing a sigh of relief that he was at least down in one piece. Thankfully, there had been no fire. His shaking hand turned off the fuel-cock, before releasing the straps and sliding from the cockpit onto the muddy field. Nothing much was bruised, apart from his ego. What would *she* have thought if she could see him now? How was he going to explain this to her? The cool damp December air started to refresh him as he removed his soft leather helmet and ruefully surveyed the crumpled machine. What now? Report to base immediately and tell them where he was, he remembered. He stumbled ignominiously across the field to the lane and made his way towards some houses nearby.

'Operator, please get me RAF Duxford, it's urgent.' An interminable silence followed, before a precise military voice enquired who he was and with whom did he exactly wish to speak.

Military voice: 'You are being put through to the Flight Commander now.'

An Avro 504K of No: 2 Flying Training School finishes upside down at RAF Duxford. Mollison's unauthorised flight to Girton College ended in a similar way.

Young pilot: 'Sir, I've landed. I'm down in a field, not far away from the aerodrome.'

Flt Cdr: 'Who the hell is that? Where are you?'

Young pilot: 'It's Mollison, sir. I got lost, sir. I'm at Balsham, about ten miles east of the aerodrome. The aircraft's damaged, it's upside down but I'm not injured at all, you see sir.'

Flt Cdr: 'You b***** fool, what are you doing over there? You are supposed to be doing circuits around the aerodrome. Wait there. We'll come and get you. And don't forget to turn the petrol off.'

The solid-tyred 3 ton RAF Crossley tender, complete with its rescue team of brown-overalled mechanics, wheezed its way into the village to find the disconsolate, young pilot waiting to guide them to the wreckage. Derisory glances were cast at the chastened young Pilot Officer as he directed them to the scene of the crime. The insolent faces of the mechanics seemed to betray their insubordinate thoughts: 'Why can't these public shoolboys with their "fraightfully" posh accents, find accessible, smooth-turfed fields in which to land? It would save us a lot of unnecessary hard work.'

The 'cortege' turned off the A505 and paused at the lowered barrier of RAF Duxford's entrance, long enough to allow the culprit time to get off. He was greeted by the duty guard with, 'The Commanding Officer would like you to report to him, sir, in his office straight away.' The Crossley tender continued towards the hangars with one slightly bent, dismantled aeroplane needing more than a few hours hard work to restore it to flying condition.

As he made his way towards the C.O.'s office his mind went back to his Glasgow Academy days. That empty, gnawing feeling in the pit of one's stomach whilst waiting to be caned came back to him. He knocked on the door and was bidden into 'the presence'.

Explanation was duly given, as best as he could muster, to the awe-inspiring WW1 veteran and Station Commander, Wing Commander Sidney Smith, DSO, who listened impassively. A long pause, and then rising from his chair the C.O. began to pace the room slowly before reminding the culprit that he had completely disobeyed orders by landing outside the gliding distance of the airfield. Furthermore, he had incurred H.M. Government and the tax-payer in the cost of several hundred pounds worth of repairs. It was no doubt more than a slight exaggeration, but effective in reinforcing the gravity of the offence. The contrite airman, now strangely dry in the throat, shifted nervously from one foot to the other as his tormentor resumed his slow pacing of the room in complete silence.

What if he were told to pack his bags and go immediately? Off the course. Off the Station. Sent back home. No more flying at the public's expense. What would his parents, grandfather and friends in Bearsden have to say about that! And then there would be the problem of getting his old job back. Employment prospects in 1923 were not exactly promising, especially in Scotland. And with a black mark from the Flying School, even worse.

Never was he more pleased than when he was dismissed from the room. He closed the door quietly behind him and with a sigh of relief made his way back to his quarters. No more had been said of his punishment. He was to be left to sweat. However much he tried to dismiss it from his mind, he could sense that a sword of Damocles was swinging uneasily over his head.

That evening in the Mess there was more than the normal amount of leg-pulling about the unauthorised cross-country flight to Girton. Would 'sir' be visiting any of his London girlfriends in a similar way? Perhaps a landing in Regents Park next time, eh? It would no doubt be a welcome break for the Motor Transport section boys. They would appreciate doing a recovery near the bright lights, rather than to these boring old Cambridgeshire villages.

Meanwhile, the Duxford delinquent downed just one more than his usual quota of whisky and sodas before turning in for the night. Relaxed by the infusion of alcohol, he was probably soon slumbering under the sheets in a fanciful world of aeroplanes and pretty Girton collegiates. Three of life's addictions were already now firmly established.

☆ ☆ ☆

That same evening in the Victorian built semi-detached residence of 85 Park Avenue, situated in one of the more prosperous middle-class suburbs of Hull, the head of the Johnson household and his wife were preparing for some important family events. Soon it would be time for Christmas celebrations, and then in January 1924 their parents' Golden Wedding. More imminently was the joyful expectation of their eldest daughter Amy's homecoming from Sheffield University, where she was in the second year of her studies for a degree in Economics. Her mother, father and sisters were probably unaware that just then she was in the first flush of a love-affair with a Swiss businessman, eight years her senior. So far it had been a liaison conducted largely through the medium of letter-writing. Little did the starry-eyed girl from Yorkshire realise that it was to last for almost six unsatisfactory years, before ending in bitter disappointment.

☆ ☆ ☆

Meanwhile, some 4,500 miles away to the west, the slim, tousled- haired youth from Detroit, Charles Augustus Lindbergh, was about to enrol as a cadet in the U.S. Air Corps Reserve. He had just enjoyed a season of barnstorming, giving $5 joy-rides in his surplus wartime Curtiss Jenny biplane to the folks in southern Nebraska. Within three short years he was to become the catalyst in the careers of the determined Scotsman, and the lovelorn undergraduate from Hull. And many others.

Chapter 2

'An Ignorant Tailor'

The Committee of Lloyd's Register of Shipping appointed three pioneering Engineer Surveyors' posts for the United Kingdom in 1874; two in England, these being in London and Liverpool, and the remaining one for the Clyde, at Greenock. For their Scottish choice they selected the well-experienced, albeit youthful James Mollison, a native of the Vale of Leven, Dumbartonshire. James had served a steady apprenticeship with James Finlayson, a well-known firm of millwrights at Gighty Burn, Angus, and following in the tradition of other gifted and adventurous expatriate Scottish engineers had, although married, subsequently sought his livelihood overseas. Upon being invited, in 1866, to accept a post as an Engineer Officer in the Imperial Ottoman Admiralty he became, in effect, a technical adviser to the Turkish Navy. He must have been quite an exceptionally gifted young man, for after four years his appointment had culminated in him being decorated by the Sultan of Turkey for 'distinguished and faithful services'.

In 1870 James returned to Victorian Glasgow with his young wife, Elizabeth (née Allan), to take up employment with the Fairfield Engine Works of John Elder & Co at Govan, on the Clyde. It was a time when the Glasgow coalfields, fortuitously allied to the local production of pig-iron, provided the resources for the rapid growth of the Clyde's shipbuilding industry – an industry that was to be without peer in the world. Britain was at the apogee of the development of its trade with the Empire as a large part of the world succumbed to pax Britannia. Empire trade meant maritime trade, and that required iron ships – lots of them, especially from the Clyde.

After a short spell as an engineer manager with George Robinson & Co, Cork, the Mollisons returned to Greenock for the Lloyd's post and there they raised their family. There were to be eight children in the Mollison household at 24 Mearns Street. Five daughters, Jean, Nora, Rachel, Katherine and Elizabeth; and three sons, Hector, Allan and Martin, the latter two dying as infants during an epidemic of diptheria. Katherine too had contracted the

7

child-killing disease and had only narrowly escaped its clutches through careful nursing. The death of their two sons made James guard his one and only son Hector, more jealously than ever. No doubt this over-protection caused the boy to be fussed over and unduly spoilt by a doting father, mother and five sisters. It was to have unfortunate consequences later on.

Although James could not trace his old Scottish surname directly back to a sept or clan, he was rather proud of his Mollison blood and dearly wanted to see the family name continue through Hector. Patronymics were the more usual form of surnames in the past, and a matronymic would normally only have been used where, for some reason or other, the father was not recognised. The name Mollison, Molison, or Mollyson, simply meant, 'son of Molly', from 'Moll', a diminutive and common pet form of Mary. If this is so, then the first record of the name was in the Derbyshire Pipe Rolls in 1204, where one, 'Walterus filius Mollie', or Molly's son, is mentioned. However, one distinguished medievalist believes that the name had a Celtic origin and is derived from the personal name Malise. It is recorded in this form in Scotland as early as the reign of David 1, circa. 1124-53. Its probable meaning in Gaelic was 'Maol Iosa', or 'tonsured servant of Jesus'. Early Scottish records confine the name to Aberdeenshire, where the principal city's town clerk in 1593 was a Thomas Molyson(e). Later records show that the name was also used further down the east coast; Francis Mollison was the member of parliament for Brechin in 1685; and David Molyson (1789 – 1834), the poet, was born in Fife.[1]

☆ ☆ ☆

Frank Robinson Addie was a wealthy young shipowner on the Clyde estuary at the turn of the century, and was the major shareholder of a line of ships running out of Greenock to all parts of the globe. More to the point, he had a very nubile sister, Thomasina, or Tommy, as she was known to her all friends. Apart from displaying all the advantages of the well-bred, her marriageability was enhanced by the fact that she was also a woman of property. She possessed quite a shrewd business head for one so young, one which enabled the impeccably mannered spinster to invest part of her dowry in bricks and mortar. Furthermore, to safeguard her investment, she had wisely arranged for her Glasgow solicitor to draw up an ante-nuptial contract when she had first started courting the young consultant engineer, Hector Alexander Mollison.

The couple were married in the spring of 1904 and settled in the prosperous suburb of Pollokshields in the county of Lanark, just two miles

Three generations of the Mollison family; grandfather James, father Hector and the infant James Allan Mollison.

south of Glasgow's city centre. Almost a year later, at 2.45pm in the afternoon of 19 April 1905, the sound of a baby's first cries were heard outside of the red-sandstoned Victorian tenement at 33 Fotheringay Road. Tommy's first and only child was to be christened, James Allan Mollison.

The arrival of a son in the family was a delight for the child's paternal grandfather and grandmother, particularly as he bore a combination of both of their surnames. The addition to the family did not however bring stability to the young couple's marriage, for it was already being stressed to breaking point by Hector's excessive drinking. Moreover, he was a man of great unpredictability. One of his less endearing habits was to invite several of his drinking partners to dinner, quite unannounced and without any forewarning to his poor wife. When drunk he could be quite violent and on one occasion he had threatened to throw his small son out of a bedroom window, and would have done so but for the timely intervention of the boy's nurse. He has been described by those who knew the family at that time, as 'a complete rotter and a drunkard'.

Being fearful for her son's safety, Tommy came to the point where she could stand her husband's behaviour no longer and she arranged for a sum of money to be settled on her alcoholic husband if he would depart from the country and leave them both alone. At first Canada was suggested as the place of his domicile, but eventually it was agreed that Hector should go to Australia on one of his brother-in-law's ships. Even when he set sail, there was to be further embarrassment for the Mollison and Addie families. Some weeks out from Greenock, Hector became bored with the monotony of the journey, and, being a close relative of one of the major shareholders and a shareholder himself, pressurised the ship's Captain to divert from his normal route and put in at a remote island. The Captain, who had been reluctantly persuaded to go ashore with the pleasure-seeking rebel, had great difficulty in getting Hector to return to the ship. As a consequence the ship was long overdue at its next port of call and was reported to the Lloyd's Register as being missing. The episode did nothing to improve relationships between the two families.

The desertion and protracted divorce proceedings were a stigma which Thomasina Mollison, with her strong Presbyterian upbringing, found hard to bear. With its accompanying loss of respectability in the eyes of one's relatives and neighbours, divorce amongst the middle-classes in Edwardian Scotland was a rarity. It was something to avoid, and the number of cases could be counted in their hundreds, not the present-day tens of thousands. Where it did occur it was usually considered to be the privilege of the aristocracy and those who could afford it. Lesser mortals who divorced were considered to be the 'black sheep' of the family. One can therefore understand Tommy's motive for moving with her child from the area. It was a move that took her across the Clyde, to the north-west of the city's centre, to a newly constructed, monolithic tenement-dwelling at 21 York Drive, Hyndland. Although now in reduced circumstances, she was able to rebuild her life, knowing that she had the family support of her married sister Ellen and sister-in-law Margaret. Both of whom had young daugters of their own and were living nearby.

It appears that on the frequent occasions when the young James Mollison was left by his mother with relatives, his arrival was not exactly greeted with approval by his young female cousins. And for a very good reason. During his visits he could leave an impression that was literally felt, for by the age of six he had acquired a nasty habit of biting his cousins' fingers. The remedy for this unsocial behaviour was swiftly administered by his own nurse, who, upon hearing of his misdemeanours and seeing it as a threat to her own employment prospects, promptly administered the cure by biting one of his fingers so hard that from thereon he kicked the habit.

One other helper in the Mollison household recalls that as he grew older, he did at least accept punishment for his misdemeanours with a certain amount of manliness and good grace. Janet Irving was employed to do washing and other domestic chores for the family, and she records that 'he was a very mischievious little boy' who occasionally got a 'skelping' from her, but to his credit was 'never a tell-tale to his mother'.[2]

Recent studies in divorce have shown that those under five, and particularly boys, tend to show greater effects of disturbance than older children. They also show that children of divorced parents may become more aggressive and demanding with their peers, thereby driving away what few friends they might have, and so making them feel even more unloved and forsaken. Readers must judge for themselves, whether these early disturbances in the aviator's childhood may have accounted for his inability to maintain intimate relationships in later life.

As the first World War approached during the late summer of 1914, the demands upon the Clyde shipyards became even more significant, with the construction of warships all along the river. Holidaymakers on the shores of the Firth were reminded of the imminence of war as they watched the Dreadnoughts steaming out for naval manoeuvres, their crews busily manning the decks. Meanwhile Glasgow's recruiting offices were being swamped by those volunteering, anxious to fight with Kitchener's army in France. Those small, stunted men from the city's slums were to be forged into a fighting force which would soon acquit itself with no little honour against the Kaiser's army.

No doubt the atmosphere of adventure engendered by these happenings was not lost on the young Mollison as he witnessed a country preparing for war. One can only conjecture on his thoughts. Did the sights and sounds of the river, a river which had transported his father to Australia and out of his life, bring a pain of heaviness to his heart? Was there emotional hurt as he contemplated his abandonment? We do know that the thought of flying filled some of the void, inspired as he was by an early reading of Claude Grahame-White's book, *With the Airmen*. He was destined to meet the pioneer aviator in 1931, whereupon he was able to tell him that not only was his the first aeroplane that he had seen in the air, but of how much the book had fired his imagination. As the war progressed, he adopted those intrepid adventurers of the Royal Flying Corps as his boyhood heroes. He admits to day-dreaming of dogfights with the illustrious members of Germany's *Jagdgeschwader* as they sought to evade the deadly and accurate guns of one small Scottish boy's SE 5A.

In March 1915, Thomasina, who had by then moved with her son a short distance away to 42 Falkland Mansions, was granted a divorce with full custody of the child from her erstwhile husband. It was given on the grounds of his desertion, and the court's affidavit showed that Hector's last known address was in Sydney, or 'elsewhere furth (sic) of Scotland'. Evidently he had taken up employment with Wildridge & Sinclair, a firm of engineering and refrigerating experts, and as far as his wife was concerned he could stay there.

Eighteen months later, her son entered form 11C of the Glasgow Academy, Colebrook Street, with Mr Hendrie as his tutor. Records do not show if he was a boarder or a day pupil but it seems more likely to have been the former for the following reason. His mother had recently met Charles Bullmore, an Engineering Lt.Cdr. in the Royal Naval Reserve, and one in whom she saw the prospect of renewed happiness. More importantly, she saw in him protection for the boy now that the war was in progress and agreements for remittance men such as Hector to stay out of the country were being broken.

The avuncular naval officer, son of Dr. Charles Forrester Bullmore of Helston, was in his early forties when he first met Mollison's mother. As a young man he had studied marine engineering in Falmouth before taking up employment in Edinburgh, and being on the naval reserve had joined up at the outbreak of war to serve on a minesweeper. The gentle, rosy-cheeked Cornishman was once described by Thomasina as a 'noble man', an epithet that often caused her son much merriment in later life. She was swift to pursue their relationship and had journeyed to Plymouth on one occasion to visit him in hospital after his ship was blown up by a mine. And so it was that on 7 September 1918, some two months before the end of hostilities, they were married at the Royal Hotel, Edinburgh. The marriage not only meant that young Mollison was to transfer from the Glasgow Academy to the one at Edinburgh, but for the next few years to he was to be known as James Bullmore.

During the summer of that year Jim was to enjoy the first of several holidays in Falmouth, staying with his step-father's cousin, Pollie Lanyon. There had been much jocular speculation in the Cornish family about Uncle Charles having 'a little widow tucked away in every port', and their curiosity was to be pleasantly satisfied when they first met Thomasina, or Aunt Tommy as she was to become known. After their first introduction, Aunt Tommy, Jim and her new husband, would arrive regularly for their summer holidays, motoring down from Scotland in Charles' baby Austin – quite an adventure in itself in those days!

Jim was more than delighted to find that he could spend the summer weeks with his host's son, Crispin, a lad near to his own age. If the weather was fine they would be driven, together with the younger cousins, Margaret and Kathleen, to nearby Gyllynvase beach, usually for a picnic. Here they would while the day away playing cricket or football, swimming, and lazing about sunning themselves on the sands. Kathleen still remembers those days, when, as a six-year old, she and her elder sister would chase the young Scot with thistles. They found him to be a light-hearted companion, never serious and always good fun. To their West Country ears, his accent, whilst never so broad that they failed to understand him, seemed enchantingly strange. They would tease him unmercifully for his 'Ach whaes' and other unaccustomed Scotticisms, all of which he would take in good part. The last visit Kathleen remembers must have been around 1922 when Jim was about seventeen. She recalls that he arrived looking terribly grown up, and proudly wearing plus-fours with rather garish, scarlet sock-tags.[3]

Back in Scotland the Bullmores settled first at 16 Park Place, and then later at 3 Dudley Terrace, Leith, where Charles was employed at the local Granton naval base. It was whilst at Granton that he became very friendly with an Admiralty overseer by the name of Fred Beales. As a consequence he and his wife, Mary, were invited to Charles and Tommy's wedding reception. A deepening friendship developed between the two families and they met quite frequently for social occasions. The Beales had two children, a son, also named Fred and of the same age as Jim, and a daughter, Betty.

Betty remembers the Bullmores coming to her home to supper where she was to meet Jim for the first time. Her recollection is that she was slightly in awe of him, as 'he seemed rather grand and sure of himself'. He was, she felt, 'a bit of a snob, very posh and a braggart'. 'Quite unlike his mother,' whom she remembers as 'a gracious, regal type of woman'.[4]

School records show that when his family decided to return to Glasgow, Jim was to leave Edinburgh Academy after only two terms and without any scholastic distinctions at all. Although Tommy was not completely bereft of family in Leith, she probably missed her closer family ties in Glasgow. Admittedly, she had a sister-in-law living nearby (Rachel Mollison had married Duncan Cran, a son of the owner of the prosperous firm of boilermakers, Cran & Somerville) but there is no evidence of any deep friendship existing between them. One can only assume therefore, that either Tommy was homesick for Glasgow, or that Charles was compulsorily transferred to an equivalent naval station on the Clyde.

No doubt Jim was glad to be back near his Mollison grandfather, who could not have been at all pleased at the young lad's change of name. The old man had by this time retired from Lloyd's and was now active in local politics as a member for Partick Central Ward. In 1917 he had been elected a River Baillie and in the following year was promoted to the Magistracy.

(Above): Engineer Lt. Cdr. Frederick Charles Bullmore, RNR.

(Below): A youthful Jim Mollison (standing on left) with his Bullmore cousins Crispin and Margaret on the beach at Maenporth Cove, Falmouth, circa. 1918.

The Bullmores returned initially to live for a short while at 388 Great Western Road, but it appears that Tommy owned 21 York Drive, for this was where the Bullmores were to eventually settle. She was quite a shrewd business woman, for even with her marriage to Charles Bullmore, she had been careful to maintain an ante-nuptial contract on her money and possessions. Perhaps it was a case of once bitten, twice shy.

Meanwhile, Jim's peripatetic childhood continued as he returned to his old school at Glasgow Academy. The constant moving from place to place, coinciding as it did with the intrusion of a step-father into his young life, did little for his emotional stability. This is evidenced from his own writings where he admits that it was at about this time that he was foolish enough to bare his soul to one of his peers on his ambitions. He confided that he wanted to become an officer in the Royal Air Force, and most probably a fighter pilot in the mould of one of his WW1 heroes into the bargain. The disrespectful confidant immediately burst into an irreverent bout of laughter, which became too much for the aspiring aviator's punctured ego to take. Fists were soon flying as the humiliated one sought his revenge, and the ensuing brawl was only brought to an end by the intervention of a vigilant prefect. Subsequently, whenever the two met again, the unrepentant sceptic would lose no opportunity to needle his victim by inquiring if the would-be airman was still 'building castles in the air'. The quarrel was only mended several years later when the two met quite fortuitously in Melbourne, whereupon the aggriever apologised, and they both enjoyed a good laugh over the whole incident. They became and remained firm friends from thereon. Jim stayed on at the Academy until 1921, admitting later that he had been a constant thorn in the side of most of his tutors.

Sometime during the next two years he dropped the Bullmore surname, with every encouragement from James Mollison senior. The original change of name had probably been a well-intentioned move by his mother in order to protect him, but no doubt it rankled in his mind and caused him a degree of humiliation. On the other side of the coin, the young Mollison must have been a constant and potent reminder to Tommy of her own failure in marriage. Unlike today, the prevailing inhibitions of that period may have denied the youngster any chance of open discussion with his mother on the subject of her divorce. As the man in him was emerging, one wonders if those early inner conflicts, which must have surely focussed upon his mother's new relationship with Charles Bullmore, had repercussions in later life. The break up of his parents' marriage and the subsequent disappearance of his father had amply demonstrated to him the fragility of even the most fundamental of relationships. It might sound trite and rather clichéd, but it did possibly set up a friction between him and his mother, which might well have had some bearing on his inability to maintain an intimate relationship with those of the opposite sex in later life. It has been said, probably not without some foundation, that a womaniser is really a woman-hater. One wonders if that trait in his character, began in his childhood.

An entry in Chambers' Biographical Dictionary shows his career upon leaving school as that of a 'consultant engineer', but at such a tender age one can only consider this to be an exaggeration. He records that his family assumed that he would go into his uncle's business at Greenock, without confirming that he ever did. One can only conclude that he spent some time in the business, but the ultimate decision on a career came on his eighteenth birthday when he announced to the family that he intended to take a commission in the RAF. Initially, it was a decision that was to be met with stiff opposition from all sides of the family, even from his grandfather. However, as time went by they relented, and it was agreed that he should apply to Cranwell for a permanent commission.

Those who knew his academic abilities best, recognised that he would stand little chance of passing the necessary examination for Cranwell. His grandfather, who wielded considerable influence in Glasgow as an ex-Baillie, began to make noises in the right quarters by suggesting that the English public schools should not be the sole recipients of RAF flying commissions. In the meantime, his mother made a direct approach to the Lord Provost of Glasgow, Sir Thomas Paxton. The outcome of the family's two-pronged attack, was that the young Mollison was nominated for a flying career in the RAF.

Jim Mollison was highly elated at the news, if a little naive about the whole affair. He was quick to rub home the point with his contemporaries, that the dull boring routine of catching a suburban train for the daily grind of a 9 to 5 office job, was not for him. Most suffered his glowing accounts of life anticipated in the junior service with a studied indifference. One or two buckled and gave him a sly satisfaction by showing a perfunctory interest. He imagined that all he must do was to wait for the call, whereupon he would don the uniform and present himself for training. It was therefore something of a shock when he received the Air Ministry's letter instructing him to present himself before a Selection Committee in London.

The young Scot was more than a little apprehensive as he travelled to London for the interview, the outcome of which would decide whether his 'castles in the air' were ever to materialise. He was acutely aware of how little he knew, for apart from a rudimentary knowledge about the theory of flight, navigation and engines, his reading had been confined to travel and adventure books.

He need not have worried, for the interviewing board were more concerned about his general standard of intelligence and knowledge, than anything specific. There came one uneasy moment however, when one of his three inquistors asked him which morning paper he read. Not being a regular reader of newspapers, he knew that it would not go down well to say as much. So, in a moment of panic, he blurted out, '*The Scotsman*, sir', hoping that that would suitably impress and deflect any further questioning on the subject. Inevitably, the original question was followed up by one asking him to tell the board about the content of that morning's editorial. Looking down to see if a hole large enough to swallow him would appear, he could only stammer a schoolboyish, 'I don't know, sir'. He remembers being dismissed from the room with a feeling of total inadequacy and anguish, wishing he had put up a better show. Anxious to restore his damaged self-esteem he left the building and made a beeline for the nearest pub, where he admits to downing his very first double whisky! It was to be the beginning of a life-long and fatal attraction. In those days the word 'alcoholism' did not appear in the dictionary.

He was more than a little relieved, when a few days later he received an official letter telling him that he had passed the interview-test and would be offered a five year Short Service Commission subject to satisfying a future medical board of his fitness. Victory was almost within his grasp but he still worried until he had presented himself to and passed the stiff medical examination. He downed his second double-whisky with greater aplomb after that occasion. It was very much a case of '*Facilis descenus Averni* – Descent to the entrance of Hell is easy'.

A letter telling him to report to No: 2 Flying Training School at RAF Duxford on 14 July 1923 duly arrived. By that date he would be aged just eighteen years and three months, making him, so he claims, the youngest serving officer in the RAF. In anticipation, he had visited a well-known Glasgow tailor and been fitted for his uniform. Already it had been worn with self-admiring approval behind the locked door of his bedroom.

It was a very proud Thomasina who stood on the platform of Glasgow's central station, whilst her son, Acting Pilot Officer James Mollison, made himself comfortable for the journey to Euston. They waved their farewells as the blast of the guard's whistle signalled the hissing steam locomotive into its first lurch towards its destination. The young officer was pleased that he had managed to find an empty carriage in which to settle, for he was still rather self-conscious about the uniform. He could see from the reflection of himself in the carriage-window that it looked embarrassingly new. He hoped that one or two soot spots and a few creases acquired on the journey would help give it a slightly more soiled acceptability.

He had the carriage to himself as far as York, whereupon an unwelcome middle-aged matron joined him. He lowered his magazine and surreptitiously lifted his eyes to assess the intruder. Took in the scene and continued to pretend to be reading. She was one of those talkative inquisitve types he thought, as he lifted the magazine even higher so that it hid his face from her. She fidgeted and fussed a bit in her seat and then asked him if he minded the window being shut. No, he didn't. Did he mind if she smoked? No, he didn't. Suddenly she leaned forward in her seat, stabbed an enquiring finger at the brevet on the breast of his tunic and said, 'You're rather young to be a qualified pilot aren't you?' He needed no reminding of his callow youth. He was well aware that he looked more like sixteen than he did eighteen. With a firm politeness, he told her that he was not a qualified pilot – yet. She was not to be deflected by this, for she then said, 'Then why are you wearing those wings on your tunic?' 'ALL officers wear these,' he explained with such conviction that she felt that she had best let the matter drop. Mollison shook his magazine with an air of exasperation, continued with his reading, and managed the rest of the journey without further interruption.

Striding purposefully out of the station at Cambridge, he looked for a cab to take him the final nine miles to Duxford. The city's taxi-drivers did a steady trade at this time of the year as they plied for custom amongst the new term pupils. Whilst waiting to be picked up, Mollison's eye was drawn to the sight and sound of a silver biplane threading its way slowly through a gin-clear sky. It sent a frisson of excitement down his spine as he considered that he too would soon be in control of a similar machine. Richthofen's ghost was about to be challenged.

Chapter 3

'Apprenticeship'

Jim Mollison paid the taxi-driver and picked up his bags to enter the austere portals of RAF Duxford. After reporting to the main gate he was ushered into the presence of the Duty Officer, whose eagle eye was immediately drawn to the unmerited brevet on the newcomer's tunic. Even before the ominous question was formed on the Flight Lieutenant's lips, he realised that his Glasgow tailor had failed him. 'Where did you learn to fly?' A pause and then, 'I've come to Duxford to learn to fly, sir.' Whereupon he was peremptorily told to remove the offending wings as soon as possible. Mollison's thoughts went back to his train-travelling companion of earlier in the day. So she was right after all. She knew more about the RAF than he did. What if he should run into her on the journey back to Scotland, whenever that might be?

Now maybe the Flight Lieutenant had not sufficiently stressed the immediacy of his instruction, or maybe the inborn intransigence of the offender prevailed, we shall never know. It appears that the young Scot found his quarters, deposited his bags, and went for a stroll around the camp before drifting into the Officers' Mess to meet other first-term arrivals.

As he entered the room there was an immediate drop in the volume of thirty chattering voices. He sensed that he had become the object of their close scrutiny, for all heads were turned towards him, especially those of the seniors who were surprised to see such a youthful qualified pilot standing in their midst. The flying course lasted twelve months and was comprised of two terms with a month's leave spaced between them. This meant that the second-term pupils, who by that time had soloed, considered themselves very much senior to their greener first-termers. It provided a pecking order that was strictly obeyed, very much, so Mollison thought, like the public school system.

Having smelt blood, three or four of the seniors appproached their unsuspecting prey and asked him the same question that he had been asked only an hour or so previously. He explained as inoffensively as he could that it was all a mistake on the part of his tailor, and that he would be removing the inappropriate brevet that very evening. He felt quite relieved when his inquistors retreated to another part of the Mess. Unfortunately, he failed to see that they were huddled together in close counsel pondering on the particular punishment that should be meted out to one who had flouted so sacred a law. A few moments later the 'criminal' was given a none too courteous tap on the shoulder and told that it had been decided by his seniors that he had committed an unforgiveable crime. He was commanded to present himself before them on the first guest night for sentencing and punishment. It had not been a very good day for his start with No: 2 FTS!

Upon enquiry, he soon discovered that he was to be sentenced to a mock court-martial, a ploy that was normally used by the seniors to extract free drinks out of unsuspecting minors who infringed the rules. He was to be allocated one of the seniors to act as his 'Defence Counsel' and he would be arraigned before the 'court' for trial. Being worried and completely ignorant about the type of punishment likely to befall him, he discreetly made enquiries from one of the more amenable seniors, only to be told that it might mean running three laps of honour around the camp in the nude. The prospect didn't exactly enthuse him.

The mock trial duly took place, much to the merriment of all the juniors and seniors present. Mollison's appointed 'prisoner's friend' put up a spirited tongue-in-cheek defence, whilst the 'prisoner' deemed it wise to keep a very low profile. As sentence was passed – two rounds of drinks for more than two dozen seniors – the defendant breathed a sigh of relief. He knew that it could have been far worse. At least the ignominy of being forced to streak naked before all and sundry had been avoided.

Amongst those present on that entertaining evening was probably one man whose future flying career was to very much parallel that of the Scot's. The six foot tall, twenty year old Londoner, Charles William Anderson Scott, had entered the RAF four months earlier than Mollison, having cut short a five year contract working on a sugar plantation in South America. Apart from being a natural born-flier, he was also a classical pianist. His father had been a Master of the King's Music, and as a consequence it was a gift he had inherited. He was also known to write poetry. Possessed as he was with a quick wit and a caustic tongue, weapons which he exercised whenever the occasion demanded, he was not a man one could easily overlook. Moreover, he was an accomplished boxer, one who was to become the RAF's heavyweight champion in the following year.

One wonders what kind of a challenge Scott must have engendered in the small-statured Celt, for there was to develop an intense rivalry between the two men over the next thirteen years. A David and Goliath confrontation. One that would continue outside of their service careers and spill over into the headlines of the world's press.

Three days after his arrival, Mollison was taken for his first flight in an Avro 504K, dual-seat trainer. Most instructors were held in god-like esteem by their pupils and for Mollison the man now sitting immediately behind him was no exception. The diminutive Flying Officer Leach was even shorter in height than his anxious pupil, and it was reputed that his piercing brown eyes did not look too kindly on any nervousness shown by his fledglings. Lack of self-confidence in the air, or lateness for lectures, quickly earned his disapproval.

As soon as the aircraft reached 2,000 feet and levelled out, the tyro placed his feet lightly upon the rudder-bar and wrapped his fingers gently around the control-column, just as he had been instructed before take-off. The muffled tones of Leach's voice came through the earphones of the Gosport communication system, commanding him to follow his mentor through the various movements of the control-column and rudder pedals, in order to get the feel of the machine. The excited youngster sensed the directional changes of attitude of the 36 foot wingspan trainer as he moved the column forward and the horizon rose between the centre section struts, and then lowered again as he brought the stick back. The port wings dropped as the column moved to his left. He was surprised how little the column had to shift to bring movement to the fabric-covered wings. And then lastly, the combined movements of right rudder pedal and column to the right brought the aircraft smoothly into a starboard banking turn. And similarly to the left for a turn to port.

It was a flight he was never to forget. Moving through the air in three dimensions. Feeling the blast from the backwash of the propeller as he moved his head slightly to one side. The smell of warm oil from the cockpit and the silky roar of the Le Rhone engine as it churned its nine cylinders in front of him. Oh what bliss.

As the biplane dipped towards the aerodrome for a landing he could see the vast expanse of the Cambridgeshire countryside spread out before him. He felt like a king surveying his empire from a mountain peak. He was hooked.

Flying was to open up a new freedom, a new beauty that he had never experienced before. It gave him a new found confidence and sense of security to which he readily responded. To his left in the cockpit's interior he could see the fuel and air-levers sliding back as his instructor weakened the mixture. The engine's note subsided into an intermittent 'brrp, brrp' as the power faded and the Avro gently stalled into a smooth three-pointer; its Palmer tyres and castoring tailskid kissing the grass simultaneously. They coasted almost to a halt before a blast from the engine with full rudder and column right back caused the aircraft to turn. Slowly they taxied back to the hangar. They had been airborne for just fifteen minutes.

A normal day's routine of training started with morning parade at 6.00am and then, weather permitting, flying would start at 6.30am and continue until 8.25am when there would be an interval for breakfast. Then more flying instruction for the rest of the morning. The afternoons were given over to lectures. Some on the theory and practice of flight, to which Mollison applied himself enthusiastically, while to others, such as meteorology, engines, aircraft rigging, Air Force law, wireless and photography, less so.

He was an apt pupil in the air, and the three instructors responsible for his training, F.O.'s, Leach, Pretty and Chief Instructor Pearce, were soon confident that the youngest member of the intake would make the grade. Once he had learned to master the rudiments of control, Leach continued by teaching him turns and gliding with the power off. And then, always a prominent feature of training in the RAF, a forced-landing in one of the pre-selected fields adjacent to the aerodrome. Landings were the most difficult part of the flying training for they were a manoeuvre which demanded good co-ordination and the ability to judge one's distance from the ground. These were given under the instruction of F.O. Pretty and involved a continuous session of landing and taking off – known as 'circuits and bumps' – around the aerodrome until the important manoeuvre was perfected. On these occasions the robustness of the Avro's undercarriage suspension was always tested to the full. Finally, came instruction in the most simple of aerobatic manoeuvres, ones which included spinning, spin-recovery and looping. Eventually the day arrived for which he and every other pupil longed. 'O.K. Mollison, that's fine, you'd better report to the Chief Instructor.'

There was always a keen rivalry amongst the members of any intake to be the first to solo, and whilst JM modestly admits that he was 'not a particularly brilliant pupil', he was by no means the last to shrug off the nursery stage. One's status immediately rose amongst the group as the restraint of dual-instruction was cast aside, and on the last day of October his turn came. His heart missed a beat as he was told to report to the Chief Instructor for a test of ability prior to going solo. A few circuits checking him out and then a landing, whereupon F.O. Pearce was satisfied.

The young Scot decided that if he was not to be the first to solo then at least he would put up a show by looping and spinning. He went into the first loop much too slowly, through not having allowed the machine to build up enough speed before bringing the column back. As the horizon dropped away beneath him the Avro hung in the sky on its propeller before lazily turning onto its back. He could feel his body drop from the seat for an inch or so as the ill-fitting straps held him, and then drop back again as the aircraft came out of the manoeuvre. He wondered why the manufacturers of Sutton harnesses didn't cater for slimly-built people like him. Regaining height, he determined to do it again, only correctly this time. Pushing the nose of the biplane down, he watched the airspeed indicator nudging 130 mph before bringing the stick back towards his stomach. The adrenalin was now pumping, and this time the centrifugal force was sufficient to keep his backside glued firmly to the bucket-seat. It was a loop that was to later earn him even the grudging praise of his instructor. And finally, a right-hand spin of two or three turns, before applying a text-book recovery of stick forward and opposite rudder, just as he had been taught.

The biplane taxied back to the hangar and eventually came to a halt on the apron as the elated pilot cut the ignition-switch. The blade of the propeller oscillated in one last blur, before coming into sharp focus as the rotary engine fell silent. Throwing his harness straps aside the young pilot levered himself up to sit on the edge of the cockpit's leather coaming. A slow smile spread across his flushed face as he pushed his goggles back and slid onto the port lower wing. As soon as his feet touched the concrete beneath him, he could sense that he was a little taller. Strangely taller than his customary five feet seven inches.

☆ ☆ ☆

Mollison soon learned that there were two important prerequisites for access to entertainment in Cambridge and for visits at the weekend to the fleshpots of London. One, was to have one's own personal transport; the other was to have money, or to know those who had it. Lifts into Cambridge were comparatively easy to get, but one could never guarantee that the return journey's car seat was not taken up by a member of the opposite sex. When this happened, it meant an expensive taxi-fare back to Duxford, and money was always a problem. Admittedly, at eighteen shillings a day, approximately £48 a day by present standards, a young Pilot Officer appeared well-off, but there were substantial Mess bills and batman's fees to be covered. In Mollison's case the owning and running of a Morgan three-wheeler which he had recently acquired, took up most of his spare cash. To run it meant having full utilisation of the car with fare-paying passengers on evening outings. Even so, he admits that most of the money spent on a night out was borrowed money, normally covered by post-dated cheques!

The Morgan was already a well-worn secondhand hack, having passed through the hands of several none too careful owners' hands before it came into his possession. However, it was put to good use, especially on the longer weekend trips to London where he and others would stay in cheap hotels, or with obliging relatives. Duxford's young RAF officers would usually make a beeline straight for the nightclubs in Soho or the West End. Obviously, the main attraction was to meet girls, and the area had more than enough to meet their need. Most of the prostitutes, or 'Fifis' as they were euphemistically known, were smartly dressed Frenchwomen. They would frequent the nightclubs and restaurants during that time, and were easily identified by the distinctive gold chains which they wore around their ankles.[5]

A great favourite with Jim Mollison and RAF officers from Duxford was the Cecil Club at Gerrard Street, popularly known as the '43 Club' by virtue of the number on its door. Here one could drink illegally beyond the permitted licensing hours, gyrate into the small wee hours on the club's miniscule dance floor and, more importantly, meet girls. The club's hostess and owner was the notorious Kate Meyrick, a rather thin and angular little woman with darting eyes that lit up when she greeted her clients. She was quite without glamour and yet was generally acknowledged as 'the undisputed Queen of London's nightclubs'. She was the daughter of an eminent Dublin doctor and had subsequently married an Irish medical student in Cork, only to separate sometime during WW1. Arriving in London in 1921 virtually penniless, and with four good-looking daughters at Roedean and two sons at Harrow to support, she had ventured into the nightclub business. The '43' was the first of a whole string of clubs that she was to own, most of which fell foul of the police at some time or other. She was sentenced to six months' imprisonment in Holloway jail in 1924, but in spite of her temporary absence her clientele continued to swell and included the Crown Prince of Sweden, Prince Nicholas of Rumania, Rudolf Valentino, Tallulah Bankhead, Jack Buchanan, Steve Donoghue, and Sophie Tucker, to name but a few.[6] The '43' had class, and was so popular with pilots from 43 Fighter Squadron at Tangmere – a crack squadron renowned for their tied-together formation flying – that by the mid-Thirties they were known throughout the RAF as 'Kate Meyrick's Own'. JM always maintained that those near sleepless weekends in London, followed by the 2am Monday morning run back up the Great North Road by the uncertain light of the Morgan's flickering acetylene lamps, laid the foundation for his long-distance record-breaking flights.

End of term exams did not come until after the Christmas-break, and Mollison recalls that cribbing, especially in the more practical subjects, was the order of the day. Excursions to Cambridge were reluctantly relegated to the back-burner as an intense period of cramming for the written-papers preceded the fateful week. Certain less colourful but more studious members of the intake suddenly found they had acquired an elevated status after they became the magnet for consultation on the more esoteric aspects of the syllabus. Although he had never been a disciplined student he was to fare moderately well overall, receiving better markings in those subjects which he considered related to flying, and less so to the more academic ones. The outcome was that after almost a month's home-leave he returned to Duxford, now a senior, to await the results. Those with the highest markings and flying aptitude were designated to become fighter pilots on the then current Sopwith Snipes; the next category would go to single-engined bombers, such as the DH 9A's and Bristol F2B's; and the remainder to the heavier type of twin-engined bombers, such as the giant Handley Page 0/400's and Felixstowe flying-boats.

The spirit of adventure was endemic in the Mollisons' blood and JM was certainly to be no exception in the family. Like his grandfather and father before him, he had itchy feet. He wanted to see the destinations of all those ships that he had watched as a small boy, steaming majestically down the Firth of Clyde. He wanted excitement. To see the world, and if possible combine it with a career in aviation. He knew that if he were to be offered a place in the top category of markings as a potential fighter pilot, then it probably meant a permanent home posting at the end of the course, for the majority of fighter stations were based in the UK. A posting into the second category, meaning light bombers, was certain to bring an overseas posting to Mesopotamia, or to India. That appealed to him. As events transpired the results showed him to be in the top category, but he immediately requested and was granted a placement into the second.

JM was on leave when confirmation was given on 14 January 1924 that he was now qualified in the rank of a Pilot Officer. Two weeks later his flying log reveals that he began training as a bomber pilot. His first familiarisation flight was under dual-instruction in an open-cockpit Bristol F2B Fighter Bomber trainer.

The F2B, or 'Brisfit', as it was affectionately known, was a well-proven old war horse developed in 1916 to combat the onslaught of Germany's

Jagdstaffeln on the Western Front. It was considered to be one of the most successful military machines ever to participate in WW1. In spite of carrying its observer/gunner in the rear seat, it had the manoeuvreability and aerobatic qualities of a single-seat fighter. Its offensive armament consisted of a single 0.303in Vickers gun synchronised to fire through the propeller, and a Scarff ring-mounted Lewis gun operated by the second member of the crew from the rear cockpit. Altogether a deadly combination for its time. Moreover, as he was to eventually discover in India, in its later Mark 1V versions it could be equipped to carry two 112 lb bombs.

The eighteen year old must have felt more than a tinge of pride when, just three days after his first introduction to the celebrated war-machine, he was allowed to go solo on a twenty minute flight. From now on it was goodbye to basic Avro trainers. What scorn might be heaped upon the head of his erstwhile Glasgow school friend when next they met! Aerial gunnery instruction was to follow, which, if live ammunition rather than camera-guns were to be used, usually meant a lengthy trip to the Air Firing Ranges at Holbeach, or Eastchurch. By mid-March his training had advanced to the stage of a seventy mile cross-country flight using a simple triangulated course of Duxford, Huntingdon, Hitchin, and back to base. It was the first of three such flights required for passing out.

Although the aerial part of Mollison's training appealed to his adventurous instincts, the discipline and regulatory mode of military life did not. Saluting, parades, correct style of dress, and compulsory Church attendance on a Sunday he found irksome. Many and varied were the unsuccessful attempts to wriggle out of the latter chore, and he was to call to mind with great relish the experience of one of his Cambridge under-graduate friends who sought a similar evasion. This young man attempted to be excused attendance at chapel by declaring himself from the outset of term to be a 'sun-worshipper'. Preening himself after the first week on having found a perfect loophole in the system, the unsuspecting truant was unaware that his absence had not passed unnoticed by the Dean's vigilant eye. The following Sunday he was awakened just before dawn by one of the college porters and given the message, 'Good morning sir, the Dean sends you his very best compliments and trusts that you will be in time for sunrise and your morning worship.' The incident was a powerful reminder to Mollison that any illegal deviation from his Presbyterian origins might not be treated with such leniency. In any event, he had arrived at Duxford in his first term with a written introduction to the station's Padre from a friend of his cousins, so he could hardly abscond.

Flt. Lt. Leslie Hamilton disappeared on a crossing of the North Atlantic in the Fokker F VIIa *St. Raphael* when he left RAF Upavon on 31 August 1927 with Lt. Col. F. F. Minchin and Princess Lowenstein-Wertheim.

The final exams at the end of June were tackled with far greater zeal than those of the first term, for every pupil knew that failure in these meant dismissal from any chance of becoming a qualified pilot. JM was determined to improve on the subjects in which he had failed to excel six months earlier, and the customary weekend jaunts to London were temporarily forsaken. It was a worthwhile sacrifice, for two weeks later the results showed that he had passed fairly high on the list with an overall 78% pass-mark. There was to be no greater satisfaction during the whole of his training than when he finally took his service tunic to the local tailor for the legitimate restoration of those much prized wings.

☆ ☆ ☆

Duxford's youngest qualified pilot was more than pleased when he saw that he had been posted to 24 Squadron at RAF Kenley, Surrey, for instruction in flying DH 9A's. Although he was only to be stationed there for a brief period of six weeks, the advantages of its close proximity to the capital's nightlife was fully exploited. At least the nocturnal return journey to base was less of an impediment than it had been previously.

The squadron operated primarily as a Communications Unit, its main function being to airlift military VIP's to various parts of the UK, but it was also used as a training unit. The DH 9A, or 'Ninak',* as it was more commonly known, was a lumbering, two-seat biplane day-bomber and a considerably heavier and bigger machine than JM had ever flown before. Unlike the 'Brisfit' it had not seen much WW1 action as it only entered hostilities during the war's final stages. However, it had become the standard equipment for home-based day-bomber squadrons in the postwar period, and was to remain in service until 1931. Although similar in armament to the Bristol machine, it carried a much heavier 450 lb bomb load. It was used extensively by the peacetime RAF during its overseas policy of 'control without occupation' against disruptive tribesmen in local wars, both in the near and far east.

Mollison's preparation for his first solo flight in the 46 foot span bomber was given in early August by F.O. Holly but permission had been necessary from the more senior instructor, Flt. Lt. Leslie Hamilton, before the nineteen year old was allowed to venture into the air alone. Hamilton was held in great esteem by his protégés by virtue of the swashbuckling way he could wring out the latent aerobatic qualities of the unwieldy Ninak. He would delight in low flying, hedge-hopping and corn-swishing over the fields of the southern counties, much to the consternation of some of his more nervous pupils.

Hamilton recognised a similar flamboyance in Mollison's handling of an aircraft to that of his own. At the same time there was an element of hero worship from his eager pupil, and as a consequence the two men soon became firm friends. It was to be a friendship which probably first sowed the seeds of the Scot's desire to become a pioneer in transatlantic flying.

Alcock and Brown in their flimsy Vickers Vimy bomber had been the first to make a non-stop aeroplane crossing of the North Atlantic, in 1919. It had been an eastward crossing of 16 hours' duration from coast to coast, and a first for Britain. Leslie Hamilton wanted to make it a double for his country, and thereby become the first across on the more difficult westward crossing. In order to do this he had teamed up with an experienced Imperial Airways pilot, Lieutenant-Colonel F. C. Minchin. They drew up plans for the flight and found sponsorship from the wealthy Princess Anne Lowenstein-Wertheim, daughter of the Earl of Mexborough. Her only stipulation was that she should accompany them on the hazardous flight.

Anne was in her sixtieth year when she put up the money for the flight and the venture was to be the fulfilment of her desire to be the first woman across the Atlantic. She had learnt to fly in 1914, in order to compete for the £10,000 prize offered on 1 April 1913 by the *Daily Mail* for the first

---

*A combination of 'nine' and the phonetic 'ack' for the letter 'A'.

transatlantic flight. However, the outbreak of war had prevented that particular attempt, and although she was now too old to act as co-pilot at the time of Hamilton and Minchin's proposal, she was prepared to risk her life as a passenger.

Their choice of aircraft was the Fokker monoplane *St Raphael* which was powered by a single Jupiter engine. Arrangements were made for them to depart from RAF Upavon, with Montreal as their final destination. They left the UK on 31 August 1927, and although a dubious sighting was reported in mid-Atlantic by one of the crew members of a tanker along the route, they were never to be seen alive again.

The first attempt at the more difficult westward non-stop crossing of the North Atlantic by aeroplane, had been made only four months earlier by the brave Frenchmen C. Nungesser and F. Coli. Lieutenant Charles Nungesser was already lionised as a national hero, even before the Atlantic attempt, for he had been a WW1 ace fighter-pilot with forty-five victories to his credit. The pair took off from Le Bourget, Paris, on 8 May in the Levasseur monoplane *L'Oiseau Blanc,* destined for New York. They flew off into the misty murk of that ocean's expanse, only to meet their watery graves. In spite of alleged sightings, many made long after their fuel would have given out, and after much searching by the ships of both the U.S. and French navies, no trace of them or their 'White Bird' was ever found.

Unfortunately, their deaths caused an outburst of recriminations from the French press, who alleged that valuable weather-reports had been purposely witheld from the aviators by the U.S. Weather Bureau. U.S. Ambassador Myron T. Herrick attempted to mollify the bad feelings that had been aroused, by prudently advising his own country against making further flights across the Atlantic at that time. His advice was to fall on deaf ears as far as Charles Lindbergh was concerned, for the hitherto unknown young man from Detroit shook the world when he landed at Le Bourget at 10.24pm on 21 May 1927, just thirteen days after the ill-fated Frenchmen had left it. It had been 33 hours and 39 minutes since the heavily laden wheels of his Ryan Monoplane *Spirit of St Louis* had grudgingly parted company from the muddy runway of Roosevelt Field, New York. Being the first successful solo crossing of the North Atlantic, it was to bring the American lifelong fame. Far from exacerbating any anti-American feeling, the flight was greatly applauded by the French public, who took Lindbergh to their hearts, especially since his first words upon arrival were to enquire about the results of the search for Nungesser and Coli. There is no doubt that all three flights, that of the Frenchmen, the American and that of Leslie Hamilton, made an indelible impression upon Mollison.

☆ ☆ ☆

After Mollison was considered competent to handle the DH 9A on his own, there came the time for formation flying. It was not an art that pupils mastered very easily for it required a great deal of concentration and careful judgment of distance between adjacent aircraft. A flight would consist of three machines, which would take up a vee-formation with the Flight Commander in the lead and his two wingmen on either side. The F.C. would expect his two wingmen to tuck in close, but not too much so. Naturally, the crew of the lead plane were always more than a trifle nervous in case their lesser experienced pupils came in too near and collided with them – a not uncommon incident in training flights. Such formation flying training consisted of six aircraft, or two flights, flying at an altitude of ten thousand feet for some four hours' duration. The route would normally involve a flight from Kenley, out through Surrey to Sussex, along the coast to Lympne in Kent, and then a return to the home station.

It was whilst Mollison was on one such flight, that the 400hp Liberty vee 12 cylinder engine of his DH day-bomber decided to misfire and eventually peter out, just as he was over the centre of Brighton. Remembering the ignominy of the Balsham forced-landing, he was determined to pick a good smooth grassy surface this time.

As he started to lose height, he could see what he thought was a suitable open piece of ground beneath him. However, as he came in closer he could see that it was in effect a children's playground area. Even worse, there were several mothers with prams and small children, now scattering in all directions to get out of his line of approach. Needless to say, as soon as he landed, the women began to express their disapproval of his unwelcome arrival in no uncertain terms. In spite of his explanation, some even thought that he had just landed there out of curiosity. However, by the time the police had arrived the crowd were made to disperse and a guard was placed on the machine whilst the corporal fitter set about rectifying the cause of engine failure.

In the meantime, Mollison was escorted to a telephone where he made contact with RAF Kenley to explain the situation and obtain the necessary permission for a take-off from the site. Arriving back at the machine which was now ready for flight, and about to climb into the cockpit, he spotted one small boy crouching in its interior. Unbeknown to the invigilating police-guard the adventurous little lad had slipped aboard unnoticed in order to satisfy his curiosity. A quick eviction sent the potential stowaway scurrying back into the watching crowd. No doubt he felt more than a twinge of regret as he watched the bomber and its crew lift off from the playing field and head northwards back to Kenley. Would any of his friends ever believe that he had nearly flown in an RAF bomber? At least he could tell them that he had sat at its controls!

By early September the young pilot's proficiency in handling the de Havilland war-machine was considered acceptable, but the next stage of training was one which he did not particularly relish. Familiarisation with the aircraft's armament, both offensive and defensive, was now required. This meant a none too popular eight-week posting to the lonely site of the Armament & Gunnery School, at Eastchurch in Kent.

It was whilst Mollison was at Eastchurch that he was to witness an accident which was to bring home to him the danger of handling an aircraft with less than the necessary respect it deserved. There was a well-known adage current in the RAF at the time which reminded pupils that, 'There are some old pilots, and there are some bold pilots. But there are no old, bold pilots.'

Jim Mollison was pleasantly surprised one day during the course at the Armament & Gunnery School to meet up with one of his old Duxford pals. Bailey had been with him on the same intake and had passed out with sufficiently high marks to qualify for training as a fighter pilot. Consequently, he had remained at Duxford to join 29 (Fighter) Squadron, which was equipped at that time with a single flight of Sopwith Snipes. The two men were soon catching up on all the gossip over a beer in the Mess. It transpired that Bailey had merely called in at Eastchurch on a training flight, and was due back at his home-station on that afternoon.

After lunch Mollison accompanied his friend across to the hangar where the solitary fighter stood waiting, resplendent in its aluminium-doped finish. The station's model T Ford carrying the Hucks starter trundled towards the nose of the aircraft for the driver to align its overhead shaft with the starter-dog on the end of the Snipe's propeller boss. A signal from Bailey as the tumbler switches for the ignition were flicked on and the driver engaged the clutch for the shaft to spin the airscrew. The giant rotary engine responded obediently and the propeller blurred as the Hucks' shaft disengaged and the vehicle backed away. Brown-overalled clad mechanics in their cheese-cutter peaked hats stood holding each wing tip as the propeller's backwash flattened the grass behind it. Wheelchocks were tugged aside and the Snipe slowly moved away toward the outer boundary of the airfield, turned into wind and paused before making its take-off run.

Sopwith's chief designer, Herbert Smith, had been responsible for some remarkable aircraft during WW1, notably the Sopwith Camel, a single-seat scout that was probably one of the most successful and manoeuvrable fighters of its time. By virtue of the torque reaction and gyroscopic effect of its 130 hp Clerget rotary engine, combining with a concentration of mass of engine, armament, pilot and fuel tanks within the front few feet of the fuselage, the Camel had a tendency to spin to the right almost without warning. This peculiarity could be used to good advantage in a dogfight in the hands of an experienced pilot. Whilst in the hands of an inexperienced pilot it could be, and often was, fatal.

The pugnacious Sopwith Snipe, with its more powerful nine cylinder 230 hp Bentley BR2 rotary engine, was in fact a heavier version of the Sopwith Camel. It was brute of a machine, and had inherited the same disturbing spin-characteristics as its predecessor. C. W. A. Scott, who had been posted to 'A' Flight of No: 32 (F) Squadron at RAF Kenley in December 1923, had already written off a Snipe on his very first day with the unit! At that time he had only logged just over sixty hours in the air and the 'black mark' could justifiably have been put down to inexperience. However, much more skilled pilots had been caught out by the aircraft's propensity to go into an involuntary spin. One such was the veteran ace pilot, Captain A. W. Beauchamp-Proctor, VC, who had fifty-four enemy aircraft to his credit at the end of the war. He was killed in a Snipe when it spun in whilst coming out of a loop during a practice with the Central Flying School's aerobatic team in June 1921.

Mollison watched with the critical eyes of someone in the same profession, as the snub-nosed fighter with its squadron's red XX markings between parallel bars on the sides of the fuselage, accelerated and bounced into the air from the far side of the aerodrome. It is understandable that a newly qualified, nineteen year old fighter pilot should want to show off, and Bailey was no exception. The silver fighter snarled over the hangars and pulled up in a steep climbing turn, before it suddenly stalled and entered an awesome spin, much like a dog attempting to bite at its own tail.

The spinning aeroplane hit the field and exploded in a ball of fire, sending a pall of black smoke across the now silent aerodrome. A Crossley fire-tender, with an ambulance in hot pursuit, raced out to make a belated attempt to rescue the pilot from the burning wreckage. Mollison arrived at the scene only to see the chemical-foamed form of his friend lying amongst the wreckage. Could this be the same young man, who, a few moments earlier, had been laughing, joking and giving him all the latest gossip on the social whirl in Cambridge. The nauseating stench of burning human flesh assaulted his nostrils and he turned away sick in the pit of his stomach.

Back in the gunnery class that afternoon, Mollison found it hard to concentrate as the lecturer droned on explaining the intricacies of the Vickers gun. The grisly scene that he had just witnessed was to leave its indelible and unwelcome mark on his memory for many years to come.

☆ ☆ ☆

The usual fever of activity and tension just prior to examination time that mid-October, was less pronounced at the A & G School than normal. In fact the exams were confidently awaited, for there had been a propitious leakage of the questions from a well-concealed source. Unfortunately, not a great deal of self-restraint was exercised by the fraudulent candidates, for, unwisely, each one sought to obtain a maximum pass-mark.

Within a few days the corrected papers, each showing an excess of 95% pass, were returned by the Air Ministry examiners marked, 'Excellent Liaison'. The class was assembled before an unamused Commanding Officer, who testily told them that they would be given just one week in which to revise before they were re-examined. Attempts were made to tap the same valuable source of leakage, but to no avail. No doubt the new paper was under close security of lock and key and beyond prying eyes this time. So down went all heads to the grindstone for what Mollison describes as one of the most miserable weeks of his life. By dint of riskily concentrating upon the revision of two or three questions that were almost certain to be on the paper, and fortunately they were, Mollison just managed to scrape a pass mark!

By this time, Mollison was considered to be a reasonably competent bomber-pilot, and on 10 November he was drafted to No: 39 (Bomber) Squadron, RAF Spittlegate, near Grantham, to await an overseas posting. The squadron was equipped with the ubiquitous DH 9A's and he appears to have spent most of the next six weeks perfecting what he admits was his deficiency in a formation-flying technique. His none too patient Flight Commander would gesticulate wildly if he tucked the lower wing of his biplane too close, warning him to pull away. The warnings became verbal in no uncertain terms when they landed, and he was soon aware that he had to work much harder to please his new tutor. F.C.'s varied considerably in what they deemed to be a 'tight formation'. Some were much more trusting of their wingmen's abilities than others, and were not happy unless their cohorts' lower wings were practically tapping the rear-gunner's head of the lead aircraft. Whilst others, who were more careful for their own necks, were far less demanding. However, by the time he was ready to go abroad he had evidently managed to satisfy his Flight Commander's standards.

Having had a spell of sitting in the bomber's draughty open-cockpit over the wintery Lincolnshire landscape, he was more than overjoyed when the official notification came through telling him that he was to be posted to India. After reporting to the Station's M.O. for vaccination and inoculations early in December, he was allowed to go home on embarkation leave.

Back in Glasgow he found it difficult to hide his true feelings of elation from his mother. In her eyes he was far too young to be visiting the potential trouble-spots of the Empire. She had probably read articles in the national press where they reported from time to time the incursion of warring Afghan tribesmen along the North West Frontier. Letters of protest had also appeared in newspaper columns, castigating Prime Minister Lloyd George for permitting RAF crews to fly unserviceable WW1 aircraft against such foes. However, apart from that, there appeared little danger for a peacetime RAF bomber pilot.

Tommy's mothering instinct prevailed enough for her to insist that she accompany her son down to Southampton where he was to board a troopship bound for Bombay. As the P & O ship *Assaye*, with some three hundred regular army troops and five RAF officers on board, inched away from the quayside, a misty-eyed middle-aged woman waved her sad farewell to her son. She had no idea that in less than ten years, he would return to these same docks as an international hero.

Chapter 4

'Never fly without one'

After a monotonous journey of three weeks, broken only by brief calls at Port Said and Suez for re-fuelling, the *Assaye* steamed into Bombay's harbour. Its long-suffering cargo of khaki-clad soldiers and airmen were more than pleased to disembark. By this time Jim Mollison was determined to spend some of the money he had been forced to save whilst at Eastchurch and Spittlegate, and he plumped for staying at the city's most expensive and plush establishment, the Taj Mahal Hotel. No doubt he was impressed, as many others had been before him, by its unrivalled waterfront position, one which gave its residents superb views across the bay. Built in 1903 and owned by the House of Tata, one of the most influential of Parsee families, it was considered to be the finest hotel in the whole of India. It stood majestically, almost opposite the triumphal archway of the Gateway of India, its clutch of red-tiled towers dominating the Bombay skyline.

Behaving much as any tourist might, JM set about taking in all the usual places of interest with relentless energy. A journey around the wide sweep of Back Bay brought him to Malabar Hill, giving him a vantage point for viewing the whole of the city. Nearby, he visited the famous Hanging Gardens, with its shrubs and bushes skillfully pruned into the shapes of animals and people. A little further away, shrouded discreetly in the wooded hillside, stood the Towers of Silence, where, somewhat morbidly, it was explained to him that the dead of the Parsees are lain. They were placed in a deep pit for the vultures and other birds of prey to pick their bodies clean, in order to comply with the Zorastrian religion which forbids its followers to defile earth or fire in disposing of its dead in the normal way.

Jim Mollison suffered something of a cultural shock during his short stay in Bombay, as most servicemen did when they first arrived in India. From the stark contrast of the ragged urchins' shrill cries of *backsheesh*, to the sight of sacred cows eating at will from the market's fruit-stalls, each experience left its unforgettable impression upon him. He was particularly intrigued by the professional letter-writers, erudite men who plied their trade amongst the illiterate, and charged them exorbitantly for their services. Eventually, after ten glorious days of sight-seeing, virtually at the expense of HM Government, and just as his money was beginning to run out, he received word that he was to report to Karachi to await a posting.

Since the unfortunate brevet incident which had landed him in so much trouble at Duxford, he had changed his Glasgow tailor. It was hardly a change for the better, for he soon discovered that he had been gullibly persuaded to purchase far more than the necessary accoutrements for survival in the East. Taking a friend's advice he quickly decided on a judicious sift and left the less necessary items in Bombay, where they were to remain until the end of his overseas tour.

An RAF officer's overseas tropical dress in those days consisted of the khaki Wolseley pith-helmet (commonly known as a 'Bombay bowler') with its *puggaree* headband. The latter consisted of a long length of fabric, which was wetted and then wound around the base of the hat so that it shrank into position. It was then fastened into position with a small piece of ribbon bearing the colour markings of the RAF. A khaki-drill jacket with matching shirt and black tie was worn with shorts during the daytime, and with jodhpurs for evening. Fox's puttees worn with black boots were *de rigueur* for junior officers, and calf-length field boots for the more senior ranks; whilst cane swagger-sticks were carried by all officers on formal dress occasions. The mandatory and uncomfortable spine-pads, worn ostensibly to absorb sweat and prevent sunstroke, were an anachronism from the Victorian era, but still in common usage in 1925. One further bulky item was bedding. Owing to the dictates of hygiene it was then current practice on one's travels to carry bedding complete with mosquito-net in a valise, for most Indian hotels did not supply such items.

JM had already been warned that he would be assailed by prospective native servants, or bearers as they were known to the military, as soon as he arrived on the railway station at Karachi on 26 January. He had been advised to resist their blandishments, for they usually took the form of 'chittys' or testimonials, mostly bogus, being feverishly waved under the prospective client's nose. Wisely, he waited until he had arrived at the Pilots' Pool at the RAF Depot at Drigh Road, where the station's Adjutant was able to recommend him to Mohammed Khan, one of his *bona fide* bearers, and one who was to serve him well.

In passing, it is interesting to note that T. E. Lawrence, or 'Lawrence of Arabia'* as he became known, almost followed exactly in the footsteps of Mollison. He arrived in India some two years to the day after the Scot, and was posted to Drigh Road, where he was employed as an Aircraft hand/ General Duties – a rank generally considered to be the lowliest recognised form of life in the RAF. Coincidentally, in May 1928, Lawrence even followed on to become a member of 20 Squadron's ground-support team at Peshawar.

The small, sinewy Mohammed Khan was from the fearsome pushto-speaking race of Pathans who inhabited an area along the North West Frontier Province bordering Afghanistan. Some twenty-five years older than his new young sahib, he had served with the British Army in WW1 and finished the last eighteen months of hostilities in a Turkish prisoner-of-war camp. Being immensely proud of his military background and Islamic faith, he looked with scorn upon his fellow Hindu bearers, who nervously treated him with a measured respect. His English was impeccable and he was reasonably honest, but, quite out of keeping with his religion, he did have a strong liking for liquor. It was a habit which he indulged in within the limitations of the standard sum of forty rupees, or approximately £3 per month, paid to him by the military.

Jim was always highly amused by his bearer's insistence that his new master be treated with the utmost deference by everyone. This meant that even if his master was unoccupied when a fellow officer called at his quarters on some matter of urgency, he would never be ushered in straight away. There would have to elapse a respectable period of waiting time before any visitor was allowed to enter. Mohammed was assisted by a junior bearer, and together they would carry out the most menial of tasks. It meant that they would assist in dressing and undressing an officer, even to the point of putting on or taking off his shoes and socks. Jim's mother had spoilt him as a child but never like this, and the whole business soon palled on him.

Unlike his stay in Bombay, he was to spend almost a complete month of idleness living on the station whilst he awaited a posting. Karachi he found to be a less colourful city than Bombay, and in view of a much depleted wallet was content to lead a conventional life on the depot. Apart from getting back in the air again on Ninaks and Brisfits during the mornings, and swimming in the afternoons, he was to spend most of his evenings drinking in the Club. Here, he and his colleagues would conjecture and speculate on the likelihood of location for a future posting. When he finally heard that it

*At that time he went under the pseudonym of Aircraftman T. E. Shaw.

was to be Peshawar, in what is now North West Pakistan, he was convinced that the soft life was over, and perhaps for good!

Mollison's first impressions of Peshawar, a town only some twenty-five miles east of the Afghan border, revived some of the more romanticised notions he had absorbed from a childhood reading of the Arabian Nights. Quite fortuitously as he arrived in the town, he witnessed the sight of a trail of dust-laden caravans threading their way slowly through the streets. He surmised that they were carrying their merchandise of silk from northern Afghanistan, or even Samarkand, having entered India via the Khyber Pass. However, these agreeable impressions were to be quickly dispelled, for his arrival in Peshawar at the end of February was an untimely one. Although tribal rebellions and bloodshed were not uncommon on the NWFP by any means, a new trouble had been brewing amongst one of the most warlike of Waziristan's hill-tribes – the Mahsuds. As a consequence he was posted from Peshawar to Tank* to join 20 Squadron, an operational unit which was equipped with some rather clapped out old WW1 Bristol F2B fighter/bombers.

Waziristan is an extremely mountainous, rugged country on the North West frontier of India, measuring some 160 miles in length and 60 miles in breadth, roughly about the size of the four counties comprising south-east England. Its irregular western boundary flanks Afghanistan along the Suleiman range of mountains, which rise to 11,500 feet; whilst its eastern border approaches the Indus plain down to the eastern bank of the river Indus itself. To the north lie the provinces of Kohat and Peshawar, whilst to the south stretched an area known as Baluchistan. Waziristan's three major rivers and valleys are the Tochi in the north; the Tank Zam running through the central part of the country; and in the extreme south the Wana Toi flowing into the upper Gumal.

During the conflict the six RAF Army Co-operation squadrons, nos: 5, 20, 28 and 31 equipped with Brisfits, together with bomber squadrons 27 and 60 flying Ninaks, were detailed to control the uprising. They operated out of seven or more airfields across the country. To the north were Bannu, and Dardoni/Miranshah; Razmak in the centre; Sorarogha, Tank and Dera Ismail Khan to the south. Most were situated alongside forts much reminscent of the fictional Beau Geste, and each airfield varied considerably in altitude, from Razmak's 6,600ft to that of Miranshah's 1,500ft. Temperatures fluctuated from almost freezing point when bombing from 10,000ft, down to ground figures of 123 degrees Fahrenheit in the shade – if any could be found. Drinking water had to be treated to prevent outbreaks of cholera and

---

*Pronounced 'tonk'.

dysentry, and other minor tummy bugs. To add to these hazards, pilots and soldiers also had to combat sunstroke, scorpions and sandfly-fever. In all, it was a thoroughly unpleasant place in which to be. Mollison found it altogether different from the time when he could sip a cool John Collins sundowner on the verandah of the quiet cantonment at Karachi!

The country was occupied by four chief tribes, all part of the brotherhood of the Pathans; the Wazirs, Mahsuds, Daurs and Bhittanis, each varying only in their degree of lawlessness. They would fight and feud amongst themselves whenever they were not making war against their common enemy, the infidel British Raj. Of the four tribes, the Mahsuds were by far the most violent, and it had long been held as a truism that whoever controlled the Mahsud, controlled Waziristan. They took their orders from the local mullahs and fakirs who would constantly urge them on into *jihad* (holy war), against all foreign intervention.

Two factors emerging from the 1914-18 War had encouraged the Pathan tribes to make more daring attacks upon the scout-posts dotted around the country. Firstly, they were not unaware that the European conflict had lowered the quality of the Waziristan militia now manning the forts. Secondly, since the assassination of the pro-British monarch Amir Habibullah in 1919, and accession to the Afghan throne of his son Amanullah Khan, there had been an increased political enmity towards the British rule in India. This had resulted in the outbreak of the Third Afghan War in May 1919, which in turn finally led to Britain's recognition of Afghanistan's independence by 1921. The Pathans, always sensitive to the feelings of their Afghan brothers, and spurred on by the anti-British attitude of the Bolshevik revolution in Russia, now looked more and more to Kabul for protection rather than to Simla.

Emboldened by the turn of events described, the Afghan tribes continued in the postwar years with their raids into the British administered territories, including Waziristan. This in its turn encouraged further uprisings by the Wazirs and Mahsuds, who would attack Army convoys travelling along the narrow valleys and passes. Armed with their long-barrelled *juzail* rifles of Afghanistan origin (a weapon which could out-distance any captured British-made 0.303in. Lee-Enfield), they could commmand the initiative by sniping from the mountainous heights along the routes. Using this type of guerrilla warfare the Pathan hill-tribesmen were a supreme fighting force – much as the Soviets were to find out to their cost some sixty years later during their incursion into Afghanistan. They knew the terrain intimately, and with their renowned marksmanship were a formidable enemy to be faced.

A Bristol F2B Fighter of 20 Squadron – the type flown by Jim Mollison on the North West Frontier Province in 1925.

Grudgingly, the British Army was compelled to recognise that the use of ground forces alone was insufficient, and the services of the RAF were increasingly called upon. One of the earliest examples of such co-operation was in December 1919, when the Afghanistan invaders were dealt a severe blow, in what was to become known as the Battle of Mandanna Hill. Here, for the first time in India, the RAF kept up a successful air offensive of bombing and ground-strafing over a five day period. On this occasion no aircraft were lost. However, on 14 January 1920, 20 Squadron was to suffer badly when three of its F2B's fell to accurate Pathan rifle fire, killing four of the six crew members involved. No doubt when the young Scot arrived at Tank, this particular story would have been related to him over a glass of warm beer by some senior member of the squadron. One wonders exactly what his reaction must have been. Maybe he thought that he should have opted for a home-based Snipe squadron after all.

Apart from the enemy, the climate and the topographical difficulties of the region, it would not have passed the notice of 20 Squadron's latest recruit that the ground-crew were far from happy about the condition of the aircraft they were supposed to maintain. Most of the machines had seen WW1 operational service in Europe, and it was not uncommon to see patches over bullet holes on the aircraft's fabric dating from that period. Funds for the supply of spare parts for the maintenance of aircraft were miserly, coming as they did under the Army vote, which in turn came under the parsimonious scrutiny of the Indian Government. It created a situation where the ground-crews were called upon to innovate and improvise to a large degree in order to keep the machines airworthy. As a consequence, pilot, fitter and rigger worked as a very close team. There was very little room for the niceties of rank in central Waziristan.

Historically, complaints about the shortage of aircraft spares and equipment in the postwar years had fallen on deaf ears. One who had made his views strongly known was Squadron Leader Arthur Harris, AFC, C.O. of 31 Squadron until May 1922, and later to become the renowned 'Bomber' Harris, AOC Bomber Command in WW2. He is on record as stating:

> We lacked practically everything which an Air Force squadron anywhere else would regard as essential for maintaining its aircraft. We came under the Army Vote and, as a result, we got little of everything and much of what we got was useless as, for instance, the photographic materials and chemicals, which had all deteriorated until they were no good. We had single ignition Rolls Royce Falcon engines (dependent on one contact breaker) when new dual ignition engines were being sold for a song as surplus in England![7]

Word reached the ears of Lloyd George, who immediately ordered an official inquiry, and as a result Air Vice-Marshal Sir John Salmond was sent to India. His subsequent report in August 1922 corroborated the spares' deficiences and in addition recommended the despatch of two extra squadrons to India. The latter part of the recommendation was only implemented some six years later. It meant that little had changed with respect to the airworthiness of aircraft by the time Mollison arrived on the scene in 1925.

In January 1925 the Abdur Rahman Khel ('khel' means clan) joined with Faridais and Maresai, both part of the Mahsuds, to attack army scout posts at Manzai, Spli Toi and Gomal. As a result, a conference of the Northern Command HQ commanders was convened at Rawalpindi on 20 February in order to instigate punitive strikes against the rebels. The remedy was to be carried out solely by the RAF, and without the customary army ground support. The air operations were delegated by AOC India, Air Vice-Marshall Sir Edward Ellington, to Wing Commander Richard C. M. Pink, OC No: 2 (India) Wing, in an action which was eventually to go down in the annals of RAF history as 'Pink's War'.

The strategy decided upon was one in which, initially, the rebels' cattle and crops would be targeted, the plan being to starve them into some form of submission. If such action did not prove effective, then attacks would be made upon the villagers' primitive mud-houses after giving them suitable warning to evacuate. Five days after the conference the first move was made to declare the zone covered by the tribes as a 'proscribed area'. This was achieved by dropping leaflets, usually informing the rebels that they had but forty-eight hours to clear out before the bombing commenced.

At 08.55 on 24 February, Flight Lieutenant Chamberlayne sat in the open-cockpit of Bristol F2B, F4602, with the twelve cylinders of its Rolls Royce engine ticking over at a steady 700 rpm. As he carried out the pre-flight check, he opened the throttle and watched the oil-pressure and temperature gauges register to his satisfaction. Magneto switches were flicked in and out for the rpm drop test, and the tailplane adjustment was set for take-off. Rudder, elevator and aileron movements responded satisfactorily to the controls before he raised a gloved hand, signalling the mechanic to remove the chocks. Behind Chamberlayne sat a rather apprehensive Pilot Officer Mollison, manning the ring-mounted Lewis gun on what was to be his first operational sortie. Stacked at his feet lay the neat bundles of leaflets printed in Pushto and Urdu, all ready for dropping over the side.

They taxied out to the far end of Peshawar's gravel runway and slowly turned for the take-off. There was a pause as the pilot pulled his goggles down into position before he gunned the throttle wide open. The engine responded with a full-throated roar, propelling the biplane down the runway and leaving a swirl of grey dust behind them. Within 250 yards they were airborne and climbing fast. On their starboard lay the peaks of Pir Ghal and Shuidar in the Suleiman mountain range and further in the distance the snow-capped peaks of the Hindu Kush, towering 20,000ft or more. Their destination – the dropping zone in central Waziristan – lay 150 miles to the south.

Although Mollison was a qualified pilot, the operational requirements of the North West Frontier demanded that a period of acclimatisation be given to new members of aircrew arriving on the squadrons. There were many things a new pilot needed to learn before he was allowed to risk his own life and that of any NCO gunner/observer. Firstly, Chamberlayne would emphasise the need for a rapid climb on take-off from the airfield. This was the time when the aircraft was at its most vulnerable to enemy ground fire from the surrounding hillsides, and especially so when the aircraft carried 112lb HE bombs under each side of the lower wings. He would also have taught his pupil that because of the accuracy and range of enemy rifle fire, it was necessary to maintain a height of at least 3,000ft above the terrain. This would often mean flying at an altitude of 10,000ft or more, where, on an early morning assignment, the temperature would be down to freezing.

As Mollison peered down upon the intricate pattern of twisting valleys and ravines beneath them, he soon came to realise that map-reading was not the relatively simple thing that it had been in England. Clusters of villages lay amongst those precipitous razor-backed mountains, each valley looking pretty much the same as another. Chamberlayne would remind him that accuracy of navigation was essential, for one could easily cause a diplomatic incident by straying over Afghanistan air space. One also had to become accustomed to studying aerial photographs that had been taken on previous reconnaisance flights, in order to avoid a mistake in the target. Dropping bombs, or even leaflets for that matter, on an incorrectly identified area could easily cause acute embarrassment to the Indian Government, and in turn to the military.

☆ ☆ ☆

On the morning of 9 March Aircraftman Lancaster probably cursed his luck and wondered what he had done to deserve being delegated to make a delivery flight with one of the rawest of the squadron's sprog pilots, namely Pilot Officer Mollison. Little did either men know that on that particular morning that Wing Cdr. Pink, now resident at the Operational HQ at Tank, was to order the commencement of hostilities.

Mollison was detailed to ferry a replacement Bristol F2B from Miranshah down to Tank, and he admits in his memoirs that it was his first cross-country flight with the squadron and that he became hopelessly lost. They were forced to put down at Kergi, an isolated and unmanned emergency landing ground somewhere in the north of the country, whereupon they leisurely discussed their navigational error, completely oblivious to the fact that they were now legitimate targets for any sharp-eyed Wazir or Mahsud warrior. Having decided in which direction their destination lay, they took off and climbed to 7,000ft. After flying south on a new compass-heading, they eventually sighted and landed at the airstrip alongside the barbed-wire encampment embracing the old square-towered fort at Tank.

The bombing of Mahsud villages was being carried out by the sixteen DH9s of 27 and 60 Squadrons, operating out of the Tochi Scout HQ at Miranshah. Whilst the Bristols of 5 and 20 Squadrons at Tank, backed this up with ground-strafing of cattle and the dropping of thermite incendiaries to set fire to the villagers' crops. JM was certainly uneasy, both morally and physically, about his involvement in the action. His conscience disturbed him for upon reflection there was little to be proud of in waging war against defenceless villages. It was not exactly a tale to tell one's grandchildren. Moreover, the mental stress caused by contemplating the physical dangers, was no doubt enough to cause him to seek some escape in alcohol – something for which he already had a predilection.

Apart from being hit by ground fire, there was always the added danger of engine failure, not an uncommon occurrence amongst the poorly maintained aircraft. Although parachutes had started to be issued in 1925 to some RAF units, they were not generally issued at this time on the NWFP. Even if one survived a successful forced-landing in mountainous territory, there was still the prospect of being taken prisoner by tribesmen to whom the niceties of the Geneva Convention were quite meaningless. The local inhabitants were not renowned for kindness, and torture before murder for those who fell into their hands was the norm. In any case the Pathan tribesmen had a very low threshold of provocation, even when capturing any of the infidel under less irritating circumstances than that of a punitive strike. As a palliative, the RAF attempted to counter the mutilation and murder of its personnel unfortunate enough to come down in enemy territory, by attaching a 'Protection Certificate' to their aircraft. The certificate was printed in both Urdu and Pushto, informing the reader that a handsome reward would be paid to the bearer for the safe conduct and delivery of the stranded crew-member back to his station.

Like many other pilots serving on the NWFP, Mollison had grave doubts about the efficacy of the so-called protection certificate. Even if one survived a forced-landing, what if those knife-wielding tribesmen running towards him were illiterate and unable to read anyway? Assuming all these difficulties were overcome, one had to consider whether the promise of money would appease those who only moments before had witnessed the destruction of their homes, cattle and crops, by someone they considered to be a foreign invader. It was not unknown for the unfortunate victim to be handed over to the female members of the tribe, who were quite adept at surgery without anaesthetics. Genitals would be unceremoniously removed and a portion sewn up in the victim's mouth, before eyes were gouged out to receive the two remaining spherical members – and this was before one was killed! As a consequence of these grisly practices, the certificate soon became known as a 'Gooli (Urdu for 'ball') Chit'. Understandably, one certainly never ever flew without it.

One rather amusing apochryphal story that prevailed amongst RAF aircrew at the time, concerned a red-haired Irish Corporal air-gunner who had fallen into enemy hands in an earlier campaign. Upon being captured, the distraught NCO imagined that he would be swiftly given 'the treatment' and despatched, not too slowly, he hoped, into eternity. However, he was quite surprised and puzzled to find that he was received with a great deal of friendliness. Unbeknown to him, his red hair was a sign of great respect amongst Muslims, for evidently the more religious of the faith who had made a visit to Mecca, were subsequently entitled to dye their hair/beard red and to prefix their name with the holy title *Hadji*. As a consequence, the captive was deemed by the women members of the tribe to be a valuable asset for stud purposes, so that he could sire red-haired sons. They considered that such children would not only earn a higher place in heaven, but would in turn confer great honour upon their mothers. Mollison was told, supposedly on good authority, that the Corporal was eventually recaptured and returned back to his colleagues with a certain amount of regret. One wonders if the thought of dyeing his own hair red, lingered for more than a moment in the mind of the young Scot!

One brief lull in the action came on 14 March, when JM was detailed to act as a member of the crew escorting the AOC India, Air Vice-Marshal Sir Edward Ellington, from Peshawar to Tank. The reason for the visit came about as the result of the leaders of the Mahsuds' desire for peace. They had indicated the day before at a *jirgha* (meeting) in Jandola that they wished to comply with the demands of the government's local political agents. However, the discussions soon broke down and the punitive action recommenced with further harsh bombing raids on the next day. JM's log records that he and Flying Officer Darvell escorted the AOC down to Multan, with a brief stopover at Deir Ismail Khan on the west bank of the river Indus. The following afternoon he flew the AOC's Bristol back the 165 miles to Tank.

Initially, it appears that JM was still considered too inexperienced to command an aircraft in action, for during the next six days he was to crew for F.O.'s James and Lester as their gunner/bomber. In this period they made eight raids along the Tank Zam valley, operating from 7,000ft for the bombing-runs on the mud houses and fighting towers, and down to ground level for cattle-strafing. He found that the baby incendaries were rarely effective, as the crops were far too green to burn at that time of the year. Moreover, they needed careful handling when dropped over the side. Two years earlier, an RAF gunner from 28 Squadron in action over Bakri Punga, had the bottom fall out of a box holding the incendaries. Several ignited in the cockpit and he managed to throw all but one over the side, burning his hands badly in the process. One incendiary however rolled back under the rear fuel tank, causing the pilot to hastily make a forced-landing in a rock strewn valley. The pilot and gunner luckily managed to escape from the wreckage just as it caught fire, and before the aircraft exploded.

Just how much action the Scot saw as a pilot is hard to verfiy, but he does record firing at a herd of stampeding cattle as it attempted to scramble up the banks of a dried up river-bed. On this occasion his NCO air gunner made good use of the Scarff-mounted Lewis gun at the rear to rake the hillside caves with fire. Most of the natives appear to have taken refuge in the numerous surrounding caverns when the RAF attacked, but the more brave would position themselves on the craggy mountain sides and take aim at the DH9s and Bristols as they flew up and down the valleys. RAF aircraft were not completely invulnerable, for on 21 March the Pathan sharpshooters managed to bring down one of 27 Squadron's DH9 bombers. The pilot, Flying Officer N. C. Hayter-Hames, must have been directly hit, for the Ninak immediately spun into the ground and burst into flames. The other crew-member, Flying Officer E. J. Dashwood, probably a sprog pilot under instruction much as JM had once been, was thrown clear from the inferno. Pluckily, he made a brave but unsuccessful attempt to rescue his colleague, suffering severe burns in the process.

Dashwood was taken prisoner by some Mahsuds who favoured going for the ransom reward, a sum which was speedily offered by the local political agent for the safe return of the two men. As a consequence the tribesmen did what they thought was necessary to keep him alive, and with the best of intentions poured brandy down the dying man's gullet. There was an inevitable and fatal result. Four days later the dead bodies of the two unfortunate airmen – they were to be the only fatalities throughout the mini-war – were brought to the post at Sorarogha. Mollison records that he witnessed their interment on a hot Indian afternoon at the cemetery in Dera Ismail Khan. They were buried with full military honours. He remembers their C.O. leading the prayers before the guard party fired a volley in salute of honour to the two men, and as a last gesture, a sepoy throwing a handful of dust down onto the lowered coffins. It came as a forceful reminder to the nineteen year old, that operational flying on the NWFP was indeed a dangerous business.

Wing Commander Richard Pink had himself composed a ditty entitled 'Waziristan 1925', which summed up the hazards of the campaign. Part of it went as follows:

> Oh smart Brisfit, Oh smart Brisfit
> What are you doing in fighting kit?
> I'm praying hard I'll avoid a konk
> On offensive patrols from a sink called Tank.

Chorus	*Up the gorges and down Spli Toi*
	Sniped to blazes but attaboy
	They call it war on the banks of the Marne
	But bless you its PEACE in Waziristan.

If they ask me – what shall I say
To the folks back home England way?

Chorus	*Don't you worry there's nought to tell*
	C'ept work and fly and bomb like hell
	With hills above us and hills below
	And rocks to fill where hills won't go
	Nice soft sitting for those who crash
	But WAR you call it? – don't talk trash
	War's a rumour, war's a yarn
	This is the PEACE of Waziristan.[8]

A decisive blow was struck against the Mahsud towards the beginning of April when the RAF decided to fly Wireless/Telegraphy (using the morse keyboard) equipped patrols, which were able to speedily pinpoint tribes on the move and signal back to Miranshah for immediate air-strikes. This successful tactic was supplemented by calling upon three of 31 Squadron's more seasoned pilots and their aircraft to operate night bombing sorties out of Tank. One of the veteran pilots to be engaged on the night missions was Flying Officer J. D. R. Hardman, DFC, later to become Sir Donald. He records:

> The squadron flew down to Ambala in the Punjab and civilisation in 1924 and was stationed there for the next two years. There was another punitive war in Waziristan and on this occasion it was to be left entirely to the Air Force and so to the squadrons then in the North West Frontier Province. But because of our knowledge of the Frontier we were asked to send three aircraft up there to try night bombing. Payne, Combe and I flew up to Tank in South Waziristan and did one night sortie each for ten days. Then it was over and I always said it was our squadron which did the trick.[9]

By 28 April the night bombing, aided by the light of dropped flares, had brought the rebels' leaders to the negotiating table. They called for further talks at Jandola, and three days later 'Pink's War' was officially ended. It had lasted for just 54 days, during which time the RAF had flown some 2,700 hours on operational sorties. Jim Mollison, along with 45 other officers and 214 other ranks, was awarded the silver India General Service Medal 1908 with its 'Waziristan 1925' clasp. It was to be one of the rarest Indian campaign medals ever to be issued.

Chapter 5

'The Missing Bedsteads'

One of the most rewarding aspects for Jim Mollison after his return to base after the Waziristan war, was to be back in the company of women. Any woman, no matter what the colour of her skin, was an attraction after three months' active service at Tank, where he had lived under the most primitive of conditions. He vividly recalls his first night back at Peshawar, where, returning to the station rather late and slightly the worse for too much liquor, he suddenly became aware of a desirable feminine form emerging from a doorway near to his quarters. The swish of a skirt and the slight fragrance of perfume from one of the officer's wives as she passed in the shadows aroused him. He turned and stared unashamedly as the silhouette of her figure merged into the darkness and was tantalisingly denied to him.

After making covert enquiries in order to identify the one who had evoked such predatory instincts, he was quite disappointed to find that his judgment of the previous evening had so deceived him. In the cool light of the early morning the provocative lady in question turned out to be singularly unattractive and undesirable. Even the feminine company that was on the station soon disappeared, as it was the custom from mid-May until late September for the officers' wives and their daughters to retreat to the cooler climate of the northern hill country.

Not wishing to spend the whole of his two months' leave in the summer heat of Peshawar, JM set out with Mohammed Khan in a borrowed car for RAF Barian, near Rawalpindi. The hill station was a favourite spot for those military personnel wishing to escape the worst of the season's humidity, or for those recovering from tropical illness. For JM it was a base from which to visit Srinagar, the delightful capital of Kashmir, and it was here that he records that he spent the two most glorious weeks of his whole stay in India. After teaming up with an Indian Army officer, the two men shared the hire of a house-boat on the Dhal Lake, a renowned beauty spot set amidst some of the world's most magnificent mountain scenery. The travel brochures of the day always referred to the area as the Switzerland of the Orient.

In times past the ruler of Kashmir had prevented the British from owning land in his province and as a result the expatriates had turned to the houseboat for use during the holiday season as a solution. These holiday homes were permanently moored at the lakeside and provided every comfort of the old home country. They were lavishly equipped and with a heavy emphasis on 'house' rather than 'boat' luxuries. It was not uncommon for them to contain elegant Edwardian furniture, and fine paintings hanging from their pine-clad walls. With chintz curtains at the windows, Persian rugs on the decks and the best bone china in their dining-room cabinets, they were designed to make their occupants feel that they were still back in Cheltenham!

The houseboat would have its food provided from kitchen-boats moored nearby and staffed by a plentiful supply of Kashmiri servants under the supervision of the occupant's bearer, in this case Mohammed Khan. In addition, each houseboat had its own *shikara* (gondola) tethered alongside and manned by a willing local native whenever one wanted to make explorations of the surrounding waterways. Mollison likened parts of the holiday to being on a trip to Venice, a place which he was to visit later on in his career. Warm, sunny afternoons were whiled away in the solitude of fishing and swimming, whilst the agreeably cool evenings were convivially spent yarning and swapping stories over drinks in the houseboat's lounge. It appears to have provided a lifestyle which met with the airman's complete approval. Waziristan, tribal rebellions and operational sorties seemed a million miles away. Perhaps India wasn't so bad after all!

JM returned to his home station to discover that he had been posted on a three month stint of duty to Kohat, the capital of the Punjab, some thirty miles south of Peshawar. Kohat was in the heart of Afridi country, an area occupied by another depredatory tribe of the Pathans who were at the time quite uncharacteristically living in harmony with the British military. The prospect of the move held little attraction for JM for it meant living under conditions equally as unpleasant as those he had endured at Tank, and yet without the excitement that the Waziristan campaign had provided. The only good news was that when he arrived there, he learned that he had been made up to a Flying Officer and that the promotion had been antedated to take effect five months earlier. At least it gave him a pleasant anticipation of some useful back pay.

It was whilst he was at Kohat that JM was introduced to night-flying practice. Unlike any of today's modern airports, runway lighting was practically unknown, apart from the use of the Ground Duty Officer's aldis lamp for signalling and a layout of 'Gooseneck' paraffin flares. These flares would be positioned by the ground erks* in the form of a 'T', with the head of the 'T' at right angles to the wind's direction. Once lit, the flares would enable the 'Brisfits' to taxy out, position into wind and then take off on the right hand side of the four flares forming the stem of the 'T'. From then on it was the GDO's responsibility not only to signal the aircraft when to land – on the left hand side of the 'T' – but also to re-align the flare path if there should be a change in the direction of the wind during the night.

During August, Mollison was crewing in the rear cockpit of a 'Brisfit', or the 'arse end' as it was popularly known, for Flying Officers A. F. James and Pilling on 'active operations' to various landing-grounds such as Lachi, Hangu and Razmak. These Army Co-operation duties would vary from reconnaissance flights over tribal areas, to that of making contact with army Scout posts. The 'Brisfit' was fitted with an under-fuselage pick-up hook for the retrieval of messages, or small packages, from isolated army outposts. Alternatively, the aircrew would hand-drop message bags. Neither operation was without its excitement, for the pilot would have to contend with unexpected air-pockets caused by the heat, and up-draughts from the sides of the valley as he made his approach. Either danger could be extremely nerve-wracking when flying low and within wing-scraping distance from the side of a mountain.

Another hazard with which RAF pilots had to contend was the dangers caused by sudden and unexpected changes in the weather pattern, since accurate weather forecasting was virtually unknown in those days. Dense cloud formations could close in without warning and shroud a mountain-side from the pilot's view. Four members of 20 Squadron had already been killed when two F2B's crashed under similar circumstances during air strikes on Razmak in July 1923. And then there was always the danger of dust storms, which could quite easily bring visibility down to 300 feet and make ground-tracking virtually impossible.

Having experienced some considerable time occupying the rear end of a Bristol F2B there is no doubt that Mollison would have had every sympathy for the role of the airgunner/bomber of those times. The men fulfilling this duty were all volunteers drawn from ground tradesmen of every description, and apart from an increase of six old pence in their daily rate of pay as a danger allowance, they received neither recognition nor promotion. During high-level bombing the gunner would have to hang over the starboard side of the fuselage in order to use the High Altitude Mk

---

*The term used for any airman below the rank of Corporal.

1A bomb-sight. Signals to bring the aircraft on course over the target were then made to the pilot by tapping him on the shoulder the agreed number of times, so that he would know the direction of change required. Not exactly WW2 standards!

During the latter part of 1925 Mollison succumbed to a mild attack of malaria. The usual symptoms of ague and accompanying high temperature were soon diagnosed and he was whisked off into the station's sick bay for ten days. Although it was only a comparatively mild attack, it was enough to weaken him and warrant a spell of recuperation, ostensibly as an Administrative Assistant, in the cool clear air of the Hill Depot at Barian. It was whilst he was recovering his strength there during this convalescence period that he became determined to make a move from Peshawar. Since childhood JM had militated against the boredom that comes from any routine that goes with constantly being in one place. He was born with itchy feet and destined throughout his entire life to be one of nature's wanderers. A person who craved for excitement and adventure.

Upon his arrival back at Peshawar, he heard that there was a vacancy for a test pilot at the Aircraft Park at Lahore on a six month detachment. The post was considered to be a highly desirable one and the envy of most pilots on two counts. Firstly, it meant a welcome variation from flying only one type of aircraft to that of piloting different types as they were tested before operational issue. This was carried out either after they had been assembled from knocked down kits brought over from the UK, or as they arrived from the local repair depots. Secondly, and more importantly for the successful applicant, it meant less personal military supervision and the added bonus of a location in what was considered to be the amusement centre of North Central India. Mollison thought that the post was too good to ignore and in spite of his age and relative inexperience, he put in an application.

His name was put forward by his C.O. to HQ, where he was selected along with five other applicants and placed as number three on their shortlist. As events turned out the favourite fell ill and the second choice was arrested pending a court-martial, which meant that JM set another record by becoming the youngest test pilot in the Royal Air Force. He was just four months short of his twenty-first birthday.

Mollison arrived at Lahore determined to make the most of his six months' freedom from the discipline and petty restrictions of life at Peshawar. Although the work was hard, he found it enjoyable after so much enforced idleness, and provided he tested the required number of Snipes, Ninaks, Avros and Bristols that were allocated to him, no one seemed to bother him. His job was to ensure that an aircraft was completely airworthy before it was passed on to any of the six squadrons then present in India. This meant a brief test flight of each machine, during which time he would put the aircraft through a simple series of manoeuvres, before marking the check-list for any adjustments deemed necessary.

Never one to neglect an opportunity for the social whirl, he records that he revelled in being able to spend entire evenings dancing at clubs such as *Stiffles*, where his partners varied in colour from every shade of whiteness to the darkest skin. His new found confidence as a test pilot at Lahore encouraged him to exploit to the full the cachet provided by the uniform and winged brevet. It was an open-sesame for meeting attractive Eurasian and white women, and the beginning of what one of his wartime colleagues later described as, 'Jim's hobby – girls'.

One must bear in mind that apart from nursery contact with his female cousins, he had been brought up almost exclusively outside of the world of women. His early upbringing as an only child, together with the male-orientated ethos of public schools and service life, created a formidable barrier which he had to surmount. Maybe his initiation into the mysteries of the opposite sex was made that much easier in India, than it would have been had he remained in the UK. Perhaps the dutch courage induced by his drinking was a factor that played some part, for not only did he develop more than a natural liking for the opposite sex and their company, but throughout his life they seemed to reciprocate in the most obliging way.

Apart from the admiration that his confidence as an aviator aroused, he seemed to be gifted with a strange chemistry as far as women were concerned. It was one that compounded a quiet gaelic charm with a dry self-effacing humour into an insouciance which certainly drew the ladies on. If blondes were to receive most of the blame for his later misfortunes in life, then it was not before he had worked his way through the dark-skinned brunettes.

The Eurasians, or Anglo-Indians as they were commonly called during the time of the Raj, had originated through mixed marriages and liaisons over the years between native women and British consorts. Such offspring resulted in a rather intelligent and handsome race of people. One which was extremely proud of its white blood. They were reasonably well-educated by Indian standards and spoke with impeccable English, so much so, that it was a commonly held view that they thought of themselves as being more British than the British. They tended to occupy the more responsible positions in society, in posts such as that of railway managers, or as government officials on the cantonments. Because of their 'foreign' blood, and favoured position with respect to employment, a mutual hostlity invariably existed between them and the native Indian. The Anglo-Indian would regard any Hindu or Muslim with a barely concealed contempt, and forbid their children to intermarry with them. However, their attractive and nubile daughters would consider marriage with any military white a most highly desirable prize. Strictly moral, they would only give themselves in marriage, and no doubt the prospect of a wedding-ring lingered for more than a moment in the minds of some of those who socialised with RAF officers at that time.

There is a rather charming if somewhat apocryphal story which is told concerning the Anglo-Indians' strong allegiance to their unseen mother 'homeland' in Britain – a country of which they were unlikely to have had any detailed geographical knowledge. Two young Eurasian women were conversing and one was heard to say proudly to the other in a Peter Sellers 'goodness-gracious-me' accent, 'I have an uncle living in the Liverpool cantonment and he cycles to work every day to his office in London.'

☆ ☆ ☆

By early June JM had come to the end of his six-month spell at Lahore and had accrued almost three months of unused leave. The normal annual service leave allowance was two months, but he also had the bonus of an extra month for his active service in Waziristan. He felt that he had had enough of India, and as adventure was beckoning him in the form of a possible trip to Malaya and beyond, he decided to take the whole three months in one go and sail for Singapore.

Immediately he pursued a hectic itinerary, taking in Rangoon and Penang as stopovers on the sea-journey, before spending several weeks in Singapore's ritzy Seaview Hotel. Determined to see as much as possible of the far east while he had the chance, he again set off to spend a further month in Batavia, the capital of Java, exploring the delights of its bars and nightclubs with the dedication of a veteran. It has been said with a fair degree of justification that Mollison probably fell off more bar-stools in nightclubs around the world than any other aviator of his period. Drink was to become an indispensable part of his social life, something which enabled him to meet people on his own terms. Moreover, it contributed to the then fashionable image of the flier as someone macho and devil-may-care. Little was known medically in those days about the long term dangers of alcohol abuse. It was all thought to be quite harmless fun and it dove-tailed neatly into his philosophy of living for the moment. He needed no reminder about the brevity and uncertainty of life, as Bailey's accident and as his own operational flying over the NWFP had so amply demonstrated. Furthermore, money was there to be used before it burnt a hole in the pocket and this was his favourite way of spending it.

By the time he had reached Rangoon where he had to change boats for the return journey, he was almost out of cash and unable to meet the rather heavy wine bill he had incurred during the voyage. Inwardly panicking at the thought of being arrested and placed into the local jail, he managed to maintain an unruffled air of composure as he went ashore without paying. He immediately made his way to the local military representative to whom he spun a convincing story of a lost wallet. Fortunately, the authorities sportingly took a chance and loaned him sufficient cash to save him from humiliation. However, his troubles were by no means over, for he had already left a very narrow margin to be back in time at Peshawar before his leave ran out. Murphy's law inevitably came into operation when the weather at sea turned rough, causing the ship to arrive back more than a day late at Calcutta.

The delay meant that he was eventually some thirty-six hours adrift by the time he reached his station in the north of India and immediately upon arrival he was placed under open-arrest for being absent without leave. Building upon the skill and experience that he had so recently acquired from the explanation at Rangoon, he managed to convince a sceptical C.O. that the overstay was due to factors completely beyond his control. Much to his relief the arrest was lifted, and he suffered no more punishment than being allotted additional orderley officer duties for the following month.

By this time he had completed almost twenty-one months of his three year tour of duty overseas. Quite mysteriously he relates in his memoirs that his health at that time was far from good, but strangely enough it was not for health reasons that he applied to be sent back to the UK. Even when he mentions the attack of malaria, some six years after contracting it, he goes on to add that he was never to suffer a reoccurrence from it. So at least that can be discounted as a reason for returning to the UK before his tour of duty was up. From statements he made later in his life and from his subsequent postings in England, there is every possibility that he had contracted some form of venereal disease during this leave period. He merely states in his memoirs that he had 'urgent private reasons' for returning home, and, more significantly, that he 'experienced no difficulty in obtaining permission to return to England'.[10] And so, on 28 September 1926, he left India for a home posting to Uxbridge.

☆ ☆ ☆

Back in peacetime Britain the old animosities between labour and employer which had been simmering since the end of the war were now resurfacing. The traditional export industries of coal, cotton and shipbuilding had declined under the restriction of outmoded equipment and work practices, all of which had resulted in low productivity and a lack of competiveness in world markets. At the same time, Winston Churchill's decision as Chancellor of the the Exchequer to restore Britain's financial prestige by returning the country to the gold standard a year earlier, had done little to improve matters.

In May 1926 the coal miners confronted the government head on and the pits were closed. A wave of sympathy, mainly from disillusioned ex-servicemen working in other industries, swept across the nation and three days later the country was lying paralysed in the grip of a General Strike. The strikers led by the TUC hoped to coerce the Government into submitting to the miners' demands, but the fight was to be short-lived and within eleven days they were forced to surrender unconditionally. The stubborn miners however fought on, suffering extreme hardship, until they too finally caved in at the end of the year.

No doubt such events made little impression on the pretty blonde head of the twenty-three year old secretary to the Manager of Morison's Advertising Agency, in Albion Street, Hull. She was far too occupied in the summer of that year planning a holiday to the home of her Swiss boyfriend, Franz, where she hoped that by meeting his mother, family and friends, he would finally make a proposal of marriage. They had been courting now for over two years and she had sought to overcome his diffidence towards any nuptial vows by various ploys. At Easter, quite unbeknown to her parents and sisters, they had spent an illicit 'honeymoon' weekend together in Scotland. She was impatient for an official engagement and more so since her younger sister had recently and unexpectedly announced that she was going to marry. Amy was very much conscious that friends and family frequently made guarded references to her own long 'engagement'.

Boarding the ferryboat to make her very first trip abroad, Amy wondered how she would be received by Franz's family. Would they approve of her – a foreigner? Would their strong Catholic leanings stand in her way of being accepted by them in a mixed marriage? She had already told Franz that she was prepared to forsake her Methodist upbringing – something she didn't closely adhere to anyway – if that was what was required. No doubt those sapphire blue eyes searched his face many times for some trace of his deepest feelings and emotions during that trip. How could she be sure if he loved her enough to marry her? She could only cling quietly to the hope that the holiday in Switzerland would accelerate her chances!

☆ ☆ ☆

After reporting to the RAF Depot at Uxbridge early in October 1926, JM was posted to the Electrical & Wireless School at Flowerdown, some three miles north of Winchester, as the Training Wing Adjutant*. No: 1 (T) Wireless School had been established on the site shortly after the Armistice, when there had also been a plan to build an aerodrome alongside it. This plan was abandoned in favour of an airfield at Worthy Down, some two miles further north of Flowerdown itself, and the station became exclusively the E & W School for some 350 boy entrant Aircraft Apprentices.

Although the political outlook in the country at this time was one of financial stringency and disarmament, the Chief of Air Staff, Lord Trenchard, and Secretary of State for Air, Sir Samuel Hoare, had, just two years previously, laid down plans for the expansion of the RAF. The principal part of that plan was to select and recruit high calibre men who would be capable of absorbing technical training of a complex nature. These airmen would form the *cadre* for an elite force, and one which could be rapidly expanded in time of war. The Aircraft Apprentice scheme was complementary to that plan, and proposals for recruitment were made through the Local Education Authorities to the schools for suitable applicants between the ages of 15 and 16 for three years' training. Although they were to become known by the somewhat derisive collective as 'Trenchard's Brats', they were to play a vital role in the nation's defences, both in the air and on the ground, and particularly so during the Battle of Britain.

Initially, the boy entrants reported to No: 1 School of Technical Training at RAF Halton, where they would spend a fortnight being kitted out and given basic military training. Those selected for training as Wireless Operator/ Mechanic, or Electrician, were then detailed to Flowerdown. Apart from a distinguishing red head-band worn around their peaked 'cheese-cutter' caps, and a brass wheel insignia worn on the left sleeve of their tunic, they wore the same regulation blue uniform of button-up-to-the-collar tunic, pantaloons, puttees and boots, as the regular serving airmen. Pay was paltry, even by standards for those times, at 1/6d (7p) per day, and was in fact reduced to 1/= (5p) during the late Twenties because of Government cuts in service pay! The boys received just three shillings of their weekly amount on

---

*This position was an appointment and not a rank.

pay-day, the other four shillings being deducted towards train fares for Easter, Summer and Christmas holidays.

Life at Flowerdown was hard, as hard as the MacDonald iron bedsteads upon which the boys slept, and the food was poor. They lived in unheated, stone-built dwellings with concrete floors and with six baths (not bathrooms) between the 350 lads on site. Even then baths were only allowed on 'bath night'. The Orderley Corporal went through each of the billets at 5.45am, and the occupants would be in trouble if they were not outside at 6.00am in P.T. kit for a thirty minute exercise period before going to breakfast.

Parade would be at 8.30am, whilst school commenced at 9.00am and finished at 5.00pm, with an hour for lunchbreak. The ten civilian and ex-navy tutors would instruct the lads in maths, english, technical drawing and basic electrical theory, supplemented by practical work on T21 and T32 military radio sets. In addition, they would be given regular arms drill, interspersed with marches to the rifle ranges on the other side of Winchester. And just to make sure that they were not bored during the evenings, the C.O. saw that their tutors set them plenty of homework.

Air Vice-Marshall Sir Thomas Shirley, KBE, CB., was a boy entrant at Flowerdown during this period and he recalls:

> We were instructed, drilled and administered by men who had served in World War 1 and whose ideas of discipline were, by modern standards, harsh. The old, badly sited war-time WAAF huts in which we lived were cold, damp and uncomfortable. Our pay and food were poor, our uniforms rough and often ill-fitting and, from the beginning to the end of each term, there was little respite from the weekly round of instruction, drill and fatigues. Yet our morale was high; or it could be that the very rigours of our training induced a high morale. Whichever it was, the results were good and to have been a Flowerdown Apprentice is now a source of pride to all of us.[11]

There is no doubt that the Uxbridge and Flowerdown postings were designed to impose some form of disciplinary punishment on the young Flying Officer Mollison. Exactly why they were imposed can only be left to speculation. He does record however, that on one occasion when he was in his cups – he does not say when or where – that he had struck a senior officer in the face.[12] Such an incident would have undoubtedly resulted in a court-martial, and as his RAF records do not verify any such incident one can only assume that a more lenient course of action was taken. The incident might well account for him being sent home from India. Those who served at

Flowerdown at the time do remember that he was known to have a reputation for being an impetuous and undisciplined young officer. Or more precisely, as one put it, 'he was a bit of a skate' – a fairly derogatory description in RAF terms!

Certainly the posting to Flowerdown was at that time considered to be 'out in the sticks' and would have afforded JM little of the social life to which he had become accustomed in India. One further punishment would be that he was now office bound and confined for the most part to 'flying a desk'. It would not however have kept him completely out of the air, for it was mandatory for officers who were temporarily placed in administrative posts to maintain their flying experience wherever possible. That this was so during Mollison's stay at Flowerdown is borne out by the only comment made on him by the Station Commander of the E & W School. It reads, 'Above the average as a pilot,' and is signed by Group Captain R. Peel Ross, DSO, AFC. The assessment must in all probability have come from observations made at the nearby Worthy Down aerodrome.

Apart from wearing his best uniform for the daily parade routine at 8.30am, Mollison would act principally as the C.O.'s secretary and general lackey. He recalls that he soon learned the art of delegation in order to avoid the most irksome chore, that of composing official letters commissioned by his C.O. He would make a beeline for the more experienced Orderly Sergeant and instruct him to compile a suitable letter or memo on whatever topic had happened to appear in his 'in' tray. He readily admits that it was an altogether too simple method of pulling rank, and one which gave him an easy life during the twelve weeks that he was at Flowerdown.

It took only one month of this deadening routine at the E & W School for him to put in an application for a Flying Instructor's course at the Central Flying School, RAF Wittering, making great play of his test flying experience at Lahore. Someone in authority must have felt that he had served his period of punishment for the request was granted. So it was that Mollison breathed a sigh of relief, when on 17 January 1927 he packed his bags and headed for his new station near Stamford.

☆ ☆ ☆

The CFS, with its bases at Cranwell and Wittering, has been aptly described as 'the birthplace of Britain's air power'. Its standards of instruction have been acknowledged throughout the world as being second to none, and Mollison revelled in being chosen to be at the school as a pupil-instructor. There is no doubt that his eventual reputation for polished flying and safe airmanship can be directly attributed to the training that he received whilst at Wittering. It probably taught him how little he really knew about flying, for he soon learned that when one is to teach others, then every manoeuvre in the air must faultless. The unsupervised flying at Lahore had lulled him into certain careless flying habits and he admits that on one occasion in India, when commencing a spinning test too near the ground, he had come close to killing himself.

At the end of the three months' course Mollison gained a creditable 79% pass mark and was given a B1 category with the comment: 'A keen hardworking pilot who has improved greatly on the course.' He recalls that it was the only time that he ever went into an examination room with any confidence and knowing that he had a complete mastery of his subject. Whenever pure flying was the sole criterion of Mollison's ability as an officer in the RAF, then he put his mind to it and excelled. But as far as the disciplinary niceties of service life were concerned, they were, for him, a complete turn off. Nothing illustrates this better than a comparison between the report he received at the end of his CFS course and one he was to receive a month later after he had attended a short course on the care, maintenance and packing of Irvin parachutes at Henlow. This one reads: 'This officer has learnt practically nothing; apparently through lack of application.' Maybe it was just as well that throughout his flying career, although very close to it on occasions, he never had to use a parachute!

☆ ☆ ☆

Mollison arrived at No: 5 Flying Training School, RAF Sealand, near Chester, in April, to enjoy his newly acquired status as the youngest qualified flying instructor in the service. He was acutely conscious of his youthfulness, but found that his reputation as a pilot quickly commanded the respect of his eager pupils, much as he had afforded those godlike, WW1 veteran instructors during his own initial flying training days. It amused him slightly when he found that by adopting the ploy of his old Duxford instructors, with their brusque and measured gravitas, he could more than compensate for the disadvantages of his youth when teaching men much older than himself. Geoff Wells recalls being under dual-instruction with the young Scot a few years later in Australia. Whenever he fell short of what was expected of him, he would hear Mollison's refined voice coming over the tube: 'Wells! You're all over the air. All over the air, damn you!'

That Mollison's flying skills as an instructor were never in doubt is readily confirmed by one who was at Sealand at the time:

Another instructor of the period was a Flight Lieutenant(sic) J.A. Mollison, yet to make his name as pioneer of long-distance flights, but his dead-stick landings were a by-word. In a Bristol Fighter at about 1,500 feet over the aerodrome he would switch off the engine and ease up the nose until the propeller stopped turning; then, descending in a series of side slips, he would make a three point landing on the grass, always perfectly judged so that the 'Biff', with only the drag of the tailskid to bring it to a halt, would just roll to the edge of the tarmac.

It appears that the Station Commander, Wing Commander Philip Babington, MC, AFC, – a WW1 veteran pilot – tended to turn a blind eye to the exuberance of such practices for the same writer recalls of one other instructor:

> Taking new mechanics out on a morning test, another expert of the same era was apt to taxi his aircraft to the far side of the aerodrome, point it directly at a hangar and open up. Then levelling off at 20 feet above the grass, he would hold the control column between his knees and use both hands to make leisurely adjustments to his goggles for the benefit of the quaking passenger in the back seat. The jest was rounded off by a last minute zoom over the hangar roof. 'Climbing the hangar walls' as this manoeuvre became known, was doubtless foolhardy and bad for flying discipline too.[13]

Apart from socialising in Chester at weekends, one of the favourite leisure pursuits of young officers was that of Padre-baiting. According to JM, the incumbent at Sealand came in for more than his fair share of their attentions. Someone had written to the agony aunt column of the local newspaper under the guise of a middle-aged bachelor to request the companionship of a young lady housekeeper, preferably blonde and buxom. The address for reply was duly given as the Reverend *******, c/o The Officers' Mess, RAF Sealand, Chester. In due course highly scented letters on coloured notepaper began to arrive, purportedly from those eligible, and were pinned on the notice-board for general reading. The embarrassed Padre was to be seen from time to time stealthily removing the 'incriminating' evidence and taking it back to his quarters for incineration.

The beginning of 1928 saw Mollison in the final year of his five year Short Service Commission contract. The tantalising prospect of getting his hands upon the £350 gratuity to which he was entitled upon release made him restless. By today's standards it would amount to some £18,000 – a sizeable sum in any young man's pocket. Moreover, he had come to the conclusion that with the benefit of the RAF's superb training behind him, he could do better for himself by following a career in civil aviation. It seems highly probable that even if he had wanted to remain in the service on a permanent commission, there was little chance that his disciplinary record would have warranted it being offered. And so his request to be transferred to the Reserve as a Flying Officer, Class C, four months before his term had expired, was duly granted. He drove out of the camp gates at Sealand on 14 March as a civilian; one determined to explore the waiting world.

☆ ☆ ☆

Over a six year period Amy had written more than three hundred intense and intimate love letters, comprising some 200,000 passionate words, to her Swiss lover, Franz. By the Spring of 1928 the prospect of their marriage had receded to the point where she considered that their affair was virtually over. He had cooled towards her and yet she never gave up hope. In March she sat down to pen a lengthy letter revealing her recriminations at the way he had treated her, but she was still loathe to end their relationship. Whilst her letters were forthright and uncompromising about her deepest feelings, they were tactful and would always end by leaving him a loophole. One through which he could still have the chance of affirming his intentions. It was something which he was never to do.

Amy slowly came to the realisation that she had been used. That her lover had merely toyed with her over their protracted courtship and that his interest in her had been purely sexual. It later transpired that Franz had openly admitted to friends behind her back that he had no intention of marrying her, although to her face he had never said as much. Her aspirations for true love, security and children were shattered and she was left heartbroken, but she never once gave him the satisfaction of knowing so. Their correspondence continued on the basis that they would from thereon remain as 'just friends'. At Easter, in one last gesture of defiance and one which she hoped would propel him into making a decision, she wrote and told him of her intention to learn to fly.

It was on a Saturday morning that Amy left her Maida Vale lodgings which she shared with Winifred, one of her old friends from her time at Sheffield University, and boarded an open-top London double-decker bus bound for Hendon. Upon her arrival at the famous aerodrome she found that there was little flying activity going on. Disappointed, she decided to travel on, via Golders Green, until she came to the home of the London Aeroplane Club at Stag Lane, Edgware.

Amy was quite surprised that she was not challenged for proof of club membership when she first wandered into the enclosure and sat down to watch the aircraft. After a while she plucked up enough courage to enquire from one of the pilots the procedure for learning to fly. Upon being told that she could join the club for three guineas, plus another similar sum for subscription, and then learn to fly at thirty shillings an hour, she was delighted and realised that with careful management it was just about affordable.

On the following Saturday an eager Amy again visited Stag Lane, and although she was disappointed to learn that there was to be a lengthy waiting list for flying instruction, she did decide to become an Associate Member on the spot. The month of June came and went and still she had not been near one of the club's DH Moths. Her patience finally ran out and she wrote off to the club secretary, Harold Perrin, seeking to persuade him to allow her to jump the queue, but to no avail; she had to wait her turn.

The start of Amy's remarkable flying career was a singularly inauspicious occasion, beginning as it did in the club's open-cockpit de Havilland Cirrus II Moth on 15 September. Unfortunately, an insensitive instructor had failed to note that she had been issued with a rather ill-fitting, soft leather helmet. This meant that the earphone inserts through which her tutor would communicate, came somewhere around her neck instead of her ears, and as a consequence his instructions were unintelligible during the whole of the flight. After thirty frustrating minutes in the air the puzzled instructor landed, taxied in, and his pupil was told quite curtly that she would never make a pilot.

☆ ☆ ☆

Almost two months had elapsed since Jim's discharge from the RAF when he descended the staircase of his modest Nice pension for breakfast. On the table, propped against the toast-rack, was an official OHMS letter addressed to him. It bore a London postmark and its Air Ministry contents informed him that not only was he now considered to be officially retired from the service, but, more distressingly, it told him to return to the Electrical & Wireless School at Flowerdown immediately, to clear up the matter of thirty-two bedsteads which had been reported as missing during his tenure as Wing Adjutant.

Now one might well wonder how an item as bulky as *one* Macdonald iron bedstead could ever go past the scrutiny of the camp-gate guard, let alone thirty-two of them! However, they were of an ingenious design inasmuch as they were capable of being dismantled down into just ten reasonably small components. The infamous iron bedsteads were always the subject of a humorous pun amongst RAF serviceman. It was said that they were called 'Macdonalds', not only because the name of their manufacturer was Scottish, but because they had so little 'give' in them. Perhaps it took a Scotsman like Mollison to prove them all wrong!

Chapter 6

'The Lotus Eater'

From the moment that Jim Mollison's suede-clad foot first stepped onto the busy platform of Nice's Gare de Provence in the Spring of 1928, he knew that he had found his true métier. Gone were the uncomfortable service boots and strangulating puttees, the irksome and petty disciplines of saluting and parades, all of which he had endured over the past five years. Now free of a uniform, he wanted to feel the sun warm on his back and bronzing his body. Undoubtedly he knew that he would miss the flying, but then maybe there was still the prospect of employment with one of the continental aviation firms. For the moment that could wait. There was a lot of living to be done. Before him, just waiting to be conquered, lay the elegant playground of the rich – the Cote d'Azur. It was to be the beginning of a long-lasting love affair with that particular stretch of sun-kissed coastline. Just now he meant to play it for all it was worth. At least until that substantial gratuity, now tucked neatly within the folds of his wallet, held out.

First impressions are usually the most lasting and those of his new-found paradise nestling in the foothills of the Maritime Alps were agreeably so. The clarity of its azure blue skies contrasted starkly with the grey overcast of Glasgow that he had so recently left behind. The heavy perfume and intense splash of colour from flowering jasmine, violets, mimosa and orange-blossom convinced him that this was his long-awaited Shangri-la. As dusk fell, he was captivated by the high-pitched drone of cicadas as they combined with the soothing sound of the waves gently lapping the seashore. Small wonder that Theodore de Bauville had said, whilst visiting this 'Queen of the Riviera' for the first time, '*On visite Nice pour une semaine, on y reste toute la vie.*'

Being a canny Scot and not wishing to waste money on what he considered to be non-essentials, Mollison eschewed the temptation of booking into one of the more plushy hotels along the Promenade des

Anglais, such as the 'Ruhl' or 'Negresco', and plumped for a modest *pension* near to the sea. The lodging provided basic accommmodation and had convenient access to the magnificent wide sweep of the plage facing the Baie des Anges. It was here that Mollison, ever appreciative of the feminine form and particularly so when displayed in a swim-suit, was to spend the sunshine hours of his two months' sojourn. His limitations with the French language do not appear to have inhibited him from chatting up foreign women, for he had soon teamed up with an attractive young seventeen year old named Paula. He had first spotted her languorous form stretched out on the beach whilst walking along the promenade, her one-piece backless costume amply displaying her tanned body, which curved in all the right places. What was more, her cool blue eyes and titian hair were equally as impressive as the rest of her. A conversation was struck up and before long they were drawn into the start of what was to become a whirlwind holiday romance.

Paula's parents were probably exiles in southern France, for although she spoke French fluently (JM admits that at this time his own was execrable) she was of mixed blood, part Russian and part Polish. Her knowledge of English was almost as poor as JM's incoherence in French, but to these impetuous young lovers their fascination for each other brooked all barriers of language. For the first time he had fallen deeply in love. So much so, that he was to admit in later years that it was probably the most genuine affair of his whole life. They became engaged and earnestly pledged that they would wait for each other and marry as soon as Jim had found regular employment. There had been a promise of employment as a pilot on a part-time basis with a French aviation firm, quite near to Nice, but it was never to materialise.*

Sadly, like so many holiday romances, their relationship was to be short-lived, and although he promised to return when he had found fame and fortune, he never did. Many sincere youthful tears were shed for 'Jeem' as he bade farewell to Paula in the casino on the jetty that evening. The next morning he was gone.

☆ ☆ ☆

Throughout the summer months he made what amounted to his Grand Tour of Europe. It included spending some time in Aix-les-Bains sampling one of their celebrated 'water cures' before moving on to Geneva. Upon his arrival in Switzerland, and quite by chance, he linked up with an old school

---

*It was in all probability the Marseilles based *Cie Air Union*, an airline which operated services out of the city to Paris and London, or the similarly based, *Agence Commercial Aeronautique*.

friend and together they toured the country sharing accommodation costs. However, after spending three weeks in Interlaken they discovered that their lifestyles were really incompatible. It appears that his colleague was even more addicted to carousing than Mollison, and would sleep in late until lunch time. This irked the Scot so much, that by the time they had reached Montreux they decided to split.

By now the gratuity money was dwindling fast and JM realised that he must make a more determined effort to find employment if he was to survive. In his memoirs he states that he had heard that there was the chance of a job with an Italian 'seaplane' firm near Venice. The Italian city and seaport was the home of *Trans Adriatica SA* who were using Macchi M18 civil flying-boats, it was also the base for *Navigazione Aerea Italiana,* a firm which operated a larger version of the M18. It is largely forgotten today that marine aircraft were extensively used during the interwar years on the Swiss lakes and in the Adriatic and Mediterranean regions for passenger and mail services. During the same period experimental flights were also being carried out between Paris and London with the Seine and the Thames providing landing areas. Indeed, it was not until after WW2 that the flying-boat was eventually dropped by the airlines as a commercial proposition. However, after kicking his heels in Venice for three weeks without any firm offers, JM finally gave up and made for Rapallo. Again he was unsuccessful in breaking into commercial aviation, and he finally decided that his future now lay either in Canada, Australia or New Zealand.

Glossy holiday brochures are always a dangerous item when they fall into the hands of adventurous young men, and more so when that man happens to be footloose. Mollison's eye alighted on one issued by a company called *Messageries Maritime* – a French shipping line with vessels sailing out of Marseilles to New Caledonia in the south Pacific. It did not pass unnoticed that one of its ultimate ports of call was Tahiti and that conveniently this was deemed to be an ideal stopover for those proceeding to Australia. A colourful description of the island brought back memories of his childhood reading – tales by Robert Louis Stevenson, Robert Keable and Pierre Loti. His mind was made up. Australia it should be.

He immediately journeyed back to Marseilles and visited the shipping line's offices in order to book his passage to Tahiti. One of the company's officials, a M. Tampier, was most helpful, even going so far as to give him a letter of introduction to Oscar Nordman, a leading member of the community in Papeete.

Mollison climbed the gangway of the 7,000 ton *Antinous* with one battered suitcase – his sole piece of luggage – to travel as a second-class passenger sharing a cramped cabin with a Tahitian boy and a gendarme. The creaking old trader slowly steamed out of the harbour at Marseilles early in August, with a complememt of several hundred troops on board for its six-week voyage to Tahiti. The ship had had a chequered and notorious history, having been pressed into service by the Germans as a commerce-raider during WW1. At one time she had passed undetected through British and French naval blockade lines and made for the Pacific, where she had inflicted considerable damage on Allied shipping before being captured. Now in her peacetime role, she was used to transport French troops for gaoler duties to the prison-settlement in New Caledonia.

With only one desirable, unattached female on board – an attractive Martiniquaise – the competition was tough, and JM was given little scope in which to indulge in any amatory exploits. He soon found that the only form of excitement on board was rather macabre in its nature and only for those with strong stomachs. As the ship was not equipped with the luxury of refrigeration, it meant that their only supply of fresh meat was provided by killing livestock that was carried on board. Once a week the ship's blue-aproned butcher would enter the arena of the after-deck, where a large crowd would gather to watch him in action. With a deft and skilful lunge, much like a matador delivering the *coup-de-grace*, he would swiftly despatch the poor bullock, or Algerian sheep, which had been selected for table consumption. Spectating at this rather bloody ritual of the abattoir struck Mollison as being quite uncivilised and an offence to his to Anglo-Saxon culture. If anything, it was, he considered, more akin to continental bull-fighting.

After two weeks at sea the ship arrived at the French colonies of Guadeloupe and Martinique, where it spent several days taking on fresh provisions after disembarking one or two Government officials and their wives. One further port of call was made at Colon, at the mouth of the Panama Canal, before sailing on past Panama City and out into the Pacific. From hereon the weather improved and most of the remaining three weeks were pleasantly spent sunbathing on deck, re-reading Pierre Loti, and watching the flying fish attempting to keep up with the speed of the ship.

The rusting hull of the *Antinous* slipped slowly past the coral reef and into the aquamarine smooth shelter of Papeete Bay, with JM leaning on the rail anxious for his first glimpse of Tahiti. Looking down into those pellucid blue waters he could quite easily discern the sea-bed at a depth of some thirty feet below the surface, whilst on the shoreline he could see a party of flower-bedecked natives strumming ukeleles and guitars as they waited to welcome them. As the passengers came ashore, the customary garlands of *leis* were offered with genuine warmth and a smiling sincerity that quite surprised him. He could not help being reminded of the island's rich and diverse history. Of Cook's visit in 1774, some seventy years before it was discovered by the French, and of Bligh's visit in the *Bounty*, the first British ship ever to find its way into that beautiful lagoon.

After depositing his suitcase and making a reservation at the port's one and only hotel, JM asked where he could find Oscar Nordman – the man to whom he was to deliver Tampier's letter of introduction. There was no difficulty in being directed to his quest for it appears that every one knew Oscar. He was known as the 'Man of Information', and the usual answer to a question no one else could answer in Papeete was, 'Ask Oscar, he knows.'

Although Nordman had been born in Papeete, he was of Swedish origin and had the linguistic flair of that race, which made him fluent in Tahitian, Swedish, French and English. He had started life as a steward and purser sailing on trans-Pacific passenger ships plying between San Francisco and Tahiti, and had settled on the island as a ship chandler and stevedore soon after WW1. As a consequence, he was known to most of the ships' captains and crews that visited the islands as a most useful and friendly contact.

JM was soon directed to Nordman's office situated in the quayside cafe, 'Mariposa'. It was owned by the Swede and named after one of the most famous ships on which he had served. Behind the desk sat a rather corpulent man in his mid-thirties smoking a cigar and surrounded by maritime souvenirs and momentoes from his earlier sailing days. Evidently the content of Tampier's letter was JM's passport to brotherly acceptance, for immediately after reading the Frenchman's message the smiling business-man thumbed his white fedora further back onto his head and eyed the young Scotsman up and down with approval. In a thick American accent he said, 'Any friend of Andre's is a friend of mine. So what can I do for you?'

Over post-prandial drinks JM soon discovered that Nordman was a man of shrewd intelligence and enterprise. He wielded considerable influence in Papeete, for not only did he run a fleet of cutters operating between Tahiti and the cluster of surrounding islands, such as Moorea and Bora Bora, but more to the point for the new arrival, he owned a hotel and several property estates to boot. Mollison's new found benefactor eventually suggested that the young Scot would be far more comfortable in one of his rented bungalows at Fariipiti than in the Papeete hotel. The proposition seemed even more enticing when Mollison learned that the accommodation costs of £8 per month, also included the services of one young female Tahitian housekeeper, Toi Mata.

JM gives a rather conflicting account regarding the duration of his stay on the Polynesian islands. In his first rather restrained memoir, *Death Cometh Soon or Late*, he records one month, whereas in the book's later revamped and unexpurgated version, *Playboy of the Air*, it is between two and three months. The former book is said to have been ghosted for him by the Fleet Street journalist William Courtenay in 1932, whilst its more lurid successor, written in 1937, was co-authored by Victor Ricketts, the air correspondent of the *Daily Express*. One cannot doubt however that these bungalow girls, or as JM terms them, 'transient mistresses', were part of the scene whilst he was there. Historically, over the previous one hundred years under easy going French rule, the island's morals had been notoriously lax. As one recent historian records:

> It was said that by 1840 some one hundred and fifty whalers, mostly American, put in to Tahiti every year. This meant about 3,000 hard drinking, undisciplined men, starved of sex, who at their best could not be controlled except by curses, fists and the butt end of a handspike. Papeete provided, hidden amongst its magnificent trees, what visiting sailors demanded; organised brothels and illicit grog-shops.[14]

Whatever moral restraints remained from JM's early Presbyterian upbringing seem to have been abandoned whilst he was on the islands, rationalised away in his own brand of hedonistic philosophy. Morality, he had concluded, was merely a matter of latitude and environment. As far as he was concerned life at *Tusi Tala* – the name given to the bungalow – was idyllic. It was a name which appealed to his Scottish chauvinism for it meant 'teller of tales', an epithet originally given by the Tahitians to Robert Louis Stevenson.

JM and his dark-eyed playmate, Toi Mata, would spend most of their days swimming from the bows of the outrigger canoe, which bore them out into the bay from the white sandy beaches. He describes the sheen on her glistening skin as she swam, and her raven, waist-length hair streaming down her brown back as they plunged into the nether-world of the coral reef below. How, wearing goggles, they would descend below the surface and stay as long as their lungs would hold them. Observing and marvelling at the multi-coloured fish that swam in those warm clear waters.

Toi Mata was only a year younger than her newly acquired lover and was part French, something which probably made communication between them not entirely physical. He was beguiled by her ready smile, the flashing white teeth and the freshly picked flower which usually adorned the side of her raven black hair. She wore no make up at all, and her clothes comprised of little more than a simple dress, or *parea*, made up from a few yards of cheap coloured material. JM entered into the spirit of things and went native, wearing nothing more than a pair of shorts and a large brimmed straw hat. I suppose by today's standards he would have been considered rather hippie. A far cry from the uniformed RAF officer of service days.

Most tropical islands with their relatively low cost of living standards and easy-going morals attract their fair share of drifters, and Tahiti was no exception in the late Twenties. They drew the adventurous and inquisitive, much like Mollison, or those drop-outs from society who, having made their pile, were now determined to enjoy their spoils. JM's natural gregariousness soon drew him into the social whirl of such people, mainly, it seems amongst U.S. expatriates. Although it might appear from his earlier memoir, where he mentions being in the company of the celebrated American author Zane Grey, that he is merely name-dropping, however, one can well imagine that the composition of such groups was as classless as he describes.

Zane Grey's visit to Papeete in his yacht *The Fisherman* happened to coincide with that of Mollison's, and the two men soon struck up a warm friendship. JM was amused to find that although the stockily built, middle-aged author was very knowledgeable and well-read, he would inevitably steer the conversation around to his pet subject, that of fishing. Little else interested him except writing and his newly discovered hobby. Grey was a prolific writer of Westerns and especially noted for his meticulous research into the times of the Wild West, having roamed that legendary land with a retired buffalo hunter. At the time of JM's meeting with the man from Ohio, he was at the height of his success, having just completed what was to be his best-selling novel, *Forlorn River*. In all, his fifty novels were to sell more than forty million copies throughout the world.

☆ ☆ ☆

Oscar Nordman's munificence was to be put to the test once more before JM left Tahiti. Never one to miss a passing opportunity, the Scot had casually suggested over dinner one evening that he would like to see how the more primitive Polynesians lived on Moorea, one of the neighbouring volcanic islands some dozen miles to the north-west. Its majestic saw-toothed peaks had aroused his curiosity – it was a case of the mountains being greener on the other side. Nordman was puzzled by his friend's request 'to go native' but agreed to take him out there with a be-it-on-your-own-head air of resignation. A few days later they set out in one of Oscar's sleek cutters, the

Avarua, and within an hour their anchor was splashing down into the shallow jade waters of Cook's Bay.

Nordman had seen it all before and stayed only for the afternoon lunch of raw shell-fish, breadfruit, papaya and coconut, washed down by liberal quantities of native rum, before returning to Papeete. However, when he returned four days later he found Mollison reluctant to leave the island, such was the hospitality he had received. The natives had treated him as a royal guest of honour, sharing what little they had with him willingly. More importantly, he had shared their simple, leisurely lifestyle of fishing and canoeing, completely oblivious to the so-called, civilised world outside.

Eventually the time came for JM to say a reluctant goodbye to Tahiti. As much as he enjoyed the life there, he had come to the conclusion that if he was to stay, then he must find a job on the island. The French authorities did not countenance vagrancy and the prospect of truck-driving* to earn his keep – apparently the only job available – did not appeal to him. When the chance of a steerage passage came his way on one of the New Zealand Union Line's boats, the *Manganui*, which was due to call in at Papeete on its way to Sydney via Wellington, he decided to take it.

A genuinely tearful Toi Mata was on the quayside to bid JM farewell on the day he left, her soft voice whispering, 'Adieu, ma cherie amie'. He admits that he too was far from being dry-eyed. Her charm had wormed its way into his affections, impressing him with her other-worldliness, her total disregard for material possessions. He compared her simplicity and artlessness with the gold-digging hostesses he had danced with at Kate Meyrick's 43 *Club* in London. He remembered that she had even been jealous when he had as much as looked at any of the other girls on the island.

Before he left he bought her a gift. In his 1937 book he describes the event so:

> Give a Broadway blonde a mink coat, or diamonds to a Parisian night club Queen. These things pale into the commonplace before the significance of the second-hand bicycle I gave Toi. Probably she rode it for a week before she broke or tired of it. By now she probably has a crop of laughing Island children whose fathers juggle shares on Wall Street or swear in fo'c'sles all over the Pacific.[15]

Once on board the *Manganui* JM realised that he had returned to a microcosm of the civilised world of respectability and convention. It was back to a culture whose shackles he had managed to throw off for the all too brief time of bliss that he had spent on the French colony. He was quickly made aware of his unkempt appearance as the ship's more stolid passengers

*Buses were always known as 'trucks' on the island.

eyed him with an air of disdain. Who was this steerage-class beachcomber in the straw hat, garlanded with coloured beads and flowered *leis*?

As he stood at the ship's stern-rail watching the silhouetted mountains of the island merge into the dusk – they seemed almost unreal, much like cardboard cut-outs – he could feel the slow pulsing throb of the ship's engines vibrating beneath his feet. The propellers were churning out a creamed wake of foam behind them as they carried him towards civilisation and Australia – away from Toi and her ephemeral world. There is a saying amongst Tahitians that if you cast your garland of *leis* into the wake of the liner, whilst still in sight of the palms, then you will return some day. As JM went below to turn in for the night, he knew that it was possible for him to return one day, but he also knew that it would never be the same again!

☆ ☆ ☆

On the evening of the second day out from Papeete the *Manganui* drew near to its next port of call, the Polynesian island of Rarotonga. It was the largest of the Cook group of islands and had been under New Zealand's control since 1901. Mollison, who by now had teamed up with an equally adventurous spirit – a young Australian by the name of Shave – was disappointed when the ship's captain announced that owing to heavy seas, passengers would not be allowed ashore. The ship would anchor in the bay for the night and be away in the morning. The two rebels were not to be thwarted however, for they seized an opportunity to visit the island when a native fruit boat moored alongside to sell its wares. At an opportune moment, as soon as trade between the boatmen and the ship's passengers had slackened off, they climbed down the rope that had been used for transaction purposes and into the boat. Having bribed the natives to carry them ashore, they hid amongst the pineapples and the boat pulled away and headed for the island.

Rarotonga was a disappointment to the two absconders, for unlike the carefree lifestyle of French rule which they had enjoyed in Tahiti, its segregation rule between white and coloured races gave it a repressive atmosphere. Moreover, it seemed to Mollison that the dead hand of the British colonial system had imposed its alien culture upon the people. Boys wore boots, and the girls were dressed in European style skirts and blouses; whilst the bare floors and spartan furnishings of its hotels were reminiscent of the worst of the Britain's public houses.

The only redeeming feature of their illicit departure from the ship was when they managed to gate-crash a native wedding. Quite fortuitously, it happened to be a wedding between a Rarotongan Princess and a Maori lawyer who were to honeymoon aboard the *Manganui*. Once the two men knew this, they realised that there was little danger of the ship sailing without them and they were able to relax and make the most of the reception festivities. Fortunately, their return to the ship the next morning in the company of the newly-weds passed unnoticed, largely because the attention of the ship's crew had been diverted by the disappearance of a young New Zealander who had been deported from Tahiti. He too had slipped ashore sometime during the night, and the ship was now forced to sail without him.

Five days after leaving Wellington, the *Manganui* sailed into Sydney harbour. One can only speculate on Mollison's thoughts at this moment, but they must have centred on the man who had deserted him as a child. He must, over the years, have often wondered just what sort of a man Hector really was, and why had acted as he did. Was it really as he had heard rumoured from family gossip, that his father was an irresponsible waster who hated the idea of parenthood? Or was there more to it than that? Maybe now he had the chance to unravel the mystery. Perhaps he knew that he would never really come to terms with his own identity until he had met this man face to face.

One who knew JM intimately towards the end of his life, remembers that he only ever once mentioned his father, and that rather briefly. Without any apparent bitterness or rancour he related how his father had returned to Scotland whilst he was still a small boy (whether they actually met on this occasion is unclear) and had promised him a cricket-bat. JM then laughingly dismissed the subject, and, as if to excuse his father's character, said, 'He never ever did send it to me.'

Although his father was most certainly still alive and resident in the country when he arrived in October 1928, there is no record to suggest that they ever met during the aviator's time in Australia.

We do know that Mollison was far from optimistic about his future when he arrived in Sydney, for he says that he was down to his last £30 and without any prospect of employment. Apart from being approached by what turned out to be a confidence-trickster, who offered him a postion as a pilot in a bogus airline in return for putting money into 'the company', the only job he did manage to find was that as a menial, bathing-beach attendant on Bondi Beach.

There came the day when he heard the all too familiar sound of a Cirrus engine. It was only faint at first and then it became a full-throated roar as a small de Havilland Moth biplane swept low over the beach. The sound of its four cylinders was like a siren-call beckoning him back to the excitement of his former RAF days. Cupping his hands over his eyes, he watched it as the sun glinted on the doped fabric surfaces of its wings and until it finally disappeared into the blue haze. At that moment he became Bondi Beach's most reluctant employee. Enquiries revealed that the plane was from the New South Wales Aero Club, and that the club had been advertising for a flying instructor. That evening JM dug out his flying-log from the bottom of his suitcase, sat down and composed a résumé of his service career and posted it off to the club. Within eight days he received a reply inviting him for an interview with their President, and although they were unable to offer him a post with the club in Sydney, they did recommend him for an instructor's post with the newly formed Aero Club at Adelaide.

The Adelaide club had been formed during the latter part of 1926, and although it had employed an instructor and mechanic it did not commence a programme of instruction until Mollison joined them in November 1928. The delay was caused when the club's committee discovered that they were to be off-loaded with Government supplied de Havilland Moths fitted with, what they considered to be, underpowered 60 hp Cirrus Mk 1 engines. They became even more aggrieved when they heard that the Melbourne club's secretary, Captain Guy Moore, stated that they had not been entirely satisfactory when his club had used them. As a result, the Director of Civil Aviation, Colonel H. C. Brinsmead, had come under considerable public criticism from the Melbourne press for purchasing the older type of machine, when the more powerful 90 hp Cirrus mark 3 engines were shortly to become available. The outcome was that the Adelaide club declined to proceed further with the movement until they were supplied with the up-dated aircraft.

Even when Mollison commenced his duties at Parafield, things still did not go too smoothly with the club, for within three days he had been grounded. The authorities at Sydney had assumed that when they interviewed him, that he possessed a pilot's commercial 'B' licence. As soon as the Department of Civil Aviation's office discovered that this was not so, they sent a telegram to the club informing them that he must not be allowed into the air as an instructor. After some speedy negotiations by telephone with Colonel Brinsmead, JM was granted the licence without the necessity of examination. It was given on the strength of his service training, and he commenced instructing on the very next day.

JM's good fortune was probably due in part to the current shortage of skilled pilots, and partly because the Director was still smarting from previous press criticisms. Obviously, Brinsmead did not relish his department being publicly exposed for its laxity in appointing the aviator, without first having made sure of his eligibility.

With almost 1,200 hours' flying time to his credit, Parafield's new instructor was soon considered to be something of a 'hot shot' pilot. Not only did he prove to be popular with his pupils, but at weekends he delighted the Adelaide crowds with his flamboyant displays of aerobatics; performing loops, spins, half-rolls and falling leaf manoeuvres. The January 1929 issue of the club's magazine, *Wing Tips*, records that JM had been busy over that Christmas:

> The Club's instructor was 'full out' during the holiday period, and with Captain the Hon. Hugh Grosvenor demonstrated night flying for the first time in this State. Mr Mollison has had considerable experience in night flying and says that a machine with side by side seats is ideal for the job.

It appears that his charm and prowess in the air earned him at least one new admirer from the fair sex, for the report continues:

> It is anticipated that we will shortly have another enthusiastic lady flier in this State, the Hon Lady Hore-Ruthven having recently been aloft in one of the Club's Moths performing aerobatics with Flying Officer J. A. Mollison as pilot. Her flight was made on New Year's day and judging from her remarks, she will be flying all the year round. She was accompanied by Lady Stalbridge and Miss Denys Daly.[16]

There is no denying that JM had some sort of pulling power with rich and titled ladies, as will be seen in later chapters. However, it seemed to matter little whether the women in his life were rich or poor for he was never without feminine company for long. During the time he was with the club he developed a strong relationship with an attractive young divorcée who had married at seventeen, some three years before he met her. She appears to have been a 'live-in' girlfriend at his rented bungalow on Glenelg Beach, and is described by him in rather glowing terms as one who would have won the heart of any selection committee adjudicating for a beauty competition.

From an account related by author Norman Ellison whilst writing about the pioneering aviation days in Australia, it appears that Mollison's impact upon his male flying colleagues may not have been quite so favourable. Sharing the aerodrome at Adelaide was a certain veteran flier named Horrie Miller, founder of the MacRobertson-Miller Airline, who happened to be flying one of the Moths on the day that Mollison was in the air. Ellison writes:

> According to those who saw the incident, there could and should have been a double crash the day Jim Mollison aeronautically locked horns with

Miller at Parafield. It began in fun. At least Mollison was having fun – flying a Moth, he 'buzzed' another Moth in which Miller had a passenger. Quickly Miller landed, unloaded his passenger, and went aloft again. He was enraged. This time he did the buzzing. Mollison was a magnificent pilot, an expert in aerobatics – also he was a fine boxer. But so furious and deft were Miller's dives and swerves at the other Moth that soon it was Mollison who came down to land. On his aeronautical heels came Miller. A minute or so after Mollison had clambered out of his machine, Miller, still in a blazing rage, rushed towards him. He told Mollison what would happen to him if ever again he came near his aircraft. Mollison never buzzed Miller again. No one did.[17]

Early in April 1929 the Club was allocated a further DH60G Moth, G-AUIB, to join the other two trainers, but this time it was fitted with the more powerful 100hp Gipsy 1 engine. This machine was to be the progenitor of the legendary and ubiquitous DH 82 Tiger Moth – the world's most famous biplane trainer during the inter-war years. History was yet to link Mollison's name inextricably with that of de Havilland's, but it is probably true to say that no single aviator ever did more to enhance this manufacturer's reputation than Adelaide's new instructor.

On the Friday morning of 25 May JM led the club on its first cross-country outing, a 400 mile flight to Essendon at Melbourne to attend the Victorian aerial pageant. On the way down, the seven small, open-cockpit biplanes ran into some unexpectedly bad weather, with winds up to 60 mph and violent rainstorms. It was what Mollison would have classified as 'real dirt' and they were forced to descend on occasions to less than 100 feet in order to keep below the cloud base. By the time they put down at Ararat, some 120 miles from their final destination and their planned refuelling-stop, the weather had not improved. Even worse, the weather-report for the rest of the journey was no more favourable and so they decided to stay for the night. Mollison was careful to stick to the rules, for whilst the club's committee had never been in favour of encouraging fair weather pilots, their instructions were that unnecessary risks should be avoided lest fatalities should lead to adverse publicity and thereby damage the cause of civil aviation.

On the following day the weather was even worse and made little improvement until the Sunday when they were able to continue to Melbourne. At least they had fared better than their Sydney Aero Club colleagues who were to suffer damage to two of their machines – one blown over upon arrival and another written off in an accident on the way home. The bad weather continued for a whole week and frustrated the Adelaide

Club's members' return but without bothering JM who had beforehand arranged to sit the examination for his category 'D' ground-engineer's licence whilst in Melbourne. The theory and 'hands on' practice which he had gained whilst studying for the course not only enabled him to pass the examination without difficulty, but was to give him an intimate and useful knowledge of aircraft maintenance. It was something which was to stand him in good stead in the very near future.

☆ ☆ ☆

Eleven thousand miles away at Stag Lane, Edgware, the London Aeroplane Club's Chief Flying Instructor, Major H. C. Travers, was discussing the weekly progress of their pupils with one of his instructors. Travers was a likeable and patient man, but he had the reputation for being a trifle over-cautious. In the opinion of most of the club's staff and pupils he was reckoned to be 'a bit of an old woman'. On this occasion, as his eye went down the flying-list he paused, looked up, and asked Matthews what was wrong with this woman – a 'Miss A. Johnson'. She had been under dual-instruction for eleven and a quarter hours over a nine month period and had still not soloed.

Matthews explained that he didn't think that she would ever make it as pilot. Moreover, he mentioned that he had told the woman as much right after her first lesson. She lacked a natural flair for the necessary co-ordination between hand and eye, and as a consequence her landings were particularly bad. But she kept coming back every weekend. After some discussion it was agreed that Travers would take over her instruction for a while during May. If she did not improve, then he would tell her to give up. He knew that most pupils soloed after eight or nine hours dual, and if they went to sixteen hours then they were just wasting their money and the instructor's time.

For the next seven flying lessons Travers concentrated on getting Amy to practice her landings. It was a chore commonly known amongst instructors and pupils as 'circuits and bumps'. If she wasn't getting it right, he would open the throttle and they would go around again until she mastered it. The aim was to initially make an approach with the correct amount of speed, height and distance. And then to reduce the flying speed until, by gently bringing the nose of the aircraft up, it stalled some six inches above the grass, thus allowing the wheels and tail-skid to touch down simultaneously into the required 'three-pointer'. As the days went by, Amy felt uneasy with

Travers and was beginning to despair, although unbeknown to her he had already come to the conclusion that she would eventually make the grade.

By early June, Amy knew that she was very close to being washed out as a pilot. She had not really mastered the art of a smooth landing and had by now logged 14 hours and 55 minutes of dual-instruction. However, she was slightly more hopeful on the 8th when Travers handed her back for a twenty minute period of instruction under Matthews. The next day, after about thirty minutes dual, again spent practising on her landings, he climbed down from the rear cockpit and signalled her to take it up alone. Her log book merely records, 'June 9th, 1929, Moth, Cirrus II, 5 minutes, "First solo".'

Chapter 7

'Airline Pilot'

When motorcycle dirt-track racing, or speedway as it later became known, arrived in Australia from the USA in the 1920's, it soon began to attract large crowds to the various events that were staged in most of the country's major cities. Adelaide was to be no exception. Its first meeting took place in February 1927 in an arena on the showground complex at Wayville, a suburb just on the border of the square mile of the actual city centre. From thereon, the Saturday evening meetings at Speedway Royal in Goodwood Road became a magnet for large crowds of spectators, varying in number from 5,000 to 20,000. One such visitor in 1929 was to be Jim Mollison.

As a spectator he was fascinated as he watched the helmeted and leather-clad riders sitting astride their Harley-Davidson, Indian and AJS machines in the pits. Mechanics scrambled around the bikes under the floodlights, busily making last-minute adjustments. Suddenly a cacophony of rasping exhausts combined to shatter the night air as the masked riders made their way to the starting line. Gloved hands were pumping throttles and levering clutches as the flag fell. With their front wheels clawing the air and a shower of dust billowing behind them the contestants hurtled down the straight and slid into the bend. Each one jockeying for position.

The partisan crowd roared themselves hoarse as their favourites battled over the three laps to the finishing flag. One, two, three across the line for qualifying points as throttles were rolled shut and fans hurriedly scribbled the race result on their programmes.

Mollison was yet to learn that each rider steered with the back wheel by keeping just the right amount of power on throughout the slide, rather than by use of the handlebars. The balance of the bucking projectile being kept under control by the rider bearing most of his weight on the right footrest, whilst the left foot steadied and trailed a plume of black grit.

In his 1932 memoirs the aviator claims not only to have been a spectator at the one third of a mile oval track – now billed as the fastest in the world – but also as a competitor. Certainly the sport had all the right ingredients for attracting Mollison into its ranks as a performer, rather than merely as a spectator. The atmosphere of speed, danger, noise and gladitorial conflict before an adulating crowd would have been a very difficult one for him to resist. More importantly, there was also what he considered to be easy pickings from the prize-money being offered. This would have been £20 for a first; £7 for a second place and £3 for a third. These were sums of money which would have compared quite favourably with an average Australian's wage of £4 per week, or the £500 a year he was probably earning with the Aero Club.

According to his written account, it was not long before he had purchased a machine and was practising assiduously whenever he was free from duties at Parafield. He tells us that he did not perform too badly on his first competitive outing, and within a few weeks he was finishing the Saturday meeting showing a small net profit after deduction of expenses for a mechanic. He goes on to say that his new found, part-time career was to be short-lived, for as soon as word of it reached the ear of the Aero Club's secretary he was given an ultimatum. Either give up speedway racing, or lose the instructor's job.

Extensive research conducted some sixty years later by Graeme Frost – a leading authority on speedway history in the Adelaide area – has thrown some doubt on the accuracy of Mollison's account of actually competing in the main Saturday evening meetings. It appears from a careful study of all the Wayville programmes, from 1927 to 1932, that Mollison's name is not recorded in any of them. These programmes are quite detailed, listing not only the starters in each race but also all the riders on the programme for that night, including the reserves.

Furthermore, Graeme Frost later found that:

> While visiting the widow of the late Frank Duckett (an early Australian speedway champion who lived in Adelaide) and reminiscing about speedway in the old days, she mentioned Mollison's name. Upon pressing her for more information on the man, she suggested that I speak with one of her friends who knew more about the aviator's involvement with the speedway.
>
> This friend turned out to be a chap in his late seventies, I'd say. His story is that in the mid to late 1920's a family called Rake had a motor garage and a farm situated at Enfield, a suburb of Adelaide. The Rake family were interested in motor bikes and speedway racing, and they marked out a rough track on their farm. On the Sunday mornings after a race meeting at

the Speedway Royal the night before, some of the riders used to congregate at Rake's farm and practice their skills on this makeshift track. Apparently there was as much beer downed as there was riding done. It was just a 'gathering of the clan', nothing official.

This chap was only a lad at the time but he and his mates used to ride their bicycles from the Yatala Prison at Northfield, where his father was a warden, to watch the speedway boys practice, hoping at the end of the day they would get a ride on the back of one of the bikes, or in one of the sidecars.

It was here that Mollison used to have a ride, and where he was considered to be a bit of a dare-devil rather than a speedway rider as such. The 'real' riders who used to give the young lads a ride round after their practising would warn them 'not to get on the back with Mollison, he'll bloody kill you'.

Apparently, while in Adelaide, the aviator went around with one of the leading lady swimmers of the time but my source was not sure of her name. She was supposedly his girlfriend but he'd say she was not the only one! Frank Duckett's widow and her friend described Mollison, as they knew him at the time, as a dare-devil and a playboy.[18]

Whilst Graeme Frost concludes from his interview with the widow's friend that Mollison never ever rode in any official speedway meetings, he does admit that it is hard to believe that a man who had achieved so much in aviation would invent or exaggerate such stories. One also wonders why, if the account of his speedway activities was false, the claim was not challenged as soon as his first book appeared in 1932, less than four years after the riding activities were alleged to have taken place? There is no evidence that they ever were challenged until now.

☆ ☆ ☆

Early in the Spring of 1929 the directors of Eyre Peninsular Airways were seeking the services of an experienced pilot, and approaches were made to Mollison. The company had been registered in the latter part of 1928 with a nominal share capital of £10,000, and it was planning to operate a regular twice a week service using a Junkers F13 L monoplane between Adelaide and Streaky Bay. The machine had already been shipped from Hamburg aboard the *Karnak* and had arrived in Melbourne on 19 June, where it was transported to Essendon for assembly and test-flown as VH-UKW six days later.

One of the EPA Directors, Albert Packer, approached the Aero Club seeking their permission for Mollison to be allowed to act as the official pilot for their company on its inaugural tour. Not wishing to be seen as hindering the advancement of civil aviation in the State, the club's officials readily agreed. They would allow him to take his annual fortnight's leave and fly for the new company. JM must have known by now that his future no longer lay with the club and on the day he commenced with EPA he wrote a letter tendering his resignation. During the nine months that he had been at Parafield he had logged 581 hours. He also had the satisfaction of knowing that he had enabled thirty-three pupils to gain their 'A' licences. It was an achievement with which he could be justifiably proud.

Eyre Peninsular's mint new aeroplane was proudly christened *Mount Wedge* and commenced its inaugural flight on 15 July with Mollison at the controls. With its gleaming corrugated metal skin surfaces (Junkers were the first in the world to operate an all-metal aircraft on passenger services, starting in 1919) and plushy upholstered seating for four passengers in the luxury of an enclosed cabin, it must have seemed the last word in airline technology. However, the pilot and co-pilot sat side by side in open-cockpits with merely the protection of a windscreen, which meant that fur-lined leather clothing was a must. In spite of this, as an aircraft design, it was far ahead of its time. When compared with other European fabric-covered, wooden biplanes then in current usage, it was most certainly a modern airliner. The German airline Lufthansa were still using the type on their Breslau to Hirschberg route, even as late as 1938.

Mollison flew the EPA Junkers on proving flights from Adelaide consecutively for the next thirteen days, cruising at 118 mph, and visiting Yorketown, Maitland, Ardrossan, Minlaton, and across the Spencer Gulf to Tumby Bay, Cowell, Elliston and Streaky Bay, before finally returning to Parafield. He then returned to the club to work out the rest of his one month's notice, before making the first official passenger services on the 19 August. The routes alternated between a 5 hour flight from Adelaide to Streaky Bay, via Wallaroo, Cowell, Point Lincoln and Elliston; and a 3 hour flight from Adelaide to Yorketown, via Maitland and Minlaton; both with an overnight stop and return on the next day.

Within two months EPA had gone from strength to strength and the company was soon seeking to expand its services to Broken Hill in the New Year. As a consequence, JM was commissioned on 29 September to carry out a proving flight and to return the next day. Albert Packer and fellow Director J. H. Moate were more than pleased with Mollison's perfomance, so much so that they made him a Director. It appears that the appointment was merely a ploy to retain his services, for JM admits that the position was purely a complimentary one and conferred no monetary reward. Whatever their motive, it did little to prevent Mollison from moving on.

By the end of 1929 Mollison had logged some 347 hours with Eyre Peninsular Airways and the novelty of flying the single-engined Junkers on the Streaky Bay run was beginning to pall. Admittedly he was still getting his kicks out of flying by giving aerobatic displays in the Aero Club's biplane Moth at weekends, but he was anxious to add to his experience as a commercial pilot. There were new opportunities to explore. One that had been beckoning was the prospect of flying bigger aircraft with Queensland Air Navigation (QAN), a new company operating two tri-motor Avro 10's out of Brisbane on an airmail-run to Townsville. Mollison applied for one of the flying posts and received a reply almost by return offering him the job. He worked his month's notice with EPA and set out for Brisbane, leaving his Glenelg playmate to look for a new boyfriend.

It was at this time that Charles Kingsford Smith and Charles Ulm came into Mollison's life. The two Australians had achieved lasting fame by becoming the first to fly across the Pacific from the USA to Australia. Together, with navigator Harry Lyon and wireless operator James Warner, they left Oakland, California, on 31 May 1928 in their Fokker tri-motor *Southern Cross* and arrived in Brisbane nine days later, where they were hailed as international heroes. They had been in the air for a total of 83 perilous hours and had flown across 7,389 miles of inhospitable ocean.

Kingsford Smith and Ulm's achievement made a lasting impression upon Mollison and earned his deepest respect. Throughout his life he was to maintain that 'Smithy', as he became known, was the world's greatest aviator. Their paths eventually converged when Smithy and Ulm's aviation plans finally came to fruition with the establishment of their own company, the Australian National Airways Limited (ANA). It was an ambitious title for an airline, one which threw down the gauntlet to the existing Queensland and Northern Territories Aerial Services (QANTAS), Western Australian Airlines (WAA) and other competitors with their limited regional areas of operation. ANA was raising the stakes by not only setting its sights on an Australian internal airway system, but it also had its eye on the possibility of an international airmail service. The company's main hangar facilities and offices were to be at Mascot airport, Sydney, with subsidiary operations at Eagle Farm, Brisbane; and at Essendon aerodrome, Melbourne. The company's inaugural flights between Sydney-Brisbane and Sydney-Melbourne were due to start on 1 January 1930, whilst their Melbourne-Hobart run would come later in that year.

Sir Charles Kingsford Smith.

Charles Ulm.

George U. 'Scotty' Allan.

Travers Shortridge.

Mollison's introduction to Kingsford Smith came within a few days of commencing work with QAN at Brisbane, and the two men immediately struck up a warm friendship. There is no doubt that there was more than a small degree of hero-worship on the part of the younger man for this quiet seemingly unflappable Australian with the disarming smile. At the same time the pacific pioneer aviator presented an unspoken challenge. He was someone for the Scot to beat. A case of . . . if he can do it why can't I?

Over drinks that evening the two men discussed commercial flying in Australia and weighed each other up. At least they had this much in common, they were both more than a little fond of hard liquor and in neither was the habit restricted solely to saloon-bars. Smithy had already been sacked from *Diggers Aviation* in his early days for drinking whilst on duty. On this occasion he had flown two passengers to an out-station where the owner's wife had just given birth to a son and heir. As a consequence, Smithy was invited to join with his passengers and the family in celebrating the new arrival. A liberal supply of champagne flowed for the next hour or so and by departure time Smithy's judgment was far from dependable. The plane swerved on take-off due to a puncture that he had either failed to notice, or had ignored, and plunged into a deep hole. Norman Ellison records the aftermath of the incident:

> The plane was smashed beyond repair. The passengers sustained facial injuries and two of Smithy's ribs were broken. There were tears on Smithy's face as the rescuers prised him out of the wreckage. 'No, it isn't hurting that much,' he explained, 'but there goes my job.' He was right![19]

One is reminded that cockpit alcoholism occurs today, although not as blatantly as it did then. It is in fact a problem as old as flying itself. At the time of writing, one reliable source in the United States estimates that since 1975 some 1,200 airline pilots have been confidentially treated for alcoholism.[20] Moreover, every major U.S. airline, in spite of the current eight hour 'bottle to throttle' rule, has its own confidential rehabilitation programme. Most of the world's major airlines are loathe to acknowledge the problem, knowing that if they did it would not be good for business. Britain's own Civil Aviation Authority will say no more than, 'there is a slight problem'.

However, on the occasion that Smithy first met Mollison he was impressed by the self-confidence of this cool 'pommie' with the Oxford drawl, and he ended their meeting by offering 'Jimmy' a job with ANA. The Australian was shrewd when it came to selecting his staff and before the year was out he had surrounded himself with some of the finest pilots of that pioneering era. Travers Shortridge and George Urqhart 'Scotty' Allan were already with the company when JM arrived, and they were soon to be joined by Pat Lynch Blosse, Eric Stephens, Eric Chaseling, Gordon Taylor and Jerry Pentland.

Mollison was delighted by an offer which gave him an annual salary of £750 and immediately promised to give in his notice with QAN. He had only been with the company for eight days and although a formal contract had not yet been drawn up between them, he was still rather apprehensive about their reactions. When he broke the news to them he admits that they were highly displeased at the unexpected resignation, although there was little they could do legally to prevent him from leaving. The matter concluded with a rather irate managing director reluctantly agreeing to him going, but not before he had cast some serious doubts upon the legitimacy of Mollison's parentage.

ANA had sunk more than half its £85,000 capital into the purchase of four tri-motor monoplanes, which were based on the successful Fokker FVIIb/3m design of the *Southern Cross* and built under licence by the A. V. Roe Aircraft Company at Manchester. It was a prudent move on the part of Ulm (now the organisational brain behind the company) to buy the British product, inasmuch as they escaped the import tariffs imposed on the Dutch built aircraft. They were designated as the Avro 10 (the 10 signifying their ability to seat ten passengers) and named *Southern Star, Southern Sky, Southern Moon and Southern Sun.* Apart from the use of the more powerful Armstrong Siddeley Lynx engines and a slight reduction in wingspan, they were almost identical to their foreign counterpart.

Such was the punctuality of the ANA service that the citizens of Sydney soon learned to set their watches by the aircraft, as on four mornings a week they clawed their way into the sky over Mascot airport. No matter whatever the weather conditions, they were bang on time. Pilot and co-pilot would sit in the open, huddled behind their oil-spotted windscreen, more often than not numbed with the cold. When it rained they would be soaked to the skin. They flew without the benefit of ground-to-air communications, or even adequate weather-reports.

Tests carried out in Australia in 1987 on a replica of the *Southern Cross* show that the aircraft needed to be flown 'hands on' throughout a flight and that the controls were extremely heavy. Particular care was needed during take off and landings due to the small fin and rudder, which combined with the large, thick wing section and large keel surface of the slab-sided fuselage, made handling difficult.[21] The passengers suffered too, for noise insulation was non-existent and they were forced to stoically endure a noisy and chilly flight. A far cry from the service of today's club-class on a 747.

Smithy and Ulm were astute enough to realise that they must place a heavy emphasis on passenger safety if they were to attract sufficient money into the creation of their new company. As a consequence, the training of pilots and technical personnel was given a high profile in ANA's prospectus, which was issued to shareholders in 1928. It meant that the two men would personally supervise newly recruited pilots during the first few weeks of their employment. Their policy proved to be a wise one, and one in which JM was soon made aware of how much he still had to learn about 'blind-flying'.

During one of Mollison's early flights as a co-pilot in the starboard seat under instruction from Smithy, they had run into some very bad weather with ice forming along the leading edges of the wings and visibility no further than the wing tips. The new pilot was peering down looking for a hole in the cloud that would enable him to see a landmark and fix their position. After a while he spotted what he thought was a recognisable geographical feature and being anxious to impress his new boss, told Smithy that he was sure of their present position. The older man nodded his approval and without comment altered course to JM's instructions. Some time later they ran out of cloud into clear weather over the sea and, as it transpired, over a hundred miles off course. Without any word of admonition at all, the older man put the Avro back onto its correct course, the one that he had been originally following. Mollison could not but help wonder how he would have reacted if the roles had been reversed.

Smithy had good reason to be lenient on the new pilot for he knew only too well the difficulties of blind-flying with the primitive instrumentation then currently in use. It consisted of little more than a compass, wind-driven Pioneer turn-and-bank indicator and an Air Speed Indicator.

JM's first three months with ANA were spent uneventfully on the airmail run from Sydney to Brisbane and return, with senior pilots Allan and Shortridge. The only excitement he could remember would be when they spotted the dark sinister shapes of sharks just below the surface of the water. Often they would see a shoal of five or six of the man-eaters and if they did happen to be near the shore they had a friendly arrangement with the bathing beaches whereby they would fire off flares as a warning.

Mollison first flew as co-pilot to 'Scotty' Allan on the ANA's Tasmanian run, and it appears that there was a fair degree of needling between the two men when they first met. Perhaps it was a case of like poles repel, for both men were natives of Scotland and former RAF pilots. Apart from their shared background, the two were vastly different in character. Allan's dourness and Mollison's flamboyance were soon set on a collision course. 'Scotty' recalls those days from sixty odd years ago:

> When Jim joined ANA, Kingsford Smith and Ulm ordered me to take him as a pupil to Launceston from Melbourne. Jim resented this and showed it by turning up late at Melbourne. In fact he had to run across the aerodrome to get on the aeroplane at 8am as I deliberately did not wait for him. We didn't speak to each other all the way to Launceston. After we had landed and all the passengers had departed, Jim quietly told me that he was going to punch me on the nose. He took up a position uphill from me and then rushed at me swinging his arms. I stepped aside and knocked him down as he lumbered past. I went forward to assist him to his feet and as he got up he said, 'I still think you're a bastard.' After that we were the best of friends.[22]

Evidently the two men eventually developed a mutual respect for each other after flying together in the *Southern Cross* on the more hazardous Sydney-Melbourne run. It was one of the ANA's most dangerous routes in the winter months, for it skirted over the Kosciusko mountain range with peaks up to 7,350ft. One of JM's most unpleasant experiences in all his time with the company was whilst he was flying at 10,000ft in thick cloud during a winter crossing of this range. Suddenly, all three engines began to lose power and finally he thought that they were going to fail completely. The tri-motor began to slowly lose height towards the critical 7,000ft level when he realised that ice had frozen onto the spark-plug leads. By sheer good fortune he happened to see a break in the clouds, with a shaft of sunlight beaming down through it. As a result, he was able to circle the aircraft in its rays for some thirty minutes, thereby allowing the sun to melt the frozen leads. The engines began to pick up and he was able to regain height and continue safely. But for that fortuitous hole in the clouds, pilot and passengers would have all perished.

Former ANA pilot Gordon Taylor describes the difficulties of navigating an airliner in the conditions described above:

> To understand and to appreciate this situation it is necessary to know that in Australia this (blind-flying on regularly scheduled flights) had never been done before; that the science of instrument flight and dead-reckoning navigation without sight of checkpoints on the earth was relatively new in aviation, and where in the United States and Europe it was regularly undertaken it was based upon radio communication and aids to navigation, organized weather reports and forecasts, and already some

Jim Mollison piloting the Australian National Airways Avro X *Southern Moon* over Mascot, Sydney, in 1930.

form of anti-icing and de-icing protection for the aircraft. Without these aids and safety provisions, regular 'in cloud' and 'on top' flying could be undertaken only by freak pilots with a new and wider perception of flight, a relentless cunning, and a rugged ability to handle the aeroplane on primitive flight instruments in the most violent turbulence.[23]

The Sydney-Melbourne route was also to present Mollison with an occupational hazard of a rather different kind. He was never known as one to pass by an opportunity for any amorous pursuit, and particularly so when flying attractive lady passengers. In fact he had soon acquired something of a reputation amongst his colleagues for being a ladies man. Some put it less politely by describing him as being 'skirt crazy'. Former ANA ground engineer, Geoff Wells, recalls that it was not unusual for him to be approached in the Essendon office by some attractive young female, asking him to tell 'Captain Mollison' as soon as he landed that she would be waiting for him in her car at the end of the road. When he did pass the message on to JM, the reply would often be, 'Oh! gosh, I'm going out this way. If she comes back, tell her I've gone. Tell her anything.' On one occasion there were actually two girls at the same time waiting to see him, one in a red Oldsmobile at one end of the road, and another in a Studebaker at the other end.

There was a time when Mollison had been eyeing up a rather stunning looking girl passenger who had boarded the aircraft accompanied by a tall powerfully built man. As he went up and sat in the front cockpit, he quietly confided to 'Scotty' Allan that this girl was the loveliest creature he'd ever laid eyes on. After a while he told his partner that he intended to chat the girl up as soon as they reached Melbourne and ask her for a date. Allan seemed disinclined to comment at first but when JM pressed him on his views on the proposed tactic, he said that he felt that it would be unwise in view of the fact that he knew the man with her was her husband. JM didn't see that the husband posed any real hurdle. That was until 'Scotty' informed him with a sly smile that the girl's husband was Lewis – 'Strangler' Lewis – Australia's current champion wrestler! Although his enthusiasm for dating was dampened on this occasion, it did little to discourage him a few weeks later.

☆ ☆ ☆

When the wheels of Amy Johnson's tiny Gipsy Moth biplane *Jason* finally bumped down onto Darwin's parched airfield on the Saturday afternoon of 24 May 1930, a legend was born. It is a legend which even today, some sixty three years later, has lost none of its potency.

Amy had flown the 11,000 miles from Croydon in 19 days and although she had not beaten Hinkler's 1928 record, she was the first woman to make the journey alone. Moreover, it was a particularly remarkable and plucky achievement in view of the fact that she had only logged 83 hours since making her first solo flight. Before she set out for Australia, she had never attempted a cross-country flight longer than the 4 hour return flight from Stag Lane to Hull!

The press began to laud her as the world's greatest airwoman, for although Lady Heath and Lady Bailey had made major solo flights from the UK to the Cape some two years earlier, they were far less arduous and made over a much longer period of time. In the case of Lady Heath's lone flight from the UK to the Cape, it took exactly three months; whilst Lady Bailey's solo to the Cape and return took almost ten months. On the other side of the world the American aviatrix Amelia Earhart was yet to make her mark upon the aviation scene. Admittedly she had been the first woman to cross the North Atlantic in 1929, but on that occasion it had only been as a passenger. Amy now reigned supreme. Here was a woman who was not only able to compete with the men, but eventually to beat them at their own game. The public loved her, and nowhere did she receive a more tumultuous welcome than in Australia.

On the Monday morning following her arrival in Darwin, Amy began a four day flight of 1,400 miles across the arid wastes of northern Australia's outback on her way to Brisbane. Overnight stops were planned at Alexandria Station, Longreach and Charleville, as she was escorted by QANTAS Airways pilot, C. W. A. Scott – none other than the same man that Jim Mollison had been with at Duxford. Scott was a man long familiar with the featureless landscape of northern Queensland and had been chosen to lead the way in one of the airline's DH50As. Whilst Amy in *Jason*, together with RAAF Flying Officer Harold Owen in the Shell Company's Gipsy Moth, flew within sighting distance behind him. The flight had all the ingredients for creating an intensely bad relationship between Amy and her escort pilot. As we shall see, it was to create a friction that would fuel the resentment that was to eventually arise between the Mollisons and Scott in later years.

Scott made little effort to disguise the fact that he resented being made to act as a mere air-chauffeur to an unknown novice flier – and a woman at that! What was more, Scott's accompanying passenger in the QANTAS airliner was Wakefield's representative, Captain S. W. Bird, who was angry that Shell's representative Owen had muscled in on the publicity and was tagging along with Amy. These two factors resulted in Scott scorching ahead in his faster and more powerful machine, so much so, that Amy and Owen in their slower machines were forced to fly flat out in order to keep up with him. Ostensibly, Scott's reason for setting such a pace was that he was responsible for seeing that Amy kept to the tight schedule of the welcoming parties that lay along the route.

To make matters worse, Amy, who had been flying almost continuously for the past three weeks with very little sleep, was not only extremely fatigued but she was also femininely unwell. Scott and Bird knew about her condition but were callously unsympathetic. On the third day out, as they were making for Charleville, Amy gave up bothering to keep pace with her escorts and deviated to follow the railway line to Quilpie, some 120 miles to the west of their destination. According to one source, she deliberately got 'lost' so that she would miss the official luncheon that awaited her at Charleville and be able to spend the time resting. The entry in her flying log for the 28th simply reads, 'Quilpie – Charleville, 1hr 40mins, Landed after dark'.

Disaster was to follow during the next afternoon on the final stage of the flight to Brisbane, where a crowd of 20,000 were waiting to greet her. Amy had already experienced being manhandled out of her plane and into a waiting car when she had stopped off in the morning at Toowoomba. Similar over-enthusiastic welcomes had awaited her at Conclurry and Longreach, and by the time she approached the airfield at Eagle Farm, Brisbane, she was in no fit state to be flying. She came in on a landing approach with far too much height and attempted to correct it by a steep side-slip. By the time the plane touched down she was heading for the boundary fence, and much to the dismay of all the onlookers her aircraft struck it and overturned.

Watched by an astonished and incredulous crowd, she unstrapped herself and slipped from the wreckage. There had been many official arrivals at the airfield before, but none so cool as this one. With true Yorkshire grit, she put on a brave face as she climbed the steps of the dais to make a speech that endeared her to the people of the city. The ordeal was not yet over however, for she was then paraded around Brisbane's thoroughfares smiling and waving from an open top car with Wakefield's representatives Cyril Westcott and Captain Bird seated alongside her. By the time she reached the privacy of Government House, where she was to spend the next five days, she broke down in a fit of sobbing. Such was the price of fame.

☆ ☆ ☆

When opportunity knocked, Charles Ulm's hand was invariably some-where near the latch, ready to swing the door wide open. As soon as he

Amy Johnson stepping ashore at Aden after arriving in the s.s. *Naldera* on 24 July 1930 and whilst on her way home from Australia.

heard of Amy's plight at Brisbane and that on doctor's orders she had now decided to continue the rest of her journey to Sydney as a passenger rather than a pilot, he immediately contacted Wakefield's Cyril Westcott. He was the man responsible for organising her tour of Australian cities and Ulm seized on the prospect of free publicity for ANA by offering to place one of the company's airliners completely at her disposal. By the time Major Hereward de Havilland had flown his company's DH Hawk Moth up from Melbourne with spares for the damaged *Jason* and offered to fly Amy down to Sydney, Westcott had already accepted Ulm's offer. Amy did not however spurn the Major's offer to fly her on from Sydney to Melbourne, Adelaide and Perth.

There is no doubt that co-pilot James Allan Mollison liked what he saw when he first met Amy as a passenger on the ANA's *Southern Sun* at Brisbane's Lytton airfield on 4 June 1930. As she stepped on board, dressed in a neat green suit, she obviously must have created a unique impression upon him. Here was a woman who combined her sexuality with unquestionable bravery. Physical courage was always something Jim admired in women, but one wonders if he experienced that same frisson of excitement when he first met Amy, as he did on the night at Peshawar six years ago when the mysterious lady had stepped out of the darkness into his path. Then it was a fantasy shrouded in the shadows. Something intangible and quickly dispelled in the cold light of the following morning. Not so now with this attractive woman in the airliner's cabin.

During the five hour flight Amy sat for most of the time with Captain Bird, Charles Ulm and his wife Josephine*, chatting around a small card-table decorated with poinsettas, whilst Mollison flew the plane.

We know little of Amy's reactions to JM – the man who was to eventually become her husband – when they first met. She makes no mention of him at all in her log book entry, merely recording that Ulm was the pilot and that she took over the controls for part of the trip. She had never flown anything larger than her own single-engined *Jason* before now, and as she sat alongside the Scot he no doubt turned on the charm. We do know that he managed to get her to promise to dance with him that evening at the Wentworth ballroom. She was to be the Guest of Honour at a reception to be given by the Australian Flying Corps Association in Sydney and he obviously knew enough contacts to get himself an invitation.

JM arrived suitably attired for the occasion in evening-dress to claim the promise of being Amy's partner in two of the dances. There was just one snag, she was being closely guarded by her chaperone the State Governor, Air Vice-Marshall Sir Philip Game. As JM approached her, he was curtly but politely told by her imperious watchdog that Miss Johnson was extremely tired and would not be dancing anymore that evening. Mollison realised that he was outgunned. Junior ex-RAF officers do not take on AVMs and win. Not wishing to cause a scene, he retired gracefully to seek some consolation at the bar. As far as he was concerned it was much like it had been with Paula and Toi Mata. He was unlikely ever to see Amy again for he knew that she was soon to move on to Melbourne, Adelaide and Perth, and within a month to leave for England.

☆ ☆ ☆

JM continued to fly for ANA throughout 1930 comforted in the knowledge that he had made the right decision when he had resigned his directorship with Eyre Peninsular Airways, for by July the company had ceased to operate. The 1930s were a time of economic squeeze and depression, not only in Australia but throughout the rest of the world, and EPA caught the full chill blast of its effect. Unlike their U.S. counterparts, Australia's airlines were operating without the benefit of subsidies, and with an extra duty on fuel, together with an imposition of a sales-tax, it had finally crippled the company.

*Charles Ulm had recently married Josephine (née Callaghan), his second wife.

Mollison knew that he had earned the respect of Kingsford Smith when he was finally selected to accompany Ulm, Allan and Shortridge as part of the company's aerobatic team. The ANA team would appear at venues such as Sydney's Hargrave Park and others around the country, where the quartet would delight the weekend crowds by putting on a display of precision aerobatics. In spite the DH Moth's less than ideal suitability as an aerobatic aircraft, they managed to include inverted flying, loops, stall turns, reasonable vertical rolls and tail-slides in their repetoire. All of these manouevres came naturally to JM from his CFS training days with the RAF, and the show would normally conclude with a display of 'crazy flying' – always a popular event with the city's spectators.

ANA entered 1931 confident that it could extend its activities by regularly linking Australia up with the services now being run by Imperial Airways on its route to India, one which had begun two years earlier. The plan however was never to be fully realised for an unexpected tragedy was soon to deal a cruel and devastating blow to the company.

At 8.10am on a wet and blustery Saturday morning Travis Shortridge pushed the throttles of *Southern Cloud* wide open and took off from Mascot airfield in a cloud of spray. He climbed to 10,000 feet, synchronised the fixed propellers with the throttles and handed over to his co-pilot. The flight was bound for Melbourne over the notorious Kosciusko range with six passengers, a load of mail and an assistant-pilot in training in the co-pilot's seat. The weather-report for 21 March predicted strong headwinds with thunderstorms all along the route, and under such conditions their ETA* was 3pm. By 4.30pm *Southern Cloud* had not arrived and the authorities at Essendon were becoming increasingly anxious, knowing that by this time the tri-motor would be nearing the end of its fuel supply. The weather that evening was so bad that no attempts could be made to fly out in a search, and all that could be hoped for was that the experienced ANA pilot had somehow managed to make an emergency landing, somewhere along the route.

Mollison and other ANA pilots were out on the next day in an aerial search scouring the mountainous region for any sign of the aircraft or its wreckage, but without success. For all they knew *Southern Cloud*, together with its eight occupants, had just completely disappeared off the face of the earth.

After ten days the search was called off, the most plausible explanation being that the airliner had strayed off course and plunged into the sea. However, knowing the accuracy of Shortridge's navigation, both Smithy and

*Estimated time of arrival.

Mollison were loathe to accept this possibility. The mystery continued and was not finally solved until twenty-seven years later, when a young man by the name of Reginald Sonter, out on a climbing expedition, discovered a tangle of twisted steel tubes and metal debris some 150 feet below a mountain ridge top.

> In the wreckage were a number of pathetic relics – a string of beads, three watches, a razor, binoculars, scent bottle, a number of sovereigns, a few calcined bones and a key ring bearing the name of Clyde Hood. Sonter had stumbled across the wreckage of the *Southern Cloud* in the wild country where Kingsford Smith thought it would be.[24]

At the court of enquiry held by the Federal Air Accidents Investigation Committee on 10 April 1931, Ulm, Mollison and others knew that the future of ANA was at stake and did their best to deflect the blame from the company. With tongue in cheek, Ulm assured the committee that every ANA pilot was capable of flying blind under *any* conditions. Equally as evasive, JM said that it was possible to 'pancake' in the most dangerous parts of the route without loss of life. However, upon further questioning, Ulm agreed that some form of air-to-ground communications would enhance air safety and if such equipment was readily available then ANA would be prepared to instal it. Even as he spoke the words he must have known that the cost of erection of radio-beacons along the route would have been beyond the company's financial resources.

The company was finally exonerated from any blame, but with the search costing £10,000, ANA was now verging on bankruptcy. The court ruled that permission for the re-commencement of the Sydney to Melbourne route should be witheld until an effective air-to-ground communication system was available. The decision was a bitter blow to ANA and although the company was invited to participate in an experimental link-up with the Imperial Airways' Croydon-India mail delivery service, when the contract was finally awarded two years later, it went to their rivals QANTAS. By the end of May 1931, Jim Mollison knew that his days as an airline pilot with ANA were numbered.

Chapter 8

'Wyndham to Pevensey Bay'

After the loss of the *Southern Cloud*, ANA's Directors, Kingsford Smith and Ulm, decided to adopt QANTAS's policy of diversifying their interests by starting up a Flying Training School. As a result of this decision Jim Mollison was detailed in April 1931 to go to Brisbane and collect Gipsy Moth 2, G-ABHY. It was a machine that they would use as the school's first trainer. Quite unbeknown to Mollison, the small biplane that he was about to collect had originally been owned by Charles Scott and had recently been used by the airman set a new England-Australia record.

When JM arrived at the Archerfield aerodrome he found G-ABHY parked outside of the main hangar ready for him to collect. However, when he made enquiries at the Flight Office, he was told that the machine could not be handed over because the transaction note had not yet been received from its previous owner. Upon asking who that might be, he was told that it belonged to 'some fella called Scott who's soon going to have a crack at the Australia-England record' and that he was expected along at any moment. Further questioning revealed that the man referred to was none other than the burly ex-RAF heavyweight boxing champion, the one who had been on the previous term's intake to Mollison's when he had been at Duxford in 1923.

Ignoring the warning not to touch the aircraft until the paperwork was in order, JM decided to carry out a test-flight whilst he was waiting for Scott to arrive. When the big man did eventually turn up, the first thing he noticed was that the Moth was missing. Moreover, as far as Scott was concerned, it was now circling the aerodrome in the hands of some upstart who had no right to be doing so.

A rapid enquiry at the flight office told him that it must have been taken by the ANA pilot who had called a while earlier. Scott was furious. By the time Mollison had landed and was taxying back to the hangar, the irate Scott was bounding towards him ready to give the pilot the length of his tongue. 'Who the hell gave you permission to fly this aeroplane?' bawled Scott. 'Oh hello Charles, fancy meeting you here,' came the wistful reply of his tormenter. Within a while the two men were at the bar laughing and joking about their former days at No: 2 FTS and marvelling that they should meet again so far from home.

Conversation soon turned to Scott's recent record-breaking flight from Lympne to Darwin in 9 days and 4 hours. On that occasion he had landed in Australia on 10 April 1931 having knocked some 17 hours off Kingsford Smith's record made in the previous October. Scott had quit his job with QANTAS earlier in the year and had sailed home, having first made an agreement with ANA that they would buy the Gipsy Moth from him, if and when he returned. The plan had succeeded and he was now debating whether to make an attempt on the Australia-England record, set by Smithy and Ulm in July 1929.

It is interesting to read Scott's own comments about his indecision on whether to go for the return record at the time of this meeting with Mollison.

> My nervous and physical qualities were impaired, there was no doubt about it, and I contemplated this return flight with great misgivings, for anyone who has not had experience of a long fast flight will hardly realise the strain and the natural reactions. Had I been allowed to rest after my arrival in Australia I should have been in a far better condition, but all these parties and evenings had given me no rest at all, so I insisted that I be left alone to prepare myself physically for this homeward flight.[25]

One wonders what Amy must have thought if she ever read this account written by Scott in 1934. The biter was bitten. So now he knew!

By the time the two men had parted, the seed of the idea to make an attempt upon the Australia-England record had been firmly planted in Mollison's mind. Knowing that the outlook for ANA as a commercial undertaking was indeed bleak, he began to reason that he had little to lose by making the attempt. If Kingsford Smith, Amy Johnson and Charles Scott could find fame and fortune by making long-distance flights, then why not him? With almost 4,000 hours to his credit in military and civil flying, he knew that he had all the qualifications necessary to succeed. Moreover, if he could master the weather conditions on the Sydney-Melbourne run, then he was more than capable of dealing with the worst likely to be encountered on a flight to England. There was just one small snag. Money. Who would finance him?

It has been said that fortune smiles upon the brave and never more so than when JM met up with the chief representative of C. C. Wakefield's Oil Co., in Australia. It was soon after the meeting with Scott, when Mollison happened to have Cyril Westcott as one of his passengers on an ANA flight into Brisbane. He seized the opportunity to invite the man to sit up beside him in the co-pilot's seat, where he explained the controls and allowed him to briefly take over the aircraft. Mollison knew that Westcott had the ear of his boss, the influential Lord Wakefield, one of aviation's greatest benefactors in the two decades between the wars. It was said by one light aeroplane club member that the oil baron 'gave away money like water', the main recipients being the various flying clubs in the UK and Dominions. More importantly for JM, he had discovered that individuals such as Bert Hinkler and Amy Johnson had been helped by the philantrophist with large sums of money towards the purchase of their aircraft.

Soon after their flight together Mollison dropped a casual hint to Westcott that he was becoming tired of flying for ANA and was contemplating an attempt upon the Australia-England record. Furthermore, he let it be known that he was every bit as capable of remaining awake and alert at the controls for as long as Smithy, Hinkler or Scott had done. After a measured pause he screwed up enough courage to ask Westcott outright if he thought that Lord Wakefield would back him in the attempt. Westcott was quietly non-committal at the time but at their next meeting a few days later, he told JM that he had asked Lord Wakefield if he would help. No one was more surprised than JM when, some weeks later, Westcott approached him with a cable from Wakefield. On it were the three brief words, 'WILL BACK MOLLISON'.

As soon as the news of Lord Wakefield's sponsorship of Mollison reached Scott's ears, an intense rivalry began. It was one which, whilst friendly on the surface, was to be fanned into a bitter feud in the years ahead. Maybe the two men were too much alike in their personalities for there ever to be any true cordiality between them. Both were wild and rebellious by nature. Their lives had strangely converged in so many ways. They had both entered aviation through the same route – a five year short service commission in the RAF at Duxford – and whereas Mollison had only just managed to keep on the right side of military law and stay the course, Scott had fared even worse and left the service fifteen months before his time was up. In his memoirs Scott admits that he left the RAF 'with many black marks in my copybook'.[26]

Scott had arrived in Australia in 1927 and started work as a £500 a year QANTAS pilot flying the air-mail on their Longreach-Conclurry-Camooweal service. He was soon to fall foul of its authoritarian Chairman, Hudson Fysh, for whilst on a special flight from Adelaide to Broken Hill in 1928 he had become dis-orientated in cloud and spun his aircraft into the ground from

3,000 feet. According to G. U. Allan, who had joined QANTAS in 1932 soon after the collapse of ANA, Scott was in an unauthorised area when he crashed.[27] The aircraft burst into flames upon impact and Scott was thrown clear, only to deliberately walk back into the inferno in an attempt to rescue his mechanic, who unfortunately died from his injuries later on. The accident had left Scott with a permanent scar across his forehead, one which passed narrowly close to his eyes.

Mollison and Scott were both noted for being able to handle themselves physically when in a tight spot, whilst at the same time they outwardly gave the opposite impression. Scott had a reputation at Longreach in his early days for his pastime of classical piano playing and for his writing of poetry. On a Saturday evening some of the rougher elements from the sheep-stations would come to town, hear about the musical poet and being ignorant of his boxing prowess seek to pick a fight with him. One observer from those days recalls that, 'Scott might have been good at Beethoven but he could also knock over an 18-stone shearer without even putting his glass down'.[28]

Similarly, JM's somewhat flashy dress-sense, small stature and rather polished Oxford accent enticed at least one unsuspecting male resident of Sydney to overstep the mark. Norman Ellison, air correspondent for Sydney's *Daily Guardian*, recalls the day when he took JM for a drink just prior to his attempt on the Australia-England record:

> The first time I took Jim Mollison to 'the blood-house' (a rather Bohemian hotel bar next door to the newspaper's offices in Phillip Street where journalists often met) for a drink, he wore a suede flying jacket and suede shoes, his trousers were 'en suite', he carried a suede flying helmet and effulgent gloves, and his hair was 'just so'. So was his voice. When I asked him what he was going to drink, he pondered for a moment and then said, 'Yes, I think I'll have a be-ah.'
> Like a flash, Olga, the barmaid, asked, 'Brown, black or grizzly?'[29]

On another occasion he was dancing with a girl in a Sydney nightclub when a six foot squatter passed a remark on JM's 'cissy' appearance, loud enough for the aviator and his partner to hear. Mollison finished his dance and then asked the man to step outside, whereupon he threw a punch that knocked his ridiculer out cold. After making enquiries from onlookers as to where the man lived, he called for a taxi and asked for 'the remains' to be delivered.

☆ ☆ ☆

The de Havilland DH 60G Moth which Lord Wakefield provided for Mollison to use on the record attempt was not a mint new machine. It was, in fact, four years old and the first Cirrus Moth to be erected in Australia. Originally it had been one of a batch of eighteen Moths built at Stag Lane, Edgware, in 1927, and shipped to Melbourne for assembly. Hereward de Havilland had made an exploratory visit to Australia in 1926 to test the market and a year later had established DH's first overseas company in some sheds in Whiteman Street. JM's machine had at the time then been registered as G-AUFT and supplied to the *Sydney Sun* for the distribution of pictures recording the opening of Canberra city. Now, re-registered as VH-UFT and with Lord Wakefield's money footing the bill, it was in the DH hangar at Mascot,* Sydney, being installed with a 120hp Gipsy 2 engine.

From all accounts when Scott returned to Sydney from Melbourne, where he had been organising supplies of fuel with Shell for the homeward trip, he did not take too kindly to the news that Mollison was now a contender for the record. Their two machines were being prepared in neighbouring hangars on the aerodrome and both were anxious to be the first away. Kingsford Smith and Ulm's record of 12 days and and 23 hours made in *Southern Cross* in 1929 was considered to be a relatively easy one to break and this made the record attempt even more enticing. On occasion each would innocently pay a visit to the other's hangar and enquire on their rival's progress, only to be spoofed with remarks such as, 'Oh, it won't be for weeks yet.'

On 20 May Scott flew off to the nearby RAAF aerodrome of Richmond to have the compass of his Moth swung. This was a process whereby the aircraft is placed on a circular concrete base on which are marked true magnetic bearings. As the metal portions of an aircraft's structure affect the accuracy of its compass, it is necessary to correct these inaccuracies by placing small magnets inside the instrument. Eight readings are taken at 45 degree intervals, adjustment made, and the deviations are then marked on a card attached to the front of the compass. This then enables the pilot to make the necessary allowances on his course-setting.

When Mollison left Mascot on 3 June he still did not know if Scott would succeed in his attempt, for his rival had been delayed when crossing Australia and was still en route for England. Scott had experienced an oil leak when a union in the oil delivery pipe fractured sometime after leaving Sydney. This had caused him to make a forced-landing at Mitchell, to the east of Charleville, where he was only able to effect a temporary repair. As soon as he arrived at Longreach the QANTAS engineers were able to fit a new part.

*Mascot aerodrome is now known as Kingsford Smith Airport.

Scott had warned Mollison that the airfield at Darwin was far too small for a take-off with an over-loaded Moth, and had advised him to use Wyndham which lay some 275 miles to the south-west. By the time JM reached Newcastle Waters in Northern Territory, having flown almost 2,000 miles via Broken Hill and Alice Springs, he had the choice of making for Darwin or Wyndham. If he chose the latter, he knew that it meant flying over relatively uncharted areas of featureless desert using inadequate maps. Furthermore, he remembered Kingsford Smith and Ulm's warning of how they had become lost in *Southern Cross* in this same area in April 1929 and had barely survived the ordeal. The Australians had been stranded on a mudbank for eighteen days and in the ensuing air-search both Keith Anderson and his mechanic H. S. Hitchcock had been killed when their aircraft crashed. Mollison therefore decided he would fly to Darwin.

JM's all-black Moth touched down at Darwin in the hot afternoon sun of 6 June where he was greeted by the news that Scott had broken Kingsford Smith and Ulm's record with a time of 10 days and 13 hours. JM now knew it would not be an easy record to beat, but he immediately instructed the airfield's ground engineer to put 119 gallons of fuel into the steel tanks that had been fitted into the space normally occupied by the front cockpit.

The total weight of a DH60G Moth was 1750 lb and normally it took but 20 gallons in the tank located in the mid-section of the upper wing. On this occasion, in order to give it a 2,000 mile range, it would be lifting approximately a 1000 lb fuel overload. One must remember that the type of aircraft used by Mollison and Scott in those days was without the assistance of flaps or variable pitch propeller. These were innovations which came later and ones which would have made the take-off much safer. The ground engineer was sceptical about the aircraft's ability to fly off the small airfield's 550 yard space with such a load and strongly advised against it. The advice left Mollison in a quandry. It had been his intention to make the 1,800 miles to Batavia (now Djakarta) in Java in one hop and it was with some reluctance that he agreed to fuel being siphoned off. However, just as a mechanic was about to insert the rubber tube into the main tank and lighten the load JM changed his mind. 'Leave it. I'm going to risk it and make Batavia non-stop.' The mechanic shrugged his shoulders with an air of resignation and did as he was told.

Having checked through his maps and prepared sandwiches and coffee for the flight over the Timor Sea, Mollison retired to snatch a few hours of fitful sleep. He admits that this was the one occasion before a big flight when he did not indulge in alcohol. It is interesting to note that his former ANA colleague, 'Scotty' Allan, states that, 'in those days JM drank very little otherwise I would have taken a piece of him'. The same man remembers their parting at Sydney before this flight with, 'When he left Mascot for England he handed me his gold cigarette case and said, "I won't want this again" – I subsequently passed it on to his ex-girlfriend.'[30]

At midnight JM was being shaken and aroused from a deep slumber. He dressed thoughtfully, knowing that out there in the darkness lay 500 miles of shark-infested sea to be crossed before dawn. A large crowd of well-wishers and one or two reporters were waiting alongside the aircraft in the light of spluttering flares as he clambered into the small space that would be his home for the next week or so. He adjusted the faint yellow light of his cockpit-lamp onto the face of the compass, knowing that its red pointer would be his sole guide for much of the trip.

One of the mechanics swung the propeller and the four cylinders of the 120 hp Gipsy engine coughed into life. Mollison's eyes hovered over the rpm indicator as he carried out the magneto drop test before allowing the engine to settle back into an even beat. Slowly he taxied out as two mechanics ran alongside, one on each wing tip. Their white faces just visible and blurred in the darkness as they guided him out to where he would commence his take-off run.

Pulling his goggles down and into position he could see in the distance at the far end of the airfield those small red pin-pricks of light. They were hurricane lamps which had been hung on telegraph poles as a guide to the the airfield's boundary. He remembered that they were supposed to be at least fifty feet below each wing tip when he passed over them.

The heavily overloaded Moth responded reluctantly at first and then gradually gathered speed as the throttle was opened. Slowly, much too slowly for Mollison's liking, the tail came up into the flying position and the red lights in the distance appeared sharper and brighter. Still she wouldn't lift. Within 300 yards the bumping of the wheels over the dusty surface ceased and he was airborne, but only just. The Moth was wrestling with gravity and lurching some seven feet above the ground. Suddenly it dropped back with such a force that it shook every bone in his body and he imagined the wheels coming through the lower wing. He cursed his luck and pulled the stick back, knowing that had reached the point of no return.

Once more the machine lurched into the air and he knew that those awesome lights were within a hundred yards of him and growing larger by the second. He was in a cold sweat for he knew that if he pulled the nose up any more the over-loaded Moth would stall and fall out of his hands. 'Please God, don't let me hit those lights.' 'Take those red demons away, out of my path.' 'Please don't let me die this way.' 'Not now at the beginning of the flight.' 'Maybe later on, somewhere over India perhaps, but not now.' With eyes shut tightly, he waited for what seemed like an eternity before the sickening bang. He expected at any moment for a deluge of aviation fuel to swamp over him. Thoughts of Bailey's shrivelled body lying stiffly and grotesquely in the froth of the fire-extinguishers at Eastchurch flashed through his mind.

The roar of the engine fell silent as it was torn from its bearers by the jerk of the wooden propeller, which bit deep into the dirt and shattered into small pieces. Wings and flying wires telescoped into an ignominious heap around him. A while later he could hear the sound of voices and running feet as he lay in the tangled mass. Slowly, he realised that the fuel tanks had not ruptured and there was no fire. Apart from his pride, he was undamaged. Fortunately, when the Moth flew into the wires and its wing had hit one of the telegraph poles, the machine had pancaked flat onto the ground. Had the biplane nose-dived, then the engine would have pushed back into his body and he would most certainly have been killed.

Mollison learned two important lessons from the Australian crash. Firstly, that heavily laden aeroplanes need enough unobstructed space in which to either get off successfully, or to abort. Darwin had provided neither. Secondly, that wherever the world's press was concerned there was no such thing as bad publicity, for whereas the report on a successful take-off would have occupied three lines in the morning's papers, his ill-fated attempt had now attracted thirty.

It is at this point that JM showed the trait for which he was to become world-famous. His sheer doggedness. That spirit of never giving in when circumstances were against him. To those looking on he had blown his chances. A lesser mortal might easily have thrown in the sponge and given way to despair. Admittedly, there was a brief period of self-recrimination; if only he had listened to Scott's advice and gone from Wyndham; if only he had taken heed to the ground engineer's warning and siphoned off twenty gallons. But early next morning he cabled Lord Wakefield and asked for a second chance. In the meantime, he pondered whether it was possible that the famous man would ever give an unknown aviator, one who had crashed on his first attempt, another try.

After a nail-biting week in Darwin waiting for a reply, the philanthropist oil baron surprisingly wired his approval of the request. One damaged Moth was shipped back to Sydney for a complete rebuild, whilst a somewhat chastened Mollison caught the train for the 200 mile journey south to Newcastle Waters. It was from here that QANTAS and Larkin Air Services, old rivals of ANA, came to the rescue and took take pity on one of their own kind by offering him complimentary flights to Brisbane and onwards to Sydney. Within six weeks VH-UFT emerged from the workshops at Mascot as good as new and ready for a fresh attempt. This time it would be from Wyndham.

☆ ☆ ☆

As a grey dawn broke over the vast expanse of the Timor Sea on the morning of 29 July, Mollison screwed his eyes to see a dark smudge on the horizon ahead which looked very much like land. Earlier in the night he had dropped smoke flares from which he had been able to determine the strength of the wind and its direction. Happily, it had confirmed that he was enjoying a tail-wind dead astern and so he had decided to ignore any slight drift and maintain a true course, one which should bring him to the island of Rotti. He had been in the air now for 4 hours since the 1am take off from Wyndham and he had estimated landfall in another thirty minutes. However, as he turned slightly towards the 'island', he reasoned that maybe the wind was stronger than he had imagined and he had arrived early. Upon closer observation it turned out to be nothing more than a cloudbank.

Just before 6am he sighted an island and he could soon recognise from its coastal contours that it was, in fact, Rotti. Its lush green tropical vegetation was in sharp contrast to the barren wastes of northern Australia that he had left only hours before, and he felt that he had already made one big significant stride on his journey. As he passed low over village after village nestling in the dark green foliage of the wooded forests, he could see natives pausing to look up and stare at the unfamiliar sight of an aeroplane. Within fifteen minutes he had crossed the island and at its far coast-line he changed course for Lombok.

As he left Rotti he descended to within thirty or forty feet of the water, for he found that the wind conditions were much more favourable at this height. As much as he tried to avoid it, his eyes did not wander for long from the fuel and oil-pressure gauges. He was forced to adopt a fatalistic attitude towards an engine failure for there was little that he could do if one did occur, knowing that he carried neither parachute nor inflatable raft. Sea-crossings were always nerve-wracking and he was relieved when he finally flew over land, no matter how inhospitable. The mischievious thought did run through his mind that if he was forced to land in the wilds, then he would become some sort of aerial Robinson Crusoe, take a native wife and hope for some other form of transport to turn up. He imagined his putative

Jim Mollison supervises the fuelling of his DH 60 Gipsy Moth, VH-UFT, at Wyndham on 28 July 1931, just prior to his successful attempt on the Australia–England record.

mother-in-law describing to the children how their father arrived in this bird from the air, now a rusting heap of metal in the jungle.

As he flew along the southern coast of Sumba, he could see the 5,000 feet peaks of Lombok rising like a barrier ahead of him. By now the fuel tanks were half depleted and the lightened Moth climbed easily to clear the mountains and to cross the island onto its northern coast. Striking across the fifty mile wide Lombok Straits, he headed for Bali and the northern coastline of Java to land at the Darmo airfield just outside of Sourabaya at half past two in the afternoon. He had now covered a distance of 1,180 miles from Wyndham, nearly a tenth of the total distance to England.

As soon as he cut the ignition switches, he realised that the assault on his eardrums from the sound of an open exhaust for the past 13 hours had left him deafened. It was one more obstacle to overcome as he sought to instruct the Dutch mechanics on engine checks and replenishment of fuel and oil. Within twenty minutes he was back in the air flying over vast areas of rice fields and following the Soco river inland to Samarang where he would pick up the coastline to Batavia. He soon noticed that the tail-wind he had so far enjoyed had in fact turned into a slight headwind and he wondered if he would make the 400 mile hop to the capital before nightfall.

By the time he had reached the port of Tjirebon the light was failing rapidly, causing him to open the throttle just that little bit wider to give a steady 2,200 rpm. He only hoped that the officials at Sourabaya had wired Batavia of his imminent arrival as promised, so that the airfield might be lit up for him. He knew that the brief period of tropical twilight would soon leave him flying in an inky darkness, something he did not relish in unfamiliar country and especially since he was still 150 miles short of his destination.

An hour after sun-down he was circling Batavia with very little fuel in the tanks and completely unable to distinguish the airport from a maze of city lights. He concluded that the message from Sourabaya had either not reached the airport officials, or they had failed to act upon it. Fortunately, he remembered that on the way in, about ten miles back in the jungle, he had flown over a large open space of ground that was lit from the flares and fires of a native village. He was now so desperate that he decided to return and make a landing there.

Having located the village he throttled back and began his glide in over the tops of the trees towards the clearing. As the plane touched down there was a loud crack as one of the wings appeared to hit something in the dark. As he switched off and climbed out to examine the extent of the damage, he could see that he had hit the branches of one or two saplings. Luckily, the damage appeared to be quite minor and he reasoned that it could easily be repaired once he got to the main airport.

Mollison's unexpected arrival soon attracted a bunch of excited jabbering natives from the local village. It was probably the first time that they had ever seen an aeroplane at close quarters. Not long afterwards they were joined by a rather helpful Dutch official, who was not only prepared to telephone the airport so that its lights could be put on, but was also able to summon the help of a number of cars to the the clearing, so that their headlamps could be used to assist a take-off in the dark.

JM was horrified when he walked the length of the area he was to use for a take-off, to discover that the ground was thick with tree stumps and shrubs. He realised how fortunate he had been in not hitting any of these during his landing run. He would certainly never have let down there in daylight. Any one of those protruding stumps would have put paid to his chances of beating Scott's time. However, the Dutch authorities were determined to assist the stranded flier in his dilemma and they soon had everything under control. About two hundred natives were set to work clearing the obstructions and within an hour they had provided him with a reasonably smooth but narrow runway. Mollison realised that the Moth's depleted fuel tanks were now an advantage, for he would never have risen out of the small clearing with any appreciable load on. As he gunned the throttle forward, the lightened biplane hit one or two nasty undulations before it finally surged into the air.

Batavia's airport at Tjililitan was now fully lit (it appeared that the wire from Sourabaya had arrived late) and after some ten minutes flying he had no difficulty in finding his aerial oasis. The airport was used by the Royal Dutch Airline's regular KLM service and acted as the terminus for their 8,737 mile route from Amsterdam via Budapest. The Dutch East Indies service had started eighteen months earlier when their renowned Captain Ivan Smirnoff had piloted their first flight across from Europe in a Fokker tri-motor. Not surprisingly, Mollison was able to find skilled Dutch hands which were soon able to repair the two broken ribs in one of the mainplane's lower wings. So far he had covered approximately 1,730 miles in less than twenty four hours. He had already set a new record, for it was the longest flight ever made in one day by a light aeroplane.

The tiredness was really beginning to tell as he took off from Batavia at midnight to face the ordeal of a 550 mile sea-crossing to Singapore. The aching eyes and leadened eyelids were longing to close in sleep. Fatigue was taking its toll and he was forced to change his body position in the small cramped cockpit every few minutes to keep awake. At least there was one crumb of comfort in knowing that the KLM office had given him a report of favourable weather ahead. Their report was the major factor in his decision to take the direct route across the sea to Singapore, rather than hug the Sumatran coast on a safer but longer journey.

One hundred and twenty five miles out over the darkness of the Java Sea he caught sight of a ship ploughing its way towards Batavia. It was well lit up and he could see one or two passengers on the deck staring up at him as he circled around her. It reminded him of his own sea journey from Singapore to Batavia five years earlier during his RAF leave. How he must have envied those passengers who would soon be retiring to their comfortable cabins for a full night's sleep. The temptation to cling to this friendly beacon of security was resisted and he turned away to resume his compass-course setting.

There was little for him to do throughout the night but listen attentively to the beat of the Gipsy's motor. Now and then he would imagine that it was running unevenly and his eyes would flick down onto the oil-presure gauge. Nothing wrong there. His mind was playing tricks. Gradually the sky lightened on his starboard wing as the dawn broke over the restless sea, enabling him to discern the faint charcoal shapes on the horizon as the islands of the Rhio and Lingga Archipelago came into view. They were just a few of the 13,677 islands that are scattered across the 3,000 miles of ocean stretching from Darwin to the Andamans off the Burmese coast.

☆ ☆ ☆

The severe buffeting started as the monsoon squall hit Mollison's machine without warning. It was the first he had ever experienced in his flying career and one he would never forget. One moment the Moth had been flying effortlessly through calm air and seconds later it was hit by a million pellets of water. It engulfed him in a blinding silver-grey mist which completely obscured his vision and drowned out the sound of the engine. Torrential raindrops beat a deafening tattoo upon the taut doped fabric of the wings and threatened to tear them to shreds. His frail craft shuddered and slewed as it was tossed around like a paper bag in a storm.

Before he had time to gather his thoughts the machine was out of control and he admits that had it not been for the brevity of that squall he might easily have plunged into the sea. His fright caused him to curse the Darwin crash and the seven week delay in getting away, for he had planned to miss the monsoon weather that was now lying in wait for him.

So much had he been concentrating upon staying alive during this frightening incident, that by the time he had flown into clearer skies he was lost. None of the islands beneath him tallied with his maps and he debated in his tired mind whether he should press on, or put down on one of them to verify his position. Caution prevailed, and seeing a strip of beach which appeared to provide a safe landing he put down.

Once more Mollison nearly met with disaster, for the beach slanted laterally across his path and by the time the Moth came to rest one wing tip was scraping the sand. Fortunately, there was no damage. Enquiries made from a local Dutch official in a nearby village enabled him to locate his true position. It transpired that the landing had not been in vain for he discovered that he had been on an incorrect course and heading for the east coast of Malay, instead of the west!

As he came in to land at Singapore on the afternoon of 30 July, there were just two gallons of fuel left slopping around in the Moth's upper wing's mid-section gravity tank. Fortunately, he had not found any difficulty in locating the military aerodrome at Seletar. As he circled the city on the way in he had even recognised the Seaview Hotel where he had spent some of his RAF leave in 1926.

It was an effort to heave his tired body out of the cockpit and he immediately sought to bring some life back into stiff and aching limbs by walking up and down stamping his feet. Intermittently, he would pause to munch a sandwich and swill some hot coffee. After a quick shower and some time spent bathing his bloodshot eyes, he listened undeterred while an RAF officer assured him that the weather up ahead was impossible. Monsoon rains were sweeping along the coastline he was to follow. After carefully checking over the engine and refuelling, he was in the air again and on his way to Alor Star in Kedah, not far from the Siamese border.

On the 420 mile flight up the western coast of Malaya he struggled to keep awake in the heat of the tropical afternoon. Without realising it he would find himself gradually closing his eyes, until a sudden jerk of the head would bring his concentration back under control. Looking down he could see the shadow of his machine being cast along the white beaches. Every now and again it would play hide and seek with him as it disappeared into the shadow of trees and then reappeared again. At the same time he kept a weather eye open for the monsoon storms that had been forecast. After his near-disaster experience over the Java Sea, he knew that it was fatal to tangle with any of these approaching rainstorms; instead he decided that he would wherever possible make a detour and fly round them.

As the sun dropped, the air grew cooler and he found it easier to shake off his torpor. He passed over Penang in darkness and when he landed at Alor Star it was almost midnight by local time. The aerodrome had excellent ground facilities and he was met by Government officials who were there to greet him. Amongst them was one whom he had known as an old friend in Sydney. JM was more than pleased to accept his friend's offer to whisk him back home for a meal, a shower and some rest. Thankful for the unexpected hospitality, he retired after giving his host strict instructions that he should be awakened in one hour. At 1.45 am he was dressing ready to leave for his next target, Akyab in Burma.

One hour out from Alor Star the normally sweet running Gipsy engine began to intermittently splutter and miss a beat. At first it was an almost imperceptible roughness and he wondered if he had in his tiredness imagined it all, but it persisted and he thought of turning back. However, after a while it cleared and the only conclusion that he could draw for its misbehaviour was that some water must have contaminated the fuel.

As dawn began to break over the Mergui Archipelago, along the Burmese border, he found himself trapped into a monsoon storm which was a repeat of the day before, only this time is was sustained and even more intense. He was now forced down to within a few feet of the sea in order to maintain visual contact with the shoreline. The downpour blasted off the propeller, peppering the windscreen and flooding back into the cockpit to soak him from head to toe. So great was the force of the storm that he feared that any moment some part of the aircraft might break away. Thankfully, it abated, and from thereon he decided that it would be dangerous to face another monsoon whilst anywhere over the sea. This meant that instead of saving time by striking directly across the Gulf of Martaban, he would now hug the coast up to Rangoon and make for Akyab over the 10,000 ft peaks of the Arakon Yomas, a range of mountains which skirt the Bay of Bengal.

More rain started to fall at Rangoon and as he flew over the golden dome of the famous Shwe Dagon pagoda he was determined to make Akyab before nightfall. Heading north-east from the capital he followed the Irrawaddy river for 250 miles and turned to cross the range of mountains somewhere near Magwe. Although the craggy peaks at this point were no higher than 5,000 feet, they were shrouded with towering cumulo-nimbus which were spilling their contents down onto the teak rain-forests beneath them. Mollison knew that it was extremely dangerous to fly through any one of those anvil-headed monsters. He knew that within seconds of entering them he would be flung all around the sky. His mind flashed back to Shortridge and the Kosciusko incident earlier in the year. If similar conditions could do that to a 71 foot span Fokker weighing 11,500 lb, what might happen to a frail, single-engined DH Moth.

In an attempt to grope a way through the dark canyons, he found himself at one point flying through heavy rain up a long narrow chasm with its tops completely obscured by menacing, black cloud. His fatigued brain told him that it was suicidal to continue and reluctantly he turned to retrace his path. Whilst he hated to admit it, he knew that he must bow to the inevitable and return to Rangoon. Nature would not be cheated. He had now been flying for almost three days continuously, during which time he had slept for no more than three hours.

Returning to Rangoon under threatening skies, JM failed to find the aerodrome and landed instead on the racecourse to the north of the city. In spite of a being surrounded by a curious bunch of inquisitive onlookers, his head went forward onto the leather coaming and he was soon asleep. O what bliss to shut those weary bloodshot eyes! Before long he was being shaken by a local policeman, who wanted to know what he was doing there. Fortunately, the man was able to show him from his map exactly where he was in relation to the aerodrome.

One of the first people Mollison met at the airport was a French air-mail pilot, who insisted on telling him exactly what he didn't want to hear. The weather ahead was unfit for flying. JM was in no mood to take any more bad news and quickly took to his bed to get the best rest that he had had since leaving Wyndham.

Refreshed by six hours of deep sleep, he set off at first light to do battle with the Arakan Yoma once more. As it transpired the Frenchman's gloomy prediction was completely accurate, with conditions no better than the previous day, and again he was forced to make several detours around the weather. As he peered over the side of the cockpit, he knew that he must be somewhere in the region where two young fliers had gone down only a year earlier.

Eric Hook was piloting a DH 60M Moth with Jim Matthews as mechanic from Croydon to Darwin in an attempt to lower Bert Hinkler's record, when they ran into similar weather JM was now experiencing. They suffered an engine failure and crash-landed into an inhospitable mountain-side. Matthews scrambled from the wreckage unscathed, whilst Hook who was not so fortunate had suffered quite serious injuries. However, after a while he found that he was able to walk to a limited degree when assisted by his colleague. The two men wandered through the mountain forests for seven days, clad only in shorts and shirts, seeking an escape route but without success. Finally, when food and water were exhausted, the injured man's strength gave out and he implored Matthews to save himself and go on alone. The following day Matthews met up with some friendly Burmese, who guided him on to the village of Prome. In the meantime they carried out a search for Hook.

Some three weeks later, the aviator's partially decomposed body was found alongside a river bed, seven miles from where the two men had parted company. News of the tragedy at home touched people's hearts and a fund was set up for Eric Hook's widow and two small daughters. One of the more generous donors was Amy Johnson, who needed no reminding of the hazards of flying over this particular type of terrain.

Mollison finally emerged from the menacing cloud-covered peaks to pick up the coast to the south of Akyab. Two hours later, Chittagong was drifting slowly under his starboard wings before he turned west on a new heading to cross the Bay of Bengal. For the next 100 miles he flew at only twenty feet or so above the sea, until he reached the eastern mouth of the Ganges.

After landing at Calcutta's Dum Dum airfield at 11.30am (local time) for fuel, Mollison was back in the air within thirty minutes. Flying north-west across Bengal he managed to circumnavigate two of the three unwelcome monsoon showers that lay in his path. He was thankful that the one he could not avoid was nowhere near as severe as those he had encountered earlier in the flight. The DH 60 Moth was never renowned for being an easy aeroplane to handle in bumpy weather and the buffeting experienced in these sudden blinding rainstorms would have been particularly unpleasant, especially for a fatigued pilot. Denied the luxury of today's electronic nav-aids, his aching eyes would have been glued for most of the time to the Moth's primitive blind-flying instruments. Keeping the bubble in the centre of the cross-level and maintaining a constant ASI, were the sole means of maintaining level flight until the datum of an horizon re-appeared.

By late afternoon he had flown into clearer, smoother air and the sun was setting as he passed over the sacred city of Benares on the Ganges. The towers and minarets of its innumerable Hindu temples and mosques, cast their long pools of tranquil shadows by the slanting light of a lowering sun. The peaceful scene reminded him of his service days in India. He had now been in the air almost constantly for the last four days, during which time he had slept for no more than nine scrambled hours. His whole being, although longing to be released from the tortuous noise and restriction of the cramped cockpit, was driven on by the thought of success. He knew by now as he neared Allahabad, less than forty-five minutes' flying distance away, that he was almost half way home. It meant that Scott's time of eleven days could be beaten. Stirrings of a latent childhood belief in 'providence' – he hesitated to use the word God – seemed to assure him that he would not have been brought this far only to fail.

JM watched the last ochre traces of daylight through the blur of his spinning propeller as the sun sank beneath a crisp horizon. In the distance he could see the confluence of the Ganges and Jumna forking around the smudged outline of the Hindu mecca of Allahabad. Within thirty minutes the wheels of VH-UFT were bouncing along the dirt field of Bamrauli's modern airport and one very tired Scotsman was taxying towards the flood-lit hangars where officials were waiting to greet him.

Mechanics were soon busy changing filters, spark-plugs and oil, and checking the security of fittings, before replenishing the tanks with fuel. Meanwhile, the fatigued pilot had accepted the hospitality of a local magistrate and was being driven away for a different kind of servicing. Mollison states that he had about two hours sleep that night before leaving at 2am for Karachi. It was now the fifth morning of the flight.

On through the night due west towards Rajputana (present day Rajasthan) on the 950 mile stretch to Karachi, he consoled himself with the thought that he was at last flying out of a monsoon area. Such comforting thoughts were however to be short-lived, for within a while he soon realised that he had exchanged the buffeting of rain for headwinds so severe that his average speed over the ground was reduced to a mere 65mph. Moreover, he found that the unpredictability of the wind required his maximum concentration. He needed a constant adjustment of the controls in order to maintain an accurate compass-heading as he passed over Jansi and Bundi towards the Aravali hills. If he relaxed for even a moment he found himself diving or climbing in unexpected directions. Taut nerves were being stretched to breaking point and by mid-morning, somewhere over the State of Jodhpur, he spotted a small unidentified aerodrome and decided to put down.

Thankfully, the airfield appeared to be deserted for there was not the usual crowd of inquisitive onlookers to greet him. As soon as he cut the ignition switch his body slumped back in the seat and his eyelids automatically closed, much like a child's doll. At he same time one hand reached down into the cockpit and his fingers closed around the neck of a bottle. Unscrewing the cap he drew it to parched and cracked lips. This time it was nothing stronger than warm lemonade. However, he does admit to having spent some of the £10 with which he set out with from Australia on liquor.

Many fliers of the period, including notables such as Charles Scott, Geoffrey de Havilland, Beryl Markham and the American Duke Schiller to name a few, were not averse to using alcohol on long-distance flights. Other stimulants such as caffein, whether in tablet form or in coffee, were commonly used by aviators. Unfortunately, these two had the side-effect of acting as a diuretic. Drinking of any kind posed a problem, for micturation within the cramped confines of a cockpit was not the easiest of tasks, especially for a woman. The usual method of transfer via funnel and rubber tube to any suitable receptacle, could, and did, present its own difficulties, particularly under turbulent weather conditions!*

JM's conscience allowed him no more than a thirty minute respite before he returned to do battle with the unabating head-winds. To make matters worse, the winds were now stirring up dust-storms as he skirted the desert of Thar, which rather spoiled his plan for keeping eye contact with the railway line to Hyderabad. As soon as he saw these conditions he began to climb and fly above the brown haze, which was now beginning to obliterate any landmarks. For three hours he flew without making a single ground reference and all the time knowing that a forced-landing, now that he was over the Sind Desert, could prove fatal.

When at last there came a break in the brown billowing clouds and he could pin-point the Mokhai Salt Lake, he was able to sight the railway to Hyderabad, having discovered that he had in fact been flying parallel with the line but some thirty of forty miles south of it. Eschewing the dangers of

*A Newark aviation mechanic confided to an aeronautical designer there, that after one of her (Amelia Earhart) long-distance solo flights her plane had reeked of urine.

the more direct flight over the Kohistan mountains, he opted for the longer but less worrying route of the railway through the delta of the Indus and landed at Karachi's RAF Drigh Road aerodrome late in the afternoon.

Once down he was on the familiar ground of his former RAF days, and ably assisted by native mechanics, he was able to carry out a thorough inspection and maintenance on the travel-stained Moth. Having lifted him faithfully across oceans, jungles and deserts, he knew that before he slept the machine's needs had to be catered for and he spent several hours working on the engine. At 9pm he retired to sleep, having arranged for a call to make a take-off at midnight.

By 3am the small black biplane was nearing Gwadur, a seaport on the Baluchistan coastline and one of the Imperial Airways' stopovers on the route to India. Visibilty was poor due to a layer of low cloud which made it difficult for Mollison to follow the contoured fretwork of the shoreline. However, as the dawn broke, conditions improved to reveal the turquoise blue waters of the Gulf of Oman. By early morning he was descending for a scheduled stop at Bandar Abbas for refuelling (again with the compliments of Wakefields Oils), but this time only to run into trouble with the Persian authorities on paperwork.

The aerodrome officials seemed to be running a lucrative racket with a form of danegelt extortion on visiting aviators, by demanding non-mandatory health certificates. Both Amy Johnson and Sir Alan Cobham had on recent flights been delayed with bogus demands – the latter for as long as two days! The more insistent that Mollison became in explaining that he was on a record-breaking attempt, and therefore it was imperative for him not to be delayed, the more adamant they became that he should stay. In desperation, JM varied his approach from aggressiveness to flattery, until eventually a levy of 100 Persian crowns (approximately £1.15) was demanded to procure the necessary health clearance. Breathing a sigh of relief, he paid up and was soon back into the air heading for Basra before they could change their minds.

After two hours' flying in the hot bumpy air along the Persian Gulf, halfway between Bandar Abbas and Bushire, he was alarmed to see that his oil-pressure gauge was reading low. As the engine was still running sweetly on all four cylinders some twenty minutes later, he reasoned that the defect could hardly warrant a forced-landing and so decided to carry on and put down at Bushire for an investigation. As it turned out, the trouble was easily remedied, but whilst working on the engine he was approached by officials demanding his papers. Knowing that it was a non-scheduled stop, he was not surprised when they finally reappeared to announce that although his papers were in order, he was to be fined 50 crowns for having landed without permission.

By now the accumulated delays had eaten their way into the precious hours of daylight and were sufficient to cause him to grope across the Gulf in the dark, looking for Basra. Once over the city he was again impeded by dust-storms, which only added to the difficulties of a night-landing. They meant that he had to circle for over thirty minutes before he could clearly distinguish the lights of the aerodrome. Upon landing, he decided to forego sleep, service the machine, grab a meal and press on. Never was there a man more determined. He was now only some 3,000 miles from home and he knew that the record was well within his grasp.

At midnight on the sixth day of his ordeal, a very tired Jim Mollison taxied out from the hangar into the swirling dust-ladened night air to the aerodrome's far boundary. Swiftly and deftly he ruddered the willing biplane to turn into wind with judicious blasts from the throttle. Within a hundred and fifty yards the tail came up and he could feel the gritty blast from the propeller's backwash stinging his sun-burned cheeks. The noise from the wheels over the gravel surface quietened as he pulled the stick back and climbed into a strong headwind. The lights of the aerodrome below gave a friendly wink back at him through the brown murk, but were soon lost as he began his climb to 5,000 feet.

Strong winds blow across Iraq for some ten months of the year and with the worst of the winds come the clouds of blinding dust. Scott recalled that anemometer readings on Baghdad's airfield, recorded gusts of up to 84mph during his crossing in April 1932. Mollison maintained that the winds were predominantly northerly and were a major factor in making an Australia-England flight more difficult than in the opposite direction. Certainly a study of record times seem to bear this out.

Around 3.15am the Moth was purring along to the south of Baghdad with the serried and lighted streets of the Iraqi capital divided by the silvered river Tigris framed in the struts and wires of its starboard wing. Mollison mused on the one benefit of flying by night in the tropics – that of knowing that he was escaping the harshness of a desert sun and the heat which would soon be beating relentlessly down on the open cockpit.

Soon after leaving the soft glow of the city's lights behind him the northerly winds strengthened, reducing his speed and causing clouds of rolling dust again to blot any visible landmarks. Climbing to 7,000 feet to avoid the worst of it he hoped that conditions would improve with daybreak. However, as the sky brightened he was forced to fly purely by compass, trusting he was following roughly along the line of the Euphrates and towards Aleppo some 400 miles to the north-west. When the dust-storms did eventually subside, he was left with a featureless landscape, no sign of the river, and an uncertainty as to his true position. The only sign of life was a cluster of black bedouin tents in the distance and he debated with himself whether he should land alongside them and attempt to verify his position. Vaguely remembering being told by an Australian friend something about the customs of nomadic tribes, whereby if one shakes hands with an Arab then he is bound by the rules of desert hospitality to assist, he decided on a landing.

Mollison picked the smoothest spot he could find and landed quite effortlessly near to the nomadic camp. Leaving the engine running, he stumbled across the sand and made towards an older man sitting on a horse, one whom he imagined to be the Sheikh. Proffering one grimy and outstretched hand, he found that the man responded with a friendly handshake as others gathered round. 'Aleppo,' 'Aleppo,' seemed to make little sense to the bemused sheikh or to any of his followers, so Mollison quickly hurried back to the plane to switch off the engine and bring back a map.

This sudden action on the part of the 'birdman' seemed to make the group highly suspicious of his intentions, but after a while they sensed that this was but a harmless, if somewhat slightly crazed, white man. Mollison tried going through the names of villages and towns on his map several times, interspersed with explanations in English and French, until finally one name appeared to evoke a response. The sheikh stabbed the air with a finger pointing to the north-east and Mollison, deciding that that was as much as he was likely to get in the way of directions, made his way back to the aircraft.

Several swings on the propeller failed to start one recalcitrant and hot Gipsy engine. It was the first time that it had mis-behaved during the flight and he cursed his luck that it should decide to play up at such an inopportune moment. It would fire for a time and then fade. Mollison knew that if another pair of hands could swing the prop, then he would be able from within the cockpit to catch the engine with the throttle before it petered out. Gesticulation and sign language to his inquisitive onlookers did not appear to convey exactly what he wanted any one of them to do. When they did finally understand, none were confident enough to even try. Suddenly, the sheikh dismounted and strode purposefully forward to make an attempt. This seemed to inspire or shame the rest of the group to each have a go, and they began to treat the exercise much like a new game that had just been explained to them. At last one man managed to swing the blade with enough force for the engine to start, fortunately, without amputating his arm or leg. The crowd stepped back quite frightened by the ferocity of the result of their colleague's actions. A cheery wave and a smile and JM was back into the air, heading in the direction that had been given him. It turned out to be reasonably accurate and by 10am he was dropping down to land at the military aerodrome at Mouslimie, an outpost near Aleppo in the French mandate of Syria. By this time Mollison was almost at the point of complete exhaustion, for he had not stretched out on a bed since the three hours' sleep in Karachi. Aleppo appears to have been his longest stay at any of his stop-overs, fourteen hours in all.

On the seventh night Mollison took on enough fuel for the 800 miles to Athens and left at midnight.

As dawn broke over a peaceful Mediteranean, he found himself skirting the Turkish coastline alongside the unbroken chain of the Taurus mountains to his starboard. Conditions were ideal and his hopes were beginning to rise as the islands of Rhodes and Cos shimmered in an exquisite blue sea and drifted slowly under the Moth's port wings. It was a perfect summer's morning with the scattered islands of the Dodecanese spread out like jewels glistening in a mirrored sea.

Mollison had been living on his nerves for the past week and he recalls that this sudden glimpse of breathtaking beauty brought home to him the utter recklessness of his life since leaving Wyndham. Whether it was the thoughts of his own mortality and the fragility of his hold on life, or the result of ingrained fatigue, he was not sure. But suddenly he was gripped by an irrational fear of being out alone over this expanse of the Aegean sea. As a result he clung jealously to the sight of each island across the warm waters of the archipelago, as if each one were a personal lifeboat that would soon be needed. The *angst* enveloped him and persisted until the coastline of the Greek mainland came into view. Never did the good earth feel better under his two feet than when he stepped down from the cockpit of the Moth onto the tarmac at Athens' airport. It was ten in the morning. A soothing breeze blew across the field, and the sun felt good.

There was no time to be wasted if he was to make Rome before nightfall and within minutes Mollison was airborne again. As he passed over the harbour at Piraeus, heading westward towards the Corinth canal, he peered down on the toy-like ships which were plying their way through the Gulf. To his right he could see the seaplane base at Phaleron Bay, where the Imperial Airways Short Scipio flying-boats landed on their way between Brindisi and Alexandria. No doubt he quite envied their passengers, who would just now be packing their suitcases in the luxurious Hotel Grande

Bretagne, before embarking for the next stage of their flight to India, or the UK. At Patras he turned north-west and followed the wild and rocky coastline to Corfu, before crossing the Adriatic to the heel of Italy.

Realising that victory was now within his grasp and that it was possible to be in England within 24 hours, he allowed his thoughts to drift toward the physical rewards that would await him. To luxuriate into the suds of a scented warm bath. To sip champagne. And then to float into a noiseless oblivion on the soft pillow of sleep. Such thoughts spurred him on. In spite of the fact that his limbs ached like mad, and he longed to stretch out, the drowsiness and heaviness of sore eyelids became more bearable. Around 2pm he flew over the harbour at Brindisi and from where he could see the aerodrome. He was tempted to land there, but instead decided to press on for the next 300 miles to Rome.

The hurdle of the mountainous range of Italy's Apennines lay ahead of him, shrouded in a barrier of low lying cloud and necessitating a climb to 8,000 feet or more. Without radio aids or eye contact with the terrain he was left solely to the accuracy of magnetic compass and dead reckoning. Somewhere over the mountains he lost his way and as the sky darkened on an obscured western horizon, nagging doubts began to taunt him. There was little that he could do but press on, trusting in his compass-course, and for this he was rewarded. One hour after dark, the clouds began to thin, leaving a gaping hole through which he could see the comforting lights of Rome spread out before him.

With less than a thousand miles from Croydon, JM allowed himself the privilege of a meal whilst his machine was being refuelled. By 11pm the Italian mechanics were pulling the chocks away from the heavily laden biplane, ready for him to taxy out into the darkness on the last stretch of his journey.

Wisely, he decided that in his present state of extreme fatigue that it would be dangerous and foolish to take the more direct route of an overnight flight across the Alps. Prudence demanded that he make the longer but safer flight over the Tyrrhenian Sea to the south coast of France, via Corsica. In the early hours of the morning, and now barely able to keep awake, he picked up the lights of Ajaccio and turned north on a heading for Nice. Skirting along the coast of the Riviera before dawn, he probably mused on Paula, the red-haired enchantress whom he had left to seek his fame and fortune only three years earlier. Was she down there somewhere, dancing the night away in the arms of a new boyfriend?

As he turned north from Marseilles and headed up the Rhone valley, he was met unexpectedly by the fuel-sapping winds of the *mistral*. A strong northerly air current was blowing over the whole of France on Thursday, 6 August, and JM knew that it was doubtful if he could make Croydon without taking on more fuel at Paris.

☆ ☆ ☆

Around 9am there came a knock on the door of the Station Engineer's office of Imperial Airways at Le Bourget airport. Lloyd Ifould looked up from his desk to be greeted by the airport's French official responsible for flight-refuelling.

'One of your compatriots is in trouble and we cannot understand what he is trying to tell us.' 'What does he look like?' Ifould enquired. 'Well, he has a Gipsy Moth, looks very tired, is unshaven, and appears to be deaf. Goodness knows where he has turned up from.' 'What does he want?' Ifould asked. 'All we can understand are two things. He wants petrol in a hurry – he keeps pointing to his watch – and he has no money to pay for it.'

Ifould rose from his chair and accompanied his colleague to meet the unexpected caller, and continues his story with:

On arriving at the other end of the aerodrome, I was introduced to the pilot, whose appearance was all that the man had described. The lines on his face and his red-rimmed, bloodshot eyes showed that he had been a very long time without sleep. He seemed to be dazed and in a state bordering on exhaustion. His machine was in a filthy condition and I saw at once that he must have come from far distant parts. I asked him what the trouble was. It was true that he wanted his machine refuelled, and also that he had no money. 'I must get to England by 2.30pm,' he said.

I informed him that the weather was bad, not only at Croydon, but that the visibility was poor all over the south of England and that our departures had been delayed one hour for that very reason. 'It doesn't matter about getting to Croydon. I will find a place to land. If it is only on the English coast somewhere it will do,' he replied.

'Where have you come from?' I asked. 'Australia,' he answered, 'and my name is Mollison. If I land in England by 2.30pm it will be alright, as I shall have beaten the record.'[31]

Ifould sportingly offered to be responsible for the fuel that was soon being poured into the Moth's near empty tanks. Moreover, he generously arranged for the aircraft to be checked over by Imperial Airways' staff before Mollison recommenced his journey. Whilst this was in progress, the tired airman was being advised by one of the IA pilots on how to avoid the worst of the fog and dark low cloud that lay before him. As it happened, the route detailed by the helpful pilot meant quite a detour from the direct crossing that JM envisaged. Dosing himself strongly with some of the remaining caffein tablets, JM debated in his mind whether the detour was worthwhile. Which would be the bigger enemy? The fatigue or the weather? He had not slept since Aleppo and by now he was heartily sick of flying. Finally, he decided to take the quickest route to the English coast, cursing the weather-front that was proving so obstinate, just when he was within sight of his goal. *C'est la vie!*

The weather turned out to be every bit as bad as he had been warned, with strong northerly winds buffeting the Moth as he arrived over the Channel towards Dieppe. Beneath him the bleached, white sands of the French coast were being blown up to meet the ragged nimbo-stratus that was blanketing the horizon. Such was his extreme tiredness, that at one point the aircraft fell into a spin from which he admits that it was by sheer instinct alone, rather than by any conscious act of the will, that he made a recovery.

After pin-pointing Le Touquet, he turned to cross the channel, heading for the aerodrome at Lympne, in Kent. He was now determined to put down at the first suitable landing ground he saw, once over English soil. Within forty-five minutes the white cliffs of the Sussex coast were just visible through the murk, and although not sure of his exact position he breathed one big sigh of relief knowing that the end of his ordeal was all but over. The strong northerly gale had caused him to drift some forty miles off course and he found that he was now circling over a large coastal town which he finally identified as Eastbourne. Flying east along the coast he decided to put down near one of the Martello towers, on what he thought were the smooth sands of Pevensey Bay.

The small, black biplane skimmed along the deserted beach and towards the end of its run tilted slowly forward onto its nose. Just before the wheels of the Moth sunk into the shingle surface of the Crumbles, JM cut the ignition. It was exactly 8 days, 19 hours and 25 minutes since he had left Australia. Perhaps it was no coincidence that he should have landed almost on the spot where William the Conqueror had first set foot on perfidious Albion, for he had knocked more than two whole days off Scott's record!

Chapter 9

'Into The Limelight'

The pebbles on the beach crunched noisily under the feet of schoolboy George Inson as he ran swiftly towards the silent aeroplane. He had been staying with his sister Molly at a bungalow owned by relatives quite near to the beach and had been walking along the coast road as the small biplane swooped in low over the sea. At first he had just thought that it was making a low pass along the shoreline of the Crumbles, and then, unbelievably, it had landed. This was definitely the most exciting thing that had happened to him since he had arrived on holiday in Pevensey.

The airman's first question was to ask, 'Where's the nearest telephone, laddie?' If George ever had a mental picture of exactly how a pilot should look, then the sight that Mollison presented on that miserable afternoon could never have matched it. The lad saw a rather dishevilled young man standing, slightly unsteadily, beside the aircraft. He was dressed in a travel-stained fawn trenchcoat, its belt tied rather than buckled around the waist, covering an unkempt, grey lounge-suit. He noticed that the man's brown shoes were scuffed and lacking polish. They would, he mused, never have met with his mother's approval. And then, there was the sunburnt, fatigue-lined face. Two red-rimmed and bloodshot eyes peered at him from beneath a brown leather helmet. The man's hands were ingrained with dirt and grease. 'Are all pilots as scruffy as this one?' he asked himself.

As Mollison stumbled up the beach followed by a crowd of inquisitive onlookers, he was directed to Mrs Goodwin's house – probably the only one with a telephone – where he was able to contact the aerodrome at Lympne. With the noise of the engine's exhaust still ringing in his ears, he managed to carry out a conversation with one of the airport officials, confirming his arrival and requesting him to pass a message on to Croydon telling them that he would be arriving after a short rest.

Meanwhile, arrangements were being made for the aircraft to be manhandled onto Arthur Tompsett's small-holding, where there would be

(Above): Mollison arrives at Croydon Airport on 6 August 1931 having knocked more than two days off C. W. A. Scott's record. Note the kangaroo perilously close to the machine's propeller.

(Below): Under Secretary of State for Air, F. Montague, MP., greets an exhausted Jim Mollison at Croydon airport.

sufficient run for a safe take-off. It needed a large crowd of willing helpers to drag the Moth from the beach, and the cutting of a hole in the hedge on the opposite side of the road, before it could be pushed to the site which was about three-quarters of a mile away. Whilst this was in progress, the owner of the bungalow where George and his sister had been staying, a Mrs Nick Prinsep,* had been alerted. She arrived in her Bentley at the Goodwin's home and with great mothering instinct immediately concluded that Mollison was in need of a fulsome, hot meal. Her offer was readily accepted and the tired aviator was whisked off in her car to a local restaurant. After driving him back to her bungalow, he needed little persuading that it was in his best interests to sleep for an hour or so before continuing his journey. In any case he knew that the Australia-England record was now in his possession.

By 3.30pm JM was back at the machine, signing autographs for the children and housewives as the shutters of the 'Brownie' box-cameras clicked to record the historical moment. A local reporter was scribbling away at his pad, with Mollison reminding him as he climbed into the cockpit, 'Don't forget that I'm not an Australian, but a native of Glasgow.'** Turning the cold engine over proved to be almost as big a fiasco as it had been with the sheikh and his fellaheen in Iraq. Mollison had spotted a young man in a painfully new RAF uniform whom he thought would be competent in assisting him to start up, but he just didn't seem to have the knack. Eventually a hefty young farm-labourer came to the rescue and after almost exhausting himself swinging the propeller, the engine finally burst into life.

Mollison taxied out to the far edge of the field, where he then detailed six young men to tug on the struts of each wing in order to hold the aircraft back as he opened the throttle. With a signal from the pilot, they released their hold and the DH60 raced across farmer Tompsett's field, its wings just clearing the chicken fence enclosure and sending the poor frightened birds scurrying in all directions in a cloud of feathers. Well before the ditch on the far side of the field, Mollison pulled the stick back and the lightly-ladened Moth zoomed over the trees. Banking sharply, he circled back over the smallholding to wave a cheery farewell to the folk who had been so kind to him, before turning north-west in the direction of Croydon.

A little after 4pm, JM realised that because of the bad weather he had overshot Croydon and was now over Mitcham. It was then that he saw one of the instructional Moths of the Rollason Aviation Company which was based at Croydon and chartered by one of the national newspapers for

*Mrs Nick Prinsep was better known as Anita Elsom of musical comedy fame.[32]
**When Mollison first appeared in the public eye it was a common misconception that he was an Australian.

photographic record of his arrival. Recognising JM's aircraft, the Rollason pilot flew alongside, signalled, and guided him in over Croydon Airport from the north of the capital.

A correspondent with *The Aeroplane* described the hazards which befell Mollison when he landed, in graphic, if not whimsical, detail.

> Mr Mollison was a tired man when he finally switched off. Needless to say there was plenty of willing – not to say officious – help for him. Someone manned a wing-tip and swung him round with such effect that Major Richard, the Chief Aerodrome Officer, was caught unawares by the tail and sent staggering. The pilot got out of the cockpit very briskly considering the circumstances, and notwithstanding all that has been printed about lifting him out with gentle hands. He apologised for being rather dirty.
>
> A kangaroo which had been brought down to infuse a quite unnecessary spice of burlesque in the affair – and nearly got killed by the airscrew at the start – was brought up and constrained to greet Mr Mollison, and we hardly knew with which to sympathise most. After all, if national emblems must be dragged in, why not lead up a haggis? Mr Mollison is, after all a Scot.[33]

JM recalls that as he walked towards the welcoming party, the boxing-kangaroo almost ruined the meal he had just eaten in Pevensey by kicking him violently in the stomach. Such bizarre happenings almost caused the proceedings to degenerate into pure theatrical farce, although from the photographic records JM appears to have remained quite unruffled. No doubt with his pawky sense of humour, he would have had a few choice words to say about a certain over-zealous, chauvinistic Australian.

Apart from a large crowd waiting to greet him in front of and on the roof of the airport buildings, the official reception party included the Under Secretary of State for Air, Mr F. Montague; the Director of Civil Aviation, Lieutenant Colonel F. Shelmerdine; and several senior RAF officers. After making himself reasonably presentable, JM was escorted to the nearby Aerodrome Hotel where a luncheon was duly given in his honour. He remembered very little of its proceedings however, for after consuming the better part of a bottle of champagne, he fell asleep literally standing up and in mid-sentence during his speech of reply. The next thing he remembered was waking up several hours later in one of the hotel's bedrooms, where he had been carried to sleep off some of his tiredness.

☆ ☆ ☆

It was clearly recognised by those who understood the niceties of fast long-distance flying that JM's flight was a considerable achievement of human endurance, skill and courage. In retrospect, one noted historian comments on the achievements of pioneering aviators such as Jim Mollison and his contemporaries, thus:

> It is doubtful, however, whether in terms of human achievement the Australian flights of Scott, Mollison and Kingsford Smith in the older type of aeroplane have ever been excelled. To cover 11,000 miles in a machine cruising at less than 100 miles an hour, flying and navigating for periods of up to eighteen hours at a stretch in the continuous battering of the propeller slipstream, and to keep this up continuously for nearly nine days, is a feat coming very near the limits of human endurance.[34]

Moreover, not only had Mollison knocked a clear two days off his predecessor's record time in an almost identical aircraft – no mean task when one considers that Scott prided himself on his athleticism – but he had performed it under the most atrocious weather conditions. Even Kingsford Smith, probably the most experienced long-distance flier of all time, commented, 'An examination of Mollison's journey convinced me that he had been unfortunate in his weather . . .'[35]

Only weeks after Mollison's arrival at Croydon, Kingsford Smith had set out in a specially built Avian biplane named, *Southern Cross Minor*, in order to beat his former employee's record. However, he found the going too tough and was forced to abandon the flight at Aleppo through sheer physical exhaustion. Furthermore, even when Charles Scott made an England-Australia flight (it was generally recognised that this was the easier of the two directions) in April of the following year and in the hope of regaining the record, he failed to beat JM's time.

Before the evening of the day of his arrival at Croydon was very young, Mollison was wide awake. He soon found that the natural rhythm of his body-clock had been so disturbed that sleep came only fitfully. Telegrams of congratulation, including one from King George V, and invitations to attend and speak at functions were coming in thick and fast. One phone call was from the chairman of the five star Grosvenor House Hotel in Park Lane, offering him the use of a suite of rooms, and for a dinner that evening to be given in his honour – all *gratis* and by courtesy of the management.

The hotel's Chairman, A. O. Edwards, was an astute Yorkshireman who was quick to catch the mood of the public's interest in their new found air-heroes and to use it to the advantage of his business. Only a year earlier he had offered similar facilities of his hotel to Amy Johnson when she returned from Australia. On that occasion she had been driven with her parents and sisters at walking pace along the twelve miles from Croydon to Park Lane, cheered by an estimated crowd of over a million people along the route. One must not forget that the public reception given to the pioneering pilots, such as Lindbergh, Earhart and the Mollisons after their record-breaking flights of the early Thirties, equalled and probably exceeded that given to the American astronauts after their return from the moon landing in 1969.

One of the telephone calls that Mollison received came from a tailoring establishment in London, insisting on clothing him as soon as he was ready. Slowly, it dawned on him that overnight he had become a celebrity. From now on the formality of 'Mr Mollison' was to be discarded for 'Jim', or 'Jimmy' Mollison. He realised that he had stepped across an invisible line, the one from obscurity into the limelight. He was determined to exploit it to the full and to enjoy every minute of it, knowing that he was virtually penniless when he arrived from Australia in 1931. Apart from the trustworthy Moth, his entire wealth amounted only to the four one pound notes in his pocket. Such offers, therefore, required very little need for a decision. Their acceptance was a necessity. The seduction had begun.

When he awoke on the next morning in the Grosvenor it was to find his suite filled by Fleet Street's reporters and journalists, each one vying for a story. A bleary-eyed Mollison sat up in bed and gave his story to the accompaniment of flashing camera-bulbs and demanding personal questions. One amusing outcome of the morning's invasion was that an attractive woman journalist who was seeking an interview, was shown in the evening newspapers poised by his bedside with the caption reading, 'Mrs Mollison with her husband in the bedroom of their luxury suite today'.

Unlike Amy Johnson, who found the relentless onslaught of such publicity enervating, JM revelled in it. He soon discovered, as some other aviators on the other side of the Atlantic had done, that celebrity-value meant big money. Publicity was there to be manipulated to one's own benefit. Tragically, he was yet to learn that fame was a commodity which carried its own penalties.

Wiley Post, the first aviator to circumnavigate the globe in one continuous staged flight, is on record as saying that Charles Lindbergh was the only American pioneer to make really big money out of aviation. Lindbergh was far too private a person ever to divulge exactly how much he made out of that one momentous solo flight in 1927, but the nominal sum of $25,000 awarded under the Orteig prize must surely have been the small tip of a rather large iceberg. Similarly, Mollison became rich overnight. It is estimated that with the gift of the plane (now hangared at Croydon free of charge), plus Lord Wakefield's cheque; together with £1,000 gift from an Australian philanthropist by the name of A. E. Whitelaw,* and an offer from the *Daily Mail* to make an instructional tour of Scotland, that the Scot had netted approximately £7,000. It was the equivalent of £350,000 in today's currency. This sum would still not have included the perks of luxury accommodation at a greatly reduced tariff in London's West End over the next five years, and other various unspecified gifts. By nature Mollison inherited none of the inclination for thrift for which the Scots are supposedly renowned. He lived very much for the moment. Money was meant to be spent, not saved.

Coincidental to the day of Mollison's welcome at Croydon, Amy Johnson arrived in Tokyo after setting a new light aeroplane record for the distance. She had flown her new cabin DH Puss Moth, accompanied by Jack Humphreys the chief ground engineer at Stag Lane's London Aeroplane Club, to Tokyo in ten uneventful days. Their route had been from Lympne, via Berlin and Moscow to cross the Urals into Manchuria and finally to land in the Japanese capital. They had beaten a comparable Berlin-Tokyo record set by a Japanese pilot by one day. The flight, however, attracted little attention in the world's press. In fact, the hitherto unknown Mollison had even displaced Amy in prominence in the London newspapers on that first morning when he awoke in the Grosvenor.

There is no doubt that Mollison was flattered when he received Amy's cable of congratulation. If nothing else it meant that she had not forgotten the dashing young ANA pilot who had chatted her up in the cockpit of the *Southern Moon* only last year. It might well have been that Amy entertained some romantic notions towards Mollison when she sent it. On the other hand, it might have been nothing more than one pilot of international renown, generously giving praise to one who had also risked his neck for fame and fortune.

Two more significant calls were received by JM on that first Friday morning in London. The first came from the air-minded *Daily Mail*, inviting him to participate in an instructional flying tour of Scotland commencing in September and working closely with their air correspondent, William Courtenay. The second was a more immediate request from the BBC, inviting him to visit that evening to make a broadcast detailing his flight from Australia.

Glasgow Corporation were not slow to honour their new hero. Its Lord Provost, senior magistrates and councillors needed little prompting from ex-Baillie, James Mollison Snr., before sending his grandson an invitation to

*The Australian manufacturer had also given a similar sum to the cricketer Don Bradman in the same year.

attend a civic reception. When he arrived on the Sunday afternoon of 16 August at Renfrew's airport in VH-UFT, the members of the Scottish Flying Club and large crowds were there to applaud and welcome him. The club had arranged for his plane to be dismantled and transported to Lewis's Royal Polytechnic in Argyle Street, where it was re-assembled and placed on display during the following week.[36] On the Tuesday evening he was honoured by the club's members at a reception chaired by the Marquis of Douglas and Clydesdale in the Central Station Hotel.

His stay in West Scotland was to last for eleven hectic days; visiting parents and the numerous Mollison and Addie relatives before culminating with the civic reception. The luncheon was attended by the Lord Provost, Sir Thomas Kelly, and some 120 guests in the Satinwood Saloon of the City Chambers. JM made a modest speech in front of a proud mother and grandfather, acknowledging that whilst it might be argued by some that there was no practical use in his flight, his demonstration of the journey in less than nine days was a powerful and visible reminder of the possibility of regular scheduled flights to Australia. He also emphasised that valuable data had been gathered regarding flying conditions and fuelling requirements along the route, and urged that the cause of aviation, still in its infancy, should receive the full support of the city in encouraging airmindedness in its citizens. The speech ended with him promising to come back within a fortnight on the *Daily Mail* tour, when he would give national air-to-ground flying lessons with the aid of wireless.

Mollison returned to London where the *bon chic, bon genre* of West End society were always on the look out for a new playmate. He was soon to become their new acquisition in Mayfair, that notorious bed of hedonism which falls roughly within an area bounded by Piccadilly, Regent Street, Oxford Street and Park Lane. He could have had no better guide than Kathleen the Countess of Drogheda, to introduce him into what he later described as 'this world of film-stars, politicians, royalty and uncaught financiers'.

The tall, statuesque Countess was some twenty years older than Mollison and recently divorced from her second husband. She was immediately attracted to the Scot, who had all the qualities she admired in a man, for she had in her youth acquired a reputation for being both physically brave and a lover of speed.[37] Amongst her closest friends she prided those who participated in speed events, whether on land, sea or in the air – men and women such as Sir Alan Cobham, Sir Malcolm Campbell, Kaye Don and Amy Johnson. A romantic by nature, she had had a succession of men-friends following her divorce from the Earl in the early Twenties, and it seemed that JM was now her latest object of hero-worship. There is little evidence to show that her attentions were ever seriously reciprocated by Mollison, but that did not seem to deter her from doting on him. She liked to be seen with him and to show him off to her friends.

Kathleen prided herself in possessing a keen awareness of dress-sense and most particularly in that of others. 'Nothing gave her greater pleasure than to choose clothes for her man of the moment – her favourite establishment of international repute being the leading men's tailors, Lesley & Roberts.'[38] Maybe it is not without coincidence that JM hints in his memoirs that she was responsible for him being led as 'a new creature dressed and groomed . . . to obtain my first insight into London's night life'.[39]

The Countess was mainly responsible for introducing him to the rich and wealthy in London's society, especially the pleasure-seeking side of it. Her silver Rolls Royce was frequently seen parked outside the 'in' club of the moment, where she could, over a drink or two, accurately rattle off the name and family gossip of most of its denizens as they arrived, even as late as at 4am.

JM had now entered a *milieu* which was all very new and exciting. He was flattered by it. The social circle in which his chaperone moved was one which fascinated and enthralled him, much like a child with its latest toy. He came to love the crowded, smoke-filled basements, where quick-fire empty chatter vied with the noise of the cocktail shaker. These were the clubs where he could gyrate the night away to the syncopated music of small jazz groups. He loved to be amongst Mayfair's 'bright young things' as they crowded onto postage-stamp sized dance floors, moving to the mellow sounds of clarinet and saxophone. The champagne would flow until they were legless, and nobody cared.

☆ ☆ ☆

It was not long after JM had arrived in England that he received a personal call at his Grosvenor suite from Squadron Leader Don. The RAF officer carried an invitation for Mollison to meet the Prince of Wales for drinks at St James's Palace.

The Prince and his younger brother, the Duke of York, had both received flying instruction with the RAF at Croydon in 1919. Although the younger man qualified and received his wings, at the last moment the King intervened and withdrew his permission for his eldest son to go solo. The decision had been made on the grounds that being direct in line for the throne it was too risky for him to fly alone. To the Prince it was the edict of an over-bearing parent, one that rankled and caused him to resent his father. As one destined to become King there was little he could do but accept the situation, and for a number of years he did so. However, after meeting Lindbergh in 1927, soon after the American's epic flight across the Atlantic, he purchased his own DH Moth and employed Don to act as his flying instructor. In spite of the King's protestations, the determined Prince went on with the flying lessons and with the connivance of Don even made an illicit solo-flight not long before he met Mollison.

JM arrived to meet the slight, golden-haired man who was destined, until his abdication in 1936, to become King Edward V111. Although in his late thirties, he still retained the air of extreme youthfulness, with a little-boy Peter Pan profile that seemed to fit his image as the world's Prince Charming. Only the premature bags under his eyes, acquired over many sleepless nights of revelling and partying, betrayed his hedonistic tendencies.

Mollison's nervousness was soon dispelled as the Prince, together with Don and the Prince's Irish equerry, Captain Edward Metcalfe, put him at ease with several gin and tonics whilst they plied him with questions. Perhaps it was not surprising that the aviator and the Prince found an instant rapport, for, apart from their mutual interest in flying, they unknowingly shared more than a little in common in other areas of their lives. It is tempting to speculate that they recognised in each other a convergence of interests. Both men were possessed of a natural ability to charm others and in both cases they exploited that gift to become dedicated womanisers. At the time of their first meeting, the Prince was in the cooling off stage of a long-standing liaison with his paramour Mrs Freda Dudley Ward, as he paralleled an affair with the desirable and titled American Thelma Furness (Thelma's friend and fellow-American Wallis Simpson was yet to appear on the scene). He was renowned for constantly falling in and out of love. In view of the fact that the future King could have had the pick of any number of titled and single partners throughout Europe, it does seem that the very inaccessibility of the married women he pursued only added to their attraction.

Both men were well-known for their hankering after the world's fleshpots and both were habituées of London's night-spots. The Prince liked nothing better than being invited (or uninvited for that matter) to take over the drums in some small jazz group performing in one of the capital's night clubs. He was a fairly regular customer at Victor Berlemont's restaurant above the 'York Minster' in Soho, an establishment, where, according to the owner's son Gaston, '. . . the party at the next table during the Twenties and

Thirties might well include film-stars, actresses, band-leaders, famous sportspeople (Amy Johnson was one), politicians or even European or British royalty – with or without their paramours. When the Prince of Wales (David) said "bonjour" to Victor on his way to the Gargoyle, he usually had a beautiful wench on either arm.'[40] Small wonder that his fitness to be the constitutional monarch was questioned by many. Sir Osbert Sitwell once criticised the protégé King's circle of friends, suggesting that they comprised 'the riff-raff of two continents . . . the rootless spawn of New York, Cracow, Antwerp and the Mile End Road'.[41]

Similarly, neither Mollison nor the Prince enjoyed a good relationship with either of their parents. The Prince never having had a warm relationship with his austere mother, the former Princess of Teck, whilst being constantly held down by his father. One illustration of his father's domineering attitude towards him being that given by one historian, who quotes a remark made by King George V to the Archbishop of Canterbury, 'After I am gone, the boy will ruin himself within 12 months.'[42] 'The boy' was then forty-one years of age!

After three months of almost continuous nocturnal partying in London's West End, the novelty and excitement began to pall on Mollison. Rarely, if ever, was he to bed before the dawn and the strain of it all was beginning to tell. He knew instinctively that if he was to retain the acclaim that he had so far enjoyed, then he could not simply rest on his laurels. The fickleness of the *dilettanti* to whom he had sold himself expected their heroes to add to their crowns. For them, Jim was becoming rather *déjà vu*. Moreover, it was being noised around that a nineteen year old slip of a girl (she was actually twenty four at the time) named Peggy Salaman, daughter of a wealthy Bayswater business-man and property developer, was about to make an attempt on the England-Cape record. The press had been giving her and her co-pilot cum navigator, Gordon Store, the full treatment. The ballyhoo headlines blazoned in the popular press read, 'The Girl With Everything Money Could Buy – Who Had Got Bored With It All', and articles even detailed the evening gown she had packed ready for her Cape Town reception.

As it transpired, Salaman and Store took off in their Puss Moth from Lympne on 30 October and landed in Cape Town 5 days, 6 hours and 40 minutes later. They had knocked more than a day off the record set up by Lt. Cdr. Glen Kidston earlier in the spring of that year. Mollison could not afford to let the record go unchallenged. After a short period of preparation, he flew down to Lympne (always the favourite aerodrome for the record-breakers because of its close proximity to the continent) in VH-UFT in early November to await favourable weather conditions. Perhaps the four day wait until Friday the 13th was appropriate, for the flight was to become a continuous succession of disasters.

JM had decided on the conventional 'all red route' to South Africa (so called because it took in all those countries in Africa that were either part of the Empire, or were mandated by the British), and that used by Imperial Airways. It meant following a route via Paris, Marseilles, Foggia, Athens, Crete, to Cairo, where he eschewed a night-landing for refuelling and decided to make the 1,000 mile hop to Khartoum with an ETA around daybreak. Under good cloudless conditions and aided by the light of a quarter moon he followed the Nile south for some ninety minutes, until things began to go wrong.

Unlike a modern car engine where the petrol is pumped either mechanically or electrically from the fuel tank to the carburetter, the Moth relied on a gravity-feed system. This operated from two ten gallon tanks positioned in the mid-section of the upper wing above the cockpit and some two feet above the engine. Mollison's aircraft had been modified so that the front cockpit space was occupied solely by a ninety gallon reserve tank. As each top gravity tank emptied, he would be required to hand-pump fuel from the large reserve tank up to the wing tanks.

Some 150 miles south of Cairo he discovered that the pump was not pushing the fuel up. He pin-pointed his position to be somewhere near El Minya, but with a known landing field still some fifty miles distant was not sure that he could make it there on the fuel remaining in the gravity tank. Reluctantly, he came to the decision that it would be prudent to pick out a suitable flat field to land in and attempt a repair on the pump.

After circling the area in the darkness for a quarter of an hour, he found what he thought was a fairly smooth maize field. What he failed to realise was that maize grows in mud, and sometimes to a height, as in this case, of at least five feet.

As he throttled back and came in for a landing with the propeller idling, he realised too late that he was about to submerge into a sea of swaying reeds. Before he could open the throttle the Moth was sinking into the crops with their darkening branches noisily scraping past the wings. The wheels bounced into the glutinous soil and the biplane careered on until it finally flipped onto its back, shedding Mollison into the mud. Fortunately, he was unhurt and able to scramble clear lest the machine caught fire.

A few moments later he was back crawling under the cockpit to turn off the petrol and to retrieve a torch which he carried for emergencies. He cursed his luck and vowed never to start a journey again on a Friday the thirteenth, for apart from setting a record time to Egypt of 37 hours, the flight seemed to be over. Realising that waving a torchlight around in the dark to attract attention when he was so deep in maize was useless, he climbed back to sit on the upturned wings to await for the morning. After sitting there for a while he became restless. And then he had an idea. 'Why not drain some fuel off and start a fire?' That was sure to be seen by someone.

Choosing a spot well clear of the stricken Moth, he tore down some of the drier branch stems and piled them into a heap. After pouring on some petrol to start a blaze, he was forced to patrol the flames in order to prevent the fire from spreading. Nonetheless, it did the trick and before long he was surrounded by a number of peasants who had come to investigate.

Eventually, after contacting the British Consulate in Minya, the plane was removed and transported to Alexandria for repairs, whilst JM followed on by train. After whiling away the best part of seventeen days in Minya, Cairo and Alexandria, the plane was ready for him to collect. If the faulty pump and the unfortunate choice of a landing site at El Minya were the first and second in a series of grave misfortunes, then the choice of route homewards was the third. It was to be even more of a fiasco.

Whilst acknowledging that there was some incentive in risking his neck with a lengthy crossing of the Mediterranean in order to capture the Cape record, he could see no point in doing so now on the return flight home. He now had the choice of two routes to England. He could either fly westwards along the North African coast to Tangier and up through Spain and France, or he could fly east along the coast to Palestine, and then northwards to follow the Syrian and Turkish shores to Bulgaria, and so on across Europe. Unfortunately, he chose the latter route.

After making a leisurely flight along the Egyptian, Palestinian and Syrian coasts, with overnight stops at El Arish and Damascus, he arrived at Aleppo, where he was pleasantly surprised to meet some of the French ground staff who had helped him during his Australia-England attempt. Mollison's arrival must have broken the monotony of routine for his Gallic friends, for such was the intensity of their welcome that he spent two whole days with them.

His plan was to make Constantinople (modern Istanbul) in one hop from Aleppo without refuelling, by flying over the Taurus mountains. It was a route he soon regretted taking for he was forced to fly at over 11,000 feet in blinding snowstorms such as he had never experienced before. The appalling cold was so severe that as soon as he had cleared the worst of the peaks, he was forced to make a landing on a deserted plateau some 3,000 feet up in order to attempt to coax some life back into his near frozen body. After some time on the ground exercising the circulation back into his stiffened limbs and studying his maps, he took off and decided to ease his navigational difficulties by following the railway line that ran from Aleppo to Constantinople. However, by the time he had reached Konia the weather conditions were no better and he decided to put down for the night. Circling around for a while, he eventually picked a suitable level spot on the outskirts of the town and landed.

The propeller had hardly come to rest before he was being approached by armed Turkish soldiers, whose officer in charge immediately made it known that he had landed in a militarised zone and was under arrest. Mollison's protestations were to no avail and he was swiftly marched into the town to the Yildiz Oteli Hotel where he was locked into a squalid little bedroom on the first floor to await questioning.

The determined Scot did not take too kindly to this kind of treatment and after surveying his surroundings, decided to escape out of the window which was some fifteen feet above the ground. By hanging on to the sill with his fingertips, he reasoned that he would not have too far to fall to the courtyard below. Just as he was about to release his hold and drop, he heard the cry of an armed soldier beneath him. As he looked down he could see that the menacing guard was about to take a lunge at him with his bayonet. JM admits that he pulled himself back up into the safety of his bedroom with more than a fair degree of alacrity.

The incident did not exactly enhance his chances of an early release when an interrogation by military officials and a police commandant followed later in the evening. From the ensuing cross-examination and excited discussions conducted in a mixture of French and Turkish, he gathered that he was being charged with espionage. Attempts to express his concern for the safety of his aeroplane, which as far as he knew had no protection from the elements, fell on deaf ears. After spending two and a half days in the hotel he was taken to a local courtroom where he was formally charged with espionage and, in addition, with some technical irregularity in his passport. Eventually an interpreter arrived and he was allowed to contact the British Embassy in Istanbul and explain his case.

After spending a frustrating and miserable seven days in Konia, he was officially told that he must dismantle his aircraft and entrain with it to Aleppo. Knowing that the dismantlement of the Gipsy Moth would cause alignment problems on re-assembly without the necessary jigs, he sent telegrams to the embassy imploring their help. The Turkish authorities were, however, unrelenting and insisted that he leave the country without the aircraft. As a consequence, he was escorted to the Syrian border under armed escort, minus the aeroplane.

After some negotiation with the British Consulate in Syria over the next few days, he was allowed to return to Konia and continue his journey by air, providing he flew outside of Turkish air space. However, such was his stubborness that when he finally took off, instead of heading south-east to Syria as instructed, he headed north-west for Bulgaria by way of the Turkish capital. From Mollison's description of the take-off it appears that he gained some satisfaction over his captors who were there to see him depart by 'waving his hand to them' in a last farewell. One wonders what caused the Turkish Commandant to shake his fist back at JM. Maybe Mollison's wave did not include all the four fingers of one hand!

JM was really pushing his luck by continuing the flight over forbidden territory and he very nearly came to grief again. Some one hundred miles south of the Sea of Marmora he ran into thick cloud, which caused him to lose eye-contact with the black weal of the railway line coiling through the mountains on its way to Istanbul. As a consequence, he was forced to land along the banks of a frozen river where he was given hospitality for the night in a nearby Turkish hamlet. The following day there was still no break in the weather and he was forced to spend another night in the hamlet, before making the Bulgarian seaport of Burgas on the eastern coast of the Black Sea.

The flight continued uneventfully via Belgrade, Budapest and Vienna towards Munich, until at Muhldorf he landed for a quick smoke and a rest. Upon attempting to taxy across the field for a take-off, one of the Moth's wheels became stuck in a deep rut. One or two local farmhands came to his rescue but unfortunately whilst assisting, one of the men came too near to the rotating airscrew and broke his arm. JM was compelled to spend a whole week in Munich sorting out compensation for the poor man's injury, and to make matters worse, he noticed that the impact had badly cracked one of the propeller blades. Knowing that a replacement could not be obtained nearer than Geneva, he decided, after testing the propeller with some run-ups on the ground, to take a chance and make for Stuttgart, hoping that it would last as far as Lympne.

Somewhere between Augsberg and Ulm the inevitable happened and the damaged blade parted company from its boss, leaving him in the air with a badly vibrating machine. It meant another forced-landing, this time in a snow-covered field. He was to spend the next two days awaiting a replacement propeller before he could depart for home. Finally, he arrived back at Lympne on 7 January 1932. It had taken him just 37 hours to reach Egypt, and 53 days to get back!

☆ ☆ ☆

Upon his return to London, Jim Mollison quickly found the truth behind the old aphorism, 'Success has many fathers, but failure is an orphan'. The crowd he mixed with were not as forgiving as he expected them to be, and he knew instinctively that if he was to enjoy the life to which he had so quickly become accustomed, then he must tackle the England-Cape record again immediately. After discussions with the de Havilland factory at Stag Lane, he decided to dispose of the open-cockpit Moth biplane in favour of one of the company's latest cabin monoplanes, the Puss Moth DH80A.

The DH80 prototype first flew in September 1929 and production of the 80A, incorporating a welded steel-tube fuselage, started in March of the following year. Unlike the Moth biplane, its more modern counterpart had its 120 horse power Gipsy 111 engine inverted, thus giving the pilot not only a clearer view ahead, but also giving the machine a much cleaner aerodynamic shape. The design improvememnts meant that it had a maximum speed of 128mph, almost 30mph faster than the DH60 biplane with the same engine. In its standard form, using the two 17 gallon wing tanks, it had a range of 300 miles cruising at 108mph. Moreover, it could carry three people (the two passengers sat in tandem behind the pilot) at a very economical twenty miles to the gallon. For record-breaking flights an additional fuel-tank was situated in the space normally occupied by passengers.

The Puss Moth had excellent handling qualities and was to become a firm favourite with light aeroplane enthusiasts throughout the world in the early 1930s. Unfortunately, its reputation was to become somewhat tarnished when instances of it shedding either, or both, of its mainplanes started to occur. One of the earliest cases of such failure occurred in Western Australia in October 1930, but at the time it was considered to be an isolated case with unknown causes. However, a similar but more publicised accident occurred in South Africa in May 1931, when the well-known pilot Lt. Cdr. Glen Kidston and passenger Cptn. Thomas Gladstone were killed at Tandjiesberg.

At the subsequent Board of Inquiry, allegations were made by an Inspector of Accidents and technical expert to the SAAF of an 'inherent weakness' in the Puss Moth's design. The charges were vehemently denied by the de Havilland Company at the time, but by the end of 1933 there had been nine known instances of wing failure. As a result, the Royal Aircraft Establishment carried out several investigations during the period 1931-34, in which the torsional stiffness of the Puss Moth wing was compared with that of other contemporary aircraft. The outcome was that the company was forced to recommend modifications to the rear spar and tank bay areas of the wings, both in production and retrospectively to existing aircraft.

A fine aerial shot of a de Havilland 80A Puss Moth over southern England (G-AAZP with owner Tim Williams at the controls). This 1930 registered aircraft was flown by its owner and Henry Labouchere from Mildenhall to Melbourne in 1984 in order to commemorate the 50th anniversary of the MacRobertson Air Race.

In spite of the modifications, the Puss Moth was never fully able to shake off its reputation for being prone to wing failure. It appears that it was most likely to occur under the combined conditions of high speed and turbulence. The same structural failure was to be responsible for Bert Hinkler's death when the port mainplane of his Puss Moth broke away over the Appenines in January 1933. The last known case was reported in June 1937, when Arthur Leavens (owner of Leavens Brothers Air Services) and two passengers were on a flight from Toronto to Detroit. 'Observers of the accident said the aeroplane appeared to lose a wing while still in the air, then hurled to earth completely out of control. It crashed on its side, cutting a huge swath in the wheat and killing all on board.'[43]

When one considers that Mollison used the Puss Moth to solo both North and South Atlantics, as well as making a hazardous solo flight across the Sahara, one wonders if he was fully aware of the machine's accident history.

☆ ☆ ☆

Even though Mollison was preparing to make an attempt on the Cape record by the untried and hazardous western route, he didn't let that interfere with his amatory pursuits. Although he had been an unknown, junior RAF officer when he visited the '43 Club' in 1924, he returned to the capital seven years later as something of an idol and was considered to be a very eligible bachelor. It was rumoured that at this time Kate Meyrick was very keen for one of her daughters to marry Mollison. However, what is far more certain is that Lady Diana Wellesley, great-grand-daughter of the Duke of Wellington was one of his conquests. The tall attractive eighteen year old debutante was the elder daughter of the late Lord Cowley by his third wife, Clare, Lady Cowley, and had met JM at a cocktail party in the West End. Diana quickly fell head over heels in love with the flamboyant aviator, and they were soon seen regularly together dancing and dining out. It was not long before they were secretly and unofficially engaged.

When the gossip of their engagement reached the ears of Diana's mother she sought to break up the liaison. In Clare's eyes JM was nothing more than a dangerous *arriviste* and any prospective union was viewed with incredulity. Such a marriage would, she felt, be a mésalliance. From the outset she was determined to end their affair.

To make matters worse, Mollison had received some very bad publicity after being charged with assault at the Marylebone Police Court in February 1932. Evidently he and two women had been standing outside of a private residence in Bayswater waiting for a taxi, when the owner of the property

Lady Diana Wellesley (she later became Lady Glentoran) and Jim Mollison at the time of their 'engagement' in 1932.

came out and ordered them to move away. According to Mollison's evidence[44] the man verbally abused the two women (probably mistaking them for prostitutes) and a fight had ensued. Immediately the police were called the women fled, obviously not wanting to be identified. Later in court when asked by the magistrate to name the two women, Mollison would only write their names down. One was a titled married lady (presumably the Countess of Drogheda) and the other a widow.

In spite of police evidence confirming that Mollison was quite sober at the time of the fracas, and the fact that the case against him was dismissed, the press account only served to harden Lady Cowley's attitude against him. Her solution was to whisk Diana and her younger sister Cecilia off to the south of France for a motoring holiday. Mollison saw this as a snub and a put down. It only made him all the more determined to break Salaman and Store's record to the Cape.

By a strange coincidence Mollison flew from Stag Lane in his Puss Moth, G-ABKG, on the morning of 19 March in the company of none other than Charles Scott. His old arch-rival was attempting to regain the England-Australia record which had been taken from him by C. A. Butler, who had made the flight in a tiny Comper Swift in 9 days and 2 hours. Both Scott and JM had picked the 20th for their departure date solely because it coincided with the benefit of a full moon.

Charles Scott recalls the affair between JM and Diana Wellesley that time with:

> The following morning the placards in the streets of Hythe bore the words, 'Famous Airman's Romance', and I bought a newspaper and showed it to Mollison at breakfast as he was the airman concerned.
>
> He left Hythe and stayed mysteriously away all day, and in spite of bad weather conditions prevailing, left for Cape Town the following morning. Publicity of this romance of his was too much for him, and he sought the security of the air and escaped.[45]

Chapter 10

'Air Lovers'

Although Jim Mollison and Amy Johnson were both living in London during the autumn of 1931,* their paths were not to cross for another six months or more. Neither, it appears, made any attempt to renew the friendship that they had struck up on the Brisbane to Sydney airliner soon after her England-Australia flight. Since that time Amy had made a 14,000 mile flight to Japan with her co-pilot cum mechanic Jack Humphreys. However, in spite of being the first to make the 1,760 miles from Croydon to Moscow and setting the fastest time for a light aeroplane to Tokyo in just under nine days, the flight aroused little public interest. The timing of her flight was unfortunate inasmuch as when compared to Wiley Post and Harold Gatty's circumnavigation of the globe, made only weeks previously, it appeared relatively insignificant. The one-eyed American pilot and his Tasmanian navigator had amazed the world by flying 15,474 miles in 8 days 15 hours and 51 minutes.

Upon her return from Japan, Amy set off with Jack Humphreys on a lecture tour of the UK, but not before instructing him to search out a suitable aircraft for a round-the-world flight. It seems that Post and Gatty's achievement had inspired her to emulate them and approaches were made to the Vickers Company at Weybridge for use of one of their Viastra twin-engined monoplanes. She let it be known that she proposed to make the flight during the following summer but nothing ever really came of her plans and the idea was eventually dropped.

By this time Amy was very much in the public eye, and being famous, young and attractive, the tabloid press were spearheading speculation about whom she might marry. In spite of Amy's close relationship with Jack Humphreys there does not appear to have been any sexual attraction between them. According to Constance Babington Smith's well-researched biography on Amy, their relationship was on a purely platonic, brother and sister level. It appears that Jack, a married man, was content to bask in the

*Amy was living at Vernon Court, London N.W.2.

reflected glory of Britain's air heroine. This did not mean that he was blind to her faults for he was all too aware that she could be a difficult person to cope with emotionally, especially when she was in what he called 'one of her black moods'.

Amy had many admirers and curiously enough, even in those so-called innocent days, not all of them were male. William Courtenay, the man who had been engaged by the *Daily Mail* to act as the organiser and adviser for her tour after her Australia flight a year earlier, was delegated to open her fan-mail during that time. Acting very much as her moral guardian, he recalls:

> Then there were strange letters from equally strange and perverted females who wished to make clandestine appointments through advertisements. For what purpose they wanted the girl may be guessed. Naturally I consigned those letters to the flames.[46]

Amy gave nothing much away to the inquisitive, for she was probably still nursing the grief she had felt when Franz had jilted her. She did, however, make it known that she would never marry a man who was only prepared to be a 'Mr Amy Johnson'. Her ideal was of a man of adventure. One who could be her equal in courage. What was more, she admitted he would be hard to find!

There are those who have attempted to cast Amy in the role of one of today's feminists, but from even a casual reading of some of the many love letters that she wrote to Franz, it is palpably obvious that she was a born romantic. Jack Humphreys had ideas that she might one day marry one of her more ardent admirers, namely, Peter Q. Reiss, a young aviation underwriter working for Lloyd's. She had met PQ – as he was commonly known by his friends – through her contacts with the Leicestershire Flying Club at Ratcliffe, where he acted as private pilot to Sir Lindsay Everard. He had acquired a reputation as a skilful pilot whilst serving in the RFC during WW1 and was a champion squash player, but there was one major snag as far as Amy was concerned – he, like Humphreys, already had a wife!

Theories have been put forward that Amy became disillusioned about marriage even before she met Jim Mollison. These tend to hinge around the embittered remarks that she finally threw at Franz when she wrote to him at the time of their break-up. In one of her final letters to her Swiss lover, she wrote that she had come to the conclusion that men only wanted women for one thing, admitting that she now despised herself for having given in to him sexually.

On quite another level, she had been deeply hurt when her younger married sister Irene had committed suicide, some two years after her wedding in July 1929. On the surface her sister appeared to be happily married, until one day, whilst her husband was away at work, she had ended her life by opening the taps on a gas-oven in the kitchen. Amy felt the loss of her sister deeply, for the two girls were particularly close in childhood (Irene was 18 months younger). Maybe, coming as near as it did to her break up with Franz, Amy blamed marriage itself for her sister's tragic death at twenty-four years of age.

After spending the Christmas of 1931 with her parents at their new home in Bridlington, Amy had only just recommenced her lecture tour of northern towns with Jack Humphreys when she was taken ill with severe abdominal pains at Bolton. Evidently she had been suffering with a gynaecological disorder for some time before this attack and had been under the care of a lady doctor in London. As a consequence, she insisted, in spite of the severity of the pain and appalling weather conditions, that Jack should drive her back to London. Two days later she was operated on in a London nursing home for what was reported to be an appendectomy. It was generally agreed, however, by several of her closest friends that the operation was in fact for a hysterectomy.

Several weeks were spent convalescing, before Amy managed to persuade her doctor that what she really needed was some sunshine. Madeira was chosen for the purpose and she sailed from Southampton on the *Winchester Castle* accompanied by her nurse. Unfortunately, when she arrived and disembarked with her luggage, she found that it had been raining on the island for the last six weeks. What displeased her even more was the fact that she could see that the hotel into which she had been booked was not going to give her the seclusion for which she hoped. In her estimation it was full of gossipy, society people, and without more ado she packed her bags and returned to the ship to continue her journey to South Africa.

Back on the *Winchester Castle* with less than a day's sailing to reach Cape Town, Amy received the news over the ship's radio that Jim Mollison was due to arrive in South Africa, after what looked to be a record-breaking flight. It happened to be the same day that the ship docked. There is no way of knowing if Amy had any romantic notions running through her mind at that time. She had only met JM briefly two years earlier and since then, apart from the telegram of congratulation she had sent him when he had arrived at Croydon, there had been no communication between them. There is no doubt he fitted one part of her image of the ideal man, inasmuch as he had proved himself to be as determined and courageous as she herself.

✩ ✩ ✩

Ever since his crash-landing in Egypt, in 1931, Mollison had turned his attentions to an alternative western trans-Sahara route to the Cape. It had one great advantage over the well established 'all red' route used by the Imperial Airways and early pioneers such as R. R. Bentley, Alan Cobham and Lady Mary Heath – it was approximately 600 tempting miles shorter! The route had never been flown by a solo aviator in a light aeroplane before and the reason for this was not difficult to explain, for it meant a dangerous crossing of some 1,100 miles over the dubiously charted Sahara Desert. A forced-landing in this area and it could be days or even weeks before a rescue team could reach a stranded flier. Bill Lancaster was to make a forced-landing there in April 1933 in an Avro Avian biplane *Southern Cross Minor*, a machine which had formerly belonged to Charles Kingsford Smith. Searches were made but pilot and machine were not found. The mystery was not solved until some thirty years later, when Lancaster's mummified body was found lying beside the wreckage, complete with a record of the final desperate days of his life scrawled in his log book.

Unlike the eastern route, with its superior airports and servicing facilities, the western route provided only primitive landing strips whose boundaries were barely marked out with just a few white-washed boulders. Even some five years after Mollison's successful flight over the route, when Alex Henshaw was surveying it for his 1939 attempt on the Cape record, fuel was carried to one of the Sahara landing spots by camel, where it then had to be buried deep in the sand to avoid evaporation.[47]

The shorter western route also entailed the additional hazard of flying over the dense jungle of the Cameroon and Congo forests. These were areas which experienced frequent and unpredictable equatorial storms, giving conditions which could mercilessly toss a light aircraft out of the sky. Not exactly the kind of weather to be welcomed in an aircraft with the accident history of the Puss Moth. Moreover, weather-forecasts were of little help in storm avoidance for they were notoriously inaccurate.

Further down the western coast and for a thousand miles south of Mossamedes, the coastline was often fog-bound, a phenomena caused by the cooler Atlantic air meeting with the extreme heat of the Namib Desert. None of this seemed to discourage Mollison, whose philosophy for success reminds one of de Tocqueville's comments regarding the politics of the impossible. *De l'audace, encore de l'audace, toujours de l'audace.*

JM left Lympne at 1.05 am on Thursday, 24 March, with 120 gallons of aviation fuel brimming in the tanks to give him a range of approximately

1,800 miles. After thrashing down through France and Spain by way of Lyons, Marseilles and Cartegena, he arrived at Oran just after noon. Within half an hour he was heading over the Atlas mountains towards his next sheduled stop, 450 miles further on to the desolate landing strip at Beni Abbés. It was his intention to fly over the French Air Force station at Colomb Bechar, but after suffering the desert heat and its accompanying turbulence for three and a half hours he succumbed to the temptation to put down there for a brief rest. At that moment JM had no reason to doubt that he would be allowed to proceed through the night. He felt secure in the knowledge that amongst the documents that he carried was a permit to cross the Sahara. However, just as he was about to take off from Colomb Bechar, the resident French Commandant informed him that not only would he not be allowed to proceed until daylight, but that he must also carry four gallons of water and sufficient food for a fortnight. No amount of protesting from JM that he was on a record-attempting flight availed. Cursing his luck, he settled down for the night wishing that he had flown on to Beni Abbés as he had originally planned.

The delay was frustrating, but once in the air he thought about lightening an already overloaded aeroplane by ditching the water and food over the side. Apart from the excess weight factor, it had been necessary to place the water-carrier between and under his legs, causing a restriction which impeded safe operation of the rudder-bar. Knowing that if he jettisoned the unwanted cargo it might hit and damage the tailplane, he dimissed the idea and set a compass-course for Reggan Oasis, some 360 miles south.

From the oasis he began what was the most dangerous part of the flight, a thousand miles of blank featureless desert. For the first three hours he had the comfort of following the trans-Sahara car track, but suddenly upon looking down it had vanished. Switching to a compass-course for the Niger, which lay 900 miles distant, the tiny Puss Moth began to ride over the bumpy air of a never ending undulating expanse of yellow sand. The sun beat mercilessly down on the glazed canopy of the cabin as JM struggled to shed some of his clothing. Ahead, in the blur of the airscrew, the horizon shimmered in a heat haze. Throughout the day the slight headwind grew stronger, causing the ground to be intermittently obscured by brown dust. It probably reminded him of the sandstorms that he had endured in Iraq eight months previously.

The final part of the Sahara route is ably described by Amy herself, not long after she had made her record-breaking flight in 1936:

Safely across the sea of sand, you then have to traverse a light plateau of absolutely flat hard earth, the Tanezrouft, in the centre of which is the loneliest landing ground in the world, Bidon Cinq, which is the French for 'Tin No: 5'.

At intervals in this vast plain you suddenly meet ranges of rocky, jagged mountains, in some instances rising to 8,000 feet above sea-level. Between the ranges run dried-up river courses, indicating that once upon a time the Sahara was abundantly watered.[48]

JM was now desperately tired and finding it difficult to keep awake. He remembered that it was Good Friday and he had had little sleep since that faraway Wednesday afternoon at Lympne. The delay at Colomb Bechar and the strong headwind now meant that he would not sight the Niger before nightfall, so he reasoned that he might just as well put down in the late afternoon for a short rest. At least the time spent on the ground would mean that by the time he reached the Niger, some two hours after dark, the moon be would be up, and, hopefully, the river would then be more visible. Flying low over the barren landscape, he picked out a smooth hard surface and landed. He slid out of the cockpit and stood under the shadow of the wing to take a swig from his brandy flask.

As he lay under the shadow of the wing smoking a cigarette and musing over the flight he fell asleep, only to be roused from his slumber when the cigarette butt had begun to burn his fingers. The brief nap did, however, take the edge off his drowsiness and he smoked two more cigarettes, all the while consciously striving to keep himself awake. After a forty-five minute break, he decided to continue his journey. Fortunately, there were no problems in starting the engine and he was soon climbing away into an evening desert sky, heading for Goa.

As he flew southwards the terrain passing under the Puss Moth's wings was beginning to show signs of sparse vegetation. Some patches of desert grass and the occasional shrub assured him that the Sahara was now behind him. Around 9pm he picked out the Niger, glistening under a waning moon, its silvery coil acting as a navigational aid as he began to follow it down past Goa, towards his scheduled stop at Niamey.

According to newspaper reports at the time the forced-landing fifteen kilometres short of Niamey was due to 'engine trouble' (JM himself records that the oil-pressure gauge was reading low). However, one cannot but help suspect that the real problem was simply fatigue. This might not have been the sole factor, for there has been much speculation regarding the quality of Mollison's night-vision, and not without some justification, for night-

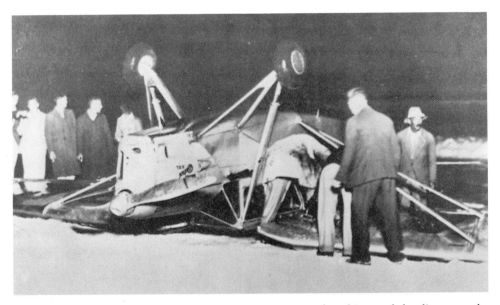

The wreckage of Mollison's Puss Moth, G-ABKG, after his crash-landing on the Woodstock at Milnerton beach, Cape Town, 28 March 1932.

landings were beginning to cause him problems, a difficulty which was to dog him throughout his flying career. It must be remembered that the testing of pilots for night myopia was not really taken seriously until the demands of operational flying began to make their effects felt during WW2. Mollison admits that his landing that night on a mud-flat alongside the bank of the river was the nearest that he came throughout the flight to losing control of the machine. It was almost a repeat of the episode at El Minyah, but his time he was luckier and the Puss Moth was not damaged.

Once on the ground, and it must have been around midnight by then, he knew that there was no possibility of getting away again until daybreak. If he had any expectations about using the enforced time of idleness by catching up on lost sleep, then they were to be short-lived. Within a few minutes he was surrounded in the dark by a hundred or more inquisitive natives, who insisted on touching the machine. Their leader's response to Mollison's enquiries made in French regarding the position of Niamey's airfield was unhelpful, and what made matters worse, the group were not content to leave him in peace. As soon as he bedded down for sleep they would creep back and start to touch the instruments in the machine's cabin, until in the end he had to squat under the wing with stick in hand ready to chase them away. Needless to say, it was a frustrating and sleepless night for the weary flier.

As soon as it was daylight JM was able to fly off the mud-flat, and once in the air soon managed to locate the reasonably smooth airfield at Niamey. Upon his arrival, there were further frustrations caused by a long delay in obtaining fuel, and then difficulties in organising the help of native labour to put the fuel into the aircraft's tanks. So much time was lost, in fact, that JM was forced to travel with his local agent into the town of Niamey in order to wire Duala that his arrival there would not be at sunset that night, but at dawn on the following day. By now he had grave fears that if he met any further delays, he would be unable to break the Cape record set up by Peggy Salaman and Gordon Store.

JM eventually took off from Niamey early on the Saturday evening, setting a course for Duala with a nine hour night flight before him. He was now flying into towering banks of rain-laden cumulus cloud over an area of monsoon weather and even at night he found the air unpleasantly humid and oppressive. If the heat on the Sahara crossing had been more intense, it was at least drier and therefore more bearable. Just before dawn there was a break in the clouds and he was able to see the Cameroon coastline outlined beneath him. After flying blind for so many hours, he was more than a little relieved to find that his navigation had been accurate after all.

The small airfield at Duala where he refuelled was literally carved out of the jungle and covered with quite long grass. Whilst it did not present much of a problem on landing, it certainly proved quite difficult on the take-off with a full load of fuel on board. On the second attempt, the heavily laden Puss Moth managed to stagger into the air, not far off the stall-speed, to clear the trees at the end of the aerodrome by an uncomfortable margin.

The 1,050 mile flight to San Paolo de Loanda on the Angola coast took up most of the daylight hours on the Sunday. By 10.00am on the following day, he was putting down at Walvis Bay in German South West Africa. The desire for sleep was now overwhelming but he knew that if he was to capture the record then he must press on immediately. Cape Town lay but 850 miles away.

Up until noon on the last leg of the journey, conditions improved with clear skies. However, during the afternoon strong winds sprang up to reduce the Puss Moth's ground speed. Mollison confesses that his eyes were now beginning to play tricks on him and by the time he arrived over Cape Town's airport at 8pm he had duplicated vision. One can only conjecture at this point whether this was caused purely by fatigue, or, as one suspects, by too much alcohol imbibed on an empty stomach during the last stages of the flight. He was certainly a man who pushed himself to the extremities of his physical endurance and maybe he was tempted to extend this limit with the support of a stimulant. On the other hand, he may well have entered into a period of fatigue where a lesser man would have given up. We shall never know.

According to his own account, the lights of the airport only served to confuse him. He says that he knew instinctively that he would never make a safe landing at Wingfield that evening, and as a consequence he turned to look for a suitable spot on the beach at Milnerton, approximately five miles away. Keeping to the seashore, where, presumably, he could see the white surf line, he then caught sight of what he thought was a jetty, though it was in reality a curving path between the golf course and the beach. Finally, he managed to scrape down on the beach after narrowly missing a taxicab drawn up on the adjoining road.[49]

Evidently the beach had a far greater slope than JM bargained for, and as he attempted to keep directional control with the rudder, the machine veered and ran into the sea to a depth of four or five feet before turning over.[50] Mollison said that he immediately kicked out one of the windows and fell into the sea, where he took in mouthfuls of sea-water. Soaked to the skin, he staggered up the beach to safety.

The astonished negro taxi-driver was soon on the scene to assist the wet and bedraggled pilot to his cab. Within minutes JM was being whisked back to the airport, where Amy was amongst the large crowd anxiously awaiting his arrival. He had flown a distance of 6,255 miles in 4 days 17 hours and 19 minutes beating the present holders, Peggy Salaman and Gordon Store, by almost 15 hours. It was a feat of great human endurance, for during this period it is doubtful if Mollison had had more than a eight or nine hours' sleep. The record flight was to be widely acclaimed as a superb piece of navigation over a particularly hazardous route. Moreover, it was a flight which firmly established him in the front rank of the world's aviators.

Just what Amy thought when she saw the exhausted and dishevilled flier walking into the airport that Monday evening is not known. He can hardly have been in any fit state to hold a coherent conversation with her, let alone convey any romantic notions. One must also consider that if Amy had been reading any of the current English newspapers, then she might well have known that they were reporting that Mollison was engaged to be married to Lady Diana Wellesley. Certainly the London *Evening News* had been printing articles by William Courtenay giving the Mollison 'romance' a high profile. However, when questioned on the affair by the Cape press, JM was tight-lipped and if anything, seemed to be backing away from any commitment to marriage.

The morning after JM's arrival, Amy spent time helping him to open the many telegrams of congratulation, and later they they lunched together in one of the city's fashionable restaurants. Inevitably, the story quickly spread to the effect that they were planning a flight across the Atlantic together. Such rumours may have originated from JM telling the press of his future plans for an east-to-west solo crossing of the North Atlantic, or maybe they were no more than speculation by one of the Cape's newspaper reporters.

The *Winchester Castle* sailed for Port Elizabeth and Durban during the same afternoon with Amy on board, by which time her nurse had caught one of the other 'Castle' liners returning to England. Constance Babington Smith tells us that the emotional turmoil of her short stopover in Cape Town caused a relapse in Amy's health, and that she admitted after the journey that during the trip to Durban she was 'on the verge of hysterics'. Strangely enough, Amy's own memories of that period seem to contradict her biographer, for she was to write only a few years later:

'. . . and once I passed through (South Africa) on a cruise I was taking for my health, visiting Port Elizabeth with its world-famous Snake Park and on to Durban, where I spent one of the happiest fortnights of my life at the home of a well-known big-game hunter, William A. Campbell, affectionately known as 'Wac' to all his friends. His lovely modern house stands on top of the cliffs, sprayed by the breaking waves of the Indian Ocean which scatter their foam just the same on picturesque African kraals further along the cliff-side.[51]

Much like Amy, Jim Mollison's company was now being sought by the rich and influential. During the short period he spent in Cape Town he was invited to lunch with Sir Abe Bailey*, one of South Africa'a wealthiest philantrophists. Sir Pierre Van Rynevald, himself a pioneer aviator and Director of Union Air Services, set the tone for the Scot's reception when he voiced his opinion that the aviator's achievement was 'as great a performance that one can imagine'. Soon after his arrival he was invited to broadcast on South African radio where he described the highlights of his flight across the Sahara and down through West Africa. The rest of his time was spent sightseeing and tasting the pleasures of Cape Town's night life, before he boarded the *Carnarvon Castle*, together with the battered Puss Moth. By the time he arrived in Southampton on 18 April, two thoughts were now uppermost in his mind. Firstly, to straighten out his future

---

*Lady Bailey, who had learned to fly with the London Aeroplane Club at Stag Lane in the 1920s, soloed from Croydon to the Cape and back during the period, March 1928 – January 1929.

relationship with Diana Wellesley, and more importantly, to be the first person to solo the North Atlantic in a westerly direction.

☆ ☆ ☆

Jim Mollison's sucessful and daring flight across western Africa to the Cape made him even more desirable in the eyes of the besotted Diana Wellesley. He was now well and truly the young girl's knight in shining armour, and her family's opposition to their engagement only seems to have made her more determined than ever to continue seeing him. However, Lady Cowley insisted on meeting the man whom her step-daughter intended to marry and he was invited to visit the family home at Seagrey Manor, near Chippenham, forthwith. In the Scot's mind the prospect of encountering the haughty, titian-haired tigress, probably required as much courage as confronting the uncharted sands of the Sahara!

JM flew down to the family residence a few days after he arrived home and landed his Puss Moth in a nearby field, where an anxious Diana was waiting to guide him into the Countess' presence. Diana waited discreetly outside in an adjoining ante-room whilst JM entered for an interview that turned out to be every bit as unnerving as any he had experienced.

Lady Clare Cowley was quite unimpressed with Mollison's flying achievements and made it quite plain that she didn't take kindly to his infatuation with her step-daughter. Moreover, she let him know in no uncertain terms that his background and family pedigree did not measure up to the tradition and breeding she would deem fitting for any proposed marriage. Maybe the press coverage of the Bayswater scuffle had been drawn to her attention, but there is no doubt she would have regarded him as completely beyond the pale. According to his memoirs he was given a third-degree questioning ranging from his present and future finances, to details of the most personal nature. As much as he tried to parry the questions, she remained adamant that marriage was not on the agenda until Diana was twenty. The result being that JM came away licking his wounds and highly dispirited. Diana it appears was almost prepared to take the plunge and elope, but not quite. As a consequence, they agreed to keep their engagement on trial for a year and wait to see if the parental opposition softened.

In the meantime, a tanned and rather animated Amy arrived back at Southampton early in May, where she was met by her mother and Jack Humphreys. Her former partner immediately sensed that there was something about her behaviour which suggested a hidden inner excitement. The mystery was soon solved, for on Sunday, 8 May, after the two of them had returned from a weekend trip to Brussels in her Puss Moth where they attended an aircraft display, Jim Mollison was waiting at Heston to meet her.

Events moved swiftly from their first meeting in the UK when Jim invited Amy to lunch the next day at Quaglino's, one of London's classiest restaurants. He was surprised by the startling change in her appearance since they last met. She was no longer the tomboy who had sat beside him in the cockpit of the *Southern Moon* on the flight from Brisbane; or the wan, tired looking girl in Cape Town recuperating from her operation. Sitting opposite him now, with those seductive blue eyes, was an elegant self-assured woman. She was, he thought, the epitome of sophistication, and there is no doubt he was completely dazzled by her. Unquestionably, their intimate conversation over that meal must have included his affair with Diana Wellesley, for Amy would most certainly have known of their relationship and would want to know the state of play. This is hinted at when JM records in his memoirs that 'we discussed *women*, aeroplanes and travel'.[52] And so it was, over a brandy liqueur in Quaglino's, that he asked her to marry him.

One can only speculate on the accuracy of the script in the 1942 Herbert Wilcox film, *They Flew Alone*, where it portrays the Quaglino scene. Anna Neagle, struggling with a mock Yorkshire accent, played the part of Amy, whilst a rather over-camped Robert Newton acted as a perpetually inebriated version of the man she was to marry. It seems that Newton's major qualification for being cast in the Mollison role, was principally because he too was renowned for being a bit of a hell-raiser, as well as an alcoholic, in real life. Their conversation at the table included JM asking Amy, 'Do you like me?' followed by a slight pause before he continues with, 'Why don't you marry me and find out?' To which Amy replies with a smile, 'I'll take a chance.' At least the film-script version of Amy's answer to the proposal accords with JM's record.

There are those today who accuse Jim Mollison of using Amy Johnson purely for his own publicity. There are others who believe that their marriage was nothing more than a business arrangement conspired by Lord Wakefield. On the former theory, one must acknowledge that of the two Amy had far more celebrity-value in 1932; however, one must not forget that Mollison had already proved himself with the Australia and Cape flights. The other theory, that their marriage was nothing more than a business arrangement, does not appear to be true from Amy's point of view. The subsequent letters that she wrote to her father just before the marriage broke up, certainly reveal a woman with a deep and genuine love for her husband.

The Mollisons' presence at public functions always drew large crowds of admiring fans.

On Jim Mollison's part, considering his extremely egotistical nature, their marriage was probably based on no more than an infatuation. It probably went as deep as he was ever capable of going with a woman.

When the news of their proposed marriage became known (they placed an announcement in *The Times* the same afternoon) it caused a ripple of excitement throughout Fleet Street. On the following morning the corridors of the Grosvenor House Hotel were buzzing with journalists and photographers wishing to interview Mollison. Meanwhile, a delighted Amy was telephoning her parents in Bridlington and contacting the *Daily Mail*, the newspaper that had done so much to promote her career. The two aviators were soon being described as 'the Flying Sweethearts' or 'the Air Lovers', and both were constantly being asked about their plans for flying as a team.

One need look no further than how cruelly and without prior warning JM broke his engagement to Diana, to appreciate how he subsequently came to earn the reputation for being the archetypal cad. The day after he had proposed to Amy, he even chose Quaglino's as the venue to break with Diana. One wonders just how she reacted as he tried to explain about Amy. No doubt he blamed Lady Cowley for his action. All credit must be given to Diana when she announced to the press, with all the stoicism and stiff upper lip of her class, that she recognised the common interests of the two aviators and wished them every happiness in the future.

Ciss Johnson had grave misgivings about the speed of her daughter's engagement and appears to have been even less happy after meeting her flamboyant, future son-in-law. Jim was anxious to show Amy off to his Scottish relatives, but before taking her up to Glasgow to meet his mother he introduced her to his aunt Katherine living in London. Katherine Mollison was one of Jim's five aunts and had married Dr W. Alexander 'Sandy' Hislop, who had a medical practice in Holland Park. Their marriage was a happy but childless one, a factor which caused them to regard Amy as almost a surrogate daughter. They were to become two of Amy's most loyal friends.

On the Saturday afternoon of 21 May the engaged couple set out from Stag Lane in Amy's Puss Moth to fly to Glasgow's airport at Renfrew. They were almost guaranteed a warm welcome for, apart from being able to meet her fiancée's family, the Scottish Flying Club was also holding its Air Pageant that weekend and some 10,000 people were expected to be there to greet them. As it happened, the weather turned absolutely foul with heavy rain and low cloud as they flew north and they were forced to put down at Catterick in Yorkshire, where they waited a while to see if conditions improved. Having decided that they could make it to Renfrew, they took-off again only to be forced down for a second time in a field at Ferryhill, near Newcastle. Luckily, the driver of a newspaper van belonging to a Newcastle Sunday paper spotted them and took them and their luggage to the Station Hotel, where they stayed overnight.

That evening in the hotel, Jim and Amy heard that the American aviatrix, Amelia Earhart, wife of publisher George Putnam, had become the first woman to successfully fly the North Atlantic alone. She had made the crossing from Newfoundland to Ireland in a record time of 14 hours and 54 minutes. Her intention had been to follow the same route across the Atlantic to Paris as that made by Charles Lindbergh,* but she had landed some 200 miles north of her intended landfall of Valencia Island, at Culmore, near Londonderry.

On the way over she had experienced icing on the wings and to make matters worse her altimeter had failed. Even more worrying she had noticed a change in the note of the exhaust in the aircraft's Wasp engine and much to her alarm had found that it was caused by a crack in one of the seams in the exhaust manifold. In itself it did not appear too serious, until she started to smell petrol leaking back into the cabin of her Lockheed Vega. By that time she had descended to within sight of the waves, figuring that it would be better to drown than to burn.

As soon as Jim and Amy read of Amelia's landing that afternoon, they offered to fly across to northern Ireland on the Sunday to pick her up and take her to the reception that would be awaiting her in London. Lady Bailey also made a similar gesture, and without waiting for acceptance flew from Croydon only to arrive in Londonderry just as Amelia left in a Desoutter monoplane chartered by Movietone News. It is interesting to note the reason for Amelia's reluctance to accept the offers she had been given. It transpired that she had telephoned her husband to announce her safe arrival, and was advised by GP not to fly to London with any of the British aviators in case they should share in her limelight!

The weather had improved by the Sunday and Jim and Amy were now able to resume their flight (their aeroplane had been flown up to Cramlington aerodrome by a member of the Newcastle club earlier in the morning) to Renfrew. Thomasina and Charles Bullmore were there in the crowd to meet their future daughter-in-law, who stepped from the plane dressed in a smart navy-blue costume. No doubt the large, single cinnamon diamond engagement ring on Amy's hand was studiously admired (Amy had bought Jim a gold cigarette case as a return engagement present) as she

---

*The date of her flight had been carefully planned by her husband to coincide exactly with that of Lindbergh's, made five years earlier.

was introduced to Jim's parents. From subsequent correspondence it appears that Amy and Thomasina struck up an immediate and genuine liking for each other, although Amy's impressions about the rest of the family was that they were 'quite likeable but rather dull'.

By June, Amy had moved out of Vernon Court having sub-let, and was now enjoying a suite of rooms at the Dorchester Hotel at a greatly reduced rate of charge. Even the cost of her meals was often borne by the largesse of wealthy residents, who were only too pleased to be seen in her company. At the same time JM was exploiting his own brand of celebrity-value at the Grosvenor. Now back in favour after breaking the Cape record, he was being lionised by London's social elite. He was living a lavish lifestyle, and money, always a commodity to burn a hole in his pocket, was being spent freely. He neither cared whether it was his own, or other people's.

It was probably at Jim's suggestion that he and Amy decided to take a holiday in Juan-les-Pins that June, but not before Amy had given her erstwhile partner Jack Humphreys notice that he was no longer required. Now that Jim was on the scene he no longer figured in her plans. If Amy needed any warning of the quality of her future married life, then maybe she should have heeded her fiancé's behaviour on holiday. The heavy drinking and irresponsible attitude towards debt were there to be seen, but she was so infatuated with the Scot and the thought of marriage, that she obviously preferred to ignore it.

The more Jim and Amy were seen together publicly, the more the press began to speculate on a wedding date. There is evidence that he was beginning to have second thoughts about going through with the ceremony, for he admits in his memoirs that he never felt the strong feelings for Amy that he had for Paula, his first love. He favoured a quiet wedding and was not prepared to give an invitation to any of his own relatives. It must be remembered that his relationship with his mother was, throughout his life, always rather strained. Their disagreement revolved largely around his drinking, something which she strongly disapproved of. She also resented his favoured ties with the Mollison side of the family, particularly the one with his grandfather. It appears that Thomasina was to be ostracised by the Mollison family right up until a period shortly before her death in 1965. There is no doubt that although she appears to have been the innocent party in her marriage failure, she was apportioned more than her fair share of the blame by Hector's parents for the divorce in 1915.

Jim's decision not to invite his family must have inhibited Amy from inviting her own parents and sisters to the wedding. In fact, she deliberately misled them by writing to tell them not to believe the newspaper accounts

Britain's 'air lovers' stroll and smile for the cameraman just prior to their wedding.

which reported an imminent wedding, even when she knew that they were true. She may have felt some embarrassment from having decided that the ceremony was not to be a white wedding. This aspect of her reluctance to invite them would not have come as a shock to her father, for he knew full well of her intimate affair with Franz. But explaining to her mother and sisters was another matter.

Another reason may have been the fear that their families might commit some social gaffe. Distasteful as it might seem, one cannot discount the fact that for both Jim and Amy there may have been an element of embarrassment at their provincial and middle-class origins. Jim's wounds would still be fresh from his meeting with Diana Wellesley's step-mother, and it is known that Amy was very conscious of her northern accent at that time. It might be easy in hindsight to condemn the couple for the hurt that they obviously inflicted upon their parents, but one must remember that Britain was a very class-conscious society in the 1930's, much more so than it is today. Social mobility in those days existed mainly for those fortunate enough to achieve stage or screen fame, or those men and women of achievement, such as Jim and Amy. Rarely did it extend to their parents and families.

The couple were married at ten o'clock on the Friday morning of 29 July, at the fashionable St George's Church, Hanover Square, London. Amy, who was given away by the Countess of Drogheda, wore a black coat-frock with silver fox fur; a matching black hat, neatly trimmed with an attractive eye-veil; and long white gloves. Jim, looking fittingly sober after the pre-nuptial celebration the night before, wore a slate grey lounge-suit. Apart from the best man, Lt. Col. Francis Shelmerdine (Director of Civil Aviation), the only other official guests were Miss Doreen Pickering (Jim's secretary) and a representative of Lord Wakefield.

Amy's parents had received a telegram from their daughter informing them of the wedding only some twelve hours beforehand. She made the excuse that they had not been invited because she wished for a quiet wedding owing to Jim's forthcoming Atlantic flight. The message was sent deliberately late with the hope that the family would make no attempt to attend. However, her deeply distraught mother, father, and sisters, (Molly and Betty) decided to travel down by car, leaving Yorkshire very early in the morning. Sadly, they were to miss the actual ceremony and arrived only in time to see the couple emerging from the back of the crowded church after signing the register. To add to their humiliation, they were unnoticed by a smiling Jim and Amy as they walked down the aisle of the church. It must

Jim and Amy outside St. George's, Hanover Square, London, on their wedding day, 29 July 1932.

have been a deep wound to the pride of Amy's parents and it probably killed any hope of a good relationship between them and their new son-in-law.

JM's lasting impression of the marriage ceremony came during the exchange of the nuptial vows when he was asked to promise to remain faithful 'until death us do part'. In the light of his forthcoming attempt to be the first person to solo the North Atlantic, he recalls that the words had a rather ominous ring to them! One cannot but help feel that the permanence of marriage was not something to which he wholeheartedly subscribed. He had witnessed the fragility of his own parents' union and he held the philosophy that promises, much like appointments, were there to be broken if need be.

Jim and Amy stepped out in front of the church to a waiting crowd of well-wishers and press cameramen jostling for shots of the 'Air Lovers'. Meanwhile, the Johnsons had slipped quietly away from the crowds and it was only during the reception in Grosvenor House later that afternoon that Amy heard word of her parents' attendance at the church. She tried desperately to retrieve the situation by having a telephone search made of London hotels but it was too late, for they had returned directly to Bridlington. To make matters worse, the presence of Amy's parents and sisters and their late arrival at the church service had not escaped the notice of the press.

At least one newspaper reported that the Mollisons would be leaving straight after the reception for a five days' honeymoon in Le Touquet.[53] Whether this was a deliberate piece of mis-information designed to ward off unwelcome pestering by the press, or whether the couple changed their minds is not known, for they eventually flew off in separate machines from Stag Lane to Renfrew. They were to spend the weekend at Kelburn Castle as guests of Lady Bowden, the wife of the Birmingham industrialist, Sir Harold Bowden.*

A most interesting side of Amy's character is revealed by one of the local newspaper reporters covering their honeymoon stay in Scotland:

> On the Saturday evening Mollison, Amy and Lady Bowden and, I think, her son, attended the Summer Show at the Barrfields Pavilion. The two aviators got a great reception from the audience, and the cast and audience saluted them by singing the song, 'Amy, Wonderful Amy'. Jim was invited up on to the stage where he made a very happily phrased speech in thanking the cast and the audience for their reception.
>
> Mr Harry Kemp, who staged the show, told me afterwards that Amy had also been asked to go on the stage, but she declined unless she was paid a fee.[54]

It was this kind of attitude that caused certain sections of the Australian press to accuse Amy of avarice during her tour in that country in 1930. At that time she was lampooned in the Sydney news magazine, *Smith's* Weekly, as 'The Gimme Gimme Girl'.

JM recalls climbing up the castle steps to its battlements and looking out over the Firth of the Clyde and beyond the Western Isles to the North Atlantic. Aware that he was supposed to be blissfully happy, he could not ignore the feeling of unease gnawing in the pit of his stomach at the prospect of the forthcoming flight. He had the disquieting knowledge that not only had no one successfully made a crossing of that vast ocean alone against the prevailing westerly winds, but no one had made it at all in a light aircraft. Only the two Americans, Charles Lindbergh, using a 220hp Wright Whirlwind J5 engine, and Amelia Earhart, using a 450hp Wasp C motor, had ever flown it alone, and that in the easier easterly direction.

It is interesting to note that of the eighteen successful, non-stop crossings, fifteen had been from west to east, whilst the three in the opposite and more dangerous direction,** were made with a crew of two or more. Mollison

---

*Their hostess was renting part of the castle from the eighth Earl of Glasgow, Patrick James Boyle, DSO.
**These were the *Bremen*, 310hp, flown by Kohl, Huenfeld and Fitzmaurice in April 1928; the tri-motor *Southern Cross*, 660hp, flown by Kingsford Smith, Van Dyck, Stannage and Saul in 1930; and *The Question Mark*, 650hp, flown by Costes and Bellonte, also in 1930.

would be flying alone in the suspect Puss Moth, powered by a mere four cylinder Gipsy III engine of 120hp, and without the assistance of radio!

Two attempts had been made by British fliers to cross the North Atlantic in light aeroplanes. Neither succeeded. Lt. Cdr. Harry MacDonald had taken off for Ireland from Harbour Grace, in October 1928, in a DH Gipsy Moth; apart from being sighted by a Dutch steamer 700 miles out from Newfoundland, he was never seen again. Eighteen months later, Squadron Leader C. S. Wynne-Eaton, DSO,[55] made an attempt in an overloaded Puss Moth and crashed on take-off at Lester's Field, St Johns – fortunately he escaped with his life.

The first successful crossing of the Atlantic by a heavier than air machine was made by the U.S. Navy flying boat NC-4, in May 1919,* but with two stopovers in the Azores. Since that crossing twenty-nine people had lost their lives in further attempts. Because of the high fatality rate, Government departments on both sides of the ocean were becoming alarmed, and in 1927 the Canadian Prime Minister Mackenzie King threatened to introduce legislation prohibiting flights from Canada.

Without specifically naming Mollison as the pilot in question, the matter was raised in the House of Commons on 11 July regarding the Government's attitude towards the forthcoming attempt by a British airman to cross the Atlantic both ways in a light aeroplane. The Under-Secretary for Air, Sir Philip Sassoon, stated that the department's policy was generally not to restrict long-distance flights by individuals, but at the same time he emphasised that his statement should not be interpreted as giving official encouragement to the venture.

*Alcock & Brown were the first to make a *non-stop* flight in a heavier than air machine a month later.

Chapter 11

'The Apogee'

It is not without justification that Mollison's 1932 crossing of the North Atlantic has been described as one of the greatest solo flights in the history of aviation. Only two other solo flights bear close comparison with it, namely, Charles Lindbergh's flight from New York to Paris in 1927, and Wiley Post's round the world flight in 1933. Not only was Mollison's flight the first solo across that ocean from east to west, but also the fastest. Moreover, it was also the first crossing in a light aeroplane and the longest non-stop flight in one.

Without disparaging the fine achievements of the two Americans, one must remember that they both had the benefit of more powerful machines, and the advantage of the prevailing winds by flying from west to east. In Lindbergh's case a 30mph tailwind for most of the way under 'freak' good weather conditions. Aviation historian Richard. K. Smith, an authority on pioneering transoceanic flying, comments on the Lindbergh crossing with:

> He found a 'window' in the North Atlantic's weather that no one else found the other 363 days of the year 1927. To be sure he was given a favorable forecast, but weather analysis was so primitive in those years that this was sheer luck. In the 1920's the Royal Navy and US Navy were experimenting with the Norwegian system of air mass analysis, and the Germans and the French were too, but the U.S. Weather Bureau was reluctant to accept it – and didn't until 1934.[56]

John P. V. Heinmuller, writing in 1944, confirms that view with:

> '. . . it is now established that during Lindbergh's flight the air conditions were perfect. Most of the time during his flight the pressure of the north winds equalised pressure from the south in such a way *as to keep the airplane almost automatically on a compass-course for many hours without drifting*. This is the first time such unusual weather conditions have been recorded by the experts.[57]

As a consequence, Lindbergh's increased speed meant that he was over the hazardous ocean for two and a half hours less than Mollison over a similar distance. And whereas Mollison had to meet the notorious Newfoundland fog-banks at the end of his journey – it took him six hours to cover 136 miles over the Bay of Fundy – the American flew into clear weather conditions where he was able to map-read from his landfall near Dingle Bay, Ireland, all the way to Paris. Admittedly, Lindbergh was airborne for three hours longer than Mollison, but even discounting the question mark over the structural safety of the Puss Moth, there is no doubt that the Scot had the more difficult flight.

De Havilland's were grateful for the publicity that Mollison had brought them with his Cape record, and were more than pleased to modify a standard Puss Moth to give it an extended range in 'still air' of 3,200 miles for his proposed Atlantic flight. To do this entailed adding two extra steel fuel tanks in the cabin; a cylindrical 75 imperial gallon one at the front end and another of 47 gallon aft (it left just enough room for the pilot to sit sandwiched between them!). These tanks were in addition to the two 20 gallon tanks carried in each wing and gave the machine a total capacity of 162 gallons.*

The modifications required the careful positioning of the tanks to maintain an acceptable centre of gravity of the aircraft, bearing in mind that the controls and instruments were moved back some four feet from their original position. Apart from these alterations, the only other major modifications were the removal of air and wheel brakes in order to save weight.

Amy, writing about her husband some years later, commented on his attitude to the hazards of taking off in overloaded aeroplanes with:

> Jim Mollison never lacked the courage to take-off on some flight with a heavier load of petrol than anyone had dared to take before. He would always say to the plane designers, 'You just put in the petrol I want and I'll get the plane off the ground,' and he always did. [58]

It is interesting to note that the Puss Moth's fuel load on the proposed Atlantic crossing was equivalent to the weight of nine men, in an aeroplane designed to carry one pilot and two passengers. It must also be remembered that the assistance of variable pitch propellers and flaps for shortening a take-off run were innovations yet to be in production in the British aviation industry in 1932. Not surprisingly, Mollison had to look around for an airfield with a suitably long runway. The RAF aerodrome at Cranwell had the best available facilities, but in view of Hinchcliffe and Mackay's fateful

---

*The press were quick to dub the machine as 'a flying petrol tank'.

transatlantic flight from the airfield four years earlier, and Sir Philip Sassoon's recent statement in the House of Commons, it is doubtful that permission would have been given. The only alternative to an airfield was a beach, and preferably one positioned as near to the Newfoundland coastline as possible.

When Charles Kingsford Smith decided to make an attempt on the westward, transatlantic crossing in June 1930, he found that the runway at Dublin's Baldonnel aerodrome was far too short for a safe take-off in their heavily laden tri-motor. As a result, he used the smooth sands of Portmarnock Strand nearby.

It was Smithy's flight that probably inspired JM to use the same venue, for early in July he flew out with Amy to inspect it. Although he felt that the beach was adequate, he was not entirely convinced that it was the best starting point. Beaches such as those at Clifden on the west coast of Ireland looked equally promising and had the advantage of being 160 miles nearer to New York. However, when he and Amy made an aerial inspection of the western coast beaches in early August, together with Captain J. P. 'Paddy' Saul of the Irish Free State Army Air Corps and W. R. Elliot, Chief Flying Instructor of the Irish Aero Club, they came to the conclusion that none were suitable. After that JM settled for Portmarnock.

The shortest distance between any two points on the globe is termed a Great Circle route* but it had two major disadvantages for Mollison flying westward. Firstly, it meant changing compass course at pre-determined points, say every hundred miles, to keep on track. Secondly, it took him a long way north of the main shipping routes and deeper into the Newfoundland fog-banks before reaching the U.S. coastline. He therefore decided to simplify his navigation by flying on a rhumb-line constant magnetic course of true bearing.** It saved him from making a complex number of calculations that would be further complicated by assessing drift. Unlike flights such as that made by Kingsford Smith, where a member of the crew could use astro-navigation, JM would not have the benefit of using a sextant to fix his position from the sun or the stars.***

Using maps supplied by the Automobile Association, 'Paddy' Saul prepared JM's route, marking a bold purple line for the 1,960 mile crossing from Golan Head on the west coast of Ireland to his estimated landfall near Harbour Grace. JM noticed that the line fell across a cluster of villages in Newfoundland, one of which was named Heart's Content. Deeming it

*Charles Lindbergh used a GCR for his New York to Paris flight.
**A rhumb-line is an imaginary line on the surface of a sphere that intersects all meridians at the same angle. By following such a course, Mollison could maintain a uniform compass heading.
***It is not impossible for a pilot flying alone to use a sextant. Francis Chichester claimed he could do it, but it would be extremely difficult to handle with any accuracy.

appropriate, he christened his aircraft by that name and had it painted on the nose of his famous silver-grey Puss Moth. One would like to think that the name reflected the relationship between Jim and Amy at that time, for later in life he was to say that the first twelve months of his marriage were the happiest. However, according to JM the name did have another less romantic connotation: 'It was in any case an apt name for a transatlantic aeroplane. You would not appreciate it unless you had seen the grey smudge far ahead that means land after you have hung ten, fifteen or thirty hours between heaven and the limitless sea.'[59]

Weather forecasting in the early Thirties was quite primitive and unlike today's aircrews, where commercial jets have the power to fly unimpeded above foul weather with the aid of blind-flying instruments, JM was forced to wait patiently for the right conditions. Surface winds over the ocean in excess of 20mph would indicate headwinds of more than 40mph at heights of 2,000 feet or more, and were unacceptable. Not only would they reduce his speed and prolong his duration over the hazards of the ocean, but far more seriously they could so diminish his fuel supplies that he might be forced down in the sea. His chances of survival if he descended into the Atlantic were minimal, for he was not equipped with either radio or inflatable life-raft and the carrying of a parachute was of little use. The Puss Moth might float for thirty minutes or so, assuming it did not break up on entering the water, but that was all.

Headwinds were not the only problem that Mollison might encounter on a flight estimated to be 3,176 miles from Dublin to New York. There was also the need to accurately judge the direction of the wind. The dropping of smoke flares, or the visual observation of white caps or foam blowing off the tops of the waves, were a fairly accurate means of determining drift in daylight but were of little use in the dark. Any serious error in assessing the aircraft's drift could mean being blown south and out of range of landfall. No doubt this could have been a factor in the disappearance of Nungesser & Coli and other aviators who had perished.

Icing was another hazard, particularly in the vicinity of the Newfoundland coast where it could well be a problem, even in what one would imagine are the good weather months. Both Charles Lindbergh and Amelia Earhart had experienced icing during their crossings in the month of May. Several years later, during the early part of WW2, military aircraft making the same ocean crossing used nothing more sophisticated than 'Killfrost' paste smeared along the leading edges of the aircraft's flying surfaces to prevent icing. In spite of this the icing of propellers could spin off lumps of ice big enough to shatter cabin windows. All these factors must have weighed heavily upon JM as he waited over an eight day period for acceptable weather conditions.

Speculation was rife concerning Mollison's rewards for accomplishing a transatlantic return flight within three and a half days. Financial reward for pilots making long-distance record-breaking flights was probably at its peak in 1932 and newspapers were reporting them to be worth £50,000 for his backers, C. C. Wakefield Oils, in advertising revenue alone. At the same time the *Sunday Express* reported that JM had received £10,000 as a wedding gift from a rich admirer just before the flight. Just how reliable these reports were is open to question. Certainly neither Jim nor Amy ever confirmed these figures in any of their subsequent writings. We do know that William Courtenay was at this time ghost-writing the aviator's memoirs in a book entitled, *Death Cometh Soon or Late*. Obviously there would be royalties from its publication later in the same year, but they were hardly likely to amount to very much.

Amy flew out from Stag Lane in her Gipsy Moth, *Jason 1V*, on 16 August to meet Jim at Baldonnel, but it was not until the following morning that weather-reports looked more promising. They forecast light westerly winds of no more than 15mph in mid-Atlantic and then a tendency to easterly winds in his favour, with very little fog. After some consultation with 'Paddy' Saul, Jim decided to wait no longer and immediately arranged with the Shell representatives for their tanker to be on the beach on the Thursday morning of the 18th ready for fuelling the *The Hearts Content*. Relieved that the decision had now been made, he celebrated the morning by taking Amy's Moth up to perform some hair-raising aerobatics over Baldonnel. No doubt it was his means of ridding himself of the tension, and a way of psyching himself up for the ordeal that lay ahead.

The next morning he flew from Baldonnel to Portmarnock to land on the beach in light rain and was pleased to find a slight north-easterly blowing down the beach. It meant that there was just enough breeze to assist the take-off in what appeared to be almost ideal conditions. He was excited by the prospect of achieving a double 'double first' for his country by making a successful two way crossing of the North Atlantic as planned. The British airship R34, commanded by Major G. H. Scott, AFC, had, in July 1919, been the first airship to make a return journey across that ocean.

Dublin's popular Lord Mayor, Alfie Byrne, together with a contingent of the Civic Guard who had arrived from their depot at Phoenix Park to control the crowd, were there to meet him as the Puss Moth taxied in. Young girls were approaching him with medallions, some of them allegedly blessed at Lourdes, imploring him to carry them in the cabin and assuring him that

Jim Mollison prepares for the take-off from Portmarnock Strand, Dublin, on the morning of 18 August 1932, for the first successful, east–west, non-stop solo crossing of the North Atlantic.

Bystanders wave farewell as Mollison's tiny Puss Moth *The Hearts Content* flies over the beach at Portmarnock before commencing its 2,650 mile journey across the North Atlantic.

they would keep him safe. Others were seen kneeling on the beach praying for his protection on the flight. Meanwhile, the newsreel cameramen were quietly positioning their equipment on top of their vehicles in order to get an unobstructed view of events.

Whilst the white-overalled Shell employees were pumping aviation fuel into his machine's tanks, JM was seen walking along the area of his take-off run, carefully checking that there was nothing likely to cause a burst tyre. After the crash on take-off at Darwin with a full load of fuel, he was taking no chances. It was probably a tip he had learned from his Scottish friend and flying enthusiast, Malcolm Campbell – the world's land speed record holder. Campbell invariably used beaches at Pendine, Daytona and the Utah Salt Lakes for his record-breaking bids, and when using the Welsh sands would get the local schoolchildren to comb the beach in order to remove any shells that might cut the tyres of his racing *Bluebird*.

Amy's car arrived just before 10am and descended onto the strand to speed along to the Martello tower at the northern end of the beach, where a crowd of some six hundred people had already gathered around the *The Hearts Content* to wait for its departure. A further crowd estimated at 5,000 people lined the beach along the intended runway. The couple greeted each other affectionately and chatted with 'Paddy' Saul and other well-wishers as last minute preparations were made to the aircraft.

There is no doubt that both Jim and Amy were extremely nervous about the outcome of the flight even if they did not show it. The risks involved had been graphically highlighted by the irascible and monocled C. G. Grey, the editor of *The Aeroplane*. Grey had never been a friend of those whom he termed 'stunt pilots', and had been chalking his cue ready to strike ever since he heard of Mollison's proposal to make the flight. He had already slammed Amelia Earhart's recent achievement, and in a nutshell his jaundiced view was that such flights were a useless display of courage. Of such undertakings he had once said:

> The deciding factor in flying the Atlantic, like going over Niagara falls in a barrel, can only be whether the instinct of vanity or instinct of fear is the more powerful. There is a kind of vanity which is so deep or so colossal, that popular applause does not count. Self-approval outweighs even publicity in such a case.[60]

Just how wrong Grey could be is demonstrated by the myopic view that he took regarding the danger of flying single-engined aeroplanes over long distances. In November 1932 he wrote, 'in time no aeroplane with a single engine will be certified as airworthy, or be saleable if so certified'. There did not seem to be much room in this philosophy for the European single-engined fighters, such as the Hawker Hurricane and Messerschmitt Bf 109, that were to be developed a few years later!

Mollison dismissed Grey's soured comments as those of an insufferable armchair critic. One who simply thought that all that was needed was to point the aeroplane in the right direction and, barring some unlikely engine failure, one would arrive on the other side. Nevertheless, such caustic remarks must have focussed the minds of the newly-weds on the dangers of the westward crossing. In spite of JM's assurance to the press that his marriage to Amy was a sign that he was confident of succeeding, deep down it conflicted with his belief that life was very much a transitory one. Privately, he would admit that ever since early childhood he had struggled with certain fears and that as a small boy he was frightened of the dark. These phobias seem to have persisted into manhood for throughout his early flying career he constantly experienced a fear of falling from the sky. One wonders if this was connected with the rumour circulating amongst his relatives at the time of his parents' divorce, that, as a young child, his father, in a fit of drunken violence, had threatened to throw him from a bedroom window.[61]

As for Amy, she revealed something of her anxiety about her husband's safety in a letter to her mother some weeks before the flight, where she wished that she could wake up a month hence and find it all over.

Just after eleven o'clock the Dublin Mayor, attired in top hat and suitably adorned with his chain of office, made a short farewell speech. Describing the Scot as 'the greatest hero of the air', he wished him God's speed and a safe journey to the land which was the home of so many of his Irish countrymen. He then handed over souvenir letters that JM had promised to deliver, one of them being to Byrne's counterpart, Jimmy Walker, the Mayor of New York.

JM, wearing a rather crumpled Sidcot flying-suit over a grey lounge suit, stubbed his cigarette into the sand and made a brief reply. He thanked his hosts for their hospitality and said that he was setting out to demonstrate the superiority of British aeroplanes over all others and to prove that the light monoplane was not only dependable, but safe. Amy posed for several shots with Jim for the busy cameramen, before he kissed her goodbye and climbed into the cramped confines of the tiny cockpit. Amy handed him chicken sandwiches, a bag of nuts and raisins, barley sugars, two flasks of coffee and a bottle of brandy to sustain him on what he hoped was a twenty-two hour flight to Harbour Grace, the planned stopover for refuelling before New York.

The Birkett Air Services' red Puss Moth, which was to escort Mollison to the Aran Islands off the Galway coast, was already in the air waiting with photographer on board as the Scot prepared to take-off. After a short warm up of the Gipsy engine the revs died down to a steady tick-over as Mollison signalled for the chocks to be removed. Slowly, the heavily-laden Puss Moth, G-ABXY, began to taxy along to the southern end of the beach with an assistant trotting alongside at each wing tip. The departure was carefully timed to make sure that JM made a landfall at early dawn in Newfoundland. This would then give him at least fourteen hours of daylight in which to make New York.

As he swung the aircraft to face the one and a half miles of sandy runway in front of him, JM remembered, somewhat ironically, the humorous comment of the RAF instructor's report on one of his pupils: 'When this pilot has taxied out and turned into wind he is then committed to a course of events over which he has no further control.'[62] JM could not help thinking that it might well apply to him at this very moment. Within a thousand yards the tail was up. A further six hundred yards and the wooden wings were lifting a ton and a quarter of aeroplane and its contents into an overcast sky.

The tiny monoplane slowly climbed to a few hundred feet before turning to tag along with the escort plane, which was now heading westwards to Galway. With a ceiling of no more than a thousand feet and low cloud over a ground-mist, Mollison was forced to follow the contours of the green valleys and low-lying ground across Ireland's central plain before he reached the open sea at Golan Head. At this moment the companion escort plane dipped in salute and turned back to the east. JM set the two P2 'Husun' magnetic compasses to 287 degrees before taking one last look back over his shoulder at the receding coast of Ireland. It might well, he thought, be the last that he would ever see of terra firma.

For the next four hours a light northerly wind prevailed with patches of low lying cloud forcing him to slowly lose height, until eventually he was only fifty feet above the white capped waves. In order to compensate for any southerly drift he allowed for a compass correction of four to five degrees.

In the late afternoon he sighted and flew over the Cunard steamship *Ascania* as she gave him a welcoming and visible blast of steam from her siren. The defeatist thought did go through his mind that if he wanted to chicken out of the flight, then this was his golden opportunity. He could always ditch alongside and swear that he was experiencing engine trouble. The temptation was resisted and within twenty-five minutes he was passing over the *Beaverbrae*, its passengers looking up from its decks as JM gave it a cheery wave and pressed on. At least the presence of the two ships, already marked on his shipping-chart, enabled him to check and confirm his own position before nightfall.

As Mollison continued to chase the sun westward at fifty feet above the waves, the once heavily-laden Puss Moth began to lighten as its fuel load lessened. Towards sunset the wind changed to a west-north-west of light velocity, as thickening blankets of low cloud down to two hundred feet made it difficult for him to keep the sea clearly in view. He had hugged the waves for as long as he dare, knowing that the velocity of the wind would be a little less at the lower altitude. But now in the twilight it would be dangerous to trust the accuracy of his altimeter at such a low level. As he pulled the stick back and began his climb to 2,000 feet for the duration of darkness, he knew that the difficulties of the journey were about to commence.

Without the benefit of the horizon to act as a datum he was now entirely reliant upon instrument flying. The luminous dials of the turn-and-bank indicator, fore-and-aft level indicator and Air Speed Indicator, now became the only substitute for the pilot's natural sense of balance. The most important of these instruments was the turn-and-bank, or 'slip-and-skid', indicator as it was commonly known. This instrument consisted of two parts which controlled two axes of the aircraft; a wind-driven spinning gyroscope operating from a vacuum supplied by a venturi tube on the side of the fuselage which detected any deviation of the aircraft from a straight line; and a sensitive pendulum which detected lateral instability. Any changes in these two axes were shown on the dial of the Reid & Sigrist instrument by two needles, vertically in line and opposite to each other. The third axis of flight was controlled by the fore-and-aft level and the ASI, indicating if the aircraft was climbing or diving. In addition, there were the two 'Husun' compasses, positioned one on each side of the cockpit at calf height, their red pointers held steady between their parallel grid lines, like sentinels guarding his track.

Engine instruments included a Smith's engine revolution counter; oil-pressure, oil-temperature and petrol gauges; and finally, an altimeter and chronometer. As he tired, each instrument began to have an hypnotic effect, as their needles danced imperceptibly beneath his eyes. There was little impression of speed, apart from when he flew through intermittent cloudbanks, and he seemed to be motionless, hanging in space. At times he would find his head nodding and then would come the almost involuntary jerk as he willed himself alert. At such times he would sing out loud, or repeat poetry that he learnt as a child. When all else failed, a nip from the brandy bottle would revive him.

Meanwhile, unbeknown to JM, the well-known ocean-weather expert 'Doc' Kimball, head of the U.S. Weather Bureau, was announcing in New York that although conditions at the start of the aviator's crossing were favourable, subsequent developments had lessened his chances. A low pressure area and storms along the New England coast had caused winds to gain velocity in their course northward, which meant that increasing headwinds, together with gales, would be directly against *The Hearts Content* for the last eight hundred miles over the Atlantic.

During the night JM found that he could occasionally take advantage of clearer skies by climbing to 2,500 feet to fly between two layers of cloud. Intermittently he caught sight of the moon, now on the wane and just past its full. Its pale white glow alleviated the boredom and gloom by giving him something, other than the instruments, upon which to focus his eyes.

Slowly, the weather began to deteriorate as first he ran into rain and then turbulence, but neither bad enough to cause him any real concern. His main worry was that as the wind strengthened, he was unsure of how much to allow on his compass bearing for drift. Twice he descended during the night in attempts at some visual contact with the sea but at four hundred feet it was still solid cloud and too dangerous to risk descending any further. Climbing back to a safer height he set his compass seven degrees to the north to allow for a southerly drift and continued throughout the rest of the night.

At approximately four and a half hours before daybreak he knew that he must be nearing the coast of Newfoundland for he suddenly ran into fog. Misty thin and slight at first, and then thicker. It became far worse than he had bargained for. Worse than he had imagined when 'Paddy' Saul first described the infamous fog-banks. Apart from the dim glow of his instruments and the faint reflection from the blue and orange flame of the engine's exhaust, he could see nothing. Even the wing tips of the plane were obscured from view and he seemed to be sitting motionless in a capsule, entirely divorced from the real world. At the same time the lack of sleep was beginning to tell, with all the old symptons that he had experienced on the Australian and Cape flights. To make matters worse, he had a splitting headache which made him feel physically sick. No doubt he must have questioned his sanity in taking on the hazards of the crossing alone. Nagging doubts began to gnaw. What if he had not allowed enough drift and should miss the southern tip of Newfoundland at Cape Race completely? It could mean flying on over the sea parallel with the Nova Scotia coast and missing it altogether. Down in the Atlantic out of fuel. Maybe going the same way that poor Leslie Hamilton had gone.

The ordeal continued for several hours before the fog finally lifted and suddenly he was topping the clouds with the moon clearly visible. Beneath him he could see floe ice, motionless on a calm sea, but no sign of land which was now due if he was really on course. Doubts began to creep up on him and believing that if one is going to die then why not go enjoying one's favourite addiction, he lit a cigarette. Not exactly a sane thing to do in a fume-laden cockpit and with a seventy-five gallon tank right in front of one. Suddenly, he could see through a break in the clouds and by the light of his ally the moon, the welcome sight of a coastline ahead of him. Landfall! His spirits immediately rose and he began to sing as he recognised the outline of Grates Point on the Newfoundland shoreline before turning south. It was 6.40am BST* and he had covered the 1,972 miles from Golan Head in nineteen hours and five minutes and was just thirty miles north of his estimated landfall.

With ample fuel in the tanks with which to reach New York, he decided not to land at Harbour Grace and pressed on for Halifax on the southern coast of Nova Scotia. At 5.45am EST he was circling low over the city in order to make sure that the registration of his aircraft was identifiable, and trusting that the message of his crossing would be speedily relayed to Amy and the Wakefield team back in London.

Mollison was now only 750 tantalising miles from his U.S. destination, but from hereon he met a stumbling block – the weather over the Bay of Fundy.

It had taken him just over twenty-four hours to reach the Nova Scotia capital and now he must strike westward to the New Brunswick coastline some ninety minutes' flying time away. From thereon he intended to follow the U.S. coastline down past Maine to Boston and on to land at Roosevelt Field, Long Island. Realising there was sufficient fuel for this last leg of the journey, he decided to forgo a landing at Halifax and press on. Victory was now well within his grasp.

JM was later to describe the next six hours, as he groped his way around the fog-laden and circuitous shores of the Bay of Fundy without continuous sight of sea or land, as the toughest part of the flight and the greatest trial in his entire experience of flying. Uncertain of his exact position and with the knowledge that high peaks fringed the coastline, he descended time and time again as low as he dare to make visual contact, only to be forced back up again. And to make matters worse, as 'Doc' Kimball had predicted, the area was in the grip of stormy electrical conditions which threw his

*It was 0.40am Eastern Standard Time.

Jim Mollison stands by as his machine warms up at Pennfield Ridge, New Brunswick, on Sunday, 21 August 1932, prior to continuing his journey to New York.

compasses into confusion. So much so that he finally had to admit that he was completely lost.

Late in the morning towards noon there was a temporary break in the weather when the fog cleared sufficiently to allow him to to recognise that he was somewhere over the New Brunswick coastline. By now he was not only physically exhausted but mentally shattered too, when he realised that he had only covered 136 miles in the last 6 hours – an average speed of 23 mph. At the same time, he had come to the conclusion that his fuel reserve was now too low under the prevailing weather conditions to enable him to reach New York with any degree of certainty. Picking a suitable spot he made a perfect landing at 11.45am local time on a large rolling meadow of a sparsely populated farming settlement at Pennfield Ridge. He had flown some 2,650 miles in 30 hours and 10 minutes and there were 10 gallons of petrol left in the tanks.

The Canadian farmer and owner of the land, Jim Armstrong, was more than a little taken aback when he discovered that the man sitting beside the Puss Moth nonchalantly smoking a cigarette had just flown from Ireland. Although at first the farmer thought that it was all a leg-pull, JM was soon being ushered into the hospitality of the farmhouse, where he was offered a full blown meal. Wisely, he declined the offer in favour of several cups of tea, but not before making a phone call to nearby St John. Within a few hours of resting he was being driven away by local newspapermen the forty miles into the city, where he was able to telephone an anxious Amy from the offices of the *St John Telegraph Journal*. She had been about to have lunch in Grosvenor House when the news first came through that his plane had been sighted over Halifax, now she was telling him in the euphoria of the moment that she would sail immediately for New York on the *Aquitania*.

JM's intention had been to rest for the night at the Admiral Beatty Hotel in St John and then fly on to New York's Roosevelt Field the next morning. However, overwhelmed by the reception given by the people of St John, and a personal invitation from WW1 flying Ace Billy Bishop, VC, to attend the fourth annual Canadian air pageant in Montreal the next day (as it transpired the fog persisted and forced him to abandon the invitation) it was not until Sunday, 21 August, that he arrived in New York.

Mollison was to spend a whole week in the city, which he later described as a Scotsman's paradise. It was unique as far as he was concerned, for although he arrived with just one ten shilling note in his wallet, he left none the poorer. From the moment of his arrival, as he banked his tiny, silver-grey monoplane vertically in salute over the heads of the crowd waiting to greet him, he was given the adulation normally reserved for one of Hollywood's movie-stars. This was the apogee of his flying career. To be landing on the famous turf of Roosevelt Field, the scene of departure for such renowned pioneer flights as that made by Charles Lindbergh, Amelia Earhart, Clarence Chamberlin and others, with a 'first' under his belt, was a victory he savoured to the full.

As the *The Hearts Content* slowly taxied in towards the hangars with de Havilland engineers Walter Rinaldo and Bill Calder running alongside each wing tip, a fellow Scot, Sergeant William Beggs of the Nassau County police and a former member of the Black Watch, sped out on his motorcycle to guide them to the waiting reception area. JM was completely non-plussed by the ferocity of the adulation he received, as microphones were jabbed in front of his face with questions such as, 'Will ya jus' say a few words here, Cap'n,' before being hoisted onto the roof of a sedan and paraded along the line of jubilant well-wishers. In spite of the attraction of the local Long Island beaches and a tennis match at nearby Forest Hills, many visitors had slipped away to see the Scot arrive. The more daring would run out from the police line and jump on the running boards of the Reception Committee's automobile and reach up to touch him.

Eventually, he was whisked away in a limousine surrounded by twelve police-mounted motorcycle escorts. The sirens on their cumbersome Harley-

Davidson machines wailing and warning off traffic as they sped their way over the Queensborough Bridge to Manhattan's Hotel Plaza. As they pulled up outside the hotel – equivalent of London's Dorchester – its entrance decorated with the fluttering flags of the Stars and Stipes and the Union Jack, JM admits that it was for him a moment of deep emotion.

Although in retrospect one might consider that Mollison was merely New York's ephemeral hero-of-the-moment, it must not be forgotten that the City was not accustomed to welcoming those air pioneers who had flown from east to west. Only three aircraft before Mollison's had succeeded in that direction and no one other than he had flown it solo in that direction before. Richard. K. Smith comments on this aspect with the following:

> It was the *arrivals* that counted with American ballyhoo artists; once arrived, they got to 'play' with their heroes for a few days. It was really a case of mutual exploitation. Indeed, in the 1950s some American sociologist shrewdly defined the many 'popular heroes' that strutted or stumbled across the American scene subsequent to 1918 (and aviators would be among them), as 'Heroes of Consumption'. They were not meant to have staying power; they were lionised 'today', consumed, and forgotten by any 'tomorrow'. James Mollison was one of these.[63]

Accordingly, for four consecutive days 'Captain' James A. Mollison made the headlines of *The New York Times* as it detailed every comment of the man and his flight. Articles sang his praises with eulogies ranging from those of 'England's Lindbergh', to 'one whose name would have a prominent place in the list of the greatly daring'. Some newspapers made great play of the small size of the aviator's 'ship' and the fact that the fuel for the journey only cost him $65, (approximately £12). Telegrams and phone calls of congratulation poured in from around the world. Britain's Prime Minister, Ramsay MacDonald; Lord Wakefield and Lord Londonderry were among the official ones, whilst probably of more interest to the Scot were those from admiring girls in Australia and elsewhere. Successful pioneer aviators of the late Twenties and early Thirties, much like the male idols of the silver-screen of the day, were always subject to the blandishments of ardent women admirers. One commentator recorded his impressions of Charles Lindbergh's reception in New York soon after his epic flight in 1927, with the following comment:

> Women literally flung themselves at him, sometimes singly, sometimes en masse. He accepted an invitation to a privileged club on Long Island, thinking he would be among well-mannered people, but he found the

Jim Mollison being greeted at Roosevelt Field, New York, by fellow-Scot, Sergeant William Beggs and DH engineer Bill Calder.

young matrons and unmarried women panting after him even harder than the girls in the street.[(64)]

Unlike Lindbergh, the Scot was magnetised towards such predatory female advances. Whilst there is no evidence that he was unfaithful to Amy during the time he was in New York, he did describe the period as 'three weeks of semi-repressed enjoyment', whatever that may have meant.

If the thirty hour crossing of the North Atlantic demanded Mollison's endurance, then the stay in New York demanded no less. Although he continually stated that he was prepared to depart within an hour's notice for the return leg of his journey to England as soon as 'Doc' Kimball gave the go-ahead on weather, the constant round of social activities left him little time to rest and recuperate. Even the journalists and reporters were finding it difficult to pin him down for interviews, such was his hectic itinerary.

On the Monday morning he made further calls to Amy, dissuading her from sailing and telling her his return flight was imminent. Later in the morning he made a visit to the hangar at Roosevelt Field, where his Puss Moth's Gipsy engine was being stripped down for minute examination in preparation for the return Atlantic crossing. Bill Calder and Walter Rinaldo had been detailed to fly down from Toronto to carry out the task and to assist him as far as Harbour Grace on his return. Surprisingly, their inspection revealed that the wear on engine components, such as crankshaft, cylinders and pistons, was imperceptible. Apart from re-lapping the valves back into their cylinder head seatings, there was little to do but reassemble.

With no real improvement in the weather over the North Atlantic being expected before the end of the week, JM took full advantage of the hospitality being offered by his hosts. New York city was footing the bill for the plushy mock Georgian suite of rooms he occupied on the seventh floor of the Hotel Plaza, as well as providing him with a well-greased reception committee to organise and supervise his every movement. They were there not only to fight off the more intrusive 'sob-sisters', but to provide transport and hone his itinerary down to a physical possibility. During the week it ranged from an aerial sightseeing trip over the city's canyons of skyscrapers, to radio broadcasts and invitations to speak at luncheons and dinners from various organisations all over the city. It seemed that everyone wanted to meet the man who had flown the Atlantic the hard way.

Mollison was eager to talk about transoceanic flying and was predicting the possibility of regular scheduled commercial Atlantic crossings within the not too distant future. The hindrances as he saw them were the necessity for a reliable ocean weather forecasting system and, initially, for some form of subsidy on the flying of ocean mail. The possibility of operating multi-engined aircraft that would eventually carry sufficient payload to make the service financially viable was something he never doubted.

Three of the more colourful meetings that JM enjoyed during his seven day stay in New York, involved two of the world's most famous characters in aviation and one from Hollywood who was making a big name for himself in films.

Charles Lindbergh had been one of the first to send a telegram of congratulation to JM, one which the Scot was to treasure. Some idea of the admiration that Lindbergh felt can be gauged by the fact that he was also keen to meet the man who had made the westward crossing alone. The opportunity came when he knew that JM was to attend a dinner given in his honour at the home of Andrew F. Carter, the president of the Shell Eastern Petroleum Company. No doubt Lindbergh would have been warmly welcomed as a guest at the dinner, but he had by virtue of recent events become a man who shunned publicity in all its forms. The American's only child, a baby son just twenty months old, had been kidnapped and held for ransom in March of that year. Ten weeks later, in spite of a nationwide hunt and large sums being paid over, the child's body was discovered by a truck driver buried in a shallow grave not far from the family's home. It meant that the grief stricken Lindberghs were keeping a low profile, especially as his wife Anne had given birth to their second child only weeks beforehand.

After telephoning the Carter's home the American arrived discreetly well before dinner and the two men talked for a short while on aviation matters in general. No doubt the conversation hinged around the proposed return flight and in all probability Lindbergh would have advised on its peculiarities. Later in the week journalists tried to find out from JM the exact details of their discussion, but the aviator would not be drawn. Quite obviously he respected and honoured Lindbergh's desire for the minimum of publicity on their meeting.

On the following day Douglas Fairbanks Jnr. arrived in New York, at the request of his employers, wishing to meet Mollison. At the time, the handsome young son of his more famous namesake father was under contract to the Warner Brothers' studios and was about to be cast in the lead role of a rather forgettable aviation film directed by William Dieterle and entitled, *The Parachute Jumper*. The film studio had chosen a relatively unknown actress by the name of Bette Davis to co-star with Fairbanks Jnr. The actor's brief was to interest Mollison in a contract, not only as the technical adviser to the film but also to act in it.

From all accounts JM did not immediately turn down the offer. He stalled the invitation by wanting to know if the contract would still allow him to continue with his flying career and to journey between the States and England as he saw fit. Whatever the outcome of his reservations might have been, no contract was ever signed. Sixty years later, Douglas Fairbanks Jnr. cannot recall the fine details of the offer but he does remember Mollison as 'a very shy and retiring, but charming young man. Quite the opposite of the "dashing hero" type that Lindbergh represented.'(65) One wonders how JM in his later life viewed the chance that he had missed of co-starring with two of Hollywood's greatest stars.

Jim and Amy had already met the tall, tousle-haired Amelia Earhart in London shortly after her solo transatlantic crossing earlier in the year. Not surprisingly, with such shared interests they had got on well, particularly the two women. At the time of JM's U.S. visit she had just flown into Newark after setting a new women's non-stop distance record by flying her red Lockheed Vega from Los Angeles to New York in a little over nineteen hours. The following day, after inspecting her machine at the airport, she took the opportunity of being in the neighbourhood to congratulate JM personally by visiting him at the Plaza.

It says something about the celebrity-value of these pioneer aviators, when one considers that even on a short social trip into the city she was accompanied by the customary motorcycle police escort. Today such ostentation is reserved for royalty, visiting heads of state or top politicians. The two met in the hotel's restaurant and over lunch compared notes of their ocean flying experiences. Much like Lindbergh, she was intrigued by anyone who had the audacity to make an immediate second attempt on such a perilous crossing as the North Atlantic. It is doubtful if there was ever any real attraction between the cool feminist and the hard drinking Scot. AE had already suffered too much in her youth from the effects of an alcoholic father, ever to be drawn towards JM.

One of the last accolades to be given to the flier before he left Manhattan, was a presentation at the Plaza of the Gold Medal of the City of New York by the legendary Mayor Jimmy Walker. The award bestowed upon him carried with it the rare privilege for a foreigner of receiving the Freedom of the City. Maybe it says something about JM's secret fears of making a successful return flight home, when, upon being asked by his admirers in St. John a few days later if they could see the medal, he told them that he was not risking losing it and he had sent it home by sea. However, at the award ceremony, during which JM handed over the letter of greeting that he had carried from Mayor Alfie Byrne, the two men seemed to strike up a real friendship.

The charismatic, if somewhat corrupt Jimmy J. Walker, had come into office with the slogan, 'I'm going to turn this town upside down'. He was highly popular with New Yorkers, having started out in life as a song-writer before becoming Mayor of the city. He and Mollison appear to have been kindred spirits, for like the Scot he too had a roving eye where women were concerned. Moreover, he had even gone so far as to immortalise his weakness for the fair sex by writing a Broadway melody with the title, 'There's Music in the Rustle of a Skirt'.* At the time of Mollison's arrival he was married to the film-star Betty Compson, and had just returned from Albany where he was fighting for his political life. He had been charged with a malfeasance which involved the taking of bribes in exchange for the placing of local government contracts. Mollison appeared to be openly sympathetic to Walker's plight and so much so that it did not pass unnoticed by the press, who were baying for the Mayor's blood. JM records that one opposition newspaper even went so far as to appear with the headline, 'Mollison Tammanay Tool'.[66] Jimmy Walker conducted his own defence at the court hearings but was eventually forced to resign within a few days of his meeting with JM. He later took exile in Britain, after being succeeded by the volatile Fiorelli la Guardia.

---

*Subsequent to his death Broadway staged a musical based on his life with the title 'Jimmy'.

In spite of JM's outward composure and cool manner in front of the U.S. media during his week's stay in New York, he was quietly and imperceptibly moving into the first stages of what was most probably a nervous breakdown. At night he found sleep difficult. The thought of the return flight bore down on him like a lead weight. How big a part drink played in deadening this dread we have no exact knowledge. No doubt it played its part. Let it be said that even at the beginning of a long-distance flight for which he was fully prepared physically and mentally, he likened the period beforehand to that of a nervous schoolboy waiting outside the headmaster's office for a caning. Moreover, his apprehension was not being helped by the fact that two recent attempts to make an eastward non-stop crossing of the North Atlantic had both ended in failure.

The two Norwegians, Thor Solberg and Carl Petersen, had set off from New York's Floyd Bennett Field for Oslo in a Bellanca monoplane named *Enna Jettick*, only to run into some real dirty weather and buffeting winds on their way north to Newfoundland. Within fifty miles of Harbour Grace they suffered engine-failure and ditched in the sea near Placentia Bay. Fortunately, they were able to cling to their machine until it drifted to the shoreline, and although it was pounded mercilessly on the rocks they managed to scramble to safety.

The other two fliers, the Americans Clyde Lee and John Bochkon, in their Stinson Detroiter *Green Mountain Boy* and also with Oslo as their destination, were less fortunate. Starting from Barre, Vermont, they too ran into bad weather on the way to Newfoundland and were forced down on the sand dunes at Burgeo where they spent the night. With improved conditions the next morning, they made Harbour Grace and spent the day preparing for departure on the following morning. They took off at dawn for what they hoped would be a thirty hour flight and with enough fuel to last thirty-nine hours. Sadly, they were only to add their names to the other twenty-nine men and women who had already perished in the attempt.

The news of the Norwegians' failure and a disappearance of two brave, young Americans did little to alleviate JM's mental anxiety. It only reminded him of those frightening hours he had so recently spent in the fog-laden skies of Nova Scotia and Newfoundland. The same regions which he soon had to confront again. At least the news of their misfortunes confirmed to him the wisdom of keeping in daily contact with and taking careful note of 'Doc' Kimball's weather forecasting. In hindsight, maybe if JM had not allowed himself to be deflected from proper resting, and the weather had not been so unfavourable during those first few days, then things would have been different. However, it was to be Sunday, 28 August, before 'Doc' Kimball considered conditions were sufficiently improved for JM to make his departure.

Mollison had already arranged with the de Havilland Toronto plant for engineers Bill Calder and Walter Rinaldo to fly with Shell employee mechanic, L. Lesterance, to Harbour Grace for the final check over of *The Hearts Content* and its refuelling. They left New York in a Sikorsky S-38, piloted by R.T. Wickford, on the Saturday with stops at Grand Manan and Port Hawkesbury before putting down short of fuel at Exploit Dam, Newfoundland. It was not until the following day that they arrived in Harbour Grace to await Mollison.

JM left Roosevelt Field at 11.48am EST on the Sunday morning for Harbour Grace with far less publicity than when he had arrived. His plan was to rest at St. John and then leave early in the morning so that he avoided an overnight flight of the Bay of Fundy on his way to Harbour Grace. Although the weather forecast given by 'Doc' Kimball was reasonable, as soon as Mollison reached Rockland on the Maine coast he ran into an impenetrable fog. It must have severely unnerved him, for as soon as he made eye-contact with the ground over New Brunswick he decided to put down. He had spotted the Canadian Pacific Railway line below and followed it as far as Nerepis, where he landed in a large field some eighteen miles short of St John. It was a clear sign that he had no stomach for the return flight, for under normal circumstances he would not have given up so easily.

The following morning weather conditions had improved, giving the prospect of a pleasant flight at least as far as Nova Scotia. However, whilst crossing the Strait of Canso, to Cape Breton Island, JM ran into a severe thunderstorm which buffeted the tiny machine around the darkened sky and convinced him that he would not reach Harbour Grace that day. As he circled Sydney desperately looking for the city's airport, the Cape Breton Flying Club sent up one of their members, Don MacPherson, to guide him down. In spite of the lead given by the club's pilot, JM decided to land on the open pastures of the Stewart Farm, three miles short of the runway. The thousands of people waiting at the airport to catch a glimpse of the Atlantic flier, were unaware that his failure to arrive with MacPherson was the sign of a man whose nerve had finally collapsed.

It was probably an act of divine providence that JM should have been offered and accepted hospitality from Dr. Freeman O'Neil on that afternoon. Without it, the Scot might well have been the North Atlantic's third victim that month. His host's medical knowledge and experience quickly recognised that Mollison, in spite of his protestations to the contrary, was suffering from extreme nervous exhaustion. The tired eyes in a deeply lined face and shaky hands belied his outward veneer of confidence, and O'Neil forbad him to fly unless he took at least a week's rest.

That evening whilst JM attempted to sleep, the doctor sent a cablegram to Amy in London which read, 'Your husband is my guest. As a medical man I strongly urge that he should not attempt the return trip until such time as he recovers complete control of his nerves. I think you should insist on this.'[67]*

The next morning an anxious Amy was on the transatlantic telephone imploring her husband not to attempt the return flight but to return on the *Empress of Britain* which was leaving Quebec on 3 September. Amy also had the moral support of Lord Wakefield who telephoned later with a similar message. They had both taken the line that whilst JM had not achieved his ultimate purpose of being the first to make a double-crossing of the Atlantic alone, he had more than succeeded by making the first solo flight westward. It was no mean achievement and one of which he could be justifiably proud. If he needed any more persuasion, then it came from 'Doc' Kimball's weather reports which stated that present conditions were unfavourable and likely to get worse rather than better over the next few days. With that, JM threw in the towel, and was quoted as saying, 'I felt as if some sickening, intangible weight had been lifted off my head.'[68]

It was a slightly refreshed and revitalised man who flew from Sydney airport on 1 September for Quebec and home. The flight coincided with a request from the residents of Pictou County for JM to break his journey and land at Trenton, Nova Scotia, in order to celebrate the opening of the town's new airport. Lew Donaldson, a member of the airport's committee, had wired JM at Sydney with the invitation, but owing to the tight time schedule for dismantling and crating of *The Hearts Content* at Quebec, the Scot declined. He did, however, promise to do a low pass over the airstrip and drop a message of congratulation to the watching crowd. The airport was later officially named and recognised as 'Mollison Field' in his honour.[69]

---

* Dr. Freeman O'Neil also ministered to the needs of Beryl Markham, when she crash-landed in Nova Scotia in 1936 after making her east-west crossing of the North Atlantic.

Chapter 12

'Anything you can do . . .'

Jim's successful North Atlantic solo flight only served to reinforce Amy's desire to add to her laurels as an aviatrix. Although she was still considered a national heroine, since her Australia and Tokyo flights she had faded somewhat out of the attention of the press. She needed little prompting therefore from her friends and advisers such as Bill Courtenay to know that another aviation 'first', or new record, was imperative if she was to retain her image in the public eye.

Amelia Earhart had been the first woman to make a solo crossing of the North Atlantic earlier in the year. Much like Charles Lindbergh's flight hers had been from west to east, which meant that Amy was now seriously considering following her husband's example and doing it in the opposite direction. However, as soon as Jim heard of her plans he did his best over the telephone to dissuade her. Contrary to popular belief, JM was not the complete male chauvinist that some have portrayed him to be, he was just concerned for her safety. On every other occasion he encouraged Amy in the planning of her record-breaking flights, even where his own records were likely to fall to her. In any case a success for either of 'the Mollisons' contained within it a reciprocity of publicity and prestige for each of them.

Amy accepted her husband's advice most probably because she realised that she lacked the ability to fly blind by the use of instruments alone. It was an essential for any long-distance pilot and a skill which Jim had acquired naturally by hard experience during his time with ANA. So determined was she to remedy this deficiency that she took the opportunity, whilst Jim was away in the United States, to enrol with the Air Service Training School at Hamble, near Southampton, for a course of blind-flying instruction.

The AST school, popularly dubbed as the 'Air University', was founded as a subsidiary of the group of companies under the control of the Armstrong Siddeley Development Co. It had been opened just over a year when Amy enrolled and she flew down in *Jason IV* to commence instruction not long

November. Jim and Amy, both snappily dressed in long black leather coats trimmed with astrakhan to keep out the cold, made their last minute inspection of her aircraft before driving away to snatch a few hours' sleep at a local hotel. Not surprisingly, the inability to sleep just before a long-distance flight appears to have been an occupational hazard with most of the pioneering long-distance fliers. Charles Lindbergh found it virtually impossible to sleep just before his New York-Paris flight, and Jim Mollison only seems to have overcome the problem by the use of generous quantities of alcohol.

Just before daybreak the silence of the airfield was shattered as the engine of Amy's *Desert Cloud* burst into life. Slowly, she taxied her plane out from the hangar towards a small, waiting crowd, where Jim, Bill Courtenay, Kathleen of Drogheda, JM's secretary Doreen Pickering and the Mayor and Mayoress of Hythe were gathered to wish her God's speed. Amy embraced her husband before he took off in his own aircraft, for he intended to accompany her as far as the French coastline.

At 6.37am the dim outline of her tiny monoplane was barely visible against the twinkling red boundary lights of the aerodrome, before it merged into the darkness and disappeared from view. Within ten minutes JM was back at the aerodrome, reporting that he had been unable to sight her at all in the murky conditions. All that he and Bill Courtenay could now do was to fly back to London and wait.

When JM returned to Grosvenor House, he found that he was being deluged with phone calls from enquirers from all over the world wishing to have news on Amy's progress. It was for this reason that he invited Bill Courtenay (he was already using the hotel as a branch office for his own private venture, Aviation Publicity Services) to stay in the Mollison suite and handle all the calls until she had safely made Cape Town.

The first messages from Reuters and the Press Association reported that Amy had put down unexpectedly at Barcelona with a suspect fuel gauge (it transpired that fuel was leaking from one of the gravity wing tanks). From thereon, she made steady progress via Oran and across the Sahara by night. One wonders how much of the instruction she had received at Hamble aided her navigational skills on this stretch of her journey. Apart from having to return back to Gao, when she discovered that one of the cabin tanks had not been completely filled, she made good time until forced to land at Benguela with low oil-pressure. Fortunately, the trouble turned out to be no more serious than a partially clogged oil-filter, but the procurement of a replacement caused her an eight hour delay. After one further refuelling stop at Mossamedes, she arrived in Cape Town 4 days 6 hours and 54 minutes after leaving Lympne. It was truly a remarkable performance on two counts. Not only had she knocked ten and a half hours off Jim's record, she even made it look easy by arriving in a black two-piece suit and white blouse, looking quite cool and fresh.

Messages of congratulation poured into Cape Town, ranging in eminence from that of King George V and Amelia Earhart, to that of her parents. Jim had never doubted her ability to better his time, but like many others he had doubted her stamina. Now, he was one of the first to congratulate her during a lengthy telephone conversation. At a speech given at a dinner in his honour by the Brooklands Motor Racing Club on the following evening, he magnaminously stated, 'I have been beaten by my wife, but it is very nearly the happiest day of my life. She has beaten my record by merit alone.'[73]

One wonders how the myth was ever established that Jim Mollison was always sullenly jealous of his wife's flying achievements!

Press reports at the time reveal that 'Johnnie' Mollison* was very much dependent upon her husband's advice on the finer points of her homeward flight. One eye-witness who overheard her telephone conversation with JM in the superintendent's office at the Wingfield airport on the afternoon of her arrival, quotes Amy as saying: 'Now I have lost the moon and have no plans . . . do tell me what to do, Jim.' It had been her original intention to wait for only two days before her return, whilst she rested and her machine was checked over. As it happened, she was not to commence her homeward flight for another three weeks. During this time, she was to be the guest at 'Sea Point', the home of some admiring friends – a Mr & Mrs Henry Hermann – whom she had met earlier in London.

In the only letter to Jim that was to survive amongst Amy's papers, and written at the time she had just arrived in Cape Town, she gently chides her husband for not corresponding with her.[74] She writes with deep affection to tell just how much she is missing *him*; not London, or the Grosvenor, but him. There is also, much like in her letters to Franz, hints that even if they were together it would all probably be spoilt by them quarelling over some trivial difference. Jim on his part was never a prolific letter writer, but he did at least on several occasions during her absence cable her with messages of considerable warmth. The only other communication in this period was a radio dialogue between the two of them, when Amy broadcast from the Cape on the day after her arrival and Jim was at the BBC in a link-up programme.

It was a bronzed and healthy looking Amy who set out from the Cape on Sunday, 11 December 1932, for Croydon. She was fairly confident of

*Amy was never really enamoured with her christian name.

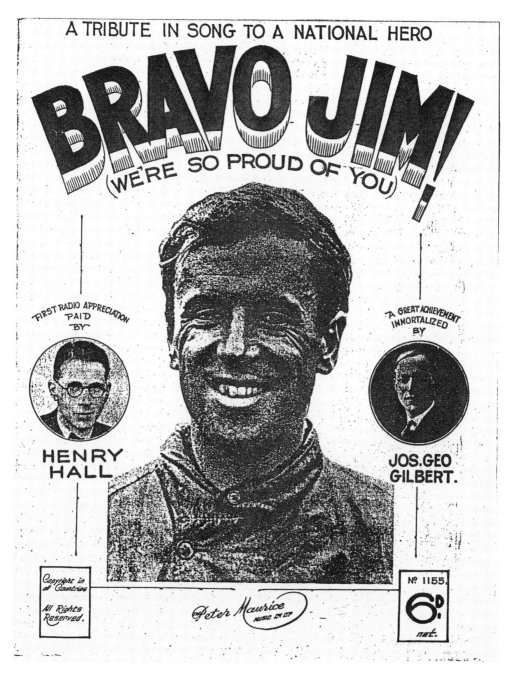

Bravo Jim was written and composed by Joe Gilbert in 1932 (he also wrote the lyric for *Amy, Wonderful Amy*).

breaking the existing record on the return flight, for she had only to beat the rather leisurely ten days set by Captain Barnard and the Duchess of Bedford in April 1930. Even so, the flight was not an easy one, for on the initial stretch she had to fight her way through severe weather between Mossamedes and Duala. Whilst over the Atlas mountains, towards Oran, she ran into blinding snow-storms which forced her to turn back and land at Beni Ounif. She eventually arrived in bright sunshine at Croydon airport at noon on Sunday, 18 December, to a rapturous welcome. It had been 7 days, 7 hours and 5 minutes since she had left Cape Town.

JM ran towards the travel-stained, silver Puss Moth as Amy taxied in. He was every bit the proud husband. They kissed and embraced affectionately, before she slid her arm in his and they walked together towards the airport crowd. On the reception platform, waiting to greet her, were her own parents, Jim's mother, Lady Drogheda, Sir Malcolm and Lady Campbell, and the usual dignitaries from the world of aviation. Amy was back on the headlines of Fleet Street's press as they recognised her gutsy performance. She had taken on the men, principally her husband,* and beaten them at their own game. She was the first woman to solo the trans-Sahara route to South Africa, and into the bargain had gained two records on a 13,000 mile journey. The crowds loved it as Jim and Amy smiled and waved from the back of their chauffeur-driven car, as it sped off towards the West End of London leading a procession of cars in its wake.

As soon as the Mollisons were back at the Grosvenor they were met by a large crowd of her fans who were gathered outside the hotel in Park Lane chanting, 'Amy, Amy, Amy'. It was all very reminiscent of her homecoming to the capital after her return from Australia in 1930. The crowd persisted, until, in spite of her extreme tiredness, she went out onto the balcony with Jim to acknowledge their applause. The ordeal was not yet over for Amy however, for the BBC technicians were already swarming around the Mollisons' suite in order for her to make a spontaneous broadcast before she was allowed any sleep.

Within a few days, Jim and Amy headed for Switzerland to enjoy a well-deserved, winter sports' holiday. On the way over they stopped off for a day in Paris, where Amy was able to meet the acknowledged Queen of *haute couture*, Gabrielle 'Coco' Chanel. The Parisian designer had recently offered to costume the aviatrix at a much reduced fee from her normal charges. In more prosperous times, Chanel's boutique on the Rue Cambon had been attracting the custom of some of the richest and most fashionable women on both sides of the Atlantic, including those from Hollywood. Now, during the

*As Amy greeted her husband, she was heard to say: 'They should cheer you Jim. They don't know how easy your advice made it.'

difficult times of the Thirties' depression, Chanel, like many other houses of fashion, was prepared to adapt her trading practices in order to survive. Amy on her part, delighted in the simple style of the couturiere's creations, especially her current fashion of the *garconne* look which employed plenty of black. Chanel was highly flattered by the Mollisons' special visit, knowing that it brought welcome publicity, and she responded by offering Amy a choice of any of her evening gowns as a personal gift.

Christmas at the sumptuous Palace Hotel in St Moritz saw Jim and Amy rubbing shoulders with some of society's *glitterati*, including Hollywood's funny man, Harold Lloyd, the beautiful Ann Dvorak and the red-haired Clara Bow. It was as well that the Mollisons' marriage was at its peak of harmony at this time for one wonders just what temptation the latter lady – known as the 'it' girl – might have posed for JM under different circumstances. She was after all the silver-screen's current, sizzling sex-symbol; the first in a long line which was to extend to that of today's Madonna.

That the Mollisons were on an equal footing with such celebrities cannot be doubted. They were stars in their own right and the public recognised them as such. Much publicity was given to the fact that each of them were soon to collect the Segrave Trophy, awarded annually to the one who had contributed the most to Britain's exploits on land sea or air. The 1932 award was to go to Amy, and in the following year to Jim. Their pictures featured regularly in newspaper and magazine articles, as well as in the weekly programmes of the *Pathe* newsreels shown at most of the local cinemas. JM had, earlier in the year, sat for the artist Margaret Lindsay Williams, and the *Illustrated London News* had featured the painting on the frontispiece of their September issue. Currently, *The Tatler* was devoting its front cover to a portrait of the aviator in hellenic pose, looking very much the intrepid airman of that era. It must be said that Mollison was quite handsome in his younger days, and one can quite understand Warner Bros' interest in his physical appeal as a potential screen actor.

Whilst Amy revelled in the winter holiday and would have been prepared to extend it, Jim, never one with a particular fondness for sports, was becoming daily more restless. He was anxious not to sit back on his reputation, but to get back to London where he was about to make preparations for his next flying adventure. Four potential prizes now lay tantalisingly within his grasp. To be the first person to solo the South Atlantic westwards, and thereby become the first to solo both North and South Atlantics. Also to be the first to fly from the UK to South America, and if possible beat the time of four and a half days to reach Brazil, set recently by a French crew flying from Paris in a tri-motor Couzinet. Not content with this, he had also agreed with Amy that they should place an immediate order with de Havillands for a twin-engined aircraft, in which they would jointly make an attempt on the world's long-distance record later in the year.

As JM prepared his Puss Moth machine during that January for the South Atlantic crossing, one piece of news must have disturbed his thoughts. On 7 January 1933, Bert Hinkler took off from the Fairey aerodrome at Hayes in an attempt to smash C. W. A. Scott's England-Australia record. Rather foolishly, he set out under atrocious weather conditions to cross Europe via the Alps, with Brindisi as his first planned stop. He was never seen alive again. After several days waiting for news of the missing aviator, an aerial search party scoured the snow-covered mountains and valleys but without success.

It became clear from the evidence found four months later at Pratomagno, in the Appenines, that Hinkler's Puss Moth had suffered structural failure in flight. The port mainplane was found several hundred yards from the site of the wreckage, and it appears that the pilot was still alive after the crash. Evidently, the little Australian had made a brave but vain attempt to crawl away from the wreckage and had died from his injuries in the extreme cold of the desolate mountainside. Whatever modifications the DH factory were implementing, the disturbing crashes were to continue, albeit sporadically and in small numbers. Perhaps it was just as well that the wreckage of Hinkler's aircraft was not found until three months after Mollison had departed for South America, for it is significant that neither Jim nor Amy ever used the Puss Moth again for long-distance flights after the cause of Hinkler's death was discovered.

The first non-stop crossing of the South Atlantic had been made by the two Frenchmen, Dieudonné Costes and Joseph Le Brix, when they flew their Breguet monoplane from Senegal on the west coast of Africa to Port Natal in October 1927. Since then, the flamboyant Italian Marshal Balbao had led a whole formation of ten Savoi-Marchetti S55 flying-boats across the ocean in order to impress the world of Mussolini's emerging air power.

Whilst a crossing of the South Atlantic presented a formidable challenge to the solo aviator, its milder and more consistent weather pattern was considered a little kinder than its counterpart to the north. On a westward crossing one had the advantage of the assisting Trade Winds, a benefit which enabled JM to state that compared to his North Atlantic ordeal, this crossing was a 'pleasure cruise'. That is not say that its weather could not be unpredictable, as he and others were to find out.

Early on the morning of Monday, 6 February, Amy's *Desert Cloud* dipped in salute, as she waved farewell to her husband somewhere near Le Touquet, before returning to Lympne. The first leg of his journey to the west coast of Africa meant two short refuelling stops; one at Barcelona in the afternoon, and another at Agadir in Morocco where he landed on the following morning. After a two hour break he left on the 700 mile flight to Villa Cisneros in the Spanish Sahara. By 5pm he was circling over the radio masts beside the white-washed fort which lay alongside the aerodrome. As he touched down on the sandy airstrip, the shimmering heat of the desert afternoon enveloped him like a hot, open oven.

However, he was pleasantly surprised to be welcomed by people milling around his machine greeting him with impeccable English accents. Evidently, they belonged to exiled political prisoners being held by the Spanish Republican Government, many of whom were of aristocratic origin. The sandy promontory containing the airfield and town was much like an open-prison, with electrified fences surrounding the area, positioned as much to keep out marauding tribesmen as to contain the security of the prisoners from escape. Mollison's arrival caused quite a bit of excitement, for these men were unused to visitors, let alone long-distance aviators from England. It was not long before they were inviting him to share with them in a glass or two of the local plonk, in order to drink a toast to the success of his ocean crossing. After sending a radio message off to Amy, he joined them for the early part of the evening, until his sleepiness forced him to snatch a few hours rest before his midnight departure.

By 8am on the Wednesday morning he had arrived at Thies, a French Sengalese military airfield approximately forty-five miles inland from the coast at Dakar. He was now well on schedule to beat the French record, and pleased that he had had his machine re-engined with the more powerful 130hp Gipsy Major of the type that Amy had first used on her Cape flight.

It was JM's intention to refuel and commence the ocean crossing without delay, but he eventually succumbed to the pleas of the French authorities when they warned him of an impending danger in the form of the notorious *pot au noir*. He needed little knowledge of their language to understand the meaning of, *C'est stupide, ca non?* when he insisted on leaving. He was suspicious at first and argued against the advice, obviously thinking this was a ploy of the French to prevent him from capturing their record. However, when it was explained that it meant severe, storm-force winds accompanied by torrential curtains of rain that would, if he took off now, strike at around midnight and just as he was nearing the Brazilian coast, he relented.

Whilst JM was not particularly superstitious, he was no doubt also influenced to acquiesce to the warning of his hosts by virtue of a forecast that had been made by R. H. Taylor, the popular astrologer of the *Sunday Express*.

Amy bids her husband farewell on 6 February 1933 as he sets out to fly from the UK to Brazil.

Naylor had predicted that an eminent aviator would die on the day intended for the ocean crossing. Although JM was sceptical of the astrologer's nonsense, it was sufficient to add to his decision not to push his luck too far.

Meanwhile, Amy was with Bill Courtenay on that evening in the Fleet Street offices of the *Daily Express*, oblivious to JM's change of plan and ready to be able to speak with her husband as soon as he landed in Port Natal (JM had agreed with Bill Courtenay before leaving, that the newspaper should have exclusive rights to his story).

They waited until 3am before the editor finally decided that it was now too late to catch the next morning's edition. Instead, he would run a story told from Amy's angle, one merely giving her reactions to the flight. There was now no point in the couple waiting around any longer. Obviously Amy was becoming worried and Bill Courtenay decided that it would be unwise to leave her on her own. They finally motored back to his home in Carshalton, where she was able to rest and wait for further news.

JM took advantage of the enforced delay and slept soundly for most of the hot afternoon at Thies. It was decided that if he left around midnight he should miss the worst of the dreaded *pot au noir*, and run into clear skies for most of the journey. Into the bargain, it would enable him to make a daylight landing safe on the other side of the Atlantic. As JM surveyed the airfield, he noticed that the wind dictated that he would be making a distinctly uphill take-off. His thoughts went back to the Darwin crash and Naylor's prediction, and he decided that there was less risk if he made a downwind take-off. Soon after midnight, the fuel-heavy Puss Moth climbed cautiously into a black, velvet sky and headed west.

Throughout an uneventful night JM was comforted by the knowledge that he had the advantage of a seven or eight mph tailwind. He smiled somewhat cautiously to himself and thought about Naylor, no doubt now fast asleep and tucked up in bed in his comfortable surburban home. What if the soothsayer should somehow be proved correct? JM imagined a troop of French soldiers at Thies firing a volley into the air for the 'tout crazy' Scotsman. Too bad he wouldn't listen.

As the long awaited dawn began to flood the horizon behind him, JM looked down on an unruffled sea. Suspended above its tranquillity and immensity only served to remind him of his own insignificance. It has been said that the best definition of religion is what a man does with his inner-loneliness. JM was not exactly a religious man, and yet on these occasions he sensed a presence greater than his own. Normally, he would drown out such thoughts with the contents of a gin or brandy bottle, now as he took the occasional swig it was insufficient to allow him to escape. He found himself promising the Almighty that if he survived just this one flight, then he would be a better Christian. At the same time, he was acutely conscious that his mother constantly prayed for his safety on these record-breaking flights.

By mid-morning, he was well aware that he was in fact flying over a tropical sea. The sun's heat began to bore down relentlessly through the transparent roof of the cabin, and he was glad to be wearing the sun helmet that he had brought along with him. Slowly, as the beads of perspiration ran down his back he started to discard some of his clothing. First his shirt went, then trousers and underpants too, until he was finally sitting stark naked. He laughed to himself as he mused on what the newsmen back in Fleet Street would report if they could see him now!

JM's first navigational check on the crossing should have occurred just over mid-way along the route with a visual fix on St. Paul's Rocks. However, as the time came for a glimpse of those black, jagged stumps that should now be protruding out of the Atlantic, he scanned the horizon in vain. After a further two hours' flying he began to have serious doubts about his position, until quite suddenly he noticed that the ocean's surface dramatically changed. Before him lay a vast mirror of aquamarine water, almost like an island of stillness within a sea, and yet lapped by the ocean's waves. It was a comforting sight for now he knew from his nautical charts that he was roughly five hundred miles from his destination. He had entered the Placid Areas, or doldrums. That strange phenomena found along the equator, and where for centuries past the sailing-ships of old had been becalmed, sometimes for weeks on end.

The good weather did not hold for very long before *The Hearts Content* was flying into the opaque folds of a grey curtain of cloud. Soon, the fabric-covered wings of the machine were resounding to the beat of a torrential downpour as rain spun off the propeller, bounced along the silvered cowling and hit the windscreen like bullets from a gun. Now and again JM would catch a glimpse of the sea, until, after what seemed an eternity, the grey blurred outline of an island appeared. Overjoyed, he realised that it was Juan Fernandez the one time refuge of the shipwrecked Alexander Selkirk, the Scottish author of *Robinson Crusoe*. It confirmed that he was now within two hours of his goal, and it was time to start dressing.

As he sighted the dark green line of the Brazilian coastline, he drank the last of the brandy in celebration of landfall and flung the empty bottle out through the cabin window. His eye followed its trajectory as it spun swirling down to burst upon the waves. Seventeen and a half hours after leaving the aerodrome at Thies, JM was circling over a large clearing amongst the dense, green foliage of the jungle, to land at Port Natal. It was 3 days 10 hours and 8 minutes since he had left Lympne, and he had the satisfaction of knowing that he had made the first flight between England and South America. Moreover, he had beaten the Frenchmen's record by more than a day.

In spite of the arrangements that had been made between Bill Courtenay and Jim Mollison, the offices of the *Daily Express* had received no report on the flight from their Brazilian correspondent by the Wednesday evening. Bill Courtenay was down in Fleet Street again on that evening and throughout most of the night, but much to his annoyance nothing came through on Mollison. What was more to his disgust, the next morning's papers revealed that the *Daily Herald*, a rival newspaper to the *Daily Express*, had scooped the entire story.

Meanwhile, JM continued his flight down the South American coast heading for Buenos Aires, where he intended to crate the Puss Moth and return home by sea. By the Saturday afternoon he was in Rio de Janeiro, where he had agreed to be prepared to take a long-distance transatlantic telephone call from Amy in Grosvenor House. Paramount newsreel had installed their cameras in the Mollison suite in London in order to film Amy speaking with her husband, whilst the *Evening Standard* had their reporter on hand for exclusive rights to the content of their discussion. After Amy had finished talking to Jim, Bill Courtenay took the advantage of speaking with him about the mix up with the *Daily Express* story. Although JM insisted that he had sent the report, Courtenay was not entirely convinced that he had done so, and even after Jim returned to London the mystery was never really cleared up between them.

☆ ☆ ☆

Whilst JM was being feted in lavish style in Rio with an invitation to meet Brazil's provisional president, Getulio Vargas, Bill Courtenay (now termed loosely as Amy's 'aviation consultant') was accompanying Amy in her Mercedes on a publicity journey to the north of England. She had been invited to her native Yorkshire for an official welcome by the city of Leeds' dignitaries. The programme included a visit on the Friday afternoon to a luncheon given in her honour by Lewis's store, where her aircraft *Desert Cloud* was on display to the public. As a counter to those who claim that Amy was really one of the early feminists, it is interesting to note from newspaper reports of the time, that although hitherto she had been known as Amy Johnson, she was not averse to being referred to as Amy Mollison. She was quite unlike her U.S. counterpart, Amelia Earhart, who was rarely, if ever, publicised by her married name.

Amy and her escort motored on over the Peninines later in the same evening to pay a visit to Amy's sister Molly, who had recently married Trevor Jones, Blackpool's newly appointed Deputy Town Clerk. Bill Courtenay tells a rather amusing account of the interview during which the Welshman, who was working for the Hull Corporation at the time, was selected for the post.

> 'Well,' said the Mayor, 'although you come from Yorkshire, we have some fine girls here in Lancashire and no doubt Lancashire can provide you with a wife.'
> 'But,' said Trevor, 'I already have a girl in Hull.'
> 'It's not Amy Johnson by any chance, is it?' said the Mayor.
> 'No, but it's her sister,' quickly rejoined the applicant for the post. Needless to say he got the job.[75]

After spending a quiet weekend with Amy's sister and brother-in-law, the couple motored back to London. Amy was in a hurry to catch the liner *Highland Brigade* before it left Southampton for Madeira. Since she had heard that her husband was sailing from Buenos Aires and that his ship was due to call in at the island, she had decided to meet him there and share a holiday together.

One or two interesting points relevant to this period emerge in the contents of the only correspondence to survive between Thomasina Bullmore and Amy.[76] In a letter sent to Madeira whilst Amy was waiting for Jim to arrive, his mother bares her soul to her daughter-in-law about her own relationship with her son. She not only admits that she has failed to understand him since he reached manhood, but also infers that her son's subsequent behaviour had hurt her badly. Whilst she is reticent to go into details, she is most probably referring to his drinking habits, since she admits that he has exhibited a good deal of his father's characteristics in his make-up. She goes on to console and sympathise with her daughter-in-law for her state of nervous tension caused by the risks her husband had taken on the two transoceanic flights. Finally, the letter makes it plain that the two women not only had a deep love for a son and a husband respectively, but also a strong affection for each other.

Chapter 13

'Seafarer'

The streetwise east London bus-driver Edward Hillman had made his mark in the early Thirties by establishing a fleet of private coaches plying for fares on a regular sheduled bus service into the city of London. Although he was a rough diamond of a man, he had managed to break the monopoly of the London Passenger Transport Board's bus service, and subsequently a sizeable portion of the city's daily commuters had forsaken the ubiquitous red buses in favour of the cheaper fares and faster transportation offered by his coaches. His success was to be short-lived however, for legislation placed restrictions upon his service to such an extent that he was eventually forced to abandon his entire bus operation. The closure was a big disappointment to him but was not without financial compensation.

Hillman was not a man to give up easily. His shrewdness and entrepreneurial flair soon enabled him to bounce back, this time with the establishment of an air-taxi business. The result was that in November 1931, Hillman's Saloon Coaches & Airways Ltd was formed. It began to operate a service to Clacton and Ramsgate from a small grass airfield at Maylands, some five miles north east of Romford in Essex, initially with two Puss Moths, and subsequently with two Fox Moth four-passenger transports.

The former bus-driver had a vision, much like his successor Freddie Laker in the 1970's, for cheap air travel for the masses. To fulfil his dream he needed bigger and more economical aircraft, and in the summer of 1932 he decided to approach de Havillands. Quite coincidentally the company had, at the instigation of the RAF's adviser to the Iraqi Air Force, begun to lay down the design for a twin-engined civil aircraft which was in fact a double version of the Fox Moth. It would use standard Moth wings for the folding portion of the mainplanes, thereby giving ease of hangarage, and be powered by two 130hp Gipsy Major engines. In its military version the eight aircraft designated for use by the Iraqis would be equipped with provision for two forward firing guns and an upper, ring-mounted open gunner's

Amy unveils Edward Hillman's DH 84 Dragon *Maylands* at the Romford aerodrome early in 1933 as Jim looks on. The portly figure of E. H. can be seen standing behind Amy on the extreme left, whilst Bill Courtenay is just about in the picture on the right.

position. The outcome of the design for civilian use was to be the DH 84 Dragon, a six-passenger light airliner of which 115 were to be built in the UK. Historically, it was the company's first multi-engined aircraft which was able to pay its way without subsidy.

Hillman took delivery of the first Dragon in December 1932, and a further six by April 1933. In a bid for publicity he invited the Mollisons to attend the inauguration ceremony of his sheduled service to Paris in that month, where Amy was duly photographed unveiling one of the blue and white liveried aircraft which had been aptly named *Maylands*. Both Jim and Amy had more than a passing interest in the occasion for the Dragon was the aircraft that they had ordered for their attempt on the world's long-distance record. Furthermore, Amy was also anxious to carve out a serious career for herself in civil aviation, and she realised that Edward Hillman might be the man who could assist her in achieving her aim.

At the time, the world's long-distance record stood at 5,341 miles, this being the distance covered by two RAF officers, O. R. Gayford and G. E. Nicholetts, when they flew from Cranwell to Walvis Bay in South Africa in a Fairey monoplane. Record-breaking was by this time becoming quite commonplace, and the Mollisons knew that if they were to achieve any distinction at all, then they must make a flight that would be truly considered spectacular. Their aim was therefore to fly from the UK to New York and thereby be the first to do so; and to then fly the 5,994 miles from New York to Baghdad non-stop for the long-distance record. With a subsequent return journey to the UK of approximately 2,500 miles, the whole flight would constitute a grand total of almost 12,000 miles. Comprising as it did a double crossing of the North Atlantic, it was sure to attract the sort of publicity that the Mollisons needed. Bill Courtenay was determined that they should receive the maximum of press coverage, and had managed to tempt the *Daily Mail* into agreeing to pay a substantial fee for the exclusive rights to their story if the flight was successful.

It was whilst the Mollisons were waiting for one of the Dragons to be specially modified at Stag Lane for its long range task, that Amy became the target for some scathing public criticism for one of her earlier flights. Her first attempt on the Tokyo record had been in January 1931, when she made an attempt to fly solo across Siberia to Japan in her open-cockpit Gipsy Moth *Jason 111* in mid-winter. It was an ill-advised flight, one which came to an untimely end when she crash-landed in a snow-covered potato field near Warsaw, damaging the undercarriage and propeller. Amy had subsequently written an article two years afterwards under her married name for the *Sunday Dispatch*, detailing the event in what was later purported to be a lurid and exaggerated manner. She had evidently described how she had at first been surrounded by a dozen or so peasants, one of whom – 'a big, dirty, bearded, evil-looking man with greedy eyes'[77] – she alleged had not only demanded money, but had attempted to drag her from a sleigh into a hut. Whether she intended it or not, her account gave the impression that she had been the victim of a near rape. When the article was brought to the attention of the Polish Aero Club, they set up an enquiry of investigation. As a result of their findings, her allegations were seriously challenged and a complaint made to the Royal Aero Club.

The outcome was that Amy was forced to admit that the facts had been grossly distorted by the newspaper without her knowledge, and in spite of a letter of apology to the Polish Aero Club in which she withdrew the allegations, she was heavily censured by the Royal Aero Club. Its secretary, Commander Harold Perrin, told Amy in a none too courteous manner that she could not evade responsibility for articles that were signed by her. Jim made an vain attempt at her defence by telling reporters that his wife had been 'made nervous' by the bearded man's action, and stressed that she had, after the incident, experienced the utmost hospitality from the Polish people. The whole story was circulated in the world's press, and unfortunately it

The Mollisons' first attempt on the world's long-distance record ended in near disaster at Croydon on 8 June 1933, when the undercarriage of their DH 84 Dragon, *Seafarer*, collapsed during the take-off run.

was eagerly seized upon and used against the Mollisons on later occasions by Harold Perrin, and by C. G. Grey in particular.

The Mollisons' DH Dragon G-ACCV, now named *Seafarer*, created quite a sensation when it was flown on a trial flight to the British Hospitals Air Pageant at Boughton, near Northampton, in April 1933, for its first public outing. The twin-engined biplane had been drastically modified by fitting three massive cylindrical fuel tanks into the space normally occupied by its passenger seats. The aluminium tanks (JM appears to have been persuaded that the weight penalty from using steel tanks was too severe) were suspended from the top longeron joints of the fuselage by steel cables, and separated from each other by sorbo rubber pads. They left a gap of only eighteen inches underneath them at their lowest point for Jim and Amy to crawl from the cabin door at the rear to the pilot's cockpit at the front. It was not exactly an easy escape route in an emergency! Small wonder that Jim had nicknamed the all-black painted machine 'the flying coffin', or that he was fond of adding that 'it only needed brass handles to make it complete'.[78]

In seeking to increase fuel-economy, the compression ratio of the engines had been raised slightly to give an additional 8hp at maximum rpm, something that was quite useful during the take-off. In addition, a mechanism had been incorporated so that the tailwheel could be jettisoned in flight to give an extra sixty miles range. The total effect was to give the machine, with its tanks topped to a 603 gallon maximum capacity, a creditable 'still air' range of approximately 6,500 miles. In order to carry the extra weight of fuel, the undercarriage was strengthened and set back four and a half inches to relieve the load on the tail wheel during take-off. However, as Jim and Amy were yet to discover, the problem was for an aircraft with a tare weight of 2,310 lb to lift an additional load of 5,024 lb on the return take-off!

The *Seafarer* went back to Stag Lane for final adjustments and further flight-trials after its first outing, and in the meantime Amy had managed to persuade Edward Hillman to loan her one of the aircraft from his fleet of Dragons. It enabled her to practise loaded take-offs from the aerodrome at Hatfield, and to familiarise herself with the machine's handling character-istics. She was all too aware that as co-pilot to Jim, she needed to be able to be able to handle the machine in the event of an emergency.

Around this period, Jim had been introduced to the Princess Arthur of Connaught at a Mayfair party (most probably by Kathleen of Drogheda) and the two had struck up an immediate and quite strong relationship. Before her marriage to the Prince in 1913, she had been the Princess Alexandria, and was in fact the daughter of the eldest daughter of King Edward V11. Jim was fond of stressing that she was the Duchess of Fife in her own right and but for the fact that certain members of the royal family had produced children, she might well have become the Queen of England. Much like her cousin the Prince of Wales, she had earned the strong disapproval of other members of the royal family through her willingness to mix with people well beneath her own social standing.

JM was once on the receiving end of the waspish wit of the Western Brothers, two stand up comedians in vogue at the time, when they drew public attention to the aviator's close relationship with the Princess. Evidently, Jim was in a West End restaurant dancing and dining with the royal lady when they became the target of the two monocled comics. During the cabaret show that followed, the two comedians concluded their mocking, semi-tuneless ballad with the line, *Hon y soit qui Mollison*. It is well attested that the Scot could be quite aggressive when he had more than a few drinks under his belt, and but for the restraint of a, 'Never mind, Jim', from his consort, he might easily have provoked a public scene. On another occasion whilst in Jim's company, the Princess was heard to pass the self-deprecating remark that, 'The Prince of Wales and I are the only two *common* members of the Royal Family.'

During JM's first meeting with the Princess, she had expressed a keen interest in flying and inevitably he offered her a flight on his next trip. She accepted, and one Saturday during mid-May, Jim took her up in a Puss Moth from Stag Lane on a joyride over the capital. JM could not resist performing one or two mild aerobatic manoeuvres which his passenger thoroughly enjoyed, and by the time they had landed she was keen for more. So it was that later in the day, she accompanied him and Bill Courtenay in a hired DH Hawk Moth for a visit to Sir Alan Cobham's National Aviation Day Display's at Leamington. As a result, she became quite air-minded and took a keen interest in the proposed *Seafarer* journey, so much so that she even hand-knitted Jim a scarf in the plane's colours of black, orange and green.[79] It was a garment of which he was to become inordinately proud, for he reasoned quite justifiably that few men could say that they wore clothing made by a member of British royalty!

At the end of May, Jim and Amy took the *Seafarer* on a nine hour cross-country proving flight in order to establish the machine's most economical cruising speed. It also gave them the opportunity to observe the result of switching fuel supplies from tank to tank during flight, and to see what effect, if any, the surging of the fuel had on the supply to the carburetters. It was estimated that they would be burning something like twelve gallons per hour at their optimum cruising speed of just over 100 mph. A wooden, tip-up bench seat with canvas backs had been substituted for the single pilot's seat normally used in a standard Dragon, so that pilot and co-pilot could sit side by side. Inevitably, it meant that they were both sitting in a cramped position, one that could only be relieved when they took turns at resting on the canvas camp bed beside the front fuel tank.

Both the *Aeroplane* and the *Flight* aviation journals were putting out disparaging comments just before the Mollisons' Atlantic crossing. Their editorial staff were not only questioning the value of the flight but also doubting the couple's chances of even surviving the ocean crossing. Amy, in whose name the *Seafarer* was registered, was already smarting under the Royal Aero Club's criticism of the Polish incident which had been reported by *Flight*, when one of its contributors, C. N. Colson, pleaded with the aviatrix in a written article to change her plans. Colson recognised that the *westward* crossing of the north Atlantic would be the most hazardous part of the whole flight. He implored her to crate the Dragon and proceed to New York by sea and *then* attempt the long-distance record to Baghdad. However, his pleas received a cool reception from the Mollisons, who pointed out that such an action would cast serious doubts upon their aircraft's capabilities, and also undermine the public's confidence in the future of aviation.

Maybe the journalist's comments were taken more seriously than the Mollisons cared to admit, for it is known that they both made out their wills just after this ominous and unwelcome advice. A trust fund was to be set up in the event of their deaths, one which would provide for a sum of money and a trophy to be presented annually to commemorate an outstanding flight of the year. It is difficult for today's air-traveller, where an Atlantic crossing in a modern jet airliner is an everyday and common occurrence, to fully appreciate what was at that time considered to be a highly risky undertaking. Jim and Amy put their chances of success at no more than 10-7. It was noticed by many, and Bill Courtenay was amongst them, that Amy was unduly worried on the eve of the flight about the prospect of their survival. If Jim did manage to hide his forebodings under the haze of a cloud of alcohol, then perhaps we should at least understand his reasons for doing so.

Somewhat naively, Bill Courtenay allowed printed invitations to be sent out to the press announcing the Mollisons' departure from Croydon on the morning of Whit Monday, 5 June. As it happened the weather was unfavourable and the flight was postponed until the following Thursday. Early on that morning, Jim and Amy hurriedly dressed and left their Grosvenor apartment suite to be driven by Bill Courtenay, who was also in residence for the night, to arrive at the airport by 4.10am. They made a brief inspection of their aircraft which was already tanked up with 450 gallon of aviation fuel and ready to go, before retiring to the Aerodrome Hotel to wait for complete daylight. Meanwhile, an excited crowd of friends and relatives had begun to assemble in the hotel foyer as Amy's parents and sisters, Jim's mother, and others arrived to see the couple off. The Mollisons' ever enthusiastic fan, Lady Drogheda, was there to slip a wrist-watch onto Amy's hand as a good-luck token. It had been worn by Brigadier-General Edward Maitland when he had crossed the Atlantic both ways as the senior passenger on the airship R34.[80] It was the first of many momentoes they were to be given on that morning.

By 5.30am the *Seafarer*'s engines were being warmed up, watched by a crowd of well-wishers and a *Movietone* newsreel van, its cameraman in position on the roof of the vehicle waiting to record the departure. Amy, dressed in white overalls, and Jim in black, exchanged farewell greetings with their relatives and friends before crawling under the cabin's fuel tanks to gain access to the cockpit. The chocks were removed and with Jim at the controls the aircraft taxied out to the far northern edge of the airfield alongside Stafford Road, to turn and face a 1500 yard stretch of grass for the take-off. They were now well outside of the normal boundary limits of the

Seafarer skirting close to the southern tip of the Irish coast (somewhere near to Mizen Head) on 22 July 1933, just after the commencement of its flight to New York.

airfield in order to gain every yard for their take-off run, but unfortunately neither Jim nor Amy had noticed a drainage-gutter which lay directly in their path on the south side of the old hangars. As the throttles were opened up, the heavily ladened Dragon began to gather speed, but had not proceeded more than two hundred yards before it struck the hidden obstacle. The sudden impact caused the port undercarriage vee-strut to collapse, and then the other leg tore away too, as the aircraft slewed to the left and finished up on its belly facing the direction from which it had started out.

For one breath-taking moment every eye was anxiously fastened onto the crumpled biplane, watching lest it should burst into flames and trap the fliers before they had time to crawl out. Almost in an instant the ominous clang of the ambulance bell rang out across the airfield as the aerodrome's blood-wagon raced towards the damaged machine. First on the scene were Bill Courtenay and the airport's senior officer, Captain Jeffs, by which time a badly shaken Jim and Amy had clambered out from one rather bent aeroplane. One other eyewitness quickly on the spot on that morning was Peter Masefield,* a young man who was working at the airport at the time. He not only recalls seeing Amy scrambling out of the *Seafarer* in tears, but remembers that Jim Mollison had been celebrating more than a little on the

*Sir Peter Gordon Masefield was knighted in 1972.

previous evening. He added, 'Perhaps it was a good thing they never got off.'[81] Photographs taken at the time, show the disconsolate pair amidst a crowd of onlookers staring in utter dejection at the twisted propellers and sagging wings.

Neither Jim nor Amy ever gave in easily to a set-back and before long they were looking around for a more suitable venue to try again. In the meantime the Dragon was back at the Stag Lane factory undergoing major repairs. Certainly the publicity had done the Mollisons' image little damage, for their plans were now followed by the public with even greater interest. Jim began to focus his attention on the possibility of using one of three suitable beaches, instead of airfields. Portmarnock Strand was eschewed in favour of a mainland runway, and Southport was deemed to be less favourable than Pendine Sands. And so, after exploratory visits to Pendine a week after the crash, the Welsh site was chosen.

De Havilland's promised that the repaired machine would be delivered to Cardiff ready for them to fly at the beginning of July. In the meantime, from a study of the moon and the tides, the first Friday in the month was set as the most suitable day for the Mollisons' departure. Apart from the distraction of flying from London to Hull to attend Amy's sister's wedding at the end of June, where Molly was to be married to Trevor Jones, Jim and Amy's eyes were firmly set on the Air Ministry's weather predictions for the month. When the all-black Dragon finally flew along the seven mile expanse of sandy beach ready to land at Pendine on the Monday evening of 3 July, they were astonished to see thousands of people thronging the golden sands waiting to greet them. As soon as the aircraft came to a standstill on the smooth hard surface, they were mobbed by autograph hunters and swarming crowds seeking to touch them. Only one local policeman was in sight and the newspapers of the time reported women and children fainting in the stampede that followed the two aviators along the beach. Holiday-makers were camping out overnight on the sands in tents, or in their cars, believing a take-off was imminent for the following morning. Bill Courtenay was alarmed at the inadequacy of police control, but finally managed to employ two teams of local men to guard the machine throughout the night. Meanwhile, Jim and Amy were booked into the Beach Hotel only to find that the privacy they needed before the flight was denied them. They found it impossible to sleep for the noise of the large crowd, who stood chattering underneath their bedroom window for most of the night.

In all, Jim and Amy were to spend eleven frustrating days waiting for a favourable weather forecast, intermittently flying the machine off the beach and back to Cardiff and then back again, before they finally gave up and entrained for London. The two weather factors they most needed – the correct direction and strength of breeze along the beach, and winds of no more than 20mph over the ocean – were missing. Understandably, the crowds completely failed to comprehend why the flight was being delayed, for during most of the time the weather was fine where they stood, but not out in the Atlantic!

There is no doubt that a great deal of inner-tension must have been building up in the Mollisons during this period of waiting. The Croydon debacle was sufficient in itself to unsettle their nerves, and the long delay in waiting for appropriate weather conditions always presented a temptation to risk making a hasty and unwise departure. Eventually, after the machine had been on view for some time in the hangars of the Cardiff Aeroplane Club at sixpence per visitor (all the proceeds went to the club), it was flown back to Stag Lane.

On the Friday evening of 21 July, Jim and Amy were alerted by the Air Ministry that conditions appeared favourable over the North Atlantic for the next few days. It had been reported that surface winds were no more than 15 mph, which indicated that at 2,000 feet, the altitude they intended to use for nightflying, the winds would be no more than 25mph. It was good enough, and urgent calls were put through to the Shell representatives for fuel and supplies to be on site at Pendine for a noon take-off on the following morning. When Jim and Amy, together with Bill Courtenay who had been sitting on the floor at the tail end of the machine, arrived around mid-morning, they found a mere two or three hundred spectators waiting to watch their departure. Ironically, extra police were on duty and rope barriers had been erected to keep back the expected crowds. The trio took a quick breakfast in the small Victorian sitting room of the Beach Hotel, whilst 415 gallons of fuel was being poured into the aircraft's tanks. Because of the undercarriage failure at Croydon, JM had now decided to take thirty-five gallons less fuel than on that occasion. Unfortunately, it proved to be a serious error of judgment on his part, and one which was to ultimately rob them of achieving their initial target – New York non-stop.

After making the usual round of interminable handshakes and farewells, Jim was heard to comment, 'If we get safely through this, I shall retire to some cottage in the country,' and then with a slight pause, 'and look twice before I cross the road.' A white-clad Amy, her hand on her head as she sought to restrain her long blonde hair from streaking back in the propeller's slipstream, looked relaxed and confident as she exclaimed for reporters, 'Now for the greatest adventure of my life.'[82]

Just before noon the *Seafarer* fanned a great cloud of sand and grit back from its prop-wash as it started its run down the beach. At 11.59am, after covering a distance of only nine hundred yards, the contour of the heavily laden tyres resumed their normal shape as Jim pulled the column back and the machine's flying surfaces bore it up on the lift of a slight cross-breeze. Four more photographic and escort planes, including a red monoplane flown by Captain George Birkett, followed their tracks to join them in the air as they headed towards Tenby. The weather report had predicted thick low cloud and drizzle over southern Ireland, and it was not long before they lost sight of Birkett. It had been his intention to escort the Mollisons as far as Mizen Head, but with the clouds down almost to sea-level and Jim holding the machine just twenty feet above the waves, they quickly lost contact.

The flight might well have come to a spectacular and disastrous ending less than two and a quarter hours after leaving Pendine. Somewhere near to Mizen Head, whilst flying in thick cloud and purely by instruments, they were both straining their eyes for a glimpse of the Irish coast on their starboard side when suddenly Amy shouted, 'Look out! Keep left.' Jim made an immediate steep climbing turn to port and narrowly missed the edge of the cliffs by only a few feet. As they climbed up through the thick layer of nimbo-stratus they suddenly emerged into bright sunshine, only to find themselves flying above a white marble carpet of cloud and surrounded by blue skies. For the next twenty hours they were to glimpse the sea only at sporadic intervals and for no more than an hour in total.

The *Seafarer* settled down to a steady 100 mph reading on the ASI at 2,000 rpm, as Jim's ear tuned in to the even beat of the two four-cylinder Gipsy engines. Both Jim and Amy knew that the Dragon was incapable of remaining airborne if one of the engines should fail. Even with a normal maximum fuel load of sixty gallons the DH 84 was incapable of maintaining height on one engine, let alone with a fuel overload of 355 gallons![83] Under such conditions it meant that with two engines they were no more secure, for the risk of failure was now doubled.

As they chased the sun westward through an extended day, Jim and Amy would relieve one another at the controls and crawl back underneath the fuel tanks to the rear of the aircraft. Here at the tail end there was almost room for someone of their stature to stand up and stretch their legs and freshen up. On the way rearwards they could, by using a torch-light, check the fuel gauges on the cabin tanks; also at the rear they carried the Royal Aero Club's mandatory sealed barograph, and a third compass by which they could verify the accuracy of the other two instruments positioned in the cockpit. There was always the need for them to keep their nerve when any one of the three main tanks ran dry, for at that instant the engines would falter momentarily. It was essential at that moment to make sure that the tank ran quite dry before switching to the next one, for the accuracy of the mechanically operated gauges then currently in vogue was never something to be relied upon.

The last-minute weather forecast that they had received on the beach at Pendine, just before take-off, had predicted that for the first eight hundred miles they would meet low cloud with headwinds, but that by nightfall they should find conditions improving. Meanwhile in New York, meteorologist expert 'Doc' Kimball was stating that there was no likelihood of storms over the North Atlantic but there would be the usual strong westerlies which make the east to west passage so hazardous. He went on to predict that they would encounter light westerly to to south-westerly winds for the first half of the ocean crossing, and then there would be a shift to the north-westerly and direct winds against them as they neared the Grand Banks of Newfoundland. As events transpired, the fuel-sapping headwinds were to become far stronger than the Mollisons had been led to believe.

As the sky began to darken, the temperature fell and Jim handed the controls over to Amy as he went back to don a warmer flying-suit and fur-lined boots. As he crawled back into the cockpit, still struggling to get his arms fully into the sleeves, Amy gave a chuckle. Jim was attempting the impossible; mistakenly, he was trying to get into her smaller size suit! Throughout the night they had hourly shifts at the controls, interspersed with noise-defying attempts at sleep lying on the camp-bed by the front tank. Jim had brought a novel along to read by torchlight, but admitted in the end that he had been far too worried to concentrate. All he did know was that the night seemed interminably long. There is no doubt that the boredom was relieved by more than a few swigs of gin passing between Jim's lips at this period of the flight.

It was approximately 9am BST by the cockpit's chronometer when the sun finally rose on the horizon directly behind them, by which time they estimated a landfall within the hour. Two hours later, however, they were flying over the majestic shapes of huge icebergs floating serenely in a sea speckled with ice-floes. At least the appearance of these floating giants confirmed that they were somewhere between Newfoundland and Labrador, the area to which icebergs are confined at this time of the year. But the Mollisons were worried. Did their silent, sea-borne companions mean that their allowance for drift was incorrect, and that they were in fact far north of their intended route? Just before noon Jim shouted excitedly, 'Land!' and peering through the screen Amy could just make out, some ten miles in the distance, a dark promontory of land jutting out into the sea as if to greet them.

Within a short while they were confirming their position as the Straits of Bell Isle at the mouth of White Bay, Newfoundland, only a few miles north of their intended landfall, and 1,200 miles from New York. Because of the unexpectedly strong headwinds they had encountered, some as much as 45mph, their average speed had been no more than a disappointing 87 mph. It meant that they were now at least two hours behind their ETA of 5pm (EST) at Floyd Bennett Field, Long Island.

The first reported sighting of their aircraft came over Nova Scotia when Jim and Amy flew over 'Mollison Field', the Canadian airfield that had been named after the Scot in honour of his solo crossing twelve months earlier in *The Hearts Content*. Max MacLeod was a thirteen year old youngster visiting the aerodrome on that day and he recalls:

> It was a hot Sunday afternoon and the local flying instructor, H. O. 'Hump' Madden, (at one time private pilot to the Duke of Windsor), was flying joy-riders at $2.00 a piece when off in the distance a larger plane was seen circling above the Northumberland Strait, some twenty miles away. Even then, I knew who it was and the instructor rushed his Fleet Finch into the air and headed towards the unidentified plane. In the meantime, Jim Mollison had spotted the field and roared past at about one hundred feet in the air en route for New York. Amy was sleeping at the time. I will always remember the thrill of seeing that black DH Dragon pass so low overhead.[84]

By this time JM knew that it was touch and go whether they would make their destination non-stop. The headwinds had taken their toll of the Mollisons' fuel supply and in order to conserve what was left, he dropped his cruising speed down to no more than seventy five mph as he headed out into the fogbanks of the Bay of Fundy.

At 4.32 pm (EST) the *Seafarer* was sighted over the U.S. at Bar Harbour, Maine, as it flew down the eastern coastline. Amy recalls that seventy minutes later the weather started to clear, somewhere near Portland. By 7pm (EST) they were sighted over Boston by two aircraft, one of which was being flown by John Polando* with four newspaper photographers on board. They circled the tired Mollisons and reported that Amy was at the controls with Jim seated beside her.

It is on record that Amy was imploring Jim to land at Boston for more fuel while there was still daylight, and then to proceed to New York, but he was

---

*John Polando had a particular interest in the Mollisons' flight, for he had crewed with Russell Boardman in July 1931 to set a long-distance record of 5,012 miles.

(Above): Caught in the act! Illegal souvenir-hunters scouring the wreckage of the Mollisons' *Seafarer* soon after the crash at Bridgeport, Stratford, Connecticut, USA.

(Below): An aerial shot of the crippled machine lying in the marshes.

insistent, perhaps understandably so, that they could do what no other British aviator had done before and make New York without putting down. There is no doubt that there were heated arguments in the cockpit and that Amy's judgment was to ultimately be proved the sounder of the two. She felt that it was far too dangerous to attempt finding a strange airfield in such a built up area as Long Island in the dark, and particularly so since the fuel reserves were now reading too low for comfort.

From Boston, Jim took over the controls and flew on past Providence and into darkness. Not long after, he discovered that every time he lifted the aircraft's nose, however slightly, the engines would begin to fade. How he must have kicked himself for not taking on those extra thirty-five gallons of fuel at Pendine!

It was around 9.30pm (EST) (3.30am BST) when they sighted the white, red and green boundary lights of the Lordship airfield, near Bridgeport, Connecticut, just fifty-five miles away from Floyd Bennett Field. There was nothing they could now do but attempt an immediate landing.

Fred Moller, the manager of the Northeastern Air Service and operator of the airport, had already been alerted of the possibility that the Mollisons might be forced to land at Bridgeport and refuel before flying on to New York. It was no surprise therefore when he heard their aircraft circling overhead. Immediately he had the 28 million candlepower floodlight turned onto the 3,000 feet long east-to-west runway as the *Seafarer* made its first approach. As soon as the airport manager saw that the aircraft was making an incorrect approach downwind, he had the rotating machinery of the airport's rotary beacon light disconnected and turned onto the windsock on the top of one of the hangars.

The Mollisons had by this time been in the air for an almost incredible period of thirty-nine hours without sleep, and both were fatigued to the point of utter exhaustion. There may have been futile attempts at sleep on the camp-bed during the flight, but these breaks had provided little more than a temporary respite from sitting in one cramped position for hours on end.

Although one can only conjecture at this point, there is every likelihood from previous known habits of Jim Mollison that alcohol had been used as a stimulant. In all probability it would have been taken to keep him awake, and also to bolster his courage in an undertaking that was now bordering on the suicidal. It was a case of a very determined and stubborn man who would push himself to the limit of his physical endurance and beyond. Now, in spite of the help that was coming from the airport authorities, neither Jim nor Amy were able to discern the correct wind direction for a safe landing.

The excess of illumination appears to have made matters worse for them by obscuring the ground's surface and making it seem all the darker. JM always claimed that there was considerable ground-fog that night which partly hid the runway, but there seems to be little evidence for this from eye-witnesses.

After the third mistaken approach, Fred Moller decided to go up in one of the airport's instruction machines and guide the Mollisons down. Once in the air the floodlight was trained onto Moller's aircraft as he circled the airfield and made a landing into wind from an easterly direction.

Neither Jim nor Amy appear to have seen Fred Moller's machine at all in the air, and when they did see him on the ground after landing, he had turned and was now taxying back to the hangar. It seems that at this instant Jim then mistakenly assumed that the American was about to take-off and therefore he set the *Seafarer* to land in that direction.

By this time they had been circling the airfield for almost fifteen minutes and were on their fifth and final attempt at a landing. There is no doubt that they were down to the last few gallons in the tanks, perhaps sufficient for twenty minutes' flying time, but still enough they realised to cause a fire if they did crash-land.

Perhaps it was because Jim Mollison was thinking at that moment of his RAF Duxford colleague Bailey, trapped in the blazing Sopwith Snipe at Eastchurch some nine years earlier, that caused him to undo his seat-belt. He recalls the immense bravery of Amy as she prepared herself for the final approach. In spite of knowing that they might both perish within the next few minutes, her face creased into a big confident grin. Whatever their marital problems might have been, or were to be, no man could have had more admiration for his wife's courage than he had at that moment. Amy remained belted as she braced herself for the uncertain touch down, all the while seeking to direct her husband as best she could.

According to one eyewitness the unlit *Seafarer* came in from a westerly direction, barely clearing the telegraph wires along the Lordship Road and pitched towards the tall saw grass in the salt swamp adjoining the airfield. Although JM had overshot the runway, he might still have made a safe landing had his course been just one hundred feet further to the left. As it happened, the Dragon bore down through the tall grass until its wheels struck an unseen, four to five feet high embankment of a drainage dyke. The plane somersaulted onto its back and slithered to a halt some three hundred yards outside of the airport's boundary.

Upon impact Jim was thrown head and shoulders through the allegedly safety-glass windscreen, badly cutting his face and head as he went, only to be left dangling head down in the marshy slime. Amy was badly bruised and cut as she was tossed against the side and roof of the cabin, and was left upside down with her head in water but still conscious.

Without realising that they had landed in a swamp, Amy imagined for one awful moment that her hair was being wetted by leaking petrol. Not surprisingly, she later described the incident as 'the most unpleasant experience of my life'. Bravely, she managed to crawl out over the tops of the fuel tanks and climb down into the marsh, where she was able to pull her semi-conscious husband clear of the machine.

Both Jim and Amy were extremely fortunate to have survived the crash for two reasons. Firstly, there had not been a fireball explosion (Jim had the presence of mind to cut the ignition switches as soon as the wheels had touched the mud); and secondly, the waters of the swamp which borders the Housatonic river and Long Island Sound were on an ebb-tide, otherwise they might both have drowned.

Rescuers were quickly on the scene to find Amy nursing her injured husband and moaning, 'He couldn't see, he couldn't see.' As they were being borne away on stretchers, hastily made from lengths of fabric torn from the wrecked aircraft's wings, souvenir-hunters were busily crossing from the road onto the marsh. Jim estimated that within two hours some 7,000 cars had been parked in the area and the *Seafarer* was literally ripped apart. Pieces of struts, landing-wires, instruments, nuts and bolts, in fact anything that was removable was taken. What parts of the aircraft that could not be removed had messages, some none too complimentary, scrawled over them.

An hour later at Bridgeport their cuts and bruises were being treated in the emergency room of the hospital before they were wheeled into a private ward, where their beds were placed alongside each other. After receiving anti-tetanus jabs they were both near to collapse and in a state of severe shock and exhaustion. Although their injuries were not considered serious, Jim's face, now showing almost two days' growth of stubble, needed thirty stitches to close a gash that ran from his left eyebrow down across his cheek and almost to his mouth. In addition, he had suffered several cuts to the head, a badly cut right hand and a score of cuts and abrasions to both legs, all of which necessitated a further seventy stitches.

Amy's injuries were less severe, with only two stitches needed to one of her fingers, a gash on her left ankle and cuts to her right shin-bone. According to one newspaperman on the spot, a rather pale-faced Amy sat in her mud-stained white overalls nervously smoking a cigarette whilst her wounds were being dressed. The observant reporter also noticed that she had a solitary, turquoise ear-ring dangling tantalisingly from her left ear lobe, and that her orange-painted fingernails were slightly tinged with the blue slime from the marsh.

Within a few hours of the news of the Mollisons' crash the south wing of the local hospital was thrown into confusion, as a swarm of newspapermen, photographers, newsreel-cameramen and representatives from various radio stations invaded its corridors. Much to the chagrin of most of the patients, the technicians began to wire the building for direct broadcasts, and for newsreel interviews with the aviators as soon as they were available.

Meanwhile, at Floyd Bennett Field in Brooklyn, an estimated crowd of 10,000 and 600 policeman had assembled to greet the man and wife team. Amongst those waiting to pay homage to the Mollisons on that evening were two outstanding pioneer aviators, Wiley Post and Marshal Italo Balbao. The one-eyed Indian from Oklahoma had already received a tumultuous welcome at the airfield only twenty-four hours earlier, having made an outstanding solo flight of 15,596 miles around the world in 7 days 19 hours; whilst the ebullient Italian was about to depart on a return journey across the Atlantic leading an armada of twenty-four flying-boats, all of which were at that moment moored in the nearby Jamaica Bay.

During a brief interview given by the Mollisons on the following morning, Jim made no attempt to cover up or make excuses for the crash. The *Bridgeport Post* quoted 'Captain' Mollison with the surprisingly unvarnished comment of, 'The crash at Bridgeport I attribute to fatigue . . . I was unable to judge my distance properly.' There was little point in him blaming a ground-mist for the mishap, for the airport manager, in an attempt to show that he had done all that was possible to assist them down safely, was quick to point out that fifteen planes from New York had landed there throughout the night and subsequent to the Mollisons' crash. Moreover, the front page of the *New York Times* featured their pictures with a leading article in which JM admitted that, 'I was so tired that I couldn't tell where I was putting her.'

Chapter 14

'Turbulence'

There has been much research into fatigue and its effect upon aviators since the Bridgeport crash-landing, and many other incidents like it. Nasa's, Dr. Curtis Graeber, in a lecture given to the Royal Aeronautical Society's Air Transport and Aviation Medicine Group in 1990 is quoted as saying:

> Each month Nasa's Aviation Safety Reporting System receives confidential reports from long-haul flight crews describing how fatigue and sleep loss have contributed to major operational errors such as incorrect altitude, gross track deviations, and landing without clearance or on the incorrect runway.

He also affirms that:

> '. . . the well known effects of sleep loss and circadian desynchronisation (better known to the layman as 'jet lag') on mood and interpersonal relations are another vulnerable avenue whereby decision-making could be negatively impacted.[85]

Dr. Graeber's last comment might go some way to explaining the content of an interview with the Mollisons that was carried out by John P. V. Heinmuller, a leading member of the National Aeronautic Association, during the week following their discharge from hospital. In it he states:

> While they were at the hotel, I had opportunities for a number of conversations with both of them about the flight and the crash landing. It seemed inconceivable to me that such experienced fliers could cross the Atlantic and navigate so skillfully (sic) all the way up to the last 150 miles (sic) and then crash clumsily in a forced landing on a small field. I sought for the reason.

> When questioned on the subject Mrs Mollison would only say that as the flight neared the end she and Captain Mollison had a disagreement, and he had refused to permit her to take over the controls. Possibly if he had let her relieve him at the time the accident would not have occurred. It

appeared obvious that they both wished to forget the matter, however, and I never mentioned it again.[86]

There is no doubt that today's British commercial airline pilot, working under the CAA's regulatory limit of flying no more than fifty-five hours in any weekly period, would find it very hard to believe that it was possible for a person to be engaged in a non-stop flight over a duration of some thirty-nine hours. Particularly so when one takes into account the primitive blind-flying and navigational aids then available. Equally, today's Concorde captain making the London-New York crossing in three and a half hours, must find it mildly amusing when he considers that the engine power then available to the Mollisons meant that the DH Dragon only averaged 80mph over its 3,190 mile route.

Maybe to fully appreciate the particular difficulties of a *westward* crossing in the early Thirties, one has only to consider the advantage of the wind direction in assisting those pioneers who made eastward crossings. As an example, Alcock & Brown's 1919 flight and Lindbergh's solo eight years later, were both made in less sophisticated aircraft than the *Seafarer*, and yet at average speeds (118 and 107 mph respectively) of 20 mph in excess of that achieved by the Mollisons in 1933.

Apart from the lack of fuel and their fatigue, which were undeniably factors in the Mollisons' failure to make their destination at the Floyd Bennett Field, one cannot discount the part that alcohol might also have played in it. There is strong evidence to suggest that JM was suffering from some form of night myopia or visual field defect, which could have been due to a vitamin A and B deficiency (nyctalopia) induced by his heavy drinking over the previous ten years. Or that he was in the early stages of severe liver disease, notably that of cirrhosis. Certainly the lack of food during the flight – some tomatoes and barley sugars appear to have been the sole source of sustenance – when combined with alcohol, would not have helped.

On the other hand, Jim Mollison's trouble might well have been purely a physiological defect with which he was born. The eye-tests that he would have undergone during his former RAF days, from 1923-28, were unlikely to have detected any form of night-blindness. For one thing, very little night flying was carried out by that service in the 1920s, and therefore it was not considered to be a problem. Another factor was that night myopia cannot be detected by an ordinary eye-test, and facilities for doing so were not then readily available. In fact, RAF screening for the condition did not come into being until the late 1930s.

According to Swedish trials undertaken in 1981, using laser techniques, tests on a random group of people between the ages of twenty and seventy

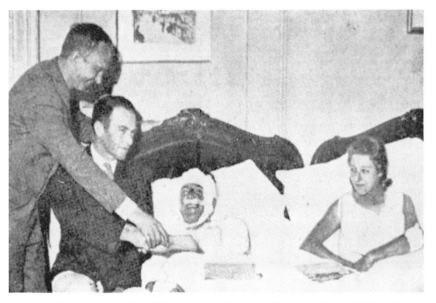

Jim and Amy being greeted by U.S. aviators Clarence Chamberlin and Clyde Pangborn in the Bridgeport hospital.

showed that one in five would have failed the standard European driving test in twilight conditions, and that the failure rate increased rapidly as the level of darkness was increased.[87] It is also on record that airline pilots have been known to have mistaken well-lit motorways for airport runways. Whether these incidents have been due to fatigue, alcohol, or some form of night-blindness, or a combination of all three, has never been fully explained.

One other factor that cannot be readily discounted in the Bridgeport mishap was that JM was a forty-a-day cigarette smoker. It is a medical fact that the excessive use of tobacco over a period of time can be associated with the atrophy of the optic nerve fibres, in a condition recognised as 'tobacco amblyopia'.

☆ ☆ ☆

Within twelve hours of being admitted to the Bridgeport hospital Jim and Amy were pressing to be allowed to continue their journey to New York. During this time Bill Courtenay had been in telephone contact with Amy, where she explained that their injuries were not as serious as had first been reported (it had been rumoured that Jim had been killed in the crash) and requested that he immediately contact their parents to this effect. As their agent in the UK, Bill Courtenay was anxious that their story should feature on the newspaper headlines as soon as possible. It was therefore a relief for him to learn from Amy that the account of their flight had been related to the *Daily Mail* representative in New York. As a result, their signed story appeared in Fleet Street on the following morning's edition of that newspaper. It was soon evident that in spite of their failure to reach their intended destination, the publicity only further enhanced the Mollisons' 'derring-do' reputation as household names in Britain.

The first visitor to the hospital had been Wiley Post, who had driven to Bridgeport through the night as soon as the announcement of the crash had been given out at Floyd Bennett Field. Spontaneously and generously, he immediately offered to loan them the use of his record-breaking Lockheed Vega, the *Winnie Mae*, so that they could still have a crack at their New York – Baghdad long-distance record. As much as they admired the man and his offer it was politely declined, for in all probability they had already received a hint from Bill Courtenay that Lord Wakefield was likely to put up £4,000 for the transportation and rebuilding of their wrecked aircraft. All they now wanted to do was to proceed to New York where an official reception was to be given in their honour.

Jim and Amy were insistent that they leave for New York the day after their crash, and much against the wishes of the hospital's medical advice they were driven by ambulance to the Lordship airfield, where one of the Shell Oil Company's Sikorsky S39 amphibians was waiting to fly them to Floyd Bennett Field. Jim was carried to the plane on a stretcher, where two of the Bridgeport doctors were waiting to accompany them on the flight. Whilst Amy was brought alongside in a wheelchair and lifted on board and into the aircraft's small cabin. As the red and yellow amphibian took off it was met in the air by three escort aircraft flying in an impressive formation. The lead plane was a Northrop monoplane being piloted by Commander Frank Hawks, famed for his U.S. trans-continental, record-breaking flights in the late Twenties and early Thirties, and for being the man who introduced Amelia Earhart to aviation.

As they landed at FBF a police motorcycle escort of ten riders sped out to meet them and the Shell amphibian was led onto the concrete apron in front of the main hangars. Newsreel-cameramen were poised on the roofs of their vans just behind the barriers, where a thousand or so well-wishers were waiting to greet the injured couple. As soon as the Sikorsky's propeller came to a standstill and the cabin door opened a loud cheer rang out from the crowd. Only when the two aviators were gently lifted out and carried to a nearby sedan, did the noise hush into a near silence. Meanwhile, a group of Scottish ex-patriates were present to welcome their fellow-countryman with the bagpipes playing, 'See the Conquering Hero Comes' and 'Land of Hope and Glory'. The onlookers were amused but no doubt puzzled as to why the couple had not been kept in the hospital for at least two or three more days. Little did they realise that the Mollisons were determined not to be kept waiting for their moment of glory a day more than was necessary.

As the couple were being lifted from the car into wheelchairs outside Manhattan's Plaza Hotel, one of the more exuberant bystanders with a strong burr of the heather in her voice shouted, 'Scotland forever, Jimmie'. It managed to raise a faint smile on Jim' face and a feeble wave from them both as they were wheeled to their suite of rooms on the fourth floor. Ten minutes later 'Captain Jimmie' and his wife were fast asleep.

Over the next few days Jim and Amy received a stream of visitors to their rooms, amongst them the cream of the USA's long-distance aviators, men and women such as Clyde Pangborn, Clarence Chamberlin and Amelia Earhart. The Mollisons had already met the tall, slender aviatrix after her arrival in England in May 1932, whilst Jim had met her at the same hotel just twelve months earlier. Without any hesitation she invited them to spend the following weekend with her and her publisher husband, George Putnam, at their luxurious mansion home at Rye, in Connecticut. It was an offer which Jim and Amy readily accepted.

George Putnam had a well-known reputation for being a self-opinionated and overbearing man, although he could, when the mood suited him, turn on the charm. Those who met him generally described him as handsome, shrewd and quick-witted. Most were impressed by his flashing, piercing eyes. His whole demeanour conveyed that he was a man who was used to getting his own way. Some ten years older than AE, he had first met the aviatrix when she was selected to be the first woman passenger across the North Atlantic, in 1928. It was generally recognised that their marriage, although not devoid of affection, was, as far as Amelia was concerned, largely a well-ordered business arrangement.

AE's husband had been born into the family of the established publishing firm of G. P. Putnam & Sons, but characteristically he had started out on his own as a freelance correspondent and 'stringer' working in Bend, then a small town in central Oregon. As well as being the owner of the town's only movie-theatre, he had before long become elected as the town's Mayor at the age of twenty-four. His agile brain and entrepreneurial skills soon saw him in a quick succession of jobs; as newspaper editor, author, film-script writer and ultimately as an 'ideas-man', not only for his family's publishing business but also for the Hollywood studios.

Prior to divorcing his first wife, a convenient move as a means to marrying AE, he had used some very dubious methods in promoting the sales of his firm's books. On one occasion when the author Francesco Nitti, nephew of a former Italian premier, was under contract to write a book for Putnam's on his experiences in one of Mussolini's prison-camps for dissidents, GP had, in order to hype the book's sales, falsely claimed that he had become the victim of a death threat. On another occasion he had attempted to gain fifty per cent of the rights of Charles Lindbergh's handwritten manuscript of a book the aviator had written to describe his 1927 solo flight to Paris. In the American idiom, he was what could be irreverently described as a huckster.

The promotion of Amelia Earhart as the world's best known aviatrix was only one of GP's more successful business ventures. No doubt on the occasion when he invited the Mollisons to Rye, he was weighing up the strength of the opposition that was to be found in Amy, something that he had already done with other women pilots of that era. So meticulous was he in guarding his wife's public image that he would advise her on exactly where to stand in a group when being photographed. By being on the right-hand edge, when the caption appeared her name would be first in the list. If ever she suffered damage to an aircraft, particularly whilst landing (something which, much in common with Amy, occurred quite often), the incident was always put out to the press as being a mechanical fault or failure in the ship. It was never put down to pilot error, that was bad for his wife's image. One wonders how he must have viewed the somewhat naive admissions, recently made by JM to the New York press, concerning the Bridgeport mishap.

Jim Mollison once referred to the chic and elegant AE, as 'that strange and charming woman'. Maybe her cool self-confidence and total abstinence from alcohol unnerved him somewhat. She was certainly not his kind of woman, any more than he was her type of man. On the other hand, Amy tended to idolise the slightly older woman, and during that particular weekend the two women appear to have formed a warm and strong attachment based on a mutual admiration for each other's achievemnets. Amy was particularly captivated by her host's all-absorbing, threefold interest; that of promoting civil aviation, feminism and pacificism. The three aviators were soon onto 'hangar talk' and it was during their conversations at Rye that they discussed the idea of forming a club for North Atlantic solo fliers. So far there were only five who could qualify; Charles Lindbergh, Amelia Earhart,

Sikorsky S39 amphibian NC-58V parked alongside a police guard with the Atlantic fliers disembarking at Floyd Bennett Field, New York. Amy can just be discerned being lifted from the machine holding a bouquet.

Jim Mollison, Wiley Post and James Mattern. Four had made it eastward, but only JM in the more dangerous westerly direction.

That weekend, apart from being their first wedding anniversary, was a memorable time for the Mollisons as they celebrated their victory in being the first persons to fly from the UK to the USA. They were asked to broadcast over NBC, with a link up to the British Empire via the BBC, giving their account of the flight. A while later they were delighted to receive an official confirmation that Lord Wakefield was in fact prepared to put up the cash for a replacement aircraft, one that would enable them to renew their attempt on the world's long-distance record. It was a great financial relief in view of the fact that the wreckage of their aircraft was already being taken on board the freighter, *American Farmer*, at New York, where it was bound for Plymouth that very weekend. Eventually, de Havilland's promised to rebuild the crippled plane using many of the major parts, such as the engines, instrumentation and fuel tanks, if Lord Wakefield would foot the bill. One further surprise came when they received a bouquet of flowers from President Roosevelt, together with a message of congratulation, part of which read, 'As time passes, your courageous achievement will be engraved in the annals of aviation, and in that there is satisfaction.'

The Mollisons were even more delighted when the message from the White House was followed up by an invitation to be the guests of the President and Mrs Roosevelt for a Sunday luncheon in their home at Hyde Park. The invitation was not to Jim and Amy alone, but was also extended to their hosts, AE and her husband. It is interesting on this occasion to contrast George Putnam's readiness to exploit the Mollisons' publicity, with the instructions given to his wife after she had completed her transatlantic solo flight to Ireland a year earlier. Then she had been warned by her husband not share her moment of glory with anyone, especially with any other woman flier.

Evidently, it was a rare privilege for anyone to be photographed at the presidential home on a Sunday, as it was normally FDR's inflexible rule not to break the Sabbath. However, pictures taken at the time show a diminutive Jim and Amy, still quite heavily bandaged, standing alongside the taller figures of the President and the First Lady with AE. Surprisingly, Amelia's husband is not in the picture. GP always had a habit of wanting to be photographed alongside his more famous wife on important occasions, and at one time the more knowledgeable photographers would muscle him out and refer to him amongst themselves as 'the lens louse'. After lunch, Jim recalls that they all bathed in the President's private pool, and that he was quite fascinated to watch the disabled Roosevelt swim effortlessly, despite his complete paralysis from the waist down.

After the weekend AE drove the Mollisons back to their Plaza suite in Manhattan, ready for their 'big day' – New York's official welcoming and reception. On the Tuesday morning they were met at the entrance to the hotel by Brigadier General John Phelan, the chairman of the Mayor's reception committee, and escorted to the Battery, ready for the parade that would commence at noon.

Richard K. Smith has some interesting comments to make on the timing of these official receptions given to visiting aviators and other celebrities:

> In the mid-1920's NY City had a police commissioner named Grover Whalen who also had a great sense of public relations and 'ballyhoo'. He discovered that if a parade was started from the Battery (at the southernmost tip of Manhattan Island), up Broadway through the financial district to City Hall at noontime when all of the office workers were out for lunch, there was an 'automatic' crowd to witness the carefully contrived event. The Mayor welcomed the Hero-of-the-Moment to NY City on the steps of City Hall. As a result the mayor got favourable exposure vis-a-vis the voters. It made for a marvellous pseudo-event.
>
> Those parades full of confetti and excitement that you see in old news photos or newsreels invariably occur during the noon hour. If they were scheduled at 10am or 3pm the streets would be almost empty! Concurrently, the office employees along the route learned to get into the spirit of things, shredding telephone directories and miscellaneous paper that they tossed out of windows into the street.[88]

Jim Mollison once said that New York welcomed aviators with a frenzy unmatched by any other country in the world. August 1st, 1933 was to be no exception. He likened the Mardi Gras type reception that he and Amy were given on that sweltering ride down Broadway, to 'a Caesar bringing home to Rome a new Empress'. Motorcycle patrolmen with their sirens blaring preceded the entourage as they sought to assist three hundred policemen into keeping spectators back onto the pavements. Only to be followed by eight rows of horse-mounted police, riding twelve abreast and leading several district police bands at the head of the procession of eleven shiny new automobiles. The excited Mollisons – Amy looking very *femme* in an eye-catching black beret and an attractive matching crepe outfit, complete with a plaid organdie bow tied at the neckline – sat laughing and waving from the tonneau of the first open vehicle as a blizzard of ticker-tape fell from the sky. Whilst the city's office workers, many of whom sat perched on

The Mollisons with President Franklin D. Roosevelt at his Hyde Park residence on Sunday, 31 July 1933.

window sills, unleashed a summer snowstorm of welcome onto the crowd of cheering New Yorkers (estimated at 200,000) lining the streets below. They were eager for a look at the first man and wife team to fly to their country from Europe, and greeted them with enthusiastic shouts of, 'Attaboy, Jim' and 'Hiya, Amy'.

Finally, the procession halted at the steps of the City Hall, where newsreel-cameramen were waiting to record the event as the Mollisons were given an official welcoming speech by Mayor John O'Brien. The man must have become a bit blasé about the whole proceedings for it was the fourth such occasion that he had officiated at within the last two weeks. However, it does appear that Amy made quite a hit with the rotund, balding mayor. The bands struck up with 'God save the King' and then 'The Star Spangled Banner', before the aviators were presented with gold medals giving them the Freedom of the City (it was the second time around for Jim). Being a woman aviator, Amy was, not unnaturally, the centre of attention. She delighted the crowds when she told them that she was 'still shaking all over' from the ride down Broadway, and pleased them even more when she said how much she admired their policemen. 'I love them all. I don't know whether to stay inside the law, or whether to break the law to get to know them better.'

It is interesting to note that the American press was giving Amy's age as twenty-five at that time, when she was actually five years older, and in fact two years older than Jim. Studying her earliest flying log book (Civil Aviation Form 24) for that period today, one cannot but help notice that the figure 'three' at the end of her year of birth in 1903, has conveniently been altered into an 'eight'. The deliberate error was probably no more than a whim of feminine vanity, but it was perpetuated in many subsequent articles and photographic captions over the years.

Much has been made of allegations that JM resented the way that the Americans took to Amy, and that as a consequence he was envious of her popularity. Furthermore, it is claimed that his jealousy contributed to the break up of their marriage and that from thereon he 'loathed America'. Although it must be admitted that the disintegration of their marriage seems to have started from around this time, one must bear in mind one or two important factors. Firstly, it must be remembered that he had already been recognised in the USA as an outstanding pioneer aviator in his own right a year earlier, and even if this had not been the case, JM was very much his own man and never one to hold on to his wife's coat-tail, or anybody else's for that matter. Additionally, one must take into account that in all of his subsequent writings, he was always most generous in his praise of Amy and her achievements. Moreover, his subsequent trips to the USA in 1935 and 1936 simply contradict the charge that he became disenchanted with America after the 1933 visit. As a matter of fact, he was fascinated and beguiled by that country, as is evidenced in his memoirs written a year after his last visit.

The second week following the Mollisons' arrival in the USA was a hectic one, for the couple were in great demand. Atlantic City, renowned for its gambling casinos, marathon dance contests and infamous Boardwalk, played host to the fliers when they arrived on a whistle-stop trip on the Wednesday. They had flown in from Newark as guests of Amelia Earhart for a luncheon and informal reception to be given by the city's mayor. Not to be outdone by their New York rivals, Mayor Bacharach was on hand to present Jim and Amy with Atlantic City's own gold medal and freedom of that slightly tacky city. Whilst in the evening they caught the plane back to New York for a dinner given in their honour at the Plaza by the Federation of Scottish Societies. Two days later they returned to Bridgeport for another public reception and to receive the tribute of having the city's airport named 'Mollison Airport' after them. No doubt Jim considered the renaming ceremony a trifle wasteful when Amy was asked to break a bottle of champagne against the hangar wall to mark the occasion!

One wonders just how much Amy trusted Jim as she bade him farewell that weekend when he embarked to sail on the White Star liner, *Majestic*. She realised that he needed to return home to supervise the building of the replacement DH Dragon, but she also knew, as did most other of her friends, that he had a weakness for the opposite sex. Perhaps she was too excited at the prospects of her stay that weekend with AE to be over-concerned. To Amy, the American aviatrix personified the emancipated woman, and there is little doubt that the example of Amelia's independent lifestyle was ultimately one of the important factors to influence Amy's estrangement from Jim.

Apart from making record-breaking flights, AE was also doing all the things that Amy had always longed to do, from fashion design and modelling, to being an aviation journalist on glossy journals such as *Cosmopolitan*. What was more, she had her foot firmly into commercial aviation – something Amy particularly envied – by becoming the first woman vice-President of an airline. AE was also into fast cars at the time of the Mollisons' visit, driving a rather sleek, little 1932 Essex Terraplane coupé produced by Detroit's Hudson Motor Company. Wendy Boase records a rather amusing incident that befell Amy and Amelia soon after Jim left for England:

> When Amy and Jim Mollison were in America in 1933, AE drove Amy to Boston to see the Boston & Maine Airways Company, in which AE had some shares. Speeding back to Amelia's home in Rye, the two were stopped by a motor traffic patrolman. AE never presumed upon her fame on such occasions, and tried to preserve her anonymity. But the officer had had a bet with his colleague as to the identity of the driver and, as so often happened, asked for her autograph, grinned, and let her go.[89]

Four days before Jim sailed from Southampton on *The Empress of Britain* to return with *Seafarer II*, Amy, dressed in the neat, blue uniform of a Trans-Continental & Western Air pilot, boarded a Fokker Trimotor belonging to one of America's main airlines. It was an opportunity for which she had longed and one which had been engineered for her by AE. Over the next seven days she was to gain forty-eight hours of valuable experience as a TWA co-pilot, using the latest state of the art in blind-flying instrumentation on flights to the West Coast. It is interesting to note Amy's comments regarding the lead that commercial airlines in the United States enjoyed in navigational and blind-flying equipment:

> In 1933, years ahead of other countries, America was flying regular schedules at night, producing and using 'blind-flying' instruments with

extremely efficient radio services. On my trans-continental flight I flew by day with ear-phones over my ears listening to the steady purr which told me I was on my course. If I wandered to one side or the other a difference in note in my ears immediately warned me. Every hour a weather report was automatically sent out over a second radio set, whilst a switch-over key enabled us to talk to ground stations or with other aircraft in flight. At night the route was marked by flashing beacons, with special ones to indicate aerodromes, each main airport having its own Morse signal.[90]

☆ ☆ ☆

When Jim came back in mid-September it was to Montreal and not New York that he arrived, for he had been persuaded at Amy's suggestion to use the five mile strip of hard sand on the edge of Lake Simcoe at Wasaga Beach, Ontario, instead of the runway at FBF. The change of departure venue was made for two reasons. Firstly, the length of runway at the Long Island airport was deemed insufficient in view of the heavy 600 gallon fuel load that they intended to carry if they were to make Baghdad in one hop. Secondly, so many record-breakers were using FBF that the flights were fast losing their news value, whilst departures from Canada were comparatively rare.

One other factor had emerged since the Bridgeport crash, and that was that Gayford and Nicholetts' long-distance record of 5,341 miles had been exceeded in August by Paul Codos and Maurice Rossi. The two Frenchmen had wisely forgone the hazardous westward crossing of the North Atlantic when they had shipped their 650 hp Bleriot-Zappat 110, named the *Joseph Le Brix*, from Cherbourg to New York. After waiting for almost six weeks for the right weather conditions, they had set out with a massive 1,400 gallons of fuel for the Iraqi capital, but once having made sure that they had beaten the previous record, they put down at a Rayak, a small airfield in Syria. It now meant that the Mollisons had 5,657 miles to better.

It is significant to note that when Jim and Amy were reunited at Toronto's Union station at noon on 15 September 1933, the press were at pains to point out that their greeting for each other appeared to be a rather cool one. No kisses, just a polite 'hello' and a handclasp were all that was observed by onlookers, before the couple made their way across the road to the nearby Royal York Hotel. One reporter covering their arrival was agreeably surprised by Amy's steel blue eyes, and whilst not forgetting to add that her photographs did not flatter her, described her as a typical English girl.

Amy and Jim Mollison with their hosts, Amelia Earhart and her publisher husband George Putnam, relaxing on one of Long Island's beaches soon after the British pilots' arrival in New York.

The Mollisons wasted very little time before they got down to serious business of breaking the world's long-distance record, for by late afternoon they had arrived with Bob Loader, the genial General Manager of de Havillands Canada, and colleague, J. Adamson, to inspect the surface of the beach at Wasaga. It had been Adamson who had suggested the Wasaga site to Amy, after she had made enquiries about using the St. Hubert airfield at Montreal during a previous visit to that city. The couple were quite impressed by the hardness of the sands but were a trifle dubious about its slightly bumpy surface. As a guide to the severity of the undulations, they got Bob Loader to drive their loaned MacLoughlin-Buick Eight along the three mile stretch at 70 mph whilst they sat in the back. After some consultation with Loader on the time-schedule for uncrating and assembling *Seafarer II*, due into Montreal the next day, and taking into consideration the advantage of a full moon, they finally decided that they would make their attempt in ten days time. In the meantime, they would relax on a two day fishing vacation as guests of a Canadian friend at his Muskoka home.

Bob Loader was as good as his word, and with the DH hangar staff at the Weston plant pulled out all the stops by working twenty-four hour shifts assembling the refurbished Dragon. Four days later the plane was ready for the Mollisons' return as promised.

As the glistening black biplane was pushed out of the hangar, resplendent with its starkly contrasting white lettering and orange and green fuselage trim lines, people were quick to notice that the G-ACJM registration contained both fliers' initials. Perhaps it was a good omen. Jim and Amy certainly hoped so.

The company's test pilot Leigh Capreol and JM wormed their way under the fuel tanks and into the cockpit for the Scot to take over the controls on its first test-flight. Accompanying them was DH employee George Blanchard, who was carried as ballast at the rear. His task was to crawl back and forth into various parts of the fuselage whilst the aircraft was in flight, in order to test the aircraft's sensitivity to a changing centre of gravity. As one of DH Canada's longest serving employees – he retired in 1978 after forty-nine years with the company – he has happy memories of those days. He remembers quite clearly that at the time of *Seafarer II*, Bob Loader and Bill Calder co-ordinated the Mollisons' wishes carefully to the factory staff, whilst his impressions of Jim and Amy were that 'they were pleasant but reserved' and 'fully absorbed with their preparation for the flight to Baghdad'.[91]

The appointed day for the Mollisons' departure came and went, for the weather conditions over the Atlantic were reported unfavourable and the take-off had to be postponed. These delays were grating on the fliers' nerves, particularly so for Amy, who was spending most of the waiting-time improving her horse-riding skills. There were several major worries at the back of Jim and Amy's minds. Would the aircraft be capable of lifting 7,334lb – more than three times the tare weight of a standard Dragon – in spite of assurances from the design team at Stag Lane that it would? Furthermore, they knew that time was fast running out on them for transatlantic flying, now that the winter weather was closing in on them. It meant that if the delays continued much longer, then it would too late to make Baghdad that year. Lastly, after Jim had made one or two exploratory flights from Wasaga in a borrowed Puss Moth, they soon realised that Adamson had failed to mention the strong cross-winds which blow predominently across the beach for most of the year.

By the morning of 3 October they had decided to hang around no longer. They had now been waiting eighteen days for favourable conditions and the Dragon was fuelled up on the beach to its maximum capacity of 608 gallons ready to go. Their destination at Baghdad lay 6,000 miles distant, with Codos and Rossi's record of 5,657 miles to beat. A few days previously the press had reported that Amy had been thrown from her horse whilst on a cross-country ride. Although her injuries had been no more than a few bruises it probably did little for her morale at the beginning of a dangerous flight. Earlier in September, she made what was to be a chillingly prophetic statement when she told reporters, 'If we're very, very lucky, we may make it, but it will have to be before the first week in October, for we are not looking for suicide. Yes, I'll fly until I die – and I hope I die flying.'[92]

On the first two runs the plane completely failed to unstick, even after having made runs of over two miles. One is not certain, but maybe Jim was just getting the feel of things. On the third and final attempt the tail rose reluctantly, and after a run of over a mile they hit a slight ridge which shot them several feet into the air. Jim later told Bill Courtenay that the drift towards the shoreline was so strong that he was forced to put the overladen plane down with a spine-rattling thud. Inevitably, there followed an ominous crunch from the protesting undercarriage. The air must have been blue with invective at that instant as JM vented his feelings with some choice expletives, for he records that Amy was telling him to, 'Keep all that to yourself!' She had no doubt heard it all before at Croydon. Such unnerving experiences and the ensuing recriminations could hardly have enhanced their marital harmony. The cruel irony of it all was that had they waited but another thirty minutes, the wind was to veer so that they would have been able to take off directly into it!

The Dragon could not have been all that badly damaged for after draining most of the fuel, the machine was flown back to the DH factory at Downsview. Close inspection revealed that the landing gear had been slightly twisted upon impact. Repairs were quickly made and the aircraft was declared ready to be flown to Wasaga at a moment's notice. However, the weather broke, and four days later Jim issued a statement to the Canadian press which made it quite clear that the flight was off and that the machine would be shipped back to England.

It was not long after this that DH Canada successfully sued the Mollisons* for garaging and assembly bills which had not been paid. Whether the unpaid bills were due to a shortage of money, or to a dispute between Jim and Amy on exactly how much each should have contributed to the costs, is a matter for speculation. Certainly JM had a reputation for leaving a trail of unpaid debts wherever he went. The Scottish pioneer aviator John Grierson once made a passing comment to Richard K. Smith on Mollison's attitude to unpaid debts. The latter remembers that:

> There was always an aspect to Mollison's career that puzzled me. By 1933 this man had done Australia-UK; UK-Capetown; the North Atlantic and South Atlantic, an almost incredible score – so why didn't he get a

---

*Much like its predecessor, *Seafarer II* was registered in Amy's name.

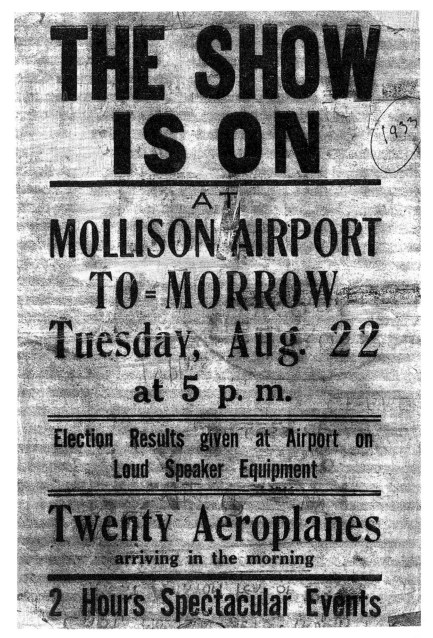

THE SHOW IS ON

AT MOLLISON AIRPORT TO-MORROW

Tuesday, Aug. 22 at 5 p. m.

Election Results given at Airport on Loud Speaker Equipment

Twenty Aeroplanes arriving in the morning

2 Hours Spectacular Events

The first of two airports to be named after the Scottish aviator in North America; Trenton Airport, Nova Scotia, Canada, became 'Mollison Airport' in September 1932; whilst the airport at Stratford, near Bridgeport, Connecticut, USA, was renamed 'Mollison Field' in the following year.

knighthood? John Grierson told me that when JM was in the RAF on a short service commission, stationed in India, and his term ran out, he left his station to return without paying his mess bill. As if that was not bad enough (it simply 'wasn't done'), he later *bragged* about it, and did so repeatedly in public. Men who do this sort of thing demonstrate that they are not gentlemen and they don't get knighthoods.[93]

JM sailed from Montreal for the UK with the dismantled *Seafarer II*, whereupon it was flown back to Hatfield to wait for a buyer.*

He immediately sailed back to meet Amy in New York, having promised her that they would spend several weeks on a holiday together in Bermuda. None of this escaped the cynicism of the *Aeroplane's* editor, C. G. Grey, who took great delight in 'congratulating' Mollison on being the first man to accompany a potentially record-breaking aeroplane on a double sea-journey across the Atlantic!

In the meantime, Amy had been admitted to a New York hospital for a checkup, ten days after the abortive take-off from Wasaga. She was described as being in a highly nervous condition and after medical examination diagnosed to be suffering from a stomach ulcer. Knowing that her stay in hospital might be prolonged, it was agreed that Jim would travel on from New York by steamship to Bermuda and she would meet him there at the end of her treatment.

Maybe it was a case of 'absence makes the heart grow fonder' for when they finally met up again early in November, Jim described those two weeks they were together in Bermuda as the happiest and most contented time of their marriage. They were to spend their 'second honeymoon' enjoying sun, sea and sand, becoming tanned and fit. Whilst by evening they would dance into the small hours – something they both loved to do – to the rhythm of the local Latin rumbas. Amy's official biographer relies upon the fact that they spent no more than two weeks out of the six that they could have been together, to support her theory that this was far from a happy time.[94] Maybe, given the volatility of their mercurial temperaments, both interpretations could equally well be true.

Although the circumstances surrounding their parting before the end of that month are uncertain, we do know that they went their separate ways for the next three months. Jim sailed from New York for the UK on the 26th, whilst Amy insisted that she continue her 'convalescence' by travelling on to Florida.

Seafarer II was purchased by James R.Ayling and Leonard G.Reid a year later and renamed *Trail of the Caribou*. It was flown by the two British pilots from Wasaga Beach in an unsuccessful attempt on the long-distance record and landed at Heston airport on 9 August 1934, having flown a distance of 3,700 miles in 30 hours and 55 minutes.

One cannot help but doubt the wisdom of Amy's action in failing to accompany her husband back to London. Admittedly, she was far from being completely recovered, and one can sympathise with her reluctance to return to the shallow life style of drinking and partying that JM was content to lead at Grosvenor House. But it was very much like allowing a mischievous, small boy alone into a sweet-shop. She must have known the temptations that he would face unsupervised by a wife. She must have also known by now about his predatorial instincts – his propensity for erotic adventuring. It is known that she had friends in London who warned her of her husband's tendencies, but she seemed to prefer not to know.

Not surprisingly, soon after JM had returned home alone, certain sections of the press were hinting that there was a rift in the Mollisons' marriage. Jim made vehement denials of an estrangement, whilst Amy was continually in correspondence with her father in order to gauge the measure of public opinion back home. They both had a great concern for their public image as Britain's romantic 'air lovers', or 'flying sweethearts'. It was, after all, a winning and lucrative formula, and therefore not one to be lightly discarded.

If their marriage had been a relatively smooth and sudden coming together, then its dissolution was to be protracted, painful and turbulent.

Chapter 15

'Black Magic Loses its Spell'

Jim Mollison's blue eyes betrayed more than a flicker of excitement as they met the page. Here was the news for which he had been waiting, ever since he had heard of the proposed England-Australia air race almost a year earlier. A British aeroplane manufacturer was at last accepting the challenge of the promoters for an event that was eventually to be known as the greatest air race in the history of aviation. The brief notice in the January 1934 issue of the trade journal simply read: 'The de Havilland Comet is now being designed for the MacRobertson England to Australia International Air Race. Orders are invited for a limited number of this long-distance type of racing aircraft.'

Although the original idea for the event had first been mooted by the Mayor of Melbourne, Sir Harold Gengoult-Smith, in order to commemorate the centenary of the founding of that city in 1834, the race was to be financed by the seventy-five year old philanthropist and millionaire, Sir William Macpherson Robertson. Popularly known to all as MacRobertson, he was the son of Scottish immigrant parents and had made his fortune from the manufacture of confectionery. He had a natural interest in the technology of transport, having earlier, in 1927, sponsored the first automobile 'Grand Tour' of his country. Now it was to be the turn of aviation. It was his desire to see improved communications between Australia and the mother country, and for him this meant the need for an improvement in the development of the long-distance aeroplane, together with the accompanying ground-support system. The incentives were to be race prizes totalling £15,000 and a gold cup for the winner.

The Air Races Committee of the Royal Aero Club was to be appointed as the chief organiser, and they were to work closely with a counterpart committee in Melbourne. The race would need to comply with the International Commission for Aerial Navigation, and safety in all its aspects was to be paramount. This meant certification of airworthiness for the contesting aircraft and proof of competence of all the competing pilots. Entries were open to men and women, and aircraft manufacturers of all nations, and had to be submitted by 1 June 1934.

Jim had already wired Amy in Florida before Christmas, asking if she was prepared to go half shares in one of the three DH Comets that were to be built. He now needed to know quickly, as the deadline for placing an order was the end of February and it was a question of first come, first served. With memories of the Croydon and Wasaga disasters still painfully fresh in her memory, Amy's initial reaction was to be sceptical of the chances of success with a British aircraft. Moreover, apart from the £5,000 needed, she had recently visited the Douglas Aircraft Corporation in California and was convinced that the U.S. aircraft industry was technically superior to its UK counterpart. Whilst there she had seen their use of advanced design features, such as variable pitch propellers, retractable undercarriages and wing-flaps being incorporated into current production aircraft. However, in spite of this she agreed to Jim's proposal, for as much as she was enjoying life in America, she was becoming homesick for England and was anxious to get back into the flying scene. Surprisingly, she also found that she was beginning to miss Jim.

As soon as Amy returned from the United States in mid-February, she was determined to lead a life after her own choosing and not that of her husband's. It is interesting to note that at this stage in her life Peter Reiss appears back on the scene. It seems that he was still carrying the torch for Amy, and when she began to show an interest in playing squash, he, being a championship class player, was the man conveniently at hand to teach her. Although she had rejoined her husband at their Grosvenor House hotel suite overlooking Hyde Park, she soon hated every minute of it. The enforced life of idleness, broken only by the constant round of invitations to parties put on by the *glitterati* of London's society, was too boring for Amy. Apart from their shared interest in making record-breaking flights, she and her husband now had little in common. Her recent friendship with the serious-minded Amelia Earhart had highlighted this fact and convinced her that she must break with all that Jim embraced so cosily. To him, long-distance flying was solely the means to a comfortable and sybaritic existence. His philosophy at that time was graphically expressed in his memoirs, *Playboy of the Air*, when he wrote:

> For a morning visitor to tear apart the dark curtains of my bedroom windows at 11.00am is for me torture. England's grey daylight spells work and offices, trams and trains, realities, punctuality, all of the things I

dislike most.

Life and enjoyment begin when daylight fades and the bright lights are atwinkle. Cocktail bars and the clubs from here to Honolulu are opening their doors to the faithful. Music, wine, moonlight through the palms, beautiful gowns, beautiful women inside them, whisperings, shaded lights. These are things only of the night.

Daylight comes to me as a break, an interval for sleeping until an afternoon drink that helps bring on another evening.[95]

It is not difficult to gather from this last statement that he was in the early stages of alcoholic addiction well before the age of thirty-five, and that in a more enlightened age, friends would have warned him of the long term dangers to his health. Whether he would have taken their advice is quite another matter.

☆ ☆ ☆

Geoffrey de Havilland's decision to go ahead with a design capable of winning the race was a very brave one indeed. A financial outlay of £50,000 was needed to build the three aircraft envisaged. This was a daunting sum of money to be spent at a time when the state of the aircraft industry in Britain was far from robust. There was no way that this money could be recouped solely by the sale of the three Comets, for he knew it was not practicable to sell them for more than £5,000 each. De Havilland was an intensely chauvinistic man and did not want to see the race given away by default to the Americans. Therefore, in the absence of any serious interest being shown by any of the other British aircraft manufacturers, apart from Airspeed, he decided to proceed. There was prestige and a sense of achievement to be gained if the company should produce a winning aeroplane, but little else. Hopefully, if they succeeded in pulling off the race, it might give a boost to the sales of their current range of aircraft. It was a bold gamble!

It says little for the British Government's foresight and understanding of the needs of its own aircraft industry at this time, that Britain did not already possess a high-speed airliner capable of winning the MacRobertson air race in 1934. Unlike the United States, which could enter heavily subsidised modern, all-metal airliners such as the Boeing 247 and Douglas DC2, Britain had neglected the development of the fast monoplane transport airliner on its empire routes. Even KLM's orders of the DC2 for use on a swift airmail service between Amsterdam and the Dutch East Indies, and Holland's development of its own Pander S-4, did not alert blinkered officialdom at the Air Ministry. Geoffrey de Havilland's warnings and the pleas of others had,

The Mollisons arrive at RAF Mildenhall in their de Havilland 88 Comet, G-ACSP, on Sunday, 14 October 1934, in readiness for the MacRobertson Air Race.

over the years, fallen on deaf ears and the Hatfield company was left to rescue its country's prestige without the benefit of a subsidy.

Geoffrey de Havilland had a tight time-schedule on his hands, for he and his design team knew that they had only nine months in which to work from a blank sheet of paper to a successful test-flight. It soon became apparent that the main design parameters of the Comet were to be determined by its need to cruise at 220mph, and for it to have a range of at least 2,800 miles.

Arthur Hagg, the DH Chief Designer and man responsible for the famous Puss Moth so successfully used by the Mollisons in their record-making flights, knew that a clean aerodynamic form was essential. As a prerequisite to achieving this it was decided to carry all the fuel in the fuselage, thereby taking advantage of being able to use a thin, low-drag section wing for cruising at high altitude. It meant that all the fuel would be carried in the fuselage and that there would be two tanks of 128 and 110 gallons in front of the cabin, plus one small tank of 20 gallons to the rear. The constructional difficulties in designing such a wooden cantilever wing with the required torsional stiffness, were ingeniously overcome by Hagg's use of a method he had discovered earlier in his career as a boat designer. This meant that the loads would be carried by a stressed-skin surface, and achieved by using diagonal cross-planking of spruce sheeting, pinned and glued across three spacer webs. It was a method rarely used before in the design of an airframe and as a result the one-piece wing of forty-four feet span was extremely light and strong.

It was decided that a centre-section flap on the trailing edge of the underside of the wing would give added lift for take-offs and assist landing approaches; and that the engine-nacelles, neatly underslung on either side of the wing, would provide access for a retractable undercarriage, so necessary in an aerodynamically clean design. As with the wing, the method of cross-planking was also used in the construction of the upper and lower surfaces of the fuselage. Little did Arthur Hagg realise at that time that the Comet was to provide the seminal design for the production of the much acclaimed wartime aircraft – the Mosquito. Some aviation historians have gone so far as to say, 'If there had not been a DH 88 Comet* in 1934, then there would not have been a Mosquito in 1940.'

Frank Halford, John Brodie and Eric Moult were the three men responsible for the design of the 230hp Gipsy Six R engines to be used in the Comet. This was a modified development of the Gipsy Six, which had itself only passed the type tests in December 1933. The 'Six' had been developed from the highly reliable four cylinder Gipsy Major, an engine whose reliability was currently being cleverly advertised by the portrayal of a pilot's gloved hand about to switch off the ignition, with the caption, 'Nothing else stops a Gipsy.'

Supercharging as a measure was considered, but discounted on the basis that the added power obtained would be offset by higher fuel consumption and concomitant weight penalty from the extra fuel carried. Frank Halford's main problem, if he was to use the Six R engine's power to its greatest advantage, was to find a suitable propeller with a variable-pitch mechanism. For by using a fine pitch setting he could obtain more power at the take-off and shorten the Comet's run – a particular necessity on elevated tropical airfields. Moreover, the subsequent coarse setting would give him the optimum cruising speed at high altitudes. Its operation can be likened to the use of a car's gearbox. One selects low gear in order to obtain maximum power for hill climbing and a higher gear whilst cruising on the level.

Finding no suitable propellers available in the UK, Frank Hearle, a Director of the company, was sent with Arthur Hagg to the United States to negotiate with the Hamilton Company at Hartford, Connecticut, for a suitable component. After spending several abortive weeks abroad they returned home empty-handed. It was now less than eight months before their deadline and things were beginning to look desperate. They had

*Not to be confused with the DH 106 Comet, the world's first jet-powered airliner.

The Bellanca Flash 28-70 *The Irish Swoop* which was to have been flown by Col. James Fitzmaurice and Eric 'Jock' Bonar in the MacRobertson, but was scratched from the race at the last minute.

encountered two major stumbling blocks during their search. Firstly, the American propellers had been designed for use with large radial engines and consequently they were far too big in diameter (whilst it was possible to crop the blades, it would have given cooling problems for the Gipsy engines). Secondly, the Hamilton pitch mechanism necessitated the use of a hydraulic system, and there was insufficient time to design such a facility into the Comet.

As a last resort Frank Halford made enquiries of a French company named Ratier, and after visiting their Paris works' came back with a suitable propeller. Its pitch change mechanism employed a somewhat crude but effective mechanical device, one which used an inflated football-bladder in the spinner to hold the blades in their fine setting for take-off. Once the aircraft was in the air and a forward speed of 160mph had been attained, a small disc protruding from the nose of the spinner was forced back to release a Schrader valve, thus causing the bladder to deflate and allowing the blade to move into coarse pitch. However, its primary disadvantage was that the blades could then only be reverted to fine pitch by re-inflating the bladder with a bicycle pump whilst the aircraft was stationary on the ground. This meant that the device could prove to be hazardous if the Comet suddenly needed to abort a landing and go round again.

By the end of February, de Havilland's had allocated all three Comets to those applicants most likely to bring them a victory. Apart from the Mollisons, the remaining two were to go to sponsors Bernard Rubin, a wealthy Australian, and to A. O. Edwards, the managing director of the Grosvenor House Hotel. Bernard Rubin intended to crew with another pilot, but owing to illness withdrew at the last moment in favour of former FAA pilot Owen Cathcart-Jones and the flying instructor Ken Waller, whom he had appointed to fly for him. Surprisingly, Edwards decided to use the Mollisons' old rival Charles Scott as his pilot and Tom Campbell Black as co-pilot, in a machine that was to be named after the hotel.

One can only conjecture at this point exactly why the Grosvenor's MD sponsored Scott and Black for his Comet and not the Mollisons. After all, Jim and Amy were resident in his Park Lane hotel and giving him the benefit of their celebrity-value at the time of the race. Furthermore, his sponsorship would have saved the Mollisons the expense of finding £5,000 from their own pockets – quite a hefty sum in 1934, especially when one remembers that their failure to succeed with *Seafarer* six months earlier, meant that the *Daily Mail* was hardly likely to have paid out more than a small proportion of the money they had promised. Although Jim and Amy were by no means on their uppers, they were not exactly flush for money either. Amy's well-stocked wardrobe from renowned Parisian couturiers and their penchant for fast and expensive cars – Amy with her Hispano and Jim with his closely guarded Buick – saw to that! It was very much a case of living for the moment, particularly for Jim who spent money as if it was going out of fashion. Bill Renwick, an international rugby player and cousin of JM, was an occasional visitor to their Grosvenor residence and he remembers that in those days 'their suite was sheer luxury. An open-house and "spooned" upon by nearly everyone.'[96]

One can only come to the conclusion that the shrewd and perceptive hotel manager recognised that whilst the Mollisons' reputation as solo fliers was unassailable, together their teamwork in the cockpit was highly suspect. In addition, their marital disputes in his hotel were hardly a tightly kept secret. One well-known London actress and friend of the Mollisons recalls receiving a telephone call from a member of the management at the Grosvenor. She was told that there had been a violent quarrel betwen the Mollisons that night and that their bathroom was found to be covered in blood from where they had fought each other.[97] Certainly they both had quick tempers and both were capable of a slugging match. Jim was known to become aggressive when drunk, and Amy was a kitten who could certainly scratch when roused. Only recently during her stay in Florida she had been pulled for speeding whilst returning to Palm Beach in the early hours of the morning from a party in Miami. Two policemen dressed in plain clothes had tagged her Mercedes, and Amy's story was that she believed that she was being chased by hoodlums and therefore drove all the faster. During the ensuing roadside interrogation, she slapped one of the policemen in the face when he tried to restrain her, and as a consequence she was driven to the local courthouse for questioning. Fortunately, she was not jailed, but two days later she was fined $50 and $20 costs.

As a consequence of Edwards' decision, plus the fact that JM had openly announced that he did not intend to make any night landings during the air race, the pundits were now placing Charles Scott and Tom Campbell Black as firm favourites to win the MacRobertson. Their prediction did little to improve relations between old rivals. Amy disliked Scott intensely for she had not forgiven him for his boorish behaviour after her 1930 flight to Australia. Jim's feelings towards Scott were no more friendly than Amy's, although differing inasmuch as they hinged more around a mutually professional jealousy.

In spite of their preparations for the race, Amy's determination to make a serious career in aviation apart from her husband was not being deflected. After her overtures to Colonel Shelmerdine, Director of Civil Aviation, had met with a cool response, she changed her tactics and with the help of her press-agent, William Courtenay, managed to land a job as the Aviation Editor of the *Daily Mail*. There is no doubt that this appointment was also assisted by JM's friendship with fellow Scot, Sir Malcolm Campbell, who was at that time the Motoring Editor for the same newspaper. Unlike her husband, Amy longed to be taken seriously. She could see that the golden age of the long-distance flier and easy money was rapidly coming to a close. Record-breaking flights were becoming commonplace and it was no longer a case of, 'From take off, to rake off', as some considered it to be. Although Amy was not a particularly gifted writer, she believed passionately in the future of civil aviation. She was well-informed in aeronautical matters and soon settled down to make a success of her new found occupation. Her contract was only for six months, which suited her for it expired just before the proposed start of the MacRobertson air race in October. Never one to be outshone, Charles Scott was appointed Aviation Editor of the rival *News Chronicle* a little later.

By May, the Mollisons had moved out of Grosvenor House for the summer and rented a country cottage at Lurgashall, West Sussex, a small village to the north of the South Downs. Although Amy still purported to be in love with her restless and intemperate husband, their married relation-

Black Magic being warmed up at RAF Mildenhall alongside Bernard Rubin's G-ACSR and Jackie Cochran's Granville Gee-Bee.

ship only seemed to survive as they led separate lives. As she admitted on one occasion to her father, her dilemma was that she was as unhappy with Jim as she was away from him. Within a month she had sailed for America. Hastily, she had decided to add another string to her bow, for now she had been offered the prospect of becoming the British agent for the Beech Aircraft Co. The American company's offer was accepted, and to show her good faith and commitment she placed an order for one of their Beechcraft B17 staggerwing cabin-biplanes. Ever an ardent americanophile, Amy promptly took advantage of combining business with pleasure by spending a brief holiday in Arizona, before returning to Lurgashall in mid-August 1934.

Whilst she was away, Jim's unsupervised lifestyle left him free to do virtually as he pleased. Although Amy suspected that he was being unfaithful to her, she always maintained that she had no definite proof of it. JM had a certain brooding sexuality which many women found to be irresistible, and his current, clandestine 'romance' was with the blonde-haired revue actress, Dorothy Ward. Considering that she was fifteen years his senior, she was extremely attractive and renowned for her 'English rose' beauty and youthful figure, which she used to great advantage in her appearances as a Principal Boy in pantomime. She was also a very versatile actress, having been widely acclaimed on the London and New York stage during the 1920s. Whether Amy was then aware of the liaison is open to question, but by the time her husband's memoirs had been published in 1937, she was left in no doubt for the book was proudly dedicated to the actress.

By late July the Royal Aero Club had issued a list of the entries for the race, sixty-four in all from fourteen different countries. It included such illustrious names as the doyen of long-distance solo fliers, the one-eyed Wiley Post; Sir Charles Kingsford Smith, Koene D. Parmentier – KLM's crack pilot; Louise Thaden, 'Chubby' Miller, Ruth Nichols, Jackie Cochran and many others lesser known. Sadly, most of these were to be scratched, and by the time of the race the list was reduced to only twenty-one.

When Amy returned from the USA, she was delighted to find that her manager's approaches to Edward Hillman for the aviatrix to be taken on as one of his airline pilots, had paid off. It was to be a short-lived arrangement, for the forty-five year old entrepreneur was to die unexpectedly from a heart attack, just before the end of the year. Bill Courtenay always maintained that had it not have been for Hillman's untimely death, then Amy would have been made a Director of the company. However, Amy was employed for a brief period as a pilot flying one of his six new DH Dragon's, operating from

Stapleford Abbots on the Le Bourget route. Her time with Hillman Airways coincided with that of another pilot, G. D. 'Flip' Fleming, who was also flying for the company at that period. He recalls that:

> Hillman ran three services per day to Paris, a daily service to the Isle of Man and Belfast, and a number of specials. It was hard work and very poor pay, but excellent experience. We worked ten hours per day in the summer, very seldom had a day off, and flew as much as 140 hours in a month, and that was without a crew; flying, navigating and working the radio ourselves.

> About this time Amy Mollison was intending to enter for the air race to Australia, and, apart from wanting a bit of flying practice, she needed a little fresh publicity, to get back to the public eye; so she made an arrangement with old Hillman to fly on his London-Paris route for a week; that also got him in the public eye.

> I do not think she became a famous pilot due to any natural gifts other than perseverance and enthusiasm for flying. Technically speaking, her flying was not above average, and her landings were erratic; her navigation and airmanship were mastered by sheer hard work and not instinct, but her courage, determination and endurance in the face of these odds was all the more remarkable.[98]

☆ ☆ ☆

As the date of the race drew nearer, Jim and Amy realised that they had to get down to some serious planning, for they were not particularly well prepared. During September they started a fitness programme and were to be seen cycling hard along the Sussex country lanes near Lurgashall in training for the event. No doubt part of Amy's plan in getting Jim away from London was to wean him off the booze into some sort of a 'dry period'. How abstemious he became during that period is open to question.

Two weeks before the start of the race Amy had written to her father telling him they had still not acquired all the equipment necessary for the flight. Apart from flying-clothing, parachutes, life-jackets, emergency flares, permits and strip-maps, they needed visas for permission to overfly nine different countries that lay along the route. One of these countries was Turkey, a land which was directly in the flight path of the first stage of the race. Whilst none of the other competitors had difficulty in obtaining permission from the Turks, a ban had been imposed on Jim since his illegal landing there in 1931. The Air Ministry had written to Harold Perrin, the

Secretary of the Royal Aero Club, in June, informing him that HM Government had made representations to the Turkish Government in an endeavour to have the ban lifted but they had failed.[99] The letter went on to warn that serious consequences were likely if JM should make a forced landing in that country; moreover, it would be impossible for the British Government to intervene on his behalf if such a situation should arise.

Jim and Amy now had a hard decision to make. Either avoid flying over Turkey altogether and make a detour of several hundred miles, thus giving the other two Comets and other competitors an unfair advantage. Or trust that their two Gipsy engines kept beating away as they crossed four hundred miles of Turkish airspace. Certainly the prospect of spending the winter in a Turkish jail, without any legal representation, was not exactly inviting.

Meanwhile, the first of the three Comets – the prototype G-ACSP which had been allocated to the Mollisons – was ready for its first test-flight at Hatfield early in September. In its day the DH 88 Comet, with its maximum speed of 228 mph at sea level, probably caused as much public excitement as Concorde was to do thirty-five years later. Whilst a technical comparison may not stand too close a scrutiny, aesthetically the two aeroplanes had a very similar visual impact. Both in the air and on the ground the Comet's lines caused the pulse of the beholder to beat that little bit faster. And even at today's airshows, an appearance of the lovingly restored *Grosvenor House*, resplendent in its scarlet livery with white markings, still brings its own distinctive brand of charisma to the aviation buffs.

DH's test-pilot, Hubert Broad, was at the controls of prototype E1 on the morning it made its maiden flight. It was carried out at an early hour in order to maintain secrecy, and although the test-flight lived up to expectation, it did give some members of the de Havilland design team who had gathered outside on the tarmac to watch, some cause for alarm. After twenty-five minutes in the air, the prototype came in as if to land but with the undercarriage still retracted. Sensing that they might be about to witness a disaster, one of the team members quickly grabbed a spare-wheel from a nearby car and held it prominently aloft as a warning for the pilot to see. Hubert Broad later told them that he was not intending to land, but admitted he had lost count of the number of turns required on the handwheel to lower the mechanically operated undercarriage. He was, therefore, making an approach, hoping to see if he could observe from the aircraft's shadow whether the wheels were up or down. From then on no one needed persuading that a warning indicator-light was necessary in the cockpit.

Jim Mollison's favourite colour for a racing aeroplane had always been black and their Comet, apart from a gold stripe along the sides of its fuselage, union jack flag on its fin and gold number disc on its rudder, was no exception. The name they chose to give to Arthur Hagg's sleek and graceful design was appropriately, *Black Magic*. The second Comet, G-ACSR, owned by Bernard Rubin and now to be crewed by Owen Cathcart-Jones and Ken Waller, was finished in an olive green with white markings and unnamed; whilst Scott and Campbell Black's G-ACSS, was painted in an equally distinctive scarlet-red and, not surprisingly, named *Grosvenor House*. De Havilland's racing stable was now complete.

☆ ☆ ☆

The starting point for the race was to be the RAF's new and partially completed grass airfield at Mildenhall, Suffolk, and all twenty-one competitors were due there for the commencement of scrutiny by 4.30pm, on Sunday, 14 October. The three Comets were the first to appear on the horizon, only to be met by strong gusting winds as they came in to land. Apart from Amy, all the crews had received 'hands-on' training, which included at least one landing at Hatfield the day previously. Owen Cathcart-Jones' approach in G-ACSR caused a brief moment of apprehension for the awaiting works' engineers as it almost scraped a wing on landing. One of the Comet's unfortunate handling characteristics was inherited from the design of its wing, which tapered sharply from root to tip. This caused a phenonema known as 'tip-stall', which, if not corrected quickly by use of the ailerons and rudder, gave the aeroplane a tendency to drop a wing on its landing approach. This was exacerbated further if a 'three point' landing was attempted, and pilots were advised on a 'wheels first' technique. Next to land was Charles Scott and Tom Campbell Black, quickly followed by the Mollisons who made an approach and then decided to go round again twice more before making an acceptable landing. Attentive, peak-capped RAF marshals ran towards the Mollisons' black Comet and positioned themselves at each wing tip as they taxied towards their station on the concrete apron in front of the hangars. This practice was especially necessary with the Comet, because the extremely long nose housing the fuel tanks, meant that once the tail was down the pilot was virtually blind in the straight-ahead position.

As soon as the parachute-clad Mollisons clambered from their cramped cabin, they were besieged by press reporters and the customary autograph-seekers. Jim, looking windswept and serious, was obviously showing some concern for the handling qualities of their brand new racer, whilst Amy,

252

A rather pensive Amy looks on in the Mildenhall hangar while Jim discusses some minor technical point with the de Havilland engineers.

wearing a black beret that enhanced her blonde hair, was quite unperturbed. She was always a magnet for the press and more so now that she was married to JM. She could play the *allumeuse* with those sad and luminous blue eyes when the occasion demanded, and she was certainly not unaware that men found her attractive.

The whole aerodrome was now buzzing with excitement as the remaining aircraft and their crews flew in at sporadic intervals throughout the rest of the day. Jim and Amy began to survey the opposition at first hand. The Dutch and American airliners aroused particular interest, for they were thought to be strong contenders in both the speed and handicap sections of the race. Parmentier and his KLM co-pilot, Moll, maintained an assumed air of insouciance, as if they were already mentally calculating exactly how many guilders the prize-money equalled. Whilst the ebullient American showman, 'Colonel' Roscoe Turner, laughed and joked, striking quite a pose with his waxed-moustache and jack-booted Ruritanian military uniform. He was giving good value to his sponsors, Hollywood's Warner Brothers, by making sure that his arrival had not been overlooked. The remaining Dutch entry was the tri-motored Pander S-4 *Postjaeger*, designed and built to give a fast service on the Schipol-Djakarta mail run. Slowly, it took its position in the line up alongside the other aircraft. Its crew, the phlegmatic Jan

Geysendorfer, and Dick Asjes, busied themselves unobtrusively with the formalities of checking in. Adding to this carnival atmosphere were the messages being passed to pilots, scrutineers, works' representatives, 'et al', from an overworked loudspeaker system.

Finally, just before dusk, the rasping note of the Pratt & Whitney radial engine from Jackie Cochran and Wesley Smith's *Gee Bee* Granville monoplane, refused to be ignored. It was the last aircraft to arrive, and as it circled for a landing all eyes were focussed on its incoming navigation lights, and not without reason. This stubby, brutish racer had been dubbed 'The Flying Brick', for its landings were anything but smooth and this one was to be no exception. Jackie was at the stick and she brought the plane in with a thud that must have rattled their teeth. Some forty years later, she had cause to recall her impressions of this aeroplane with the following acerbic remarks:

> *Gee Bee* stands for Granville Brothers, a Springfield, Massachusetts, airplane company which made fast, unstable, dangerous planes in the Thirties. The nearly cute nickname is a sham. They were killers. There were few pilots who flew *Gee Bee*'s and then lived to talk about it. Jimmy Doolittle was one. I was another.[100]

Just to add to the pre-race tension, Jackie's relationship with one of the other entrants, fellow American pilot Clyde Pangborn, was not exactly a cordial one. He had been the original nominee to fly the *Gee Bee*, but difficulties with the manufacturers and a more lucrative offer from Roscoe Turner to act as co-pilot in the Boeing, meant that he had withdrawn his option. However, he was demanding a sum of money from Jackie for the transfer of his entry and she was not yielding. Her comment on the incident is best summed up in her own words. 'If I had been a man, we would have gone out behind the hangar to fight it out.'[101]

The next five days were to be as hectic as the race itself, with Jim and Amy motoring in each day for the many tasks that still had to be done. Between the intervals of weighing-in, fuel-consumption checks, preparation of equipment, poring over maps and discussing the intricacies of the route, Amy managed to get in two solo flights in *Black Magic*. Jim knew that these practice flights were vital for Amy, for apart from her role as navigator she had to be able to handle the machine in case of emergency. However, he much preferred that she didn't fly alone and he did his best to talk her out of it for fear that she would crash the machine. It was only when Will Johnson intervened by reminding Amy that she had put fifty per cent of the money into the venture, that she dug her heels in and insisted that she fly the Comet solo. Rumour was rife that JM attempted to increase the amount of insurance cover once he knew that she was determined to go ahead with her plan. Knowing that his wife was never particularly noted for her landings, the best that he could do under the circumstances was to seek refuge at the bar of the Royal Aero Club's refreshment tent. Some of the Mollisons' less charitable colleagues had even coined the adage, 'Amy doesn't land – she just arrives!'

If it was a busy time for the pilots, then it was even more so for the de Havilland engineers and mechanics who worked like trojans labouring through the long cold nights. Often it meant them having to push the three Comets out of the hangar into the night, so that the effect of carburetter-jet changes could be verified by observing the colour of the engines' exhaust flames. Correct carburation was essential. Too weak a mixture would mean overheating and possible piston failure, whilst an over-rich mixture would reduce range with equally disastrous results. The inevitable, last-minute modifications were found to be necessary, and these included the fitting of improved magneto-covers and the installation of larger oil tanks. Adding to their difficulties was the need to repair the damage done to G-ACSR, when, less than thirty-six hours before the start of the race, Owen Cathcart-Jones landed with a partially retracted undercarriage. Sir Geoffrey de Havilland was to record in his autobiography many years later that, 'I don't think that any of us would care to live again through the weeks that preceded the start of the race.'[102]

Four days before the start of the race, saw the belated arrival of the last entrant, the controversial and ill-fated Bellanca 28-70 monoplane, named *Irish Swoop*. It had been specifically designed by the American company for the MacRobertson air race and entered by the Irish Hospitals Trust, sponsors of the Irish Sweepstake. Unfortunately, some exaggerated claims had been made for its performance and a certain amount of ballyhoo had preceded its arrival. This adverse publicity had not escaped the monocled and imperious eye of Charles Grey, editor of the weekly journal *The Aeroplane*, who had caustically nicknamed it the 'Shamrocket'. However, as James Fitzmaurice taxied it towards the hangars on that day in its green and white livery, its potential as a serious contender must certainly have attracted the attention of more than a few. One such was Jim Mollison. Little did he realise that within almost two years to the day, he would be preparing for a record-breaking transatlantic flight in virtually the same machine.

The event was now arousing international interest and Fleet Street's reporters and air correspondents from other countries were much in evidence at Mildenhall. Curiosity was being shown in the romance rumoured between Scott's co-pilot, Tom Campbell Black, and the highly

255

The Mollisons with their all-black and gold-trimmed Comet early on in the race week and before the name of the aircraft had been painted on the nose cowling.

Note the small discs mounted on the front of the propeller hubs. These were part of the rather crude Ratier mechanism which was used for changing the blades from fine to coarse pitch during flight.

nubile comedy-actress, Florence Desmond, popularly known to her set as 'Dessie'. She had been one of 'C. B. Cochran's ladies' and had made many successful appearances on the London stage, her forte being the impersonation she gave of famous Hollywood stars of the time, such as Tallulah Bankhead, Mae West, Greta Garbo and other celebrities. They were delivered with devastating satirical effect, and unfortunately for the Mollisons her repertoire also included a thinly disguised version of Amy, complete with Yorkshire dialect – an accent which Amy's elocution classes had failed to eradicate. No doubt this was the background to Florence Desmond's description of the continued needling that existed between the two rival Comet contestants, when she recalls:

> Before the London-Melbourne race Tom had a piece of grit in his eye. Seeing that Mollison had a neatly pressed handkerchief in his breast pocket, he asked if he might borrow it. Mollison took out the handkerchief, blew his nose on it and handed it to Tom. Tom simply let it drop to the ground, he never liked him after that.[103]

On the day before the start of the race, King George V, Queen Mary and the Prince of Wales travelled from Sandringham to speak with the competitors and officials. Naturally, their visit attracted even bigger crowds of spectators and Florence Desmond recalls the atmosphere at that time:

The day before the race I motored from London to Mildenhall. The roads were parked with lines of traffic . . . suddenly the whole world seemed to be interested in the race. That morning the King and the Prince of Wales had been to Mildenhall . . . to wish the competitors God-speed. These keen pilots, the best the world had to offer, were about to compete in a race which would make flying history. Champagne corks were popping, but neither Tom nor Charles took a drink, they had been 'on the wagon' for many weeks. There were three Comets in the race . . . As I looked inside that tiny space which was to house Tom and Charles for the next three days, I wondered just how two men could stand the physical strain of operating a plane while being cooped up like that for so many tedious hours.[104]

Jim, smartly attired in black leather coat with astrakhan collar, and Amy, appropriately dressed in a warm tweed suit against the damp, blustery weather, stood patiently alongside *Black Magic* as they waited to be presented to the Royal party. White-overalled mechanics, busying themselves on the Comet's wing as they carried out the final refuelling, paused from their vantage point to stare as the Mollisons were introduced. The two aviators were no strangers to the 'sailor King' and his son, for both had been in their company on previous occasions, and they chatted informally with them as they discussed their chances in the race. Amy humorously suggested to the King that they could manage to squeeze him in alongside as a passenger on their flight. With a wry smile the King replied that he was far too old for such adventures, but perhaps they would be kind enough to convey his regards to his son the Duke of Gloucester when they finally reached Australia.

That afternoon Jim and Amy felt that they had every chance of being the first to Melbourne. Their spirits were lifted even higher when it was later announced that they had drawn first place in the ballot for starting positions.

Bill Courtenay readily appreciated that his charges would need an early call, and more importantly that they would need to be in close proximity to the airfield for the following morning. Kindly, he offered them the use of his own bedroom at Mildenhall, which was in the home of his friends, Walter Clarke and wife. It caused him little inconvenience for he was already booked for that evening to drive to London, where he was to make a broadcast on the race for the BBC. It was also agreed that Jim and Amy would leave their cars at their hosts' home, so that Bill Courtenay could arrange for the vehicles to be driven back to London. Perhaps it says something for the strained state of the Mollisons' finances when Courtenay records that '. . . neither car was licensed since the expiry date of September 30th, and the fourteen days' grace were both up before the race started on October 20th'.[105]

It is highly doubtful whether this worried Jim overmuch as he pulled the Clarke's household bed-sheets up under his chin and sought a few hours of fitful sleep.

☆ ☆ ☆

Hangar doors squealed noisily as they were pushed open along their tracks, causing a widening shaft of light to pierce the gloom of another autumn dawn. Outside, a steady stream of rain was gently falling onto the Suffolk countryside. The 'met' men had been forecasting bad weather and thunderstorm conditions for central Europe during that week, and they did not appear to be wrong. The DH works' engineers and mechanics had toiled on all three of the Comets through the last six long nights, but this dawn was different, for it heralded the start of the contest. One by one the machines were pushed silently out onto the tarmac and their engines primed ready for warm-up.

Six miles away, the Mollisons had been given an early call at 3am. They dressed hurriedly and finished their breakfast just before Bill Courtenay was knocking at the door ready to drive them to the aerodrome. Even at that early hour the roads were jammed with traffic as some 60,000 sightseers began to converge on the RAF station.

There had been an element of excitement during the night, for race officials had decided at the last moment that the increased gross weight of the *Irish Swoop* disqualified it from the race. James Fitzmaurice and Jock Bonar needed an extra two hundred gallons of fuel to make Baghdad in one hop, and the officials ruled that it was unacceptable to carry it without fresh load tests. Since there was insufficient time to conduct these tests, the aircraft was scratched. Now there were twenty!

Will and Cissie Johnson, Amy's parents, were at the start just before 6.00am to wish the pair good luck. They mingled with the crowd gathered around the *Black Magic*, which was now in line ready for take-off. As the Mollisons were helped into the narrow confines of the cockpit, one observer on starting duties, Flying Officer Jeffrey Quill, recalls: 'I saw Jim and Amy climb into their Comet. He looked as white as a sheet and as if he had been sloshed for forty-eight hours – which I suspect he was. She looked very nervous and apprehensive and I felt desperately sorry for her having to climb in behind that raffish character for such a venture as this.'[106]

During the last minute preparations, Roscoe Turner and Clyde Pangborn's Boeing 247 came alongside the Mollisons' aircraft, and next to them the green Comet of Cathcart Jones and Waller. Tom Campbell Black had made a last minute decision that the slippers he was wearing might not be sufficiently durable for a long walk through the desert, should he and Scott be forced to bale out, and was exchanging them for a pair of boots. Whilst Jackie Cochran, who had also opted for light footwear, found she was getting her feet wet walking through the long grass on the way to her *Gee Bee*. She was soon rescued by one of the student apprentices, who gallantly carried her over his shoulder to her waiting aircraft.

Sir Alfred Bower, London's acting Lord Mayor, stood with the unfurled flag ready to hand as the minutes ticked towards 6.30am. At the same time Jim busied himself in the front cockpit, double checking that both front fuel-tank cocks and the mixture control were set correctly. Adjusting his seat height so that the rudder pedals moved comfortably under his feet, he lowered the air-flap lever two notches to give more lift for the take-off run, and set the air intake to the 'cold' position. This sleek monoplane might well have been specifically tailored to fit his small frame.

An RAF marshal leaned forward from the port wing and helped Jim and Amy to fasten their Sutton safety harnesses before swinging the canopy shut. Amy settled herself for her navigational tasks and prepared the strip-maps ready for the initial flight across Europe, whilst her husband glanced slowly from side to side checking the movement of the ailerons as they responded to the stick between his knees. He was pleased to see that the rain had eased a little and that a strongish wind was now blowing. It would give more lift. His eyes scanned the long sweep of those graceful wings which would soon lift them and 258 gallons of precious fuel into the overcast sky, and then refocussed sharply onto the neat orderly instrument board. He was checking the rev counters, oil-pressure and fuel guages carefully, knowing that their round glinting dials would become as familiar as the faces of old friends over the next three days.

The flag fell and the two Gipsy motors responded smoothly and eagerly to the throttles, much like a dog straining on the leash. Behind them the wet grass flattened out into a fan shaped semi-circle as the black Comet slowly accelerated away. Noise from the tailskid's scraping surrendered to the intermittent thumping of the undercarriage as the machine's wheels sped over the rough turf and the tail lifted.

Carefully countering any tendency for the Comet to swing, he could now see the far side of the aerodrome directly ahead of him. The disturbing noise from the wheels became less audible and then ceased altogether as he eased the stick back. After what seemed like an interminable run they were airborne in 650 yards.

Holding the aircraft on a steady climb, he raised the flaps and immediately began to wind on the large handwheel to his right. On the fifteenth laborious turn and after winding for a full five minutes, the undercarriage came up. They turned onto their south-easterly setting, nosed down slightly so that the increased airspeed changed the propellers into coarse pitch, before beginning their climb to 10,000 feet. Ahead of them lay Baghdad, the longest leg of the race and 2530 miles distant on a great circle course.

The remaining aircraft were flagged away at forty-five second intervals, watched by a giraffing crowd of raincoated spectators. The big Boeing followed the Mollisons, and then Cathcart-Jones and Waller's green Comet made its run spitting white flames from its exhausts. It swung wildly and was forced to return to the line for another attempt. Parmentier and Moll's DC2 went next, climbing effortlessly into an unwelcoming and overcast sky with three passengers on board. KLM was determined to demonstrate that a perfectly standard airliner could compete on equal terms with any of these specialised racers. Scott and Campbell Black were then away in the red Comet, and within a half an hour the youngest and final competitor, the twenty year old Australian C. J. Melrose in a Puss Moth, was gone.

The race conditions stipulated that all the aircraft must cover the 11,300 miles to reach Melbourne within 16 days to qualify for an award, and in order that slower and smaller aircraft could compete, there were to be two races run concurrently within the event. One was for speed and the other for handicap, the latter being determined by a formula embracing the variables of engine horse power, weight, payload and wing area. The course had been planned with five mandatory control points; Baghdad, Allahabad, Singapore, Darwin and Charleville, each with a decreasing distance between them so that allowance could be made for the crews' tiredness. In addition there were eighteen further optional 'check-in' points spaced across the route so that the aircraft with reduced range could compete.

Meanwhile, Amy was making sure that *Black Magic* was on course for the Iraqi capital. Unlike the two American airliners, all three Comets eschewed the carrying of radio equipment in favour of extra fuel. This meant that Amy's navigation relied primarily on the 'dead-reckoning' method, calculating the course by use of an aperiodic compass, known airspeed and estimated drift, and hoping for visual landmarks to corroborate her position on the air-map. Arthur Clouston, destined to become the most experienced of all Comet pilots, believed that it was best to ignore drift because of the unreliablity of forecasting wind strength at various altitudes. He found that the variations generally cancelled each other out. Nevertheless, Amy had the use of an additional aid for she was skilled in the use of the sextant, and if they did get a glimpse of the sun above the clouds on that murky day, she would have been able to get a positional fix. Heavy cloud blanketed Germany and it was not until they skirted Bratislava to the east of Vienna, that a break in the cloud enabled them to visually pin-point their first landmark, the Danube.

The route was a familiar one to Amy for it closely followed that taken on her England-Australia flight just four years previously. Then she was single and in control, now she was married and just one member of a team captained by her unpredictable partner. As Jim peered over the port wing, she was reminded by the long scar on his left cheek of the Bridgeport crash. Now, seeing his head jerk back as he took a swig from the bottle she was reminded of another fear, his heavy drinking. She had admitted privately to friends that she too had often over-indulged in order to obliterate her disgust at his drunken stupors. Drinking in a night-club was one thing, but in the air it was another matter. It must have worried her considerably.

As they climbed to 14,000 feet to clear the shrouded Transylvanian Alps ahead of them, she knew that her husband's eyes would never be far from the most vital of all flight instruments – the oil-pressure gauges. Charles Lindbergh had stuck a piece of paper over the oil-pressure gauge on the instrument panel of the *Spirit of St Louis* during his Atlantic crossing in 1927, it worried him that much. A fall in pressure was the first indication of engine failure, but at least the Mollisons consoled themselves that the Comet was powered by two Gipsy engines. The failure of one engine might not have been disastrous, but it would certainly have meant a time-consuming detour for there would have been difficulty in maintaining sufficient height to clear these Alps. And whilst their parachutes gave them some added security, neither relished the thought of baling out over the hostile, snow-covered mountains that now lay beneath them.

Around 3.30pm GMT, soon after crossing the Black Sea, they flew into heavy turbulent thunderstorms over the Taurus Mountains in northern Turkey, and they were forced to climb to 16,000 feet in order to escape the worst of them. With such foul weather conditions and dangerous terrain beneath them, the lack of a Turkish visa was probably the least of their worries. Finally, they emerged into clearer skies and were able to pin-point Aleppo, before making a south-easterly heading to follow the Euphrates as it snaked towards Baghdad. Both Jim and Amy were highly relieved to see the familiar sun-baked landscape beneath them, for she had traversed it in the

Black Magic being frantically worked on at Karachi airport after it had returned with a jammed undercarriage. It was a piece of misfortune which probably denied the Mollisons a victory over Scott and Black in the MacRobertson air race.

same direction in 1930, and he the opposite way a year later. They now knew that they could survive a forced-landing, should the need arise.

The heat and glare began to bear down on the cramped, glass-canopied cabin, contrasting favourably after the cold and blinding rain of northern Europe. Realising that Baghdad only lay some five hundred miles ahead of them, their spirits began to rise. Their only immediate concern now was fuel supply. This caused Jim's attention to focus for most of the time on the fuel-gauge, which was registering what little was left in the front nose tank. He was aware that de Havilland's had not had time to carry out accurate fuel-consumption tests on the Comet, and so was hoping that this instrument was not misleading him. Fuel-gauges were notoriously unreliable at this period in aviation. However, they probably took some crumb of comfort from the knowledge that they had the advantage of the prevailing northerly wind, one which blows across Iraq for most of the year.

The wheels of *Black Magic* met the stony surface of Baghdad's airfield to a perfect landing at precisely 7.10pm, sending two plumes of red dust trailing behind them. A split-second later the swirl was joined by a third as the protesting tailskid ploughed its noisy furrow, aiding the braking and bringing the racer and its weary crew to a halt. Turning and taxying towards the floodlit control point, they were met by an eager crowd of officials who later confirmed that they had covered the distance from Mildenhall in 12 hours 40 minutes at a speed of 199.77 mph. As one of the works' mechanics clambered onto the wing to swing the canopy aside, the engines were cut. Jim's first words were, 'Have any of the others been here before us?' With the noise of the engines still ringing in their deafened ears, they received the reply that they were longing to hear. 'No, you're the first.'

Before they had left England the newspapers had reported the reaction of the middle-eastern countries that lay on the route of the MacRobertson air race. One of the corresondents on the *Daily Express* in its coverage had luridly reported that 'hundreds of tribesmen are riding day and night by horse and camel to the aerodromes of Aleppo and Baghdad, where the competitors are scheduled to call. Strange rumours spread over the ancient trade route, but now the bazaars are aflutter with anticipation . . . the tribes have realised and approved the sporting nature of the contest'.[107] Sure enough, the Mollisons were given a warm welcome at the capital's aerodrome and after they had been escorted to the airport hotel, where they indulged in the luxury of a bath, they emerged to respond to a call for speeches from the press before an excited crowd. Amongst the members of the welcoming party were the Mayor of Baghdad, and Government ministers bringing a message of welcome from the young King Ghazi especially for Amy.

News was coming in from some of the less fortunate competitors. Jackie Cochran and Wesley Smith in the fast but unpredictable *Gee Bee* were flying at 14,000 feet over the Carpathian mountains when the engine cut out within seconds of switching to their reserve fuel-tank. In the ensuing panic their first reaction was to bale out, but when Wesley realised that his partner's canopy was jammed, he chivalrously decided to stay with the machine. Jackie then discovered that the fuel switch had been incorrectly marked, and that 'on', in fact meant 'off'. In spite of surviving the scare, they hardly needed any persuasion to put down at Bucharest, for they were extremely cold and had been wearied to the point of exhaustion by the noise from the big 'Hornet' engine. Worse was to come however, for when they made their landing approach, with Jackie at the controls, they found that one of the trailing-edge flaps was jammed. She made two attempts at a landing but the imbalance of the controls forced her to go round again. On the third and final approach with one flap down, she hit the turf with all of the aircraft's customary clumsiness and needed the whole length of the runway in which to pull up. They were relieved to retire with no more than a damaged undercarriage.

Other competitors were straggled across Europe. Soon after leaving Mildenhall, the Airspeed Viceroy flown by T. Neville Stack and S. Turner was down at Abbeville with engine trouble, but after repairs flew on to Le Bourget. There the crew were greeted by the Australians Ray Parer and G. Hemsworth, whose obsolescent Fairey Fox was suffering from a similar problem. Neither of these entrants were a threat to the Mollisons. Their main concern was the two other Comets, and the fast American and Dutch airliners.

Jim and Amy were back in the cockpit of their refuelled aircraft within ninety-five minutes after landing, and departed confidently into a velvet night sky at 8.50pm GMT (11.50pm local time) knowing that none of their rivals were even in sight. Unwisely, they decided not to fly directly to the next control point at Allahabad, 2,300 miles distant. Maybe the non-arrival of any of the other competitors, particularly that of Scott and Parmentier, had induced a degree of complacency into their planning, for that night they set a compass-course for Karachi. It was to be a fatal flaw in their strategy, and one which was to cost them dearly.

Meanwhile, Charles Scott and co-pilot Tom Campbell Black had cautiously put down at the RAF station at Kirkuk, a town 130 miles to the north of Baghdad and allegedly the site of the biblical fiery furnace incident recorded in the book of Daniel. Earlier on they had become lost in bad weather over Angora and quite fortuitously had found this airfield on their way south. Deeming it unwise to continue further and risk a forced-landing through insufficient fuel, they decided to land and take on twenty gallons.

Ten minutes after the Mollisons had left Baghdad, the beam from the Harley landing-lamp in the nose of *Grosvenor House* appeared as a pin-prick of light on the darkening horizon. Minutes later the thirsty Comet was on the ground being replenished for the long haul to Allahabad. So near were the two men to seeing their arch-rivals that Scott was to comment: 'There they told us the Mollisons had left fifteen minutes earlier *on a course for Jask*. The dust kicked up by their Black Comet still overhung the aerodrome; she had shaken it from her dainty fabric with a vengeance.'[108]

Within half an hour Scott and his companion were ready for take-off. Not for them the effete toiletries and reception of the 'Flying Sweethearts', for they were determined to close the gap, and had in fact already salvaged one precious hour on the Mollisons when they departed at 9.33pm.

Little did Jim and Amy realise as they settled down for the overnight flight by way of Jask, that Cathcart Jones and Waller's Comet had overshot the Iraqi capital by some 240 miles to the south-east. G-ACSR had become hopelessly lost and was forced to make a hazardous night-landing in the desert near Dizful, in Persia. There they waited until dawn before they were able to fly back to the mandatory control point at Baghdad. Meanwhile, the DC2, Pander and Boeing had preceded them, hard on the heels of the two remaining Comets.

By choosing to overfly Jask on the coast of the Gulf of Oman on their way to land at Karachi, and then to proceed to Allahabad, the Mollisons were now conceding not only an increased distance of 180 miles, but the time-delay involved in an additional stop. There could only have been two possible motives for this decision; either they believed that Scott was out of the race completely, or they were determined to add the England-India record to their laurels. Maybe it was for both reasons. Scott, however, with the benefit of knowing that the Mollisons were now making for Karachi, had boldly decided to go the 2,300 miles to Allahabad in one direct hop and take out his rivals' lead.

At precisely 4.43am GMT (9.11am local time) on Sunday 21st, the Mollisons touched down at Karachi. It was exactly 22 hours and 13 minutes since they had left Mildenhall, and they had set a new time for the England-India distance by knocking 28 hours off the previous record. Neither Jim nor Amy were strangers to the present day Pakistani capital, and they were warmly received by the awaiting European and Indian crowd. Jim had served there in the RAF during the 1920's and had landed at the aerodrome when he broke Scott's Australia-England record three years previously. Whilst Amy had been welcomed at Karachi when she arrived six days after leaving Croydon in May 1930, thus reducing Bert Hinkler's time by almost two days.

Within an hour the Mollisons' aching limbs and sleep-deprived eyes had been partially refreshed and they were shoe-horning back into their cramped compartment. Refuelling, engine-checks and correct propeller pitch change had all been made and they were airborne by 5.49am heading for Allahabad. It was then that disaster struck. As soon as JM tried to wind on the hand-wheel to raise the undercarriage he knew that something was wrong, for the wheels would only partially retract before they jammed. Thankfully, they would go fully down, so there was no alternative but to return to Karachi, and this they did only fifteen minutes after their departure. Mechanics were soon working frantically to rectify the fault and by noon they were on their way once more. And then the unbelievable happened. After two hours in the air the black and gold Comet was seen returning again to Karachi for the second time. Ground crew and officials were perplexed. What were the Mollisons up to? Were they deliberately throwing the race away? Officials and spectators gathered round anxious to hear the irate fliers give their reason.

History records two variations for the explanation given on their unexpected return; the first being that they had forgotten a vital map, and the second, that the maps were 'unsuitable'. All we do know is that a dejected Jim Mollison was to tell reporters, 'Rather than carry on with suspect landing-gear and inadequate charts we will spend the night here.' He knew that an immediate departure would mean attempting a night-landing at Allahabad and this he was not prepared to risk. Maybe the memories of the Connecticut landing had unnerved them both. To add to their troubles a heavy mist was now settling over the aerodrome, so they decided to go to a local hotel and snatch a few hours sleep while they could.

Exactly how they assessed their chances at this time we are not sure, but they must have known by now that the race was quickly slipping from their grasp. Their morale had been lowered throughout the day as they had seen first the DC2, and then the Pander and Boeing relentlessly arriving and departing from Karachi without hold up.

By midnight local time they were being roused from their slumber for a return to the airport, where they received the devastating news that Scott and Black had left Allahabad twelve hours earlier, and in all probability were now flying down the Malaysian coast towards Singapore. The Mollisons only consolation was in seeing Bernard Rubin's Comet being worked on as they left. They had now lost sixteen precious hours.

Ahead of the Mollisons and in the blackness of that night was the radio-assisted Boeing of Roscoe Turner and Clyde Pangborn, which was having great difficulty in finding the Bamrauli aerodrome at Allahabad. It was a modern well-equipped airfield using a powerful flashing beacon to assist incoming aircraft at night, and one which reportedly could be seen from a distance of up to seventy miles away. Unfortunately for the Americans, the flashes of lightning from thunderstorms across India that night, confused and nullified the guiding effect of the beacon. For Jim and Amy the weather was to have far graver consequences. After holding an easterly setting for two hours they noticed a discrepancy between their two compasses, no doubt due to the electrical disturbances from the thunderstorms which they were now encountering. It will be recalled that on their joint Atlantic crossing a year earlier, they had purposely carried three compasses in *Seafarer*, in order to resolve the very problem thay were now confronted with.

Tempers were now flaring, aggravated by tiredness, and a heated argument ensued between them. Adding to their difficulties was an

Charles Scott arrives at Allahabad delighted to find that the Mollisons were now well behind him in the race to Melbourne.

unrecognised drift from a strong northerly wind, for which they had not been adequately briefed. Soon they were hopelessly lost in the all-enveloping Indian darkness. It was an inky blackness which was relieved only by the incandescent glow from the engines' exhausts.

Sighting the lights of a town, they wisely decided to circle above it until there was sufficient light from the dawn to risk a landing. As soon as he was able to pick a suitable site, Jim put the Comet down safely in a field on the outskirts of what turned out to be Jabalpur, some 175 miles to the south-east of Allahabad. By now relationships between the husband and wife were at breaking point, and with only the remotest hope of retrieving the lost time, all caution was thrown to the wind. Fuel-tank levels were low and with little prospect of acquiring aviation fuel, they took on commercial petrol from the local bus depot. By 10am (local time) on that Monday morning of the 22nd, Mollison took off with throttles wide open, overdriving the aircraft at a low altitude and with Amy protesting that it would only result in damaging the engines, which it did.

As the Mollisons were approaching Bamrauli, the red Comet of Scott and Campbell Black was skirting the coastline of Java on its way to Darwin. Much to the chagrin of Jim and Amy, their arch-rivals were to take the first prize in the MacRobertson air race with a time of 70 hours and 55 minutes from Mildenhall to Melbourne. They were followed by the KLM airliner twenty hours later, and then into third place came the Boeing, less than three hours behind their Dutch rivals. The Pander had withdrawn at Bamrauli where it made a crash-landing, skidding to a halt when the port undercarriage wheel failed to fully lower. Less fortunate were the crew of the straggling Fairey Fox, who perished when their biplane crashed at Foggia in Italy.

Upon their arrival at Allahabad, the Mollisons' Comet was found to have damaged several of its cylinder-heads and pistons through overheating, a problem caused by the use of the low-octane fuel. The engine replacements that were needed were not immediately available and Jim and Amy were definitely out of the race. Maybe the use of incorrect fuel was not the sole culprit, for Arthur Swinson records how Aircraft Inspector Randall '. . . noticed three empty whisky bottles lying by the side of Jim Mollison's seat and convenient for his right hand'.[109]

Perhaps the most poignant summation of the Mollisons' predicament is given by Jehangir Tata, founder and Chairman of 'Air India', who was at Bamrauli on that day acting as one of the marshals.

> I was present when James Mollison and his co-pilot wife Amy arrived after some hours delay. After landing, they remained for quite a while in the middle of the airfield, whereupon an Indian Air Force NCO was sent in a jeep to enquire what the trouble was and to help them. He brought them in, leaving their Comet behind to be towed in later. He told us that when he had gone to them on the airfield he found them having a heated and loud discussion, or quarrel, as to who was responsible for their engine trouble, later found to be due to their having refuelled at Jabalpur with ordinary petrol. Amy left the same day, but Mollison remained in the reception tent for most of the time during the next two days, unchanged and unshaven, not having brought even a change of shirt with him. As was to be expected, he was not in a very happy or communicative mood and I, naturally, didn't inflict myself on him.[110]

Truly, *Black Magic* had lost its spell!

Chapter 16

'Baling Out'

By now it must have been all too obvious to both Jim and Amy that not only was their flying partnership a disaster, but also that their marriage was clearly disintegrating. Admittedly, they had picked up the minor record-breaking honour of setting the fastest time to India, but the finance and publicity they so much wanted in winning the MacRobertson had frustratingly eluded them. As a consequence, a tearful Amy immediately stormed off alone from the aerodrome to the English Club in Allahabad, where she wired Lord Wakefield for a loan of the £100 she needed for the cost of a single air-ticket home, by KLM or Imperial Airways.

Meanwhile, Jim roughed it under canvas for a few days at Bamrauli as Jehangir Tata describes, whilst trying to obtain engine spares in order to fly the damaged Comet back to the UK. Initially, his efforts met with little success, for whilst Rex Pearson (Bernard Rubin's appointed engineer at Allahabad) was in possession of some engine spares, he was specifically at the aerodrome for the servicing of Cathcart-Jones & Waller's Comet. Furthermore, he had been instructed by Bernard Rubin not to assist the Mollisons until they had officially and publicly retired from the race. Rubin had stressed that it was necessary that Rex Pearson held what engine spares he had, until G-ACSR and its crew had made Allahabad on their return trip home from Melbourne. RP recalls that his first impressions of JM were those made by his rather polished accent, something which he summed up in the phrase, 'he was certainly a bit upper crust'.[111]

In the meantime, tempers had cooled somewhat between the Mollisons and they decided to put a brave face on events by travelling together to Calcutta, where accommodation was deemed more civilised for Amy, and where Jim could wire the DH factory at Hatfield for new cylinder-heads and pistons. A week later the spares had been flown out on an Imperial Airways sheduled flight and by early November Rex Pearson had successfully ground-tested the Comet's Gipsy R engines. By this time relations between the Mollisons had improved enough for Amy to decide to accompany Jim in the Comet on the homeward flight. It was a decision that she was soon to regret.

Such was the popularity of the Mollisons that they received quite lavish sympathy from the world's press and the public as they slowly made their way home. Their arrival at Baghdad happily coincided with an official welcome being given by King Ghazi of Iraq to the Crown Prince and Princess of Sweden, who were currently making a tour of the near-east. General Nuri-es-Said, the pro-British Iraqi Prime Minister and the man responsible for JM's release from a Turkish jail three years earlier, was quick to arrange not only for the Mollisons to be accommodated at the home of the King's physician, but also to extend to them an invitation to the official reception being given that evening for the Swedish royal couple. Although Jim and Amy readily accepted, there was just one snag, neither had any suitable formal clothes for the occasion, for the amount of luggage space in the Comet was miniscule.

There was little difficulty encountered in getting Amy fixed up with a borrowed dress from the wife of their host, but when it came to providing Jim with an evening suit, things became more tiresome. Eventually, pleas to Nuri resulted in a suit being offered from his own wardrobe. There was just one snag. Although he was only a little taller and of similar shoulder width to Jim, he was of a much more generous girth. As a result the jacket fitted reasonably well but the trousers were so voluminous around the waist that when Amy saw her husband dressed she was horrified. Other than pleading an indisposition – something Jim was loathe to do with all that free drink about to flow – there was little he could do other than to follow her advice and keep one hand in his pocket in order to pull the trousers up and in. It caused more than few wry smiles and giggles that evening when Jim was introduced to the white-uniformed young monarch.

As the evening wore on and as the glasses were constantly refilled, the formality of the occasion melted and the recently crowned twenty-two year old King Ghazi, at one time uncle to the present-day King Hussein of Jordan, was soon in deep conversation with the two luckless aviators. He had been educated at Harrow and being anxious to bring about the modernisation of his country, was keen to know all he could about aviation. Jim was quick to promise him a flight in *Black Magic* before they left, and although he readily accepted the offer, he was diplomatically dissuaded by Nuri on account of the risks involved. Ironically, the young King was to be tragically killed in a motoring accident only five years later, whilst Nuri was to be assasinated in 1958 during an Iraqi Army revolt led by the rebel Brigadier Kassem.

Amy and a rather bedraggled Jim Mollison pose with friendly Iraqi Government officials during their stopover at Baghdad and whilst on their way back to the UK. They had been forced to retire from the race at Allahabad.

Rex Pearson had in the meantime left Allahabad on a KLM flight bound for Croydon, but had stopped off overnight at Cairo. Quite fortuitously he met up with the Mollisons again during their homeward flight, whilst they were staying at the Heliopolis Hotel in Cairo. During a conversation in the hotel lounge, he recalls that Amy was bemoaning the cramped conditions of the Comet and the fact that there was 'barely enough room to carry a toothbrush'.[(112)] In a chivalrous gesture RP offered to swap places with Amy and give her his seat on the KLM flight, if she would deliver his luggage to Croydon. It was an offer she was quick to accept.

It is interesting to note Amy's revealing comment as recorded in her book, *Skyroads of the World,* some details of that particular KLM flight. 'I was lucky enough to have him (Cdr. Ivan Smirnoff) as pilot on the KLM plane which brought me home in 1934 . . . We became firm friends during this trip and I envied him *his remarkable imperturbability* no matter how bad the weather, or how irritating the passengers.'[(113)] No doubt Smirnoff's unruffled behaviour was not lost on Amy, for it must have contrasted sharply with that of her husband's over the previous three weeks!

Jim Mollison's newly acquired companion on the journey from Cairo still remembers quite clearly, even over fifty-five years later, the fine details of that eventful homeward flight, and how on numerous occasions he acted as the 'auto-pilot'. He recalls that they were delayed for a while at Athen's Tatoi aerodrome whilst replacement elevator hinge-pins were fitted, and that as soon as they took off, Jim waggled the control-column signalling him to take over the controls. To which Pearson, who was not a qualified pilot, replied, 'You get her over the mountains first!' From thereon the engineer was content to fly on any compass-heading that was given him, acknowledging that, 'JM was a jolly good navigator.' He seems to have been unperturbed by the fact that, 'Jim always had a bottle of gin in the air , and a bottle of brandy on the ground.'[114]

They arrived at Rome on 7 November and after a brief stopover set off for Lyons. They had not been in the air long before they flew into fierce thunderstorms and were forced to return when one of the engines developed magneto trouble. It meant booking into a local hotel in spite of neither of them having any money, and RP remembers that he was only able to cash a cheque after visiting the British Consul. They shared a bedroom together and RP recalls that he was more than a little alarmed on the first morning when, after taking a bath following JM's use of the bathroom, he was asked if he had ever had VD. 'It's no bother,' assured the Scot cooly, 'I go to Glasgow – I have a friend there who cures me when I've got it.'[115] From this remark one cannot but help suspect that it might well have been the contraction of venereal disease that caused JM's repatriation from India in the latter part of 1926.

From Rome the two men flew on to Brussels, where it seems that RP became a victim of Mollison's carelessness. As RP came to hand-swing the engines on the morning of departure, one of the Gipsy engines failed to start and he signalled the Scot for 'switches off'. There was some mis-understanding, for although he remembers JM confirming, 'Switches off', they were in fact 'on'. As a consequence, when RP slowly turned the blade of the Ratier prop the engine fired and the blade caught him under the arm. He subsequently spent two days in hospital before they were able to proceed to Lympne.

Meanwhile, it was a rather forlorn and footloose Amy who stepped off the Imperial Airways plane at Croydon on a rainy afternoon two days later. She was without luggage (RP recalls that he was rather peeved when he did finally collect his suitcase at Croydon airport, for it had been broken into) and wearing an ill-fitting overcoat that she had borrowed from an Army officer in India – not exactly Schiaperelli! By this time she had quite made up her mind that she was not going back to live with Jim, either at the rented Lurgashall cottage, or at the Grosvenor. Things were never to be quite the same again in their marriage, for although they were both prepared to keep up a pretence of marital harmony, it was purely for the sake of their public image. She was however encouraged to find Bill Courtenay and Dorothy Ward waiting on the tarmac to greet her, and after being whisked off to lunch, soon became her normal cheerful self. The fact that Amy was offered and accepted an invitation to stay at Dorothy Ward's home for the next few days, seems to bear out Peter Glenville's view that his mother's relationship with Jim was never more than platonic.

Finances were low in the Mollison camp and they were forced to sell their DH 88 for as much as they could get for it. From de Havilland's point of view the successes of the three Comets – an outright win, a fourth, and an India record – had enhanced not only the company's prestige but also the value of each individual machine on the second-hand market. As a result, the three aeroplanes were in strong demand, not only from the Air Ministry but also by foreign countries. *Black Magic* was flown to Hatfield for a complete overhaul, before being sold to the Portuguese Government in February 1935. To the last it still retained its black and gold livery, only now re-registered as CS-AAJ and bearing the name *Salazar*, after that country's Prime Minister. Whilst the exact price the Mollisons received for their machine is not known, if the sale of the victorious *Grosvenor House* is any guide then it probably earned them a considerable profit,* even after making an allowance for the cost of engine replacements.

In the weeks preceding the sale of *Black Magic,* money was so tight that Jim had written to the Royal Aero Club asking for the return of his £50 air race entry-fee.[116] One cannot help but detect in the tone of the letter of reply from the Mollisons' old protagonist, secretary Harold Perrin, that there was an element of rubbing salt in Jim and Amy's wounds. After assuring JM that he will receive his fee in the course of the next few days, Perrin goes on to invite both him and Mrs Mollison to attend a banquet that was to be given at the Grosvenor Hotel in honour of Scott and Campbell Black. With something of a sting in the tail, he adds, 'By the way, we hope on this occasion you will make a point of turning up to time – eight o'clock.'[117] Perhaps here, we catch a glimpse of Hector. Like father, like son.

Apart from them both participating in an aviation debate organised by the Women's Engineering Society early in January 1935 (Amy had been elected President for the period, 1934-37), Jim and Amy saw little of each other until the summer of that year. Without any word of warning to his wife, Jim sailed off to the USA late in January after being interviewed by the *Daily Telegraph,* to whom he had announced that he was 'about to attempt a stratosphere flight'.[118] It was in fact a feeble ploy to give some respectability to their

*A. O. Edwards sold his Comet to the Air Ministry for £7,000 – a profit of 40%.

separation over the next four months. Amy reacted by spending a brief riding holiday with her sister Betty in Malvern, before sailing in search of sunshine in Madeira.

Jim arrived in New York in the depth of winter, where he began linking up with some of the old cronies he had met in 1932 and 1933. At the time of his first 1935 visit, the laws of Prohibition had been repealed, and with it had gone much of the corruption that had dominated that big city. However, it did little to quench his fascination with crime, and the slightly sadistic and prurient streak that was part of his nature. This comes out quite forcibly in his memoirs, *Playboy of the Air*, where he describes being privy to police raids on Harlem drug parties in New York's 43rd precinct, reputedly one of the toughest in that city. He was also invited to attend identification parades where the unrestrained use of the rubber truncheon was commonplace. The book is liberally sprinkled with descriptions of 'niggers' and 'coons' in a way that would be branded as overtly racist by today's standards. Perhaps in all fairness one should hesitate from attacking JM for failing to measure up to today's climate of political correctness. He was after all a man of his time, brought up and moulded by a class-consciousness that was quite prevalent amongst those from his background.

JM goes on to give his impressions of leaving New York deep in snow and ice, only to step from an airliner at Miami into a world of palm trees and bleached beaches that compared with the best he had seen at Bondi. All the predatory instincts of Mollison the womaniser are revealed, as he eulogises the tanned high-heeled beauties of Miami Beach and Palm Beach. Poor Amy. In the latter town he appears to have been welcomed by the affluent members of the snobbish '400 Club', an elitist group as exclusive as any amongst the British aristocracy, and where he boasts that the rich vied for his patronage as their guest.

One particular facet of American society that particularly seems to have fascinated him, was the elusiveness of classifying the social position and status of a person by their accent. In Britain it presented little difficulty. One knew instantly by the voice alone if one was speaking to a shop-girl or a Baroness, but not so in the States. On one occasion he was seduced and fooled by the dulcet and honeyed tones of someone he later considered to be his social inferior, when the hotel's female receptionist purred over the room-service telephone, 'Yes, Cap'n Mollison, can I help you?' It was an innuendo not lost on the Scot! Small wonder there was an outrage when these encounters were described in his book in 1937. One can imagine how incensed Amy must have been. Her first reaction was to issue a writ for libel, but she was restrained from doing so by a legal friend who advised her that such an action was unlikely to succeed. It is doubtful if she ever forgave him for embarrassing her in the way he did with these 'kiss and tell' revelations.

Never one to stay in one place for too long, JM decided to sample the fleshpots of the Bahamas before returning home, and sailed from Miami to the capital of Nassau on New Providence Island – playground of the rich. There were no scheduled air-links in those days, but this did not stop the steady influx of wealthy American tourists who came in the winter months to gamble at the casinos, such as the Bahamian Club, and to laze their days away on Paradise Beach.

It was in Nassau that JM teamed up with Lord Tredegar, purportedly one of England's richest peers, and his erstwhile companion, Crown Prince Paul, brother of the exiled King George of Greece. Jim and Amy had become quite friendly with the monocled monarch whilst he was living as a near neighbour in London. He had been forced to abdicate his throne in 1924 for his pro-German sympathies, and did not return to his own country until a general plebiscite was taken in November 1935. Although he was reputedly a great admirer of the Germans, it was not long before he had been anglicised by the Mayfair set – he even had an English mistress – to the extent that Mussolini would always refer to him derisively as 'that Englishman'. There is no doubt that JM, always one to exploit his fame as an aviator and notoriety as a playboy, used his contact with the monarch to introduce himself to his brother in Nassau.

Lord Tredegar seems to have made a strong impression upon JM, not for his wealth, or his ability to keep up with the Scot's capacity for drinking, but for his professed psychic powers. He told the aviator that he would never become the victim of a violent death in the air. It was a remarkably accurate prediction in view of the precarious nature of the flying that Jim Mollison was to pursue, and in a career that totalled over 8,000 flying hours.

☆ ☆ ☆

Jim returned to London and the Grosvenor in May, to learn that Amy had just moved into the Savoy Hotel after her Madeira holiday. She was trying her best to forget him and was absorbed in flying her recent acquisition, a fast, four-seater Beechcraft B17L cabin biplane. Popularly known as the 'Staggerwing', due to the unorthodox reverse layout of its wing positions, it was powered by a 225hp Jacobs radial engine and featured a fully retractable undercarriage. As the British agent for Beechcraft, Amy thought that it would be a good form of advertising to own one, but unfortunately it was an aircraft she was never able to fully master. It was not long before she had made a crash-landing, after forgetting to lower the undercarriage.

Apart from the American franchise, her other interests included lecturing and writing, but none of these activities could quite blot out the misery she was going through in living apart from Jim. At one time she implored him to go back with her, but he would merely say that he preferred to live a bachelor life. His excuse was always that he could do little right in his wife's eyes, and that she was too demanding and quick-tempered. However, in July, he relented and came back to live with her at the Savoy. It was a short-lived reunion, for one evening whilst she had gone to the theatre, he had invited a girlfriend back to their apartment. Amy returned home earlier than she was expected and found the two of them lying on the bed in her bedroom. Whilst it was not exactly a case of discovering her husband *in flagranti delicto*, a blistering scene followed in which the woman hurriedly left. JM pleaded that nothing had happened between them and that they were merely sleeping off the effects of too much drink. In the ensuing row Amy ordered her husband to leave immediately but he refused, still protesting adamantly that he had not been unfaithful to her. With her suspicions now fully aroused, Amy left the hotel early the next morning and went to stay with a friend living in the country, leaving Jim to his own devices.

Whilst an outwardly polite relationship was maintained between the Mollisons over the next four months, they lived apart and there was never a true reconciliation. Amy must have been determined to go her own way from now on, for during this period Amy's flying-log shows that she began making quite long flights in her Beechcraft to Paris, Biarritz, Vienna and Budapest. In one of the entries the name 'Diana' appears, no doubt referring to the socialite Diana Caldwell, who was at this time in a whirl of activity mixing with the aristocracy of Europe. Earlier she had run a small cocktail club called 'The Blue Goose' in Bruton Mews, just off Bond Street, a club which was probably frequented by the Mollisons. Famed for her *femme fatale* persona and classic good looks, she was destined to become the woman most heavily involved in the infamous Lord Erroll murder trial in 1941.

James Fox, in his compelling account of Kenya's Happy Valley set, *White Mischief*, throws some light on the kind of circles that Amy was now moving in: 'She (Diana Caldwell) led a hectic social life, and used her aeroplane to pursue it across Europe. She flew with the famous aviatrix Amy Mollison. She fell in with an exclusive group of aviating aristocrats, one of whom was Prince Stahremberg, the Austrian Vice-Chancellor. They would meet in Budapest and the *Tatler* correspondent was somehow always there . . .' [119]

Amy presents the Mollison Trophy for aerobatics to Victor Ercolaine, circa. 1934. He eventually won the trophy outright after three successive wins in his Avro Sports Avian.

Note the Beechcraft 17, 'Staggerwing', in the background – in all probability Amy's G-ADDH.

It was most certainly around this time, and in the Paris or Budapest *milieux*, that Amy first met Francois Dupré, a wealthy Parisian hotelier and owner of a stud-farm for the breeding of race-horses. Dupré, some fifteen years older than the aviatrix and her most ardent admirer. He was determined for her to be his wife, or failing that his mistress. Amy must be given full credit for the way she conducted herself during the two years of her liaison with the Frenchman. She remained inviolate, in spite of the many wiles he pursued to seduce her, mainly because she did not love him. Admittedly, she played along with his plans and prospered financially, especially when he helped her to establish her own 'Air Cruises' air-tour company, but throughout the whole affair she retained her self-respect.

By November 1935 Amy had rented the furnished Belgrave Cottage residence near Eaton Square, although she still had the use of a suite of rooms provided for her by Francois Dupré at his Hotel George V in Paris. JM visited her in London as soon as she returned, still protesting his fidelity towards her, before sailing for New York on the *Champlain*. During the serious discussion they had before he left, Amy had suggested that they divorce, but JM's answer to this was that they should wait for a further six months until he returned from his round the world trip. Probably with one eye on her public image, Amy agreed.

☆ ☆ ☆

One prominent press release at the time of JM's departure for the USA, early in November, discreetly reported, 'Jim Mollison going round the world to look at some aeroplanes.' It was a bland enough statement for public consumption, and revealed nothing of the acrimony that now existed between the two fliers. Indeed, the reason given was even partially true, for both Jim and Amy had in fact been invited by Amelia Earhart and her husband George Putnam to attend an Aero Exhibition in Los Angeles. The offer included using the Americans' North Hollywood home as a base. Understandably, with the marital hostility now existing between the Mollisons, Amy had declined the invitation. Jim, however, grabbed the opportunity with both hands, for there had been little prospect of making the headlines in any long-distance flights since his return from India, and the chance of free accommodation in California fitted in with the itinerary he had already loosely planned.

Prior to his departure on the French luxury liner *Champlain*, JM had happily made the acquaintance at the Savoy Hotel of Maurice 'Tex' Moore, a wealthy American lawyer. He was the senior partner in Cravath, de Gersdorff, Swaine & Wood, one of the most celebrated legal firms in New York and famous for conducting lawsuits on behalf of the big-name stars in Hollywood. Over drinks at the hotel's bar, JM soon discovered that 'Tex' was also an official of the ruling Democratic party in his native state. As the brandy flowed, Jim, who had a keen eye on visiting that part of the States, was more and more intrigued when told that there was no bother in him being granted a full Colonelship in the Texan Army. The hoopla greatly appealed to JM's sense of humour and fun, especially when he heard that Ginger Rogers had recently been made an Admiral of that state's ship-less navy. In due course, his Texan friend began to apologise by explaining that the award would, unfortunately, be no more than that of a 'Lootenant-Colonel'. JM, never one to look a gift horse in the mouth, took the letter of introduction intended for State Governor Alldred, grateful for small mercies.

At New York, JM eschewed the parties and nightclubs – after the surfeit of roistering on the crossing, their prospect had probably palled on him anyway – and made the train journey southwards. Even the enticement of his old friend Harry Richman, owner of Broadway's Club Richman, was not enough to detain him.

Overt racial prejudice was rife in the USA at the time, with lynch laws still operating in Kentucky, Georgia and Texas, and the full impact of such tyranny was brought home forcibly to him when his train passed through the 'Mason and Dixon's line'. This imaginary line, not seen on any ordnance survey map but coincident with the boundary separating Pennsylvania and Delaware, divided the free from the slave-holding states. In November 1935 it was still the practice for all coloured passengers to be segregated from the whites, by being forced to change coaches.

After redeeming the 'Tex' Moore pledge, an award that seemed to have brought more imaginary benefits to the Scot than any real ones, JM proceeded to explore the sleepy, small border towns of Piedras Negras on the Mexican side of the Rio Grande, and further north to Juarez. Apart from sampling the local brew of tequila and observing the futile attempts of the Texan law enforcement officers to prevent the Mexicans smuggling their hooch across the border by night, there was little to satisfy his native curiosity. He must move on.

☆ ☆ ☆

The sun glistened on the burnished aluminium-alloy surfaces of the American Airlines' Douglas DC2 airliner as it slipped in over the San Gabriel Mountains and touched down on the oil-streaked runway of Glendale's Grand Central airport. JM's first glimpse of the sunshine state and its lifestyle came as he entered the main lobby of the imposing faux-Spanish Colonial air terminal building. Its Zig-Zag moderne tower dominated the landscape and was possibly already slightly familiar to him from being a backdrop for many of Hollywood's early movies.*

The terminal had opened in February 1929 when the first airline service fron southern California to New York was inaugurated. On that occasion Charles Lindbergh had piloted a TWA Ford trimotor with Mary Pickford and Douglas Fairbanks, Snr. amongst its passengers on the opening flight. Amelia Earhart had also been a regular visitor to the airfield long before it had become a scheduled airport, and had competed there with her Kinner biplane in an air rodeo in 1923. In those days the area was a WASP stronghold, one that did not baulk at employing blacks for the menial tasks of airport baggage-handlers, etc, so long as they were out of town and on the other side of the tracks by nightfall. In nearby Burbank, one former resident remembers that as a ten year old he 'was sent home one hot summer day by a policeman for not wearing a shirt in a downtown area'.[120]

As soon as JM entered the airport's restaurant, his head was swivelling with all the consummate skill of a film-studio talent scout. It didn't take him

---

*The airport closed in 1959 due to the fact that its 3,400 foot runway could not take the larger jet airliners. However, the terminal tower still exists and functions as an office building in part of a development known as the Grand Central Industrial Center.

long to realise that he had found his El Dorado. It seemed as if he had stepped right into the middle of a movie-lot. He quickly discovered that there was no bigger magnet for the glamour of aspiring film-actresses than this particular part of Hollywood. After being shown to his seat by a slinky hostess comparable to a Constance Bennett, and waited on by a Hedy Lamaar look-alike, it began to dawn upon him that this was the unbelievable norm of the San Fernando valley. It was very much a case of being spoilt for choice.

After a brief interview with the airlines' press agent, 'Colonel' Mollison was boarding a cab for the Putnams' home in Toluca Lake, North Hollywood, leaving his interviewer to fabricate what was lacking in hard facts. Ballyhoo was at its peak in the movie capital in the mid-Thirties and Mollison was not slow to appreciate the fact. He records that the ensuing article brought him a plethora of invitations, as well as giving American Airlines the publicity they were seeking. There is no doubt that he was welcomed on two major counts. Firstly, Hollywood's dream factories loved a pukka, 'dammit, sir', English accent – a whole colony of British actors and actresses were already there to prove it – and secondly, the film industry covertly welcomed notoriety. Mollison happily qualified on both counts.

JM had an open-sesame to meeting many of the stars of the silver-screen during the eight weeks that he was to spend in Los Angeles. Apart from the employment offer that he had received and turned down from Warner Bros in 1932, he was never short of good contacts for the purpose of visiting film studios. His host, George Putnam, had first become involved in the film industry in 1927, when he was employed on location in Texas as an adviser in the making of the classic aviation film, *Wings*. Even today its black and white photography is still considered by film buffs to provide some of the finest aerial dog-fighting scenes ever portrayed of World War 1. Currently, he was working for Paramount studios as a script-writer on *Go West Young Man*, a film starring Mae West and Randolph Scott. Small wonder that JM was to be seen sitting alongside the audacious, blonde sex-goddess at the ringside of Hollywood's Legion Arena fight-stadium, on several of the Friday night boxing contests.

A visit to Hollywood's most expensive and exclusive night-club, the Trocadero, along with some of the film industry's important executives, found Mollison being introduced to MGM star Clark Gable. By that time 'the King' was a big box-office draw and his latest film, *Mutiny on the Bounty*, was just being released. JM, ever an acute observer of the methods of opportunism operating amongst his fellow human beings, was struck on that occasion by the selectiveness of lingering glances and lipsticked smiles that were generously lavished upon his easily recognisable companions. Apart from the stars themselves, these film directors and executives were well-known as men of power in Hollywood, and they were targeted unashamedly. It must be remembered that the USA was still emerging from the great Depression that had followed the Wall Street crash of 1929, and that there were some thirteen million unemployed at the time of Mollison's visit. Hence these attractive waitresses and check-out girls, most of whom had migrated to California from the big cities, were in a frenzy to make it into films, and to make it quick. It struck Mollison as being all rather pathetic. They were playing a scene that was tinged with as much pathos as any that might appear before the film studio cameras.

There was another aspect of the film industry which touched a sympathetic chord with Hollywood's latest arrival. On 9 January 1936, during the time of his visit, the *Los Angeles Times* reported the premature death of actor and screen idol John Gilbert. The unfortunate forty-one year old star, at one time in the top bracket of the industry and now living the life of a self-imposed recluse, had been found dead in his luxury Beverly Hills home. He had died of a heart attack, allegedly brought on by the stress of finding the transition from silent to sound movies difficult. This reason might have been only partially true, for it was common knowledge that the studios often used this 'quality of voice test' as a pretext for getting rid of certain people who had fallen from favour with the film bosses. On top of all this, John Gilbert had suffered three failed marriages and a frustrated, highly publicised, albeit one-sided love affair with Greta Garbo. His screen career had collapsed and he had turned to alcohol for a refuge. From then on it was down hill all the way. Maybe, when JM looked back on the tragedy in later life, he recognised that Gilbert's demise held some portent for him. Confronted with this illustration of the unacceptable face of Hollywood, showing that obscurity could come as swiftly as success and fame, Jim Mollison saw and recorded it in his memoirs, but unfortunately he failed to take it seriously.

Through her husband's connections, Amelia Earhart had recently acted as an adviser in the RKO production *Christopher Strong* – an early feminist aviation movie starring Katherine Hepburn as a tough pioneer aviatrix. In addition, AE's close professional association with Paul Mantz, Hollywood stunt-flier and near neighbour, gave her ready access to the film studios. One can therefore safely assume that these two people must have also provided readily tappable sources for her inquisitive British guest.

JM recalls that during this time he met the little man with the cane and the baggy trousers, the inimitable Charlie Chaplin. He was impressed by the

A carefully coiffured Amy in an unusually sophisticated pose. It is hard to imagine this same woman delving into the intricacies of an aero engine.

man's quiet, serious demeamour, more often than not the hall-mark of the world's funny men. The comedian had met Amy soon after her 1930 flight to Australia, and Jim was quick no doubt to remind him of the picture he had seen in Amy's photograph album, showing Amy arm in arm with Chaplin, Lady Astor and George Bernard Shaw as a foursome outside of the House of Commons.

Other British actors with whom JM became close friends during this time were Alan Mowbray and Victor McLaglen. The former was to play over four hundred small parts in films, usually as the imperious man-servant, and later in prominent TV shows in America. Most notably he featured in *Becky Sharp* with Miriam Hopkins and Cedric Hardwicke (another British actor) in a screen adaptation of Thackeray's *Vanity Fair*, a film historically important for being the first feature-length film in Technicolour's three colour process. The tough but warm-hearted Victor McLaglen had already scored a popular success in 1935 in *The Informer*, a story about the IRA, and one in which he had won an Oscar. However, it was his staged Hollywood parades that intrigued JM most of all. Known as Victor's private army, it formed a regular cavalcade of horsemen, accompanied by leggy and booted drum majorettes in their eye-catching blue tunics, complete with their military high hats.

JM enjoyed the benefit of one further important contact in the film capital, namely the American actor Robert Montgomery. The Mollisons had already established a firm friendship with the MGM star during one of his transatlantic trips to London when he had stayed at the Grosvenor, and the aviator was never one to be slow at exploiting such a relationship. The suave leading man of the Thirties was at the time of JM's Californian visit at the height of his career, having partnered some of the screen's most glamorous actresses, including Greta Garbo, Norma Shearer, Constance Bennett and Joan Crawford. Much like his Hollywood colleague Ronald Reagan, he was eventually to become disillusioned with the razzamataz of show business, and during the post-WW2 years entered politics.

It is not particularly difficult to detect thinly disguised references to Robert Montgomery in JM's 1937 memoirs. In a chapter philosphising on the mores of the Mayfair set, JM describes a favourite ploy of one of its less scrupulous predatory females who was out to get her man. Quick to spot the chance of enticing a visiting Hollywood star under her spell, the confident huntress glides alongside her intended victim who is now sitting at the bar alongside friends. As she purrs, 'Say, Bob, fancy meeting you here of all places. The last time we met was in Palm Springs, wasn't it, do you remember?' She is now playing for high stakes and knows that the credibility of her line being accepted depends upon two factors. Firstly, that her target is slightly the worse for drink and therefore his memory is not functioning as smoothly as it might, and secondly, that if he is still cold sober, then there is a real possibility that he will mistakenly believe that he has met her somewhere before, and that he might fear committing a social gaffe if he flatly denies knowing her. If either of the two conditions are met, and she is attractive enough, she is in.

Such tactics appealed greatly to Mollison's impish sense of humour, and also let it be said, to a sneaking admiration he had for its sense of a fair play on his scale of justice. He considered that everyone had a 'racket', and in that respect he and the woman in question were kindred spirits. His danger was in risking his neck on an Atlantic or Sahara desert solo crossing, and hers was of a similar nature inasmuch as she worked alone. Added to that, he was swift to recognise that her profession needed similar nerve and audacity to that of his own, albeit its failure had possibly less disastrous consequences.

It is probably germane at this point to mention JM's introductory visit to one of Hollywood's less reputable establishments, made in the company of someone whom he described as 'a handsome film star internationally known to millions of repressed women'. Having dropped the star's wife back at their luxurious home after a party, JM was driven by his host for a peek into some of the activities of one of the many high-class brothels, or 'Call Houses' as they were discreetly and euphemistically termed. In this case a pseudo-Moroccan style villa with its fifteen rooms, was typical of many such disorderly houses that were dotted around those sun-kissed valleys of Hollywood – its proprietress, a certain Madame Francis. Its sophistication and pretence was all a far cry from its nearest Soho equivalent – Kate Meyrick's '43 Club' in Gerrard Street. Reading JM's account of his visit reminds one of the description given in David Niven's book, *Bring on the Empty Horses*, where he details the activities of 'Mary Lou' and 'the Baroness' from the same period.[121]

JM and his host were ushered into an expensively furnished lounge to the accompaniment of soft music wafting in from one of the latest auto-changing radiograms playing on the outside patio. Jim's eyes lingered for a little more than politeness demanded, at seeing girls serving drinks who would not have disgraced any local film lot. Over a leisurely round of cocktails, he was introduced to the elegantly gowned hostess, who was assured by JM's colleague that they were but passive observers, and that their visit was purely to satisfy the Scot's curiosity. Stranger requests had come her way, and she was happy to comply.

The chief source of amusement appears to have been in watching the Madame as she flicked through the pages of her well-thumbed private telephone directory. The charms and attentions of the starlets and aspiring film extras contained therein were but a telephone call away, even in the early hours of the morning. It appears that at least one star of international screen fame had started with her foot on the ladder by providing such a service. JM was assured that the LA Police Department had tacit instructions from the bosses of the film studios to turn a blind eye to such activities.

On 23 January 1936 the *Los Angeles Times* featured a picture of 'Colonel' James A. Mollison, alongside an article giving the aviator's views on the appointment of King Edward V111 as the new monarch of half a billion subjects of Great Britain and the Commonwealth. There was a fever-pitch interest in the USA in the new King's appointment at this time, owing to his much-publicised liaison with the American divorcée Wallis Simpson. It was too good a publicity opportunity for JM to miss, and he was able to share some of the personal anecdotes of his meeting four years earlier with the man who was then the Prince of Wales.

A week later the same newspaper carried a much less flattering article, reporting that the aviator had been charged in the Beverly Hills area for drunken driving.[122] JM was evidently on his way from a cocktail party to a nightclub when he was stopped, and being unable to pay the $10 fine he was taken into custody. Contrary to the opinion of those who said that he could often be extremely aggressive when under the influence of drink, he seems to have surrendered to authority without qualm on this occasion, and his fine was paid the following morning by friends. It must be said, that his arrest appears to have been far less painful than that of Amy's skirmish with Florida's police force a few years earlier.

☆ ☆ ☆

Having bid farewell to the Putnams, JM sailed out of San Francisco Bay on a blustery evening early in February on the SS *Lurline*, bound for Honolulu and eventually Australia. Matson Line's luxury liner, dubbed by its owners as the 'Queen of the Pacific', had been instrumental just over twelve months earlier, in assisting the passage of another distinguished long-distance flier in the opposite direction – albeit that she was not a passenger on that occasion. Amelia Earhart had set out from Hawaii in January 1935 in her Lockheed Vega, determined to be the first person to make the 2,098 mile transoceanic flight to Oakland alone, when she met up with the *Lurline* unexpectedly mid-way along the journey. Evidently AE's navigational skills

Dorothy Ward.

were none too finely honed, and at the time of the ship's sighting she had become quite unsure of her position. After signalling the ship's captain for a navigational fix, he had obligingly turned his ship around to point her in the correct direction. Jim Mollison's navigational difficulties were far less worrying on that windy evening as the ship slipped under the Golden Gate and headed into the far from peaceful Pacific. His route presented no greater hazard than finding his way back from the bar to his cabin.

It appears that JM's short stay in Honolulu was somewhat marred by the fact that he was virtually an unknown amongst the island's transient pleasure-seekers, and therefore he was forced to foot the bill for all of his own expenses. Not even the majestic view of Waikiki Beach from the balcony of his Royal Hawaiian apartment, with its wide sweep of curving white coral sand, fringed by palm trees and pounded by clear blue waters, could compensate for the agony of the basic hotel charges of £3 a day without food! Ruefully, he admits to getting through a total of £20 daily (£800 to £1,000 in today's currency!) with more than a few twinges of pain. It was all a far cry from being a repeat of the easy-going time he had enjoyed in Tahiti eight years earlier, and there were few regrets when he finally boarded the *Mariposa* bound for Sydney.

There is no doubt that during the Pacific sea crossing Mollison's thoughts turned to the business of making fresh record-breaking flights. He had now been inactive and away from the flying scene for almost sixteen months, and such an absence carried with it the double-edged penalty of reduced publicity, and more importantly, a drain on his financial resources. Wiley Post's outstanding solo circumnavigation of the globe in July 1933 was still a challenge to Mollison, who was keenly aware that it had only been made at a northerly latitude of between 45 and 60 degrees, thus giving it a distance some 10,000 miles less than one made at the equivalent of the equator. In all probability, if the one-eyed Indian from Oklahoma had lived (he was killed in a plane crash with the celebrated Will Rogers in 1935), the full equatorial distance would have been his next target.*

JM knew therefore that to be newsworthy such a plan had to include a full transoceanic flight across the Pacific. As he surveyed that seemingly endless waste of inhospitable ocean from the ship's rail, he must have mused not only on the possibility of finding a suitable aeroplane, but also on the flight's navigational difficulties whilst flying alone. Charles Ulm, his old ANA colleague, had perished even with the assistance of a crew on a flight from Oakland to Australia only fifteen months earlier. Amelia Earhart was soon to go the same way whilst attempting the 2,556 mile hop from British New Guinea to Howland Island. On that occasion she too had flown with the assistance of a navigator.

After brief stops at the islands of Pago Pago, Fiji and New Zealand's north island, JM stepped ashore at Sydney late in February 1936. During several interviews with the press over the next few weeks, he announced that he was in Australia merely to renew old friendships and to clear up some family matters that had arisen since the death of his father, some eighteen months earlier. Later on he outlined his plans for a round-the-world solo flight, giving his likely route as London, Australia, Fiji, Honolulu, Los Angeles, New York and back to London. It is interesting to note that at no time did he give any hint of a rift between himself and Amy. The nearest he ever came to doing so was when he emphasised that although he and Amy were still a man and wife team, they would, in future, be making record-breaking flights separately.

There is no doubt that he was a willing conspiritor in wanting to keep up the pretence of marital harmony, for at this particular time Amy was planning to stage a 'come back' by attempting to recapture her old England-Cape record. It had recently fallen to the genial and popular Flt. Lt. Tommy

*At that time the Australian Charles Kingsford Smith was the only aviator who could claim to have truly circumnavigated the globe by air, albeit in four stages. These flights were made between May 1928 and July 1930, and totalled a distance of approximately 25,000 miles.

Rose in February of that year. Amy was acutely aware that she was no longer holding the media's attention as the Empire's favourite aviatrix, at least not since Jean Batten had soloed the South Atlantic in the previous November. The plucky little New Zealander, six years younger than Amy, had piloted her silver Percival Gull monoplane along the same route as that followed by JM to Natal, and had knocked almost a whole day off his record. Bill Courtenay was now back on the scene acting as Amy's manager and was anxious that her plans be kept secret until she had actually commenced the flight. He had also advised her to write to her husband, warning him of the danger to her public image if news of a rift should leak out just before a major flight. JM obviously saw some mutual advantage in playing ball with the idea, and he even went so far as to announce that his wife might shortly fly her Beechcraft to Australia and join him.

Just how faithful JM was to Amy during the whole of his overseas trip is very much open to conjecture. There is every likelihood that he would have attempted to renew some of those 'old aquaintanceships' that he had known as an airline pilot in Sydney, Adelaide and Brisbane, and even to make one or two new ones. He was once asked by an enquiring female admirer whether he ever remembered the names of his many conquests, to which he replied, with his customary laconic wit, 'My dear, I never ever ask them their names.' We do know, however, that he received an invitation from Josephine Ulm, the aviator's widow and teacher at Sydney's Double Bay Public School, to speak to her pupils on his aviation exploits. It appears that the schoolchildren were particularly keen to know how he managed to keep awake for so long on his transatlantic flights. One small boy, who was keen to follow in the footsteps of his hero, had asked if it was possible to eat and fly at the same time, and was quite relieved when told that it was.

JM's plans to sail back to the UK were changed in favour of flying home, when he received a letter from Amy informing him that she was due to commence her second attempt on the Cape record from Gravesend early in May. After telephoning her, he caught the scheduled QANTAS flight from Brisbane to Singapore via Darwin, where he then had the opportunity of continuing the rest of his journey, either by Imperial Airways or KLM.

Upon his arrival at Singapore's Seletar aerodrome, he was met by one of his former Grosvenor cronies, the Sultan of Johore, ruler of the British protectorate and rubber producing state bordering Singapore. His wealthy host had a car waiting to whisk him off, all expenses paid, to an iced-champagne welcome preceding a three week holiday in one of his old stamping grounds, the Seaview Hotel. The liquor must have flowed quite freely during his stay there for the press were soon to report a fire in one of the bedrooms, caused when its occupant had fallen asleep with a lighted cigarette in his hand.[123] Fortunately for JM, a Chinese servant had been alerted by seeing smoke emanating from under the aviator's bedroom door, and had entered the smoke-filled room to put out the smouldering bedding and mosquito-net.

As soon as the partying was over and JM was prepared to depart, he made enquiries at the Imperial Airways' desk for the cost of a flight from Singapore to Croydon. Their response, however, did not quite match up to his expectations. He reasoned that any airline should be prepared to pay for the honour of his patronage and offer a discount on the standard £156 air fare accordingly. Disgruntled, he stormed off to the KLM desk where he was offerd and accepted a slightly better bargain. As soon as the local British press correspondents got hold of the story, they questioned his patriotism in flying on a foreign airline. JM argued that the Royal Dutch Airline offered a speedier service in more modern American airliners – they were making the journey to London in two days less than their British rivals – and that one could carry out a normal conversation in flight, without the necessity of shouting to be heard. Newspapers at home and abroad were soon carrying the headline, 'Mollison attacks Imperial Airways'.[124] It was an outburst that was to ultimately cost Mollison dear in the wartime years.

Undeterred, JM climbed the steps to board the Douglas DC2 airliner with his luggage prominently displaying the colourful KLM logo. Making his way up the aisle to the pilot's cabin, he was delighted to find the aircraft being captained by the well experienced Evert van Dyck. The Dutchman had been Charles Kingsford Smith's co-pilot, along with navigator Paddy Saul and radio-operator John Stannage, in the *Southern Cross*, during its memorable east-to-west crossing of the North Atlantic in 1930. With so much in common to chat over, the boredom of the journey must have passed much more speedily than it might have done. Fortunately for JM, the KLM flight touched down at Croydon airport just two days before Amy was due to leave for South Africa. The 'dutiful husband' had returned home.

Chapter 17

'The Dorothy'

Amy's first attempt at the Cape record in April 1936 had ended in near disaster when she ground-looped her brand new Percival Gull, G-ADZO, whilst making a take-off run at Colomb Bechar soon after refuelling. She had failed to correct the aircraft quickly enough from veering under a gusting desert wind, after it had hit a bumpy patch in the aerodrome's rough stony surface. As a consequence, the small pale blue monoplane spun around violently in a cloud of dust, tearing off its starboard undercarriage before its propeller dug in to tip the aircraft ignominiously onto its nose. Amy was left weeping in the cockpit and stranded 1,500 miles from home in Algeria, but not for long. Displaying a similar grit and fortitude that she had shown during her momentous Australian flight, she had, with the assistance of the admiring Peter Reiss (from Amy's flying log it seems that he appeared back on the scene during JM's absence), managed to fly the damaged Gull back to the UK.

Jim must have wondered just what kind of a reception he was about to receive from a justifiably aggrieved wife, when he rang the doorbell of her newly rented Gate House cottage at 59a Ennismore Gardens in Kensington, that Spring. In view of the imminence of her departure for South Africa which was timed for the next full moon, and the risks that she was about to undertake, it is unlikely that there was any enthusiasm for scathing recriminations on her part. They agreed on a temporary truce between them until she returned, whereupon they would make a serious re-appraisal of their marriage commitment. Amy certainly appears to have accepted the situation with commonsense and more than a little good grace, for she is on record as telling her parents that her husband would look after her affairs whilst she was away.[125]

Jim was more than pleased to play his part in the publicity exercise that Bill Courtenay was anxious to stage-manage for Amy on the morning of her departure from the aerodrome at Gravesend. Under the watchful eyes of

Fleet Street's reporters and news-cameramen, the couple embraced in a farewell kiss, before Amy, elegantly clad in her Schiaparelli designed oxford-blue outfit with matching culottes, stepped into the cockpit. From thereon, she was to be back in the nation's headlines intermittently for the next ten days. She smashed the previous record on the outward flight by one day, fourteen hours and forty minutes; and by over two days on the total time for the completed return journey. Jim was there at Croydon to be photographed jubilantly greeting her by running alongside her aircraft, hand on wing tip, as she taxied towards the airport buildings and the waiting crowds. Some have said in later years that he was only cashing in on his wife's popularity and fame, whilst others, who served with him during his wartime service and knew him intimately, would argue that he was genuinely pleased with her successes.

Upon Amy's return, the Mollisons got down to some very straight talking on their marriage prospects. Jim decided that the best policy was to make a clean breast of all his past infidelities, even admitting to their commence-ment within one month of their wedding. Amy could hardly have been unaware of his behaviour for it was bruited around quite freely amongst their friends, but, there is no doubt she was taken aback by the extent of it. Francois Dupré had been urging her for some time to start divorce proceedings against her husband, doubtless with the motive of leaving her free to marry him. Peter Reiss, and no doubt many other admirers, were waiting in the wings for the marriage's final collapse. In spite of Amy's gullibility in accepting JM's promise to turn over a new leaf, they did not have to wait long for the impending crash.

The commonly held view of JM's character was that he was a cad, or a bounder, or both. They are nouns that were very much in vogue from Victorian times until the late Thirties to describe a character who indulged in such unscrupulous sexual behaviour. Harold Macmillan's biographer, Alistair Horne, recalls that the former Prime Minister once held finely graded definitions of these two terms, explanations which had a graphic way of illustrating the difference between them. For him, a bounder was a man who went to fight on the front in time of war, and where he wins numerous outstanding decorations for bravery. He then goes on leave, during which time he seduces his colonel's wife. On the other hand a cad manages to dodge enlistment altogether, but seduces the colonel's wife anyway. On that score JM would almost certainly qualify as a bounder!

Temptation was soon to be placed in JM's pathway, not long after his reconciliation with Amy, when Beryl Markham arrived in London. The tall, willowy blonde – something of a Vanessa Redgrave look-alike – had piloted a Leopard Moth from Nairobi to London in several stages whilst accompanied by Baron Bror von Blixen-Finecke. Her companion had at one time been the husband of Beryl's friend, the authoress Karen Blixen, renowned for her classic book *Out of Africa*. Bror was more or less hitchiking a ride on his way home to his native Sweden, whilst Beryl had come to the UK to make plans for becoming the first woman to solo the North Atlantic westward. Another reason for her visit was to pursue her old flame Tom Campbell Black. The aviator had taught her to fly whilst he was working for Wilson Airways in Nairobi and they had soon become lovers. However, after his winning coup with Scott in the MacRobertson air race, he had dropped Beryl in favour of the actress Florence Desmond.

Perhaps it was inevitable that Beryl Markham and Jim Mollison should be thrown together, for, apart from the heavy drinking, they were in many ways aviation's male and female counterparts. Both managed to be sexually promiscuous without any pangs of conscience, even when married. Both were possessed with an inordinate amount of courage when it came to making hazardous long-distance flights. As an enthusiastic member of Kenya's notorious Happy Valley set, Beryl had earned a reputation for cool permissiveness. Her first husband Jock Purves had tried unsuccessfully to tame her wild ways, and it was rumoured that he had angrily knocked nails in a post outside of their front door in order to shame her, each one representing her many lovers. Similarly, she and JM were irresponsible in matters of finance, inasmuch as they were both completely uninhibited when it came to leaving a trail of unpaid debts behind them. JM had been introduced to Beryl by Tom Campbell Black as someone who would be able to advise her on the navigational aspects of an Atlantic westward crossing. Not surprisingly, the Scot was more than willing to help such an attractive competitor.

With Fleet Street showing a renewed interest in the Mollison name ever since Amy's return from South Africa, Jim and Amy began to set their sights on fresh fields to conquer in aviation. They had no doubt heard rumours of Amelia Earhart's determination to be the first to make a full encirclement of the globe, and yet they knew that with the navigational complications of a long Pacific crossing, it was too hazardous for it to be undertaken by either of them solo. Accordingly, they floated the idea of their interest in acquiring one of the DH Comets for the purpose, but it came to nothing. With Nazi Germany now beginning to flex its military muscles in Europe, rearmament of the RAF had become a top priority. Hitler was becoming increasingly strident in his demands for what he termed as *lebensraum* and had, earlier in the year, moved three battalions of the Wehrmacht into the demilitarised zone of the Rhineland in defiance of the Locarno Treaty. As a consequence of the military threat from Germany, the design office staff of the country's aircraft industry were now more concerned with perfecting machines such as the Hurricane, Spitfire and Blenheim, than they were with the luxury of developing long-distance record-breaking aircraft.

Britain's pre-occupation with rearmament, also thwarted the Mollisons' attempt to find suitable aircraft for them to compete individually in the forthcoming England-South Africa air race. This event had been planned to rival the MacRobertson of 1934, and had been sponsored by the wealthy industrialist, I. W. Schlesinger, with a donation of prize money totalling £10,000. Its aim was to celebrate the opening of the Johannesburg Empire Exhibition, and at the same time give the British aircraft industry a chance to display its wares in South Africa. But it was ill-timed, and the fact that entries had been restricted to competitors flying British hardware, meant that there was eventually to be only nine competitors. Jim's interest in the race finally waned when he realised that only the three extremely fast, single-seat Percival Mew Gulls had any chance of success, and that these had already been allocated to South Africans, Captain Stan Halse and Major Allister Miller, and to his old rival Tom Campbell Black.

During the summer of 1936, Jim and Amy made every effort to give the public all the outward appearances of being a contented married couple. The mask was to slip, however, on more than one occasion. They accepted the usual invitations to attend social functions around the country, and at the end of May they flew to Hedon to visit Amy's parents. Will and Ciss Johnson had now retired to live by the sea at Bridlington, and it was a convenient stopover for Amy to perform the official opening ceremony at Sewerby Hall on the following day. Pictures taken at the time show a rather bored-looking Jim Mollison sitting alongside his sister-in-law Molly, the Mayor and Mayoress and other official town dignitaries, whilst a crowd of some 10,000 listened to Amy's speech. After her death in 1941, her parents were eventually to present most of her trophies and memorabilia to the Hall, where they remain to this day in a room devoted to her memory. Significantly, very little remains to show that she was ever married to Jim Mollison, a good indicator of her husband's unpopularity with the Johnson family.

The Mollisons' attempt to keep up with the charade is further exposed during this time by the memories of one particular Bolton businessman, William Davies. He had gone with three friends to stay at the Norbreck Hydro, Blackpool, for a golfing holiday. Evidently Jim and Amy were also booked into the hotel and he recalls that:

In those days the Norbreck was teetotal and the nearest place that you could get a drink was across the fields at the 'Red Lion' on the edge of Bispham village. During the night Jim Mollison had returned and there was a blazing row. Jim and Amy were arguing outside, which woke many of us up. Jim was unsteady on his feet and fell back into the ornamental pond outside the entrance, with the result that Amy became hysterical and was shouting about going somewhere. She left in a car and apparently went to the airport at Stanley Park where she attempted to fly off in her aeroplane. Fortunately, she failed to do so. Someone there was able to persuade her that she was in no fit state.[126]

In one last desperate attempt to save her marriage, Amy decided to spend the whole of August 1936 on holiday with Jim at Juan-les-Pins on the Riviera. As far as she was concerned it was his last chance to change his ways, but as the adage goes, the leopard never does. Whilst we have no record of his misbehaviour on the holiday, it was evidently sufficiently bad enough for Amy to approach her solicitors upon her return home, instructing them to commence divorce proceedings immediately. There is every possibility that there was an undisguised flirtation going on during this holiday between JM and the woman who was soon to become the second Mrs Mollison.

☆ ☆ ☆

Guiseppe Mario Bellanca was born in Sicily in 1886, and had emigrated to the USA along with many of Europe's other 'huddled masses' to settle in Brooklyn in 1910. From an early age he had had a passion for flying, and with the extensive engineering knowledge that he had acquired in Italy, was soon into designing his own aircraft. Acclaimed by the American press as 'the genius of the aerofoil', he was to become one of the world's finest aircraft designers during the late 1920s and early 1930s. But for the intransigence of his arrogant partner, Charles Levine, he might well have had the honour of supplying Lindbergh with a Bellanca machine for his 1927 New York-Paris flight, rather than the Ryan monoplane the American eventually used. Lindbergh had initially approached the Italian in order to purchase a promising Bellanca design, installed with the proven Wright Whirlwind engine. Levine had told him that the price was $15,000 and the young man from Detroit had departed hotfoot to raise the cash from a group of businessmen in St Louis. After returning to New York, he placed a cheque on the desk in front of Levine sufficient to cover the cost. By this time Levine had moved the goalposts and was stipulating that although he would sell to Lindbergh, he still retained the right to choose the pilot who flew it. Without any fuss, Lindbergh cooly picked up his cheque and left the office to catch a train for San Diego, home of the Ryan Company. The rest is history.

After breaking his partnership with Levine, Bellanca went on to design a series of successful aircraft, including the record-setting Columbia – the first aircraft ever to make two Atlantic crossings – and Pacemaker and Skyrocket types in 1932 and 1933. Jim Mollison had first become aware of the potential of the factory's designs, when he inspected the Irish Hospitals Trust entry for the MacRobertson air race at Mildenhall in October 1934. Their powerful Bellanca Flash 28-70,* a two-seat monoplane with a range of 3,000 miles and cruising speed of 235 mph at 15,000 feet, and named the *The Irish Swoop*, was to have been flown in the race by Colonel James Fitzmaurice, formerly of the Irish Air Corps, and ex-RAF Sergeant Pilot, Eric 'Jock' Bonar. It had, however, been disqualified by the Royal Aero Club's race committee at the very last moment because of its lack of certified approval for full-load landing tests. The only alternative the officials would permit was for the load not to exceed 5,400 lb, but Fitzmaurice complained to no avail that this be increased to 8,000 lb if they were to compete on equal terms with the three Comets. The decision caused much bitterness because the American authorities had already deemed that such tests were really unnecessary. Their argument was based on the fact that the machine's main 400 gallon fuel tank was fitted with a dump valve, which could jettison its entire contents within 20 seconds.

Jock Bonar had eventually accompanied the aircraft back to the Newcastle factory at Delaware aboard the *Majestic*, where it was to undergo further tests with different engine cowlings. It was during one of these tests in April 1935, with Bonar at the controls, that the aircraft was badly damaged in a landing incident. The wreckage was subsequently dragged into the corner of the hangar, where it was to languish until the summer of 1936. By then Guiseppe Bellanca had heard of Jim Mollison's plan to have another crack at the North Atlantic record and immediately wired the Scot, giving him the aircraft's performance figures and promising him an early delivery date. JM, never one to dally, wired back a deposit on the offer price of $28,000, approximately £5,600 in those days of a strong sterling currency.

His ambitious plan was to fly the Bellanca in three spectacular stages. One from New York to Croydon, via Newfoundland, and thereby hopefully setting a new Atlantic record. And then after a brief stop for servicing, to proceed down the continent of Africa trusting that he would break Amy's Cape record on the way. Finally, he proposed, after the minimum of delay at Wingfield, to fly on to Australia. The only major changes to be made to the

*The designation signified a wing area of 280 square feet, and the use of a 700 hp Pratt & Whitney Twin Wasp R-1830 engine.

Mollison's Bellanca Flash 28-70, *The Dorothy*, named, much to the chagrin of Amy, in honour of his actress friend Dorothy Ward.

aircraft, now registered NR 190M, were the strengthening of the wings and the shortening of the two kingposts, now linked together into a longitudinal skid-member and carrying the lift wires on the underside of the fuselage.

Unfortunately for Mollison, the Bellanca Flash was not to be ready before the end of September. It left him little time for familiarisation with his new purchase and very close to the time when Atlantic weather conditions were considered to be well past their best for a solo crossing, especially in an unproven single-engined aircraft.

☆ ☆ ☆

After making her last attempt at a reconciliation with her husband, Amy had, not unnaturally, asked him to leave her Gate House residence. Reluctantly, he had moved out and into the Hyde Park Hotel. It was during this period, whilst he was waiting for the Bellanca to be prepared, that JM spent much of his time with his current 'romance', Beryl Markham. It seems rather ironical that she had throughout that summer been employed by none other than Francois Dupré. Her introduction to the wealthy Frenchman had been made through her estranged husband, Mansfield Markham, who was a very good friend of the hotelier. As a result, she had become Dupré's personal pilot with the Air Cruises company – the venture in which Amy was so anxious to become a partner. One wonders whether the promise to the two women of a partnership in the financier's aviation company, was but a bait and crude blandishment for the return of covert sexual favours. Whether Beryl was more compliant in this respect than her successor Amy Mollison, is not known. She was however acknowledged to be the archetypal enchantress, and had quickly learnt from an early age that doors readily swing wide open for pretty blondes with charm. This is most clearly illustrated by the fact that she even cajoled her ex-lover and mentor, Tom Campbell Black, who was at this time recently married to Florence Desmond, into giving her practical flying tuition in Dupré's luxuriously equipped DH Dragon. Although she had logged approximtely 2,000 hours over a six year flying period in Africa, mainly as an aerial wild game spotter in Tanganika and Uganda and on various flights to South Africa, they were all accrued on single-engined aeroplanes. It was therefore an expertise she needed in order to obtain her licence rating for twin-engined aircraft.

Beryl had also managed to find a sponsor for her proposed Atlantic crossing through the generosity of the wealthy Kenyan planter and keen amateur pilot, Lord Carberry. The two had known each other in Nairobi, and during a dinner party in a London hotel, Carberry spontaneously offered to loan Beryl the Percival Vega Gull that he had ordered for the Johannesberg air race. His only stipulation was that she must fly non-stop from England to New York and return the aircraft before the start of the race, which was due to commence in late September.

JM was her constant companion just before the flight, for who better than he to advise her on the difficulties that she was likely to encounter on a solo westward crossing. Although the news of the Mollisons' impending divorce had not yet officially broken, gossip was rife after photographs appeared in the London press showing Jim and Beryl partying together just before her departure. She had decided to fly from RAF Abingdon, and Edgar Percival, accompanied by engineer Jock Cameron, had flown Lord Carberry's silver and turquoise Vega Gull, *The Messenger*, from Gravesend on September 1st in readiness. Weather forecasts over the Atlantic continued to be unfavourable but by Friday the 4th Beryl decided to wait no longer.

With JM at the controls of a hired Puss Moth and Beryl seated behind him, the couple flew in from Croydon under a storm-laden sky. He did his best to persuade her to delay the flight but to no avail. Just before she climbed onto the wing of her aircraft in the late afternoon, JM unstrapped his gold wrist-watch, the one he had used on his own Atlantic crossing in 1932, and handed it to her with the wry comment: 'Here Beryl, don't get this one wet.' It was more than a friendly gesture or lucky charm, for it enabled her to wear it set with a five hour time delay registering Eastern Standard Time, whilst her own watch was set to GMT. JM felt that it would prove helpful once she had made a landfall on the Newfoundland coast and as she made her way down to New York.

At 6.50pm she opened the throttle wide and splashed down the mile-long, puddled runway. The small monoplane lifted its 185 gallons of fuel into a grey overcast, which was grudgingly allowing weak shafts of sunlight to penetrate its gloom. Twenty-four hours, forty minutes and 2,700 miles later, the tiny Vega Gull upended noiselessly onto its nose in a peat bog near Baleine Cove, Cape Breton, just one hundred yards from the shoreline. The flight had been an amazing demonstration of the woman's courage and navigational skills, and equally worthy of the other two British 'firsts' – namely, those of Alcock & Brown and Mollison. And whilst she did not make New York non-stop, at least she had the satisfaction of knowing that she was the first woman to make the solo crossing westward.

Unfortunately, Tom Campbell Black never lived long enough to congratulate Beryl personally on her achievement. Two weeks after her successful crossing, he was killed in a rather stupid flying accident at the Speke aerodrome. Evidently, he was taxying the Percival Mew Gull, G-AEKL, *Miss Liverpool*, so named because of its sponsorship by John Moores, owner of the Liverpool football-pools syndicate, when he was struck by an incoming Hawker Hart two-seat light bomber. A combination of errors, whereby Black was studying a map whilst taxying towards a take-off position, at the same time a young RAF pilot was landing with the sun directly into his eyes, resulted in the Hart landing on top of the sporty squat racer. The bomber's propeller sliced the Mew Gull almost in half, mid-way along its fuselage at the cockpit. Black was rushed to hospital but succumbed to his injuries within a short while. His newly wed wife Florence Desmond was devastated, and one wonders just what effect it also had on Beryl when Jim telephoned her in New York with the tragic news.

With ten days to go before the commencement of the Johannesberg air race, Amy Mollison announced that she was prepared to fly the *Miss Liverpool* if Percivals could repair the damaged machine in time. In spite of Amy protesting that her intention to fly it was in honour of Tom Campbell Black, she was bitterly criticised. Many thought that she was just cashing in on Florence Desmond's grief, in an attempt to outshine the publicity that JM was receiving on his forthcoming Atlantic crossing. As it transpired, her proposal did not materialise because the Percival factory was unable to do the work in time. Strangely enough, Jim Mollison was to purchase the rebuilt racer two years later, whereupon, with a fair degree of nostalgia for his old ANA flying days with Kingsford Smith, he renamed it *Southern Cloud*. He even offered it to Amy in 1938, along with all his maps and equipment, when she was going through a bad patch, and so that she could re-establish her finances by making a long-distance flight in it. She declined the offer however, for by then she had lost all zest for such ventures. G-AEKL was to be an ill-fated machine as far as JM was concerned. At the outbreak of war it was hangared at Lympne and destroyed by fire when the aerodrome was attacked by Stukas during the late summer of 1940.

☆ ☆ ☆

Jim Mollison sailed into New York on 25 September, ready to collect the Bellanca Flash from the Newcastle factory at Delaware as soon as possible. He was anxious to make the eastward crossing before the weather conditions made it too hazardous an undertaking. The reader may find it hard to believe that regular scheduled passenger flights across the North Atlantic were still over two years away in 1936. Early October was deemed the latest for such a venture in those days, and it appears that there was a delay in the rebuilding and testing of the aircraft of at least three weeks beyond its promised delivery date. To use JM's phrase it was 'a rush-built job'.

When the aircraft had been used by James Fitzmaurice and Jock Bonar as the *The Irish Swoop*, it had been liveried with a white fuselage and yellow cowling, together with green wings. As *The Dorothy*, its colour scheme became even more garish, with an orange fuselage, fin and rudder, complemented by green wings and tailplane. One can only conjecture, a half a century later, on the reason for JM's instruction to the factory to use this particular colour scheme. There is a strong possibility that Dorothy Ward put some money into its purchase, as is evidenced by the name he gave to the racer, in which case the aircraft's livery might well have been made in deference to Dorothy's Irish husband – the actor and comedian, Shaun Glenville. On the other hand, knowing JM's contempt for C. G. Grey, it might well have been used to ruffle a few feathers of his journalistic protagonist. The irascible editor of *The Aeroplane* was a constant critic of hazardous long-distance flights made by solo aviators, particularly those of the Mollisons. Moreover, in spite of spending his early years in Dublin as the son of an ex-patriate Northumbrian functionary, he was almost paranoid about all things emanating from the Emerald Isle.

There is no doubt that the attractive Dorothy Ward, doyenne of pantomime's principal boys, was infatuated by the playboy Jim Mollison.

The actress's son, film director and Broadway producer Peter Glenville,* believes that their affair was a romance, but not a flagrant one. In his opinion, their relationship might best be described as being one of passionate friends rather than lovers. During a telephone conversation he added:

> Remember, that at forty-six my mother was 'on the edge', and therefore quite flattered by his attentions as he was by hers. It was no more than a highly-geared mutual flirtation. She was very kind to Amy and admired the Mollisons greatly. Amusingly, whenever she recalled Jim, she would demurely refer to him as *that splendid cad.*[127]

By the time JM flew *The Dorothy* on the short flight from the Bellanca works in Delaware, to the Floyd Bennett Field in Brooklyn, Amy had told the press that she and Jim had agreed to separate. She had crashed her Beechcraft a few days earlier at Chelsfield near Orpington whilst returning from Paris in bad weather and low on fuel, and as a consequence, she had let the story out to reporters who were gathered at her Gate House residence. She told them that from now on, she wished to be simply known by her maiden name of Amy Johnson. On the following morning, Fleet Street's newspaper headlines were reading, 'Mollisons to Split'.

The effect of her press release was to encourage a great deal of unwarranted but welcome sympathy for JM in the USA. Amy had left herself in a no win situation. She was now seen as kicking her husband in the teeth at the very moment when he was about to risk his life on a dangerous crossing of the Atlantic, late in the autumn of the year, and in an unproven and hitherto troublesome aeroplane. Should he not survive the crossing, and subsequently she mourned him, then she would be seen as a hypocrite. Should she show no public grief, then she would be slated as hard-bitten and uncaring. The possibility of JM's early demise was far from improbable, for earlier that month the Swedish pilot Kurt Bjorkvall had almost perished in a similar flight, when he was forced to ditch his Bellanca Pacemaker about one hundred miles from Ireland. Prior to the flight most of the empty spaces in the aircaft's structure had been filled with ping-pong balls, as a precaution for something that was to become a reality. Bjorkvall had left Floyd Bennett Field on the 6th, aiming to make an estimated 25 hour flight to Stockholm non-stop, when a blockage in the fuel supply caused engine failure. Miraculously, the machine floated for many hours, until late in the afternoon the aircraft was sighted by a French trawler and the pilot rescued.

JM enjoyed the unsolicited publicity from Amy's statement while he could, as the New York press and its sob-sisters clamoured for an interview.

---

*Peter Glenville directed Richard Burton in the film *Becket*.

Dixie Tighe of the *New York Mirror*, known for her opportunism and hyped up reporting methods, portrayed JM as the wounded husband. She was the wife of Cecil Thompson, Beaverbrook's New York representative, and it was probably through this connection that JM received the offer of an accompanying co-pilot. The Hon. Max Aitken, Lord Beaverbrook's son, (later to be decorated with the DSO and DFC during WW2) volunteered to occupy the rear cockpit on the Atlantic crossing, but by then JM had learned a trick or two from George Putnam and was not about to let anyone steal his thunder. He would go alone, or not at all.

Jim kicked his heels around in New York for two days awaiting a suitable North Atlantic weather report from Doc Kimball. The Scot was by now an old hand at Atlantic crossings, having already made three, and he had developed an amazing patience when it came to waiting for the right moment to go. Knowing that his reputation was at stake, he had determined that if all else failed he would fly back to Croydon via the more clement South Atlantic route. In the meantime, he hit the New York night scene much like a prisoner facing execution, with the consolation of being offered the indulgence of his last whim.

On the night that he was to depart for Harbour Grace, Newfoundland, he had visited the Club Richman, where his old friend Harry Richman ran one of Manhattan's glitziest nightspots. The two men had much in common. Both were ardent womanisers. Harry, who at one time had been engaged to Hollywood's celebrated 'It' girl – the sex-goddess Clara Bow – had been Broadway's original song and dance man. The straw hat, cane, high kick and lisping voice were his stock in trade, long before Frankie Vaughan was born. He had appeared in the film *Putting on the Ritz* with Joan Bennett, even before Fred Astaire had made the song famous. He had also been the star of several Broadway shows and as a consequence his club now attracted the rich and famous. Moreover, he was hooked on the flying scene, having accompanied Eastern Airlines pilot Dick Merrill on a return Atlantic flight*, which was made only weeks before his 1936 meeting with Mollison. It was, therefore, inevitable, that JM should be magnetically drawn towards Richman.

The forty-one year old Jewish night club owner specialised in putting on spectacular floor shows at the Richman,** and on the night that JM entered

*On 2 September 1936, Henry T. 'Dick' Merrill and the New York entertainer left Floyd Bennett Field in the Vultee monoplane *Lady Peace* to cover the 3,300 miles to Llwyncelyn, Wales, in 18 hours and 38 minutes – a record time. Their return flight was made from Southport beach, Lancashire, on 14 September, but they were forced to land at Musgrave Harbour after flying 2,300 miles in 17 hours and 24 minutes. After repairs to the aircraft they flew on to New York, thereby becoming the first to make a return North Atlantic crossing.
** Joan Crawford had worked for Harry Richman as a chorus girl under the name of Lucille Le Sueur, long before making her break into films.

the club, he had matched him up with one of his more glamorous girl dancers. Maybe it was all part of the aviator's carefully stage-managed publicity, who knows? According to JM, he and the girl had then left the club on a spree which took them from bar to bar. Knowing that a favourable weather report meant an imminent departure, he managed to leave a message with each bartender of his intended whereabouts.

By the early hours of the morning, he and his brunette girlfriend were back at her Brooklyn apartment when the message came through that weather conditions were the best that he was likely to get. Not wanting to waste time in going back to his hotel for a change of clothes, he hurriedly covered his black tuxedo with a loaned pair of grey flannels and a borrowed raincoat, before phoning for a cab. As JM and his transitory paramour made their way through the silent empty streets to the airport, the first yellowish streaks of dawn began to break over the city's skyline.

They were met by the usual crowd of voracious news-reporters and gossip columnists milling around to get their story, especially now that Amy had announced her decision to go her own way. Awaiting him at the Floyd Bennett Field was a cablegram from Amy wishing him good luck on the flight. At least she had done the polite thing and not ignored the danger he was now facing. Instructing the brunette, who was now warming to the occasion, to move discreetly into the background, – she didn't exactly fit in with the image of the distraught husband – Jim traded witticisms with his inquisitors, one of whom had by now spotted the partially hidden dinner clothes.* 'Oh, yes, I'm ready for dinner invitations as soon as I arrive in London.' 'I do my best flying at night, so you see I am properly dressed.' 'What if I meet icing of the wings on the way over?' 'Well, it'll come in useful with the brandy and soda.' They loved it. It was just what their readers liked. What they didn't know, was that Guiseppe Bellanca had already warned him that he had no permission to fly *The Dorothy* outside of U.S. airspace. Moreover, he had been advised by the self-effacing little Italian, that he must remove the U.S. registration markings and re-register the aircraft with the British authorities before leaving. Such niceties had little importance for a man now anxious to be on his way before the winter weather conditions closed in on him, and they were duly ignored.

---

*William E. Parsons, author of *The Challenge of the Atlantic*, was present at Harbour Grace when Mollison landed on the afternoon of 28 October 1936. He maintains that the aviator was wearing ordinary clothing under his flying gear. The two photographs of Mollison which appear in his book, certainly do show him wearing a lounge suit over a cricketer's type, vee-necked pullover with collar and tie. However, with all due respect to the author, these pictures appear to have been taken on the day *after* his arrival, by which time he had probably changed his clothing.

After buckling on his parachute harness over the heavy flying suit, one that had once belonged to the late Charles Kingsford Smith, JM climbed into the front cockpit of the wire-braced monoplane. Earlier, when he sought to put on the rubber boots that went with the flying suit, he found that he had lost one somewhere along the way. There was no time to go back looking for it now. With a wave of the hand the chocks were pulled and he was away.

The first leg of his journey would take him some 1,200 miles to the northeast. To the desolate and frozen 4,000 feet long airstrip at Harbour Grace, which was experiencing its first cold spell of the winter. Bill Parsons, correspondent for Associated Press and International Newsphoto Service, was covering the flight from Newfoundland on the afternoon when JM flew in 6 hours and 41 minutes after leaving New York. He recalls that:

> Shortly before 5.00pm on October 28th *The Dorothy* was sighted over the airstrip at Harbour Grace. It circled three times and headed westward right into the eyes of the glazing light of the setting sun. Skimming the promontory at the eastern end and landing on one wheel, and by skillful manoeuvering, the craft came to its balance and stopped about halfway up the runway . . . The first thing he asked for when he stepped down from the airplane was a cigarette.
>
> As the only communication system from Newfoundland at the time was by a commercial cable through St John's. I usually visited the local postal telegraph office to see if any information on the flight was available. The operator gave me a telegram for Jim Mollison and in consequence of this I made sure that I reached him upon arrival (I understand that the content of the telegram was relative to their impending divorce).
>
> In conversation with him for a line on his flight, he informed me that coming east on the Newfoundland leg he experienced a lot of rain and flew quite a distance with the hood open; and said that his charts were wet and would I kindly see that they were dried off. As he was taking them from the chart-box there was a flask of *Four Roses* whiskey which he gave me. A friend and I soon made quick work of it.[128]

Bill Parsons might well have been wrong in his surmise on the content of the telegram, for it is on record that Doc Kimball and others cabled JM the news that he could expect further rain and sleet 500 miles out to sea, as well as high winds. On the strength of that, Mollison decided to spend the night at Harbour Grace. The machine was tanked up with 610 gallons ready to go, and JM took dinner in the Archibald Hotel with one or two local aviators and businessmen, before retiring for the night onto a cold, hard bed in the nearby Cochrane House. One can glean from the various newspaper accounts of the time that JM was far from confident about his chances of survival. All four weather reports, each from a different source, agreed on one point, and that was that conditions over the Atlantic were unfavourable. Some would say suicidal. They only differed inasmuch as they predicted winds of between 30 and 60mph, and whether there would be snowstorms, or sleet, or ice somewhere along the way. Inevitably, thoughts of Bjorkvall's miraculous escape a few weeks earlier must have been uppermost in his mind. This time there would be no ping-pong balls or rubber dinghys, just a parachute for the slim and unlikely chance that if anything went wrong, then he might be near to a ship.

During the late afternoon of the following day, JM made a last minute decision to wait no longer. Jock Bonar recalls how JM later described that particular period, with the following:

> By the time he arrived at Harbour Grace, Newfoundland, he didn't feel like going because not only had he been without any real sleep for two days, the weather reports were now no longer as optimistic. All the local inhabitants were waiting to see this celebrated airman take off and the place was full of reporters. Jim went into the toilet to put on a jersey and pull a pair of serge trousers over his dinner suit, hoping to give himself added warmth on the flight. At the same time he was thinking, 'If I hang around in the toilet long enough, they will all go away and I can chicken out without too much loss of face.' When he finally came out, they were all still there. He told me later, 'You see Jock, I had to b***** well go.'[129]

According to Bill Parsons, JM was in such a hurry to leave on that afternoon that he failed to clear customs 'because of the loss of time that would have been involved'. It is far more likely that JM realised that he might well have been forbidden to leave the country owing to the stipulations of which Bellanca had already warned him. Small wonder that the newspaper reports of the time describe him as being nervous and depressed just before he left. As it transpired, the Harbour Grace authorities slapped a $200 fine on him for failing to clear their customs. It was not the last time that he was to be in trouble with customs' evasion.

At precisely 4.40pm (EST), and after 'only a short warm up of the engine, JM took off downhill in a westerly direction, did a slow climbing turn and headed out to sea without circling the field'. The hurried take-off had been made with the assistance of maximum boost from the engine's supercharger. It was a device which enabled *The Dorothy* to lift its incredibly heavy 4,276 lb load of fuel, oil and equipment – not to mention at least one bottle of brandy – into an already darkening sky. JM craned his neck around to snatch one

Jim Mollison arrives at Croydon in *The Dorothy* on Friday, 30 October 1936, having set a new transatlantic record time of 13 hours 17 minutes for the solo crossing.

brief glance below, as the flickering lights of the small fishing town slid into the gloom of the landscape.

During the first hour he made a long, slow climb to 15,000 feet with the canopy hood wide open and levelled off into a clear moonlit sky. He was cruising at 220 mph on a steady compass heading for the next two and a half hours, until he began to run into sleet, and then worse. At first he noticed that spots of oil from the engine began to freeze into an icy film over the screen, whilst ice also started to form along the leading edges of the wings. Ahead of him lay an occluded front, a dark mass of vicious looking cumulo-nimbus, into which he was now loathe to enter. It warranted him taking a few gulps of brandy, before circling for the next forty-five minutes trying to find a belt of warmer air, all the time aware that he was using up precious fuel. Eventually, he took the plunge and entered the uninviting black towers, whereupon, for ten stretched out minutes, the adrenalin was pumping overtime. As he emerged into a clear sky and welcoming moon, he cursed the weather men for the time he had wasted. The clearer skies enabled him to confirm his position from the stars, and as it became lighter he could check his drift from the waves below as he pressed on.

Just before dawn, he caught his first sight of land on the eastern horizon after 2,000 miles of inhospitable ocean – it was the Valentia lighthouse in southern Ireland. It confirmed that his navigation was spot on and he could now relax as he made for the Welsh coast and skirted the Bristol Channel. His map-reading became a trifle sloppy from hereon, and he ended up some twenty miles to the north of London, over Hatfield, before he realised he was off course.

At 9.57am the wheels of the faithful Bellanca skidded as they tore at the grass of Croydon's runway at 90 mph, only sixteen minutes after his estimated time of arrival. It was the first direct flight from the north American continent to London, and he had set a record time for the Atlantic crossing of 13 hours and 17 minutes, in spite of the unnecessary delay due to icing. Over the entire 3,498 miles from New York, he had averaged 173 mph, the fastest yet.

Several hundred people were there in front of the main airport building to greet him, including Bill Courtenay, but no Amy. One reporter, a little bolder than the rest, asked the fatigued pilot if he would like him to telephone Amy on his behalf and received a curt, 'Certainly, not'. His first request was for a stiff drink but unfortunately the bar of the 'Aerodrome Hotel' was not yet open and he had to be content with a ginger beer. It was not long before representatives of the *Daily Express*, the newspaper which had purchased the world copyright on his story, whisked him away to his Hyde Park Hotel for a press interview. There must have been quite a commotion as they entered the hotel foyer, for as a porter went to assist him with his gear, he lifted the parachute by its ripcord handle and the contents of its silk canopy spilled out across the floor.

As a PR man, Bill Courtenay was no slouch when it came to the packaging of his clients' image, particularly that of the Mollisons. Not only did he secure the *Daily Express* contract for JM but he also arranged for him to make a BBC broadcast in their *Radio Gazette* programme on the Saturday morning. What is perhaps even more surprising, is that he conducted an interview with JM two days later in front of the television cameras during the opening of the first regular television broadcast to be made in Britain. They appeared together in the first programme of *Picture Page*, a weekly feature which went out during the evening from Alexandra Palace.

Dorothy Ward was currently appearing in pantomime at the King's Theatre, Edinburgh, and one can gauge the depth of her feeling for the Scot, by the fact that she took the trouble to catch a train to London to greet her admirer during the evening of his arrival. On the following morning, he accompanied the glamourous actress to Croydon, where they boarded an Olley Air Services aircraft for Turnhouse, near Edinburgh. Press photographs taken at the time show Dorothy dressed to kill in a full length fox fur, complete with a rather appealing William Tell style hat tilted jauntily over one eye. That afternoon she led him onto the stage of the theatre at the end of her matinee performance to a loud applause. For the 'King of the Air' it was all a far cry from his early days as a rebellious schoolboy at Edinburgh Academy.

As JM boarded the Olley Air Service DH Rapide on the following day for the return flight, he was surprised to find that the aircraft was being piloted by someone who had recently acquired almost as much notoriety as he had himself. Four months previously, Captain Cecil Bebb had been the man who had flown the Nationalist leader General Franco from out of exile in the Canary Islands to Morocco, where the initial uprising against the Republican Government had begun at the outset of the Spanish Civil War. JM had already made it known through the press, that he had now decided that he would take a co-pilot along with him on his proposed attack on his wife's Cape record. Letters from various enquirers, some with no flying experience whatsoever, were piling up on JM's bedside table at the Hyde Park Hotel. Two were from young women, one of whom strongly appealed to JM's baser instincts by offering 'to go anywhere and do anything'. Cecil Bebb was obviously the ideal candidate for co-pilot on the South African adventure, but the astute Welshman declined as soon as he knew that the Scot was not offering any financial reward, just the honour of flying with him.

That evening JM sought some consolation in Bebb's refusal by dining out in one of Mayfair's plushier restaurants with Beryl Markham, where they were duly spotted by the parapazzi and photographed tête à tête. One cannot help but wonder, whether on that occasion he attempted to entice her along with him on the Cape flight.

☆ ☆ ☆

The thirty-seven year old passenger Edouard Corniglion-Molinier smoothed his carefully cultivated black moustache against his tanned face as he settled back in the seat, ready to become immersed in his favourite magazine. He flicked through its pages as he waited for the remaining nine passengers to board the Wibault 282 *Voile d'Or*, one of Air France's most modern, three-engined monoplanes currently in use on the Croydon to Paris run.

As JM took his seat behind the pomaded Frenchman, he noticed not only that his companion was reading an aviation magazine, but also that there was a slight flicker of recognition from the man's inquisitive eyes. Not long after they were over the Sussex coast, the pomaded head craned round to

enquire of JM, 'M'sieur Mollison, non?' and to introduce himself with an abbreviated and rapid, 'C'rnlion-Molinier'. JM must have immediately recognised the name, for the Frenchman had been one of the entries for the Mildenhall to Melbourne MacRobertson Air Race just two years previously. On that occasion his entry with co-pilot Captain L. Challe had been scratched, along with forty odd other dubious entries, most of whom had encountered difficulties in acquiring a suitable machine in time.

The two men were soon deep in conversation as Edouard explained that he was just the man Mollison needed for the flight to 'the Cap'. JM wasn't so sure. However, the more they talked, the more JM became interested. He learned that his gallic friend had not only been a seventeen year old, WW1 fighter pilot with seven citations for bravery and the Legion d'honneur to his credit, but had also more recently been engaged on archaelogical reconnaissance flights in Africa. As the plane touched down at Le Bourget, the wealthy Frenchman invited JM to be his guest for dinner at his home on the Avenue Matignon that evening. It was an invitation that was readily accepted.

By the early hours of the next morning, Edouard had thoroughly dispelled any doubts that JM might have entertained about his ability as a suitable co-pilot and navigator. JM admitted that he was forced to the conclusion that if his charming host could guide him unerringly through most of the city's nightspots that evening, including the Sphinx, then a 6,000 mile flight down to the Cape was a cinch. They would fly together.

In the meantime, in spite of *The Dorothy* having been re-registered with the British authorities as G-AECP, Guiseppe Bellanca had issued a writ on 5 November for the return of the aircraft. One can only assume that Mollison still had an outstanding debt on the plane, one which he had promised to repay as soon as he arrived in the UK but had failed to do so. From subsequent events in the story, one can only conclude that JM kept to his normal practice and, as with any other debt, he simply ignored it.

For three days prior to the Cape flight JM lived at the Aerodrome Hotel, Croydon, monitoring the servicing needs of the Bellanca, until Eduoard joined him there with his auburn-haired, half-English wife, on Saturday, 28 November. On the Sunday morning of their departure, JM was highly amused to see his companion appear in a blue leather coat covering a teddy bear coat, and both worn over a sports suit. Jim found that his co-pilot was also carrying a number of highly perfumed toiletries and deodorants in a hold-all for use on the journey, a habit strangely superfluous in Jim's estimation. It appears that the Frenchman was determined that if he was going to die, then he was going to die smelling sweet. The Scot was also intrigued by his companion's wearing of a rather complicated French parachute, one in which the normal method of opening by a ripcord handle was supplemented by a static-line for attachment to the aircraft. The theory being, that if one were knocked unconscious whilst baling out, a line would extend for a length of some 400 feet to open the chute independently of the operation of the person wearing it. They both hoped that it was a theory that neither would have to put to the test.

Just before the engine was fired up and as the two men were climbing into their cockpits, a customs official hurried towards the plane with a handful of letters and telegrams. JM opened the first one, which was from an aspiring co-pilot, half read it and then tossed it along with the rest of the pile to a waiting reporter. On the following morning the *Daily Express* bore a picture of Mollison, over which a reproduction of a customs and excise telegram was superimposed. Its content was pithily worded to reveal that due to non-payment of customs on the importation of a foreign aircraft, *The Dorothy* must not be flown from Croydon until £2,170 had been paid. By the time that readers were opening their morning newspapers to read that piece of news, JM and CM were tracking their way along the bumpy air of the Nile heading for Kisumu.

One wonders exactly why JM chose to fly on the longer eastern route to the Cape, instead of the western one that he had pioneered in 1932. Admittedly he had more speed in hand than Amy's Percival Vega Gull when he set out to beat her time of 3 days 6 hours and 26 minutes. Possibly he was seduced into thinking that the Imperial Airways all-red route would provide better ground support facilities. Or more probably by that time, the fact that the French authorities were loathe to give permission for a Sahara crossing without the deposit of a substantial sum of money for any likely rescue work, cash that JM was obviously unable or unwilling to provide. What he had not bargained for, however, on the eastern route, were the difficulties that the Bellanca would encounter in lifting heavy fuel-loads from the heat and rarified atmosphere of aerodromes at high altitudes.

The two men set out at a cracking pace and soon saw the airport at Le Bourget disappear under the green shapely wings of *The Dorothy* at 10.28am, just 55 minutes after leaving Croydon. They were averaging a creditable 216mph without particularly pushing the noisy Pratt & Whitney engine too hard. Mollison had already achieved speeds as high as 272 mph in the Bellanca during test-flights at Croydon, and it is worth noting that these speeds compared quite favourably with Britain's single-seat Hawker Hurricane, which was currently being advertised at the Paris Air Show as a 300mph fighter.

After a two hour stop at Marseilles, they struck out for a direct night crossing across the Mediterranean to Egypt. Their route would have taken them across the toe of Italy to Alexandria, but at 11,000 feet whilst over Sardinia they ran into unexpectedly severe weather and strong headwinds. At this point the two men made a quick decision to curtail the long, hazardous sea-crossing and make for Tunisia. After circling the airport at Tunis so that their arrival and deviation of route could be reported back to London, they followed the north African coastline eastwards. JM cursed his luck as he thought of the extra 500 miles it would put on the journey.

By around 3am they were over the aerodrome at Alexandria, only to find to their dismay that it was in complete darkness. The prior arrangements for the switching on of boundary lights had not been honoured and there was no way in which JM could be tempted to make a night-landing under such conditions. If only they had carried radio equipment they would have been able to signal their plight. To add to their consternation, the fuel-guages were reading inexplicably low. What they did not know at that time was that one of the tanks had ruptured and precious fuel was seeping away into the night air. There was now no alternative but to make for Cairo's well-lit, main airport at Almaza, another one hundred miles to the south-east. JM recalls the cool manner in which his companion greeted his shouted instruction to be ready to jump should the fuel give out. There was nothing but a submissive 'Airright' from the Frenchman as he adjusted his parachute harness straps.

After two hours respite on the floodlit aerodrome at Almaza for a smoke and a drink whilst the aircraft was being refuelled, they left at dawn for the long 2,100 mile flight to Kisumu in Kenya. An hour after overflying Khartoum, JM began to smell fumes of high-octane fuel in the cockpit, even with the hood open. Craning around he could see that CM's face had already turned a ghastly pallor as the poor man mouthed the words 'Benzine'. Looking down, JM could see that fuel was beginning to seep along the floor to the rear cockpit. To make matters worse, the intense tropical heat of the day was now bearing down on the plane. There was little they could do but look for a suitable spot to land along the banks of the White Nile and try to make a temporary repair. After a brief inspection on the ground at Kosti, they decided that, apart from knocking a hole in the floor to allow the noxious liquid to drain away, there was little they could do but return to Khartoum. Hopefully, someone there amongst the station's RAF ground staff would be skilled in the intricacies of the aircraft's fuel-system.

As events transpired, the 400 mile detour was to no avail, for at 10pm local time they took off from Khartoum having failed to find the cause of the leak.

With the front hood open to allow the cooler night air into the confined space of the cockpits, they managed to suffer the fumes until they reached the 5,000 feet high aerodrome at Kisumu, early on the Tuesday morning. In theory, the Bellanca should have been able to make the 2,800 mile flight from Kisumu to the Cape in one hop. However, there were two major obstacles. Firstly, the danger of attempting to lift over 600 gallons of fuel off the small, elevated airfield in the heat of the day with the propeller striving to bite at thin and rarified air. And, secondly, the problem of the fumes and their effect upon the already physically weakened co-pilot. JM decided on the wiser course of taking on only enough fuel to make the 1,200 mile hop to Broken Hill.

As they taxied out to the far boundary of the aerodrome at Kisumu, the full strength of the equatorial sun bore down onto the two men under the open canopy of the oil-streaked monoplane. The air was breathlessly soggy, and the windsock hung limp at its moorings. JM was more than a little apprehensive about the hazard of the trees that now lay shimmering in a heat-haze at the far end of the runway. Now, he thought, was as good a time as any to test the integrity of Guiseppe Bellanca's much acclaimed aerofoil. It was a wing design which was renowned for its ability to combine the qualities of lifting of heavy loads, whilst at the same time coping with a wide speed range.

As they neared the trees, still flying only a few feet off the ground, CM pondered on whether to brace himself against the bulkhead for the inevitable crash, or just to let himself go limp. *The Dorothy* staggered into the air just skimming the tree-tops as the plucky Frenchman relieved his tension by bellowing out, *Vive le France et les pommes frites*. Whilst the Scot describes that hairy take-off in his memoirs with the classic, Mollisonian understatement of: 'So I dragged the stick back and wished I hadn't come.'[130]

After flying through heavy rainstorms, they landed at Broken Hill around 5pm local time, with CM now in a bad way from inhalation of the poisonous petrol fumes. However, after resting for nearly twelve hours at a local hotel, he was game enough to continue and they returned to the airfield. This time another disaster befell them. Mollison, now showing visible signs of fatigue with a badly sunburnt face and bloodshot eyes, carelessly struck one of the red boundary lamps as he attempted go outside of their limits in order to gain as much take-off space as possible. Worse still, he had bogged the machine down in the surrounding mud. Help was needed in the form of a rescue party, comprising of a crowd of natives and two cars employing tow-ropes, before they were finally extricated.

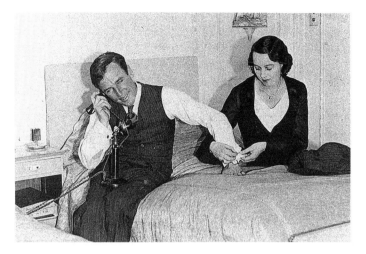

Marcelle Adkings the Swiss-born manageress of the 'Aerodrome Hotel' fusses over one of her more famous customers.

The original print of this press photograph was mischieviously autographed by the aviator with the inscription: 'Marcelle, many thanks for the intimate services rendered, Jim Mollison.'

By the time they reached the diamond town of Kimberley, late on the Wednesday morning, the Frenchman was in a state of collapse and had to be carried to the aerodrome's clubhouse, where he was laid out on a table. It took a local doctor some thirty minutes to revive him, whereupon he was advised not to continue with the flight. Stubbornly he refused, for he knew that they were still within striking distance of breaking Amy's record. It was around noon and they now had only 500 miles to cover before 5.57pm, the deadline. All that was now needed was for JM to keep awake and follow the railway line from Kimberley to Cape Town.

Around 12.45pm they were ready to depart when the Bellanca's engine failed to start. After fifteen minutes of tinkering they were in the air, only to be seen by eyewitnesses to be heading south-easterly, almost ninety degrees in the wrong direction. Some members of the press conjectured that they had flown the one hundred miles to Bloemfontein before discovering the error, and had then flown a parallel course to their true Cape heading. JM however, subsequently denied this allegation, (certainly his aircraft was never reported to be seen over Bloemfontein) and one finds it hard to believe that a navigator of his calibre, even taking into account his fatigue and the carrying of a sick passenger, could make such a major blunder. However, from a study of the map, one can see that the railway line running south from Kimberley to the Cape branches off at Beaconsfield towards Bloemfontein, and he could have possibly become careless and followed it. It seems far more likely that he did in fact follow the wrong branch of the railway line initially, before discovering his error and correcting it.

They had little difficulty in making eye contact with the line down as far as Beaufort West, some 300 miles from the Cape's aerodrome at Wingfield, but from hereon they ran into atrocious thunderstorms. The 11,000 feet Hex mountain range ahead of them was completely obscured by vicious spirals of turbulent cloud formations, their anvil heads betokening a rough reception for any aircraft foolish enough to enter them. At this point they were some three hours in front of Amy's record time.

For the next hour or so the tiny monoplane was buffeted around the skies, as JM clawed his way along canyon after canyon of towering black cumulus seeking a way through. His eyes were never far from those bracing wires which were now being tested to their full capacity as they helped support wings to fuselage. This part of the country was renowned for violent weather patterns, and he had heard hangar stories from some of the Imperial Airways' pilots of passengers being thrown around in their airliners whilst making this last stage of the flight. He had been assured that on one trip the dents in the roof of the cabin gave ample proof of where their heads had made contact! Now he could believe it.

Eventually they flew through the turbulence into smoother but cloud-laden skies over Cape Town. JM records that at around 4pm he made three attempts to land at Wingfield, where the Duty Staff were waiting to confirm their official time of arrival. However, it was not to be. On each occasion he claims to have descended to within 500 feet without breaking cloud in an attempt to find the airfield, but with the uncertainty of their exact position and the possible proximity of high ground, he was forced eventually to abandon all hope of locating the airfield.

Setting a south-easterly course they flew away down the coast and did not break through a rift in the clouds until they were over Cape Agulhas, the southernmost tip of Africa. Although they had taken on enough fuel for four hours' flying time at Kimberley, ample for the intended journey, they were now running low with only an estimated five gallons wetting the tanks.

As they flew along the coastline looking for a suitable place in which to put down, they spotted a solitary Boer farmhand trudging across the fields near the fishing village of Arniston. JM scribbled a note requesting the man to notify Cape Town that they would be landing somewhere nearby, stuffed it in one of his gloves, and threw it from the plane. Circling the spot he saw the man stoop to pick up the note and wave an acknowledgement before they flew inland. Minutes later, at 5.10pm local time, they were touching down on Dickie Swart's farm at Weesdrift, some twenty-five miles west of the small town of Bredasdorp. The farmer found them both two hours later, fast asleep in the shadow of *The Dorothy's* wing.

Tantalisingly the record had eluded them, and Amy's record remained unbroken.

Chapter 18

'Second Time Around'

If Jim Mollison had entertained any hopes of a reconciliation with Amy upon his return to London at the end of December, and there is every reason to believe that he did, then they were quickly dashed when he discovered that she had entered a Swiss clinic to undergo treatment for nervous exhaustion.

Events had taken their toll on Amy, for earlier in October she had been returning alone from Paris on a late afternoon flight in her Beechcraft, when an unexpectedly heavy ground-mist had obscured the Kent countryside beneath her. In vain she had scanned the horizon looking for the security of the red and green boundary lights of Croydon's aerodrome, but there was little that she could pin-point as a landmark as she passed over the outskirts of the capital. Realising that she was hopelessly lost, she finally decided to put down into what looked like a reasonably smooth open field. As soon as the wheels started to hit unsuspected ruts and ridges, in what turned out to be a site being prepared for building development at Chelsfield, she applied the brakes rather too fiercely and the machine turned over and slid along on its back. As a consequence she was left dangling from the straps, her clothes soaked in petrol, and having suffered cuts to her face and damage to her left shoulder.

The after-effects of her accident and the combined stress of the publicity surrounding her estrangement from Jim, had no doubt resulted in her taking medical advice to recuperate abroad. Wisely, she had taken her younger sister Molly along with her to act as a chaperone, now that Francois Dupré was openly on the scene. She was in fact stringing him along with no intention of consummating the affair, in spite of his determined efforts to seduce her. It was, in effect, a finely balanced performance of coquetry. As her wealthy suitor, Dupré was urging her on to divorce her errant husband, for he was now incorrectly sensing his chances of taking over where Jim had left off.

Whilst she had no real love for the middle-aged Frenchman, there was probably an element of revenge against her husband incorporated in her cultivation of Dupré's attentions, for Jim was openly flirting in London with Beryl Markham at the time. Although the press had been pre-occupied with the news of the King Edward V111's recent abdication,* they were not too busy to picture Jim and Beryl *tête à tête*, or dancing the night away in the capital's nightspots.

In spite of her recent transatlantic solo success, the sybaritic Kenyan aviatrix was practically insolvent during the spring of 1937. It was, however, something which did little to deter her from leaving a trail of debts wherever she went, principally amongst some of London's classier dressmakers and milliners. As a result of being broke, she was more than grateful to accept an invitation to share a flat with the comedy-actress Florence Desmond. It was a strange partnership of two women who both consoled themselves with having been deeply in love with the same man.

Coincidentally, during the time of Beryl's liaison with JM, the actress was appearing with Leslie Henson in *Seeing Stars* at the Gaiety Theatre, a show which was then being produced by William Mollison. JM always claimed that the the stage Mollisons (another was the actor Clifford) were his distant cousins, although Thomasina always declaimed, with a fair amount of scorn, that they were unrelated. The connection may or may not have had some bearing upon the fact, that Dessie returned from the theatre one night to find Jim and Beryl in her sitting room.[131] The unexpected sight of Jim in her home revived feelings of animosity in Dessie, stemming from the time of his rivalry with her late husband Tom Campbell Black. Beryl quickly sensed the troubled atmosphere and asked Jim to leave, but such was JM's state of drunkeness that he could barely stand, let alone leave to find a taxi on his own. Fortunately, Dessie was courteous enough to allow him to stay to sleep it off, and she made up a bed for him in Tom's old room for the night. Beryl was soon told, in no uncertain terms, that she was never to do that again!

The Scot appears to have been chasing the demon in the glass with a vengeance at this footloose period in his life. The mischievous Jock Bonar recalls a rather humorous incident which occurred when JM was living at the 'Aerodrome Hotel', at Croydon, with the following:

> As I remember it, Charlie Allen** had a very good taste in good-looking
> young ladies when he was based at Croydon airport. Jim was staying there
> at the time and on this particular evening he had gone to bed early in his

*Having failed to secure the agreement of the Government and the Church for a morganitic marriage, the King had finally spurned the crown for the American divorcée Wallis Simpson – the woman he so desperately wanted to marry.
**Charlie Allen was the owner of Air Taxis, a small charter firm based at Croydon, and for whom Mollison was to work just prior to the outbreak of WW2.

Beryl Markham – the first woman to make an east–west, non-stop solo crossing of the North Atlantic – exiting from her Percival Vega Gull.

usual state. The young lady arrived to wait for Charlie Allen's return.

Now I thought to myself: 'It's not right for a nice girl like this to be messing around with these two.' So I decided to play a bit of a trick on both of them. I said to the girl: 'Have you ever met Jim Mollison?' (all the pilots were very well known in those days) 'Oh, no,' she said. 'Come on then, and I'll introduce you to him.'

Now Jim always slept without any pyjamas on, and as I walked into his bedroom with this charming young girl, I shook him awake and said: 'Jim, there's a lady here to see you.' Jim roused himself from his drunken stupor, sat up, and with that impeccable accent of his, said: 'How do you doo?' As soon as the young lady saw Jim starting to climb out of bed stark naked, she screamed and took to her pretty heels out of the building. Charlie Allen was never to see her again![(132)]

By the time JM arrived back in London from South Africa, during the early part of 1937, he had earned enough from the proceeds of the sale of his transatlantic and Cape flight stories to the *Daily Express*, and from general advertising, to clear the outstanding customs' debt. He also had enough to appease Guiseppe Bellanca's writ for money outstanding on the plane. What next? Two projects were uppermost in his mind.

The French Government had not been slow to notice that the tenth anniversary of Charles Lindbergh's historical crossing of the North Atlantic, from Roosevelt Field to Le Bourget, coincided with the Paris International Exposition planned for 1937. As a result, they mooted the idea of an aerial derby to be flown over the identical course during the period 21-22 May, and to be officially known as 'The Lindbergh Memorial Air Race'. The prize money was certainly big, with £30,000 to the outright winner and a further £20,000 for additional prizes. As in the Mildenhall-Melbourne Air Race it was to be a massed start and open to contestants flying solo or with a crew.

JM's other prospect of earning money came when he was approached by the *Daily Express*'s Air Correspondent, Victor Ricketts, with an offer to assist him in the updating of his 1932 memoirs, *Death Cometh Soon or Late*. It was to result in an unexpurgated version of that volume, complete with the slightly salacious title of *Playboy of the Air*, and pulling no punches in what one might now term pure 'kiss-and-tell' journalism. Reading it in today's permissive moral climate it appears fairly innocuous, but at the time it shocked. Not least of all it shocked Amy and her family. For whilst it had nothing but praise for her as a flier and as a person, its uninhibited revelations of her husband's promiscuity certainly belittled her. Moreover, its dedication to Dorothy Ward especially rankled. Not surprisingly, with the Mollisons' relationship now in open conflict, Amy resumed her maiden name officially by deed poll. Towards the end of March, she initiated divorce proceedings before sailing for the United States.

JM and Beryl Markham were quick to announce their entries in the forthcoming Lindbergh Memorial Air Race. They were at that stage undecided on whether they should crew together in the Bellanca, or in any other plane that she was able procure through sponsorship. Amy was not to be outdone, and Bill Courtenay had suggested she compete in the twin-engined Scottish Aircraft & Engineering Co's *Clyde Clipper*. However, as the twin boomed 'Flying Wing' aircraft was unlikely to be ready in time, she had finally accepted Dupré's offer of using his recently acquired low-wing passenger monoplane, a sleek, red and silver liveried Caudron Goeland. It appears that she felt the need of improving her navigational skills for the race, for, unlike Jim and Beryl, she was acutely aware that she lacked transoceanic flying experience. The main reason of her U.S. trip was, therefore, apart from obtaining treatment for her teeth from a New York dentist, to attend a two-week course at the Weems System of Navigation at Annapolis. The school had been founded by Commander Philip Weems of the U.S. Naval Academy, an authority in celestial navigation and tutor of both Charles and Anne Lindbergh. During this period the school was also employing the skills of Harold Gatty as its manager. The Australian was an expert in precision flight instruments and had acted as Wiley Post's navigator on his 1931 round-the-world flight in the *Winnie Mae*.

By April of that year, with some twenty-one entries already accepted, reactions in the United States to the proposed air derby were clearly hardening against the event. Memories were still fresh in the minds of government authorities of the disastrous 'Oakland-Honolulu Dole Derby' air race of 1927. On that occasion ten lives had been lost, but not before costly, massive air and sea rescue searches had been made for survivors who might still have been alive after ditching in the Pacific. It meant that the date for the start of the Lindbergh Memorial race was postponed from 21 May until the summer, as firstly the U.S. Bureau of Air Commerce and then its Canadian counterpart stiffened in their opposition. Added to this were the voices of disapproval from two eminent individuals in the world of aviation; those of Doc Kimball of the U.S. Weather Bureau, and more importantly, Charles Lindbergh himself. The latter had already fled from his own country at the end of 1935 to settle in England, in order to avoid the glare of unwelcome publicity over the kidnap and murder of his baby son. Consequently, he was anxious lest the proposed race should disturb the relative anonymity he now enjoyed. The argument for and against the proposed race continued, until finally the U.S. and Canadian Governments declared that the event would not be allowed to start in either of their countries.

In spite of protests from Amy, and some of the other disappointed competitors who were accusing the U.S. authorities of being over-cautious, and covertly wishing to protect Pan American Airways – they were about to commence their own proposals for a transatlantic service – the race across the North Atlantic was cancelled. The French promoters quickly stepped in and announced an alternative race to be flown over a 4,000 mile course, commencing on 20 August from Istres (Marseilles) to Damascus and finishing at Le Bourget (Paris).

By this time JM, Beryl Markham and Amy had lost interest and the only British entrant was that of Flying Officer Arthur Clouston and Flight Lieutenant George Nelson in the ageing DH Comet G-ACSS.* Jim and Beryl's enthusiasm for the flight had no doubt waned in view of the predominance of fast civilian versions of military aircraft being entered by the Italian and French governments. More importantly, there had been a vast reduction in the prize money being offered. With war clouds now looming large on the horizon in Europe, and the Spanish Civil War now almost a year

*Formerly *Grosvenor House*, now renamed *The Orphan*.

old, it must have surely dawned on the long-distance aviators that the Golden Age of record-breaking and easy money was all but over.

On 17 April 1937, Jim Mollison flew *The Dorothy* with Baron Segonzac as a passenger from Croydon to Meaux, Esbly,[133] an airfield just sixteen miles to the east of Le Bourget. Never one to do things by halves, it was the first stage in his plan to make an east-to-west crossing of the North Atlantic, with or without Beryl, and in preparation for the start of the Lindbergh Memorial race. According to *Les Ailes*, whilst he was there awaiting a resolution of the debate on whether the race should take place, he made two trips to London in the Bellanca. On one of these flights and whilst returning to Meaux (either on 24 April or 24 May – the exact date is uncertain), he suffered an engine failure and was forced to make a dead-stick landing.[134] It might well have been as a result of this unnerving experience, that JM was eventually persuaded to crew with Beryl in what he hoped might be a more reliable aircraft. Gerald Howson, author of the brilliantly researched *Aircraft of the Spanish Civil War, 1936-39*, confirms that Mollison flew to Meaux on 24 May in order to confer with Beryl Markham about the proposed transatlantic race.

In the meantime, Beryl was, according to her biographer Mary Lovell, putting many irons in the fire with attempts to cajole a succession of possible rich backers for a sponsorship. Amongst them was the manager of the Irish boxer, cum actor-singer, Jack Doyle; a friend of Dupré's; and a South African syndicate including the industrialist I. W. Schlesinger. None of these quite materialised, and eventually she sailed for the U.S. in June at the instigation of the syndicate to try her fortunes over there. Finally, she came up with a backer who was prepared to purchase a Northrop Delta 1C, at that time registered as SE-ADI and owned by the Swedish ABA airline based at Malmo.[135] Soon after, she announced that she would fly it in the race with Jim Mollison as her partner. However, by the time the single-engined low-wing monoplane was flown from Stockholm to arrive at Meaux early in July,* the transatlantic race had been called off. Beryl didn't bother to return to the UK but remained in the States until the end of December; whereupon she sailed to Africa, via Australia, arriving in Durban in February 1938.

As soon as the race was cancelled, JM decided to cut his losses and sell the Bellanca to the highest bidder. The bright lights of the Riviera with its nightclubs and accessible women were beckoning, and he needed the wherewithal to indulge in them. Fortunately for him that was not too difficult a task, as at that time the Spanish Republican Government was scouring the arms-dealers of Europe to purchase aircraft, either military or civil, in order to stem the advances of the Nationalist forces. From its

---

*Earlier in the year the Northrop Delta had been kept in the hangar of Personal Airways at Croydon.

outbreak, the bloody civil war had quickly polarised into an international conflict. On the one hand, the rebel leader Franco was being supported by men and equipment supplied by the dictators, Hitler and Mussolini; whilst the Soviet Union and France, together with a conglomeration of mercenaries, were backing the duly elected left-wing Republicans. After receiving an appeal for arms from the beleaguered government in Madrid, the French Premier Léon Blum, leader of a government already sympathetic to the Republican cause, sought to limit the support being given by Germany and Italy by proposing an International Agreement of Non-Intervention. It was an agreement doomed to failure from the start, for apart from its observance by the USA and a lukewarm response by the British government – who were concerned lest it jeopardised Britain's strategically placed base at Gibralter – it was virtually ignored.

Two conflicting reports are on record regarding Jim Mollison's disposal of the Bellanca. One explanation is that he sold the aircraft to the Spanish Republican government sometime during the summer of 1937 and that it was subsequently shot down, or caught fire in the air, whilst being used on high-speed reconnaissance work over the Madrid sector.[136] Another explanation is that the plane was sold to the UK Air Ministry in June 1939, and subsequently impounded throughout the Second World War. However, when one carefully sifts the facts and considers the backgound to the history of the Non-Intervention Agreement, and the chicanery surrounding it, one can only conclude that the former account is the correct one. The latter, as we shall see, is merely a mis-interpretation of the former.

Several factors lead one to this inevitable conclusion. Firstly, it is an established fact that Lejeune Aviation, a company operating from the aerodrome at Meaux, was known to be not only covertly training Spanish pilots to fight for the Republican cause but also one which procured and smuggled aircraft to them. Secondly, it has also been firmly established that Beryl Markham's Northrop Delta was flown from Stockholm to Meaux, after its Swedish registration was cancelled on 13 July. In spite of it reportedly being sold to the Iraqi government on 27 September 1937 with the registration YI-OSF, evidence currently remains showing this same aircraft in Spanish markings during the time of the civil war. Furthermore, ex-LAPE (Lineas Aereas Postales Espanoles) pilot, Jose-Maria Carreras, recalls that he flew the plane in September 1938 with the Republican Premier, Juan Negrin, on board, to conduct peace negotiations with one of Hitler's officials in Zurich.[137]

It is also known that in December 1937, an order was placed at the Newcastle factory in Delaware for the supply of twenty-two Bellanca 28-

Thomasina Bullmore and her son Jim Mollison. This picture was most probably taken at Edinburgh in November 1936.

90Bs* by the SETA (Societe d'Exploitations Techniques et Aeriens) agency in Athens. The timing of the order appears to confirm that the Republicans had been impressed with the performance of the Mollison Bellanca. The documentation, including Greek import licences, was subsequently found to be a forgery and the crated aircraft were impounded by the U.S. authorities. They remained on the dockside at Wilmington until the early part of 1939, when they were eventually sold to the Mexican government.

The Northrop and Bellanca deceptions illustrate quite clearly to what extraordinary lengths the various agencies were prepared to go in order to circumvent the Non-Intervention Agreement, and so that they might obtain aircraft for the Republicans. They also possibly show the reason why Jim Mollison's solicitor, when confronted with an Air Ministry questionaire headed 'Impressment Review of Aircraft', just prior to the outbreak of WW2, guardedly stated that the Bellanca had already been sold. The AM official seemed quite satisfied with the explanation, and merely recorded the owner's statement with the words, 'Noted as sold 23.6.39'. Maybe, in hindsight, if the official had added a comma after the word 'sold', it would have saved a lot of confusion for those now researching the history of the aircraft's disposal!

*The 28-90B was a later development of JM's 28-70, one which incorporated the larger 900hp Wasp engine, a fully cantilevered wing instead of the externally braced type, flaps and improved undercarriage fairings.

The accuracy of the story is put beyond doubt by the recent record of a meeting which took place in December 1939 between JM and Freddie Kent, a former Director of Rollason Air Services, Croydon.[138] Evidently when JM first flew *The Dorothy* into Croydon, after setting the transatlantic record on 30 October 1936, Rollasons serviced the aircraft. By some oversight, JM had left a valise in the cockpit containing his white canvas flying helmet, goggles, several AA flying maps and his 'B' licence. The valise was removed during servicing and thrown into the corner of their hangar, where it remained forgotten until some time later. Freddie Kent did not meet up with JM again until he happened to be working on the repair and servicing of Fairey Battle bombers, at the company's Stockport factory, soon after the outbreak of war.

During the weekend of his stay in the north, Freddie was invited to the Grosvenor Hotel in Manchester, and as he walked through the hotel's main lounge, he chanced to see the familiar profile of a man dressed in the ATA uniform, sitting at the bar chatting up a rather attractive blonde. As he neared the couple, he recognised Mollison immediately, and slapping him on the shoulder remarked: 'Well of all people, it's Jim, where have you been for the past three years?' 'I haven't seen you since you flew the Bellanca into Croydon.' 'What have you been up to?' JM duly explained that he had been spending much of his time in the south of France enjoying the proceeds from the sale of the Bellanca. According to FK it transpired that he had sold the aircraft to the Spaniards for £6,000, some £400 more than he paid for it originally. During the course of the conversation, Freddie asked him if he had missed his 'B' licence. He had, and perhaps Freddie would be kind enough to post it on to Barton aerodrome where he was now working. He could keep the valise and the maps, etc., (they are still in his possession to this day) but he would like the licence back. It was duly sent. The last time the two men were ever to meet again was a few years later at Abbotsinch, when Jim was delivering Blenheims.

☆ ☆ ☆

By the end of 1937, Amy had broken her rather fragile relationship with Dupré after two major rows had erupted. The first one had come soon after her return from the USA in June, when she assumed that she had first call on the use of his Caudron Goeland. On this occasion she became infuriated, and her quick temper got the better of her when she found out that he was departing in the new aircraft on a lengthy trip, just as she was about to use it. There was a partial reconciliation between them for a while, until finally in the August, there came an embarrassing show down in the Carlton at

Cannes. Dupré had found out, quite by chance, that Amy was also holidaying in the resort with one of his close friends. The break up caused a financial shock-wave from which Amy never quite recovered. For the past seven years she had enjoyed an extravagant life-style without having to worry too much about money. At first with the proceeds from her Australian flight, then with the two flights made with Jim, and finally from her association with Dupré. Once deprived of these sources of income, she found it extremely difficult to manage her own affairs.

The ever faithful Peter Reiss, still carrying the torch for Amy, recalls how desperately hard up she was in 1938.[139] It came to the point where she was too embarrassed to visit London pawnbrokers, in order to sell some of the jewellery she had been given after her Australian flight, for fear of being recognised. As a consequence, she asked him if he would do it for her. Peter Reiss dutifully did the rounds touting for a quote, until he finally settled for an establishment in Victoria that seemed more generous than the rest. When he reported back to Amy, she was shocked at the cut-throat prices that she was being offered, but had no alternative other than to accept. Worse was to follow, for the ignominy of the sale was further compounded for Amy when her companion returned to the shop with the goods. He was told that as the jewellery so obviously belonged to a woman, then the lady herself would have to be present to sign 'the usual forms', before they would pay up. Early the next morning, PR and a heavily muffled Amy, with hat pulled well down onto her forehead, stood before the assistant who presented the form and asked her to sign her christian name and surname. It was obvious to PR that the assistant, had recognised her immediately. Amy just scrawled, 'A. Johnson', thinking that that would suffice. 'We do need your full name Madam,' he said, and then added tactfully, 'perhaps I can help by suggesting Amelia, would that do?' 'That's fine,' said Amy. She collected the money and they quickly left the shop.

Jim Mollison knew of Amy's plight and made her the offer of borrowing the Percival Mew Gull that he had recently purchased from Giles Guthrie, so that she could make a new attempt on her Cape record, but she declined. Such action on his part, certainly demolishes the long held myth that he was always jealous of her flying achievements. His magnaminous gesture did at least bring them back into a warm and friendly relationship. Many believed that she never really got over her love for him, and there were rumours right up until the time of her death that there was the possibility of a reconciliation between them, even though he was by then married to Phyllis. However, the break up was now irrevocable and the decree absolute was granted on 24 August 1938. From then on it appears that she had a number of liaisons with

Amy Mollison and her ardent admirer Peter Reiss, circa. 1936.

various men, but in none of them did she ever find true happiness. Sadly, it is probably true to say that the only man with whom she ever attained a stable relationship was her father.

The summer of 1938 saw JM living the bachelor playboy role as irresponsibly as ever. It appears that he worked his way through France much as he had done ten years earlier, only this time he was an internationally known figure. With the proceeds from the Bellanca, he was to be found in the casinos of Le Touquet, spending as if there were no tomorrow and hitting the bottle as hard as ever. It was whilst he was in the northern resort in June, in the company of millionaires C. R. Fairey and the Maharajah Kapurthala, that he was fined for putting on an uninvited aerobatic display whilst drunk.* Part of his time was spent on the Riviera and it was whilst he was there that he met the thirty-four year old heiress and socialite, Phyllis Louis Verley Hussey. Their first meeting took place in August, probably at the Carlton Hotel in Cannes, for, apart from being one of Jim and Amy's old stamping grounds, it was, according to Phyllis's daughter, her mother's favourite summer idyll.(140)

The slender, willowy, blonde divorcée was reputed to have an income of £20,000 a year from her father's legacy, and was undoubtedly considered by

*He was later summoned to appear before a court in the Montreuil-sur-Mer Town Hall, where, on 29 March 1939, he was fined and given a suspended prison sentence. His defence attorney was a M. Satchell.

most bachelors to be quite a catch. With her wealth and good looks, she was every unattached male's dream-girl. For Jim Mollison, now obviously looking for a marriage partner, she could hardly have been overlooked. Although their first meeting was but a brief one, it was, according to the account he later gave to the press, the proverbial case of love at first sight. Known to her friends as Lydia, (the initial for Louis conveniently provided the assumed christian name) she was a prominent figure in Jamaican high society and a member of the distinguished Verley family. According to official records, her grandmother founded the Verley home by bequest, and Phyllis subsequently inherited the large banana plantations on the Mona estate employing some 1300 workers. In addition, her father had been the wealthy owner of a stable of race-horses on the Caribbean island.

Her first marriage had been to Lieutenant Commander Thomas Andrew Hussey, RN,* in the early Twenties, and by whom she had a son and a daughter. Just how big a part her wealth played in JM's attraction to her, is left for the reader to decide. He had always told the press that he would marry again, but only if the right girl came along. Maybe, as in the case of his marrriage to Amy, there was an element of mutual exploitation between the two people concerned. There is no doubt that a linkage with Jim Mollison's name at that time, could provide a woman with a certain cachet in the social whirl, albeit a rather uncertain one.

Soon after, Jim returned to London,** thinking that his meeting with Phyllis had just been one of those holiday romances that are soon forgotten. To his amazement, the new tenant in his Mayfair block of flats turned out to be none other than Phyllis Hussey. From then on a brief courtship began, one that lasted just seven days before he proposed and she accepted. Having decided to marry, they flew to Paris for the ceremony, but when they arrived they found that three weeks' residential qualifications were necessary.

Once back in London, Phyllis moved out of her flat into the Claridges Hotel until the wedding took place. Fleet Street was hammering out articles with captions such as, 'Jim Mollison to wed millionairess after whirlwind wooing', and at the same time reporting that he was planning a record-breaking, round-the-world flight. Just how serious Mollison's claims were on such a venture, are open to question. Admittedly, there had been others such as Amy and Beryl Markham who had declared an interest since Amelia Earhart and Fred Noonan's death in the Pacific a year earlier, but in each instance they had failed to secure the financial backing necessary. In Mollison's case, the Mew Gull he possessed was hardly a suitable machine

*He was later to become Lord Mountbatten's equerry during WW2.
**He was writing a gossipy night-spot column for the *Sunday Chronicle*, at that time.

Jim and Phyllis Hussey outside Caxton Hall after their wedding on 12 November 1938.

for lenghty over water flights. One is, therefore, left to speculate on whether he saw Phyllis's money as a ready source for such an undertaking.

A few weeks before the date planned for the wedding, Jim broke his leg whilst playing cricket, and as a result the ceremony was delayed and did not take place until the Saturday morning of 12 November. Although JM's public image had been waning since his 1936 flights, Fleet Street's press cameramen were there in force, jostling for position, as the couple came out onto the steps of London's fashionable Caxton Hall after signing the register. Phyllis, looking very chic, wore a stunning black outfit consisting of a woollen suit and matching black hat, complete with pearls glistening around her elegant neck. Over the suit she wore a contrasting lime green, three-quarter-length coat, trimmed with dark fur at its edges. Jim was as ebullient as ever, as he waved to the crowd and cracked jokes with the cameramen; whilst the ever faithful Bill Courtenay busied himself giving interviews to reporters who were keen to know of the couple's honeymoon plans.

David Hussey has vague memories of meeting Jim Mollison for the first time in 1938, soon after his mother's wedding to the aviator. Prior to that, he had only read of Mollison's exploits in the newspapers, and then more recently of his mother's intending marriage. At the time, he was a preparatory school student at Clifton College, Bristol, when his mother invited him to lunch with her and her new husband in a local hotel. It was on a Sunday, just prior to their departure by sea from Avonmouth to Miami on their honeymoon trip, and he recalls that JM 'seemed to be a good-natured, baby-faced, short and pleasant man'. He does, however, cast doubt on the accuracy of the newspaper reports at that time, especially where they describe his mother as an heiress. As far as he can remember, 'she only had a small 500 acre banana plantation in Jamaica, which was taken over by the mortgagees shortly after the second world war'.[141] Inevitably, the blockade of the Atlantic by German U boats during the war, crippled the fruit trade between the UK and Jamaica because shipping space was needed for more important cargoes. In fact, bananas did not reappear in Britain's greengrocers' shops until well after the war had ended.

The nearest David Hussey ever came to meeting Jim Mollison again, happened in London in 1956 (by this time his mother had been divorced from Jim for more than seven years), when he paused to have his shoes cleaned in Piccadilly. The 'shoeshine', who had never set eyes on his customer before in his life, happened to say to his client during the usual small talk: 'I bet you can't guess whose shoes I have just cleaned before yours?' To which came the desultory reply: 'No, tell me, who?' One can imagine the sense of shock that his customer received when the cleaner retorted: 'Jim Mollison's'. David Hussey paid his money and walked away into the crowded street with a faint wry smile still lingering on his face.[142]

☆ ☆ ☆

After German troops had marched across the frontier into Austria on 11 March 1938, in an annexation of the country in what Hitler euphemistically termed *die Anschluss*, there was little doubt, except amongst a few willfully blind politicians, that a major war in Europe was now inevitable. One of its consequences, was the announcement in July by the British Government of its far-sighted Civil Air Guard scheme, due to commence on 1 September. It was part of a National Defence programme in which men and women between the ages of eighteen and fifty, would be trained at some sixty local flying clubs throughout the country, for use as pilots in time of war and as a supplement to the RAF. Effectively, it was the RAF's equivalent of the Territorial Army. Owing to an unexpected rush of applicants, numbering some 35,000 in the first few months, an appeal was also made for qualified instructors. JM had, during the week prior to meeting Phyllis again in London, been one of those offering his services to the CAG. It was a duty he was never to fulfil, for with his marriage and forthcoming honeymoon, he

Jim and Phyllis on their honeymoon in Miami, December 1938.

was to be out of the country for the next seven months. By the time he returned, the CAG had served its purpose and in May 1939 the scheme was dropped.

The couple's honeymoon vacation took them first to the resort of Miami Beach, where they stayed for a while at the plushy Roney Plaza Hotel on Collins Avenue, then on to Havana in Cuba for a brief visit, before sailing back to settle on the Verley estate at Kingston. From hereon, little is known about their marriage relationship, except that it was to be a short-lived affair. Jim was on the drink as hard as ever and Phyllis just could not cope with it. Her only references to Jim, made in later life to her son, was that her second husband was a hard-drinker and an inveterate womaniser.

For a time JM attempted to reform by becoming a member of the Oxford Group. It was a religio-ethical movement based on a liberal form of Christianity and popularly known in the late Thirties as Moral Rearmament. Founded in 1921 by the American Lutheran minister, Dr Frank Buchman, it advocated an idealogy based on the four absolute moral standards of honesty, purity, unselfishness and love. Buchman aimed for people of position and power as his converts, claiming that the 'up and outs' needed what his movement had to offer, just as much as the 'down and outs'. As a consequence, MRA attracted world leaders in over fifty countries to its ranks; men such as Chiang Kai-Shek, Dr. Konrad Adenauer, Rear Admiral Richard E. Byrd; and in the world of aviation, men such as Captain Eddie Rickenbacker.

Maybe JM was ripe for such a 'conversion', for by this time even he must have recognised that he was almost totally dependent upon alcohol. Furthermore, he was vulnerable to such a movement, for he had a strong religious side to his temperament. This can be seen in the not infrequent references to God, and promises to be 'a good Christian' in his memoirs. Such thoughts of the Creator and promises to Him usually came at those times when he was lost somewhere over the notorious Newfoundland fog-banks. Not surprisingly, once the danger had passed, he reverted back to his old ways. Of course, one can dismiss this side of his character as exhibiting no more than a 'fox-hole religion', but that would be to ignore his strong Scottish Presbyterian background. Again, if it is true that the best definition of religion is what one does with one's inner loneliness, then JM had had plenty of opportunities to discover a creed for himself. Not only in the loneliness of the cockpit, on those long, frightening flights across the North and South Atlantics, but also in the loneliness, despair and self-loathing that only the alcoholic knows.

In the summer of 1939 JM returned to the UK leaving Phyllis in Jamaica. Maybe she was just expecting too much from a man with such notoriously itchy feet. To sit and vegetate on a Caribbean island was not for Mollison. Or maybe, as some have suggested, it was the discovery of a latent patriotism within himself. For, apart from his loyal wartime service in the ATA, it is often quoted that he had punched a man senseless in a Bermuda nightclub, for not having stood to his feet during the playing of the national anthem. The years appear to have mellowed the rebellious young man from the Clyde, into some sort of orthodoxy. Whereas he was once content to be the rebel with left-wing socialist tendencies, it was now a case of Britain calls, and a man must do his duty.

Chapter 19

'Ancient, Tattered Airmen'

By the time Neville Chamberlain had returned from his meeting with Adolf Hitler at the Munich Conference in September 1938, it was obvious that war was imminent. Fortunately, few were foolish enough to believe Britain's wimpish Prime Minister, as he stepped from the plane holding the worthless document containing the Fuhrer's signature and promise that he was not seeking war. In a wavering voice, bereft of any confidence, the British PM proclaimed that there would be 'peace in our time'. Most knew that it was now a matter of staving off the enemy for as long as possible, whilst the country rapidly rearmed.

During the subsequent months leading up to the outbreak of World War 2, the issue of civilian gas-masks and domestic air raid shelters throughout the country, together with the announcement of evacuation plans for women and children from the likely war zones, had highlighted the subject of air defences, or perhaps more importantly the lack of them. Even before the so-called 'Munich crisis', people's imagination had been stirred during their weekly visits to the local cinemas, where newsreel films showing air attacks upon defenceless cities, in both China and Spain, were a regular feature. Perhaps none had been more graphic than those showing the merciless 'terror attacks' of the Luftwaffe's Condor Legion upon Guernica and Teruel in 1937. On the notorious Guernica raid, forty-three aircraft had destroyed over seventy per cent of the buildings and had left about a thousand dead in the streets. The sight of the legendary, gull-winged Stukas, peeling off to descend on civilian targets in near vertical dives with their sirens screaming, was to become all too familiar on Britain's cinema screens.

One of the less obvious consequences of a heightened awareness of the need for air defences, was to be seen when the Air Ministry began placing rather lucrative contracts with civilian aircraft companies for work on Army Co-Operation duties. It was deemed that the RAF were too busy with more important matters, and civilian aircraft were hired to fly on fixed courses above AA defence units which would practise tracking and ranging their guns and searchlights on them. The small, air charter company, Air Taxis Ltd of Croydon, run by Charles Allen, was one such firm.

According to the script of the Herbert Wilcox film, *They Flew Alone*, which was made in 1942, JM had attempted to rejoin the RAF but had been turned down. If true, it is hardly surprising, for in all probability he would have been considered too old for flying duties. Apart from that, his previous military record was, from a disciplinary point of view, far from satisfactory and would have gone against him. Furthermore, drink had had a marked effect upon him physically. Pictures taken at the time show him with his hair thinning prematurely and aged beyond his thirty-four years. The incessant drinking was taking its toll and he was obviously not in good physical shape. It meant that he was glad to accept the rather menial flying duties being offered by Air Taxis, and he commenced employment with them towards the latter part of August, flying one of their Puss Moth's in the Brighton area.

As soon as hostilities commenced on 3 September, the Air Ministry immediately impressed all civilian aeroplanes. At the same time they set up a new department known as National Air Communications, which took over most of those firms which had been employed on Army Co-operation work. The rationale behind the creation of NAC was that with the expected heavy bombing of the UK mainland, there would be an urgent need to keep the military lines of communication open. As events transpired, the bombing did not happen until a year later, and so the duties of the new organisation were extended to include a freight and mail service between Britain and France, as well as the transportation of men and equipment within the UK. As a part of the re-organisation, Air Taxis was evacuated out of Croydon to Ringway at Manchester, and it was from here, and at Barton aerodrome near Eccles, that JM worked on Army Co-Operation duties for the next twelve months.

By 14 June 1940, triumphant German troops of the Wehrmacht and its armoured columns were parading through the tree-lined avenue of the Champs Elysees in Paris. Seven days later, with Hitler, Goering, Ribbentrop and Hess present, a delegation of French Generals were listening submissively to General Keitel as he read out the harsh surrender conditions, euphemistically termed at that time as an Armistice. To rub salt into an already sore wound, the Boche ensured that the signing took place in the glade of the Forest of Compiègne in the same railway carriage that had been used to accept Germany's defeat in November 1918. The Allied armies had been routed in less than a year by new methods of modern warfare based on the rapid movement of highly mechanised forces. The magnitude of Hitler's military commanders' success in their *blitzkrieg* attack, can be gauged by the fact that the Germans suffered losses of 27,000 dead, to that of 135,000 by the Allies. Things started to look black in Europe as Hitler now turned his full attention on the British Isles.

With the fall of France the work of NAC began to lose its importance and finally its *raison d'être*, as the military took over most of its duties. JM was virtually out of a job by that summer, and like most NAC civilian pilots, he looked to serve his country by joining the recently formed Air Transport Auxiliary.

☆ ☆ ☆

The ATA came into being as the result of an action initiated in 1938 by the Director-General of Civil Aviation, Sir Francis Shelmerdine. His plan was to utilise those airline and civilian pilots, who for reasons of age or fitness would be unacceptable to the RAF, for service on a national basis for communications work during wartime. By the end of June 1939 he had managed to get Treasury approval for the formation of a Civil Reserve of Pilots, one which was initially under the control of Imperial Airways and British Airways, but with the amalgamation of these two organisations on 1 April 1940, came under the direction of the British Overseas Airways Corporation. Finally, it was decided to appoint Gerard d'Erlanger, a Director of British Airways, to recruit suitable candidates from those pilots holding 'A' licences. So it was that the plan was approved, and on 3 September 1939 the ATA was born.

It was proposed that these civilian pilots should be between 28 and 50 years of age, with a minimum of 250 hours' flying experience, and that they should report for final selection at Whitchurch, near Bristol. If suitable, they would be paid at the same rate of pay as junior officers in BA – approximately £350 to £400 per annum – and be issued with a similar uniform. Their duties would include the transport of dispatches, mail, medical supplies, and important civilian personnel. In addition, they would co-operate with the police and fire brigades.

The ferrying of aircraft from the manufacturers' airfields to the operational squadrons was not, initially, a part of the ATA's remit, for since the end of WW1 this duty had been carried out on an 'ad hoc' basis by RAF squadron pilots themselves. However, during the pre-war expansion of the RAF, a scheme was inaugurated in which thirty-two RAF pilots, operating from two Ferry Pools at Hucknall and Filton, and equally shared between them, were ferrying aircraft from the factories to the RAFVR schools, and into and out of several storage units. This continued throughout 1939, until such was the pressure on these service pilots, that the work was partially handed over to the ATA, in what were termed mixed pools. Before long the whole of the work was given over to the ATA and it became their main role.

Inevitably, with the creation of an all-male staffed ATA, the voice of a small but significant band of women pilots was soon demanding to be heard. Apart from Amy, there were many other lesser known but equally capable women such as Pauline Gower, Dorothy Spicer, Mona Friedlander and Mildred Bruce, who had already carved for themselves a career in aviation, albeit, most only in a minor role. This was a war in which they were determined to serve as pilots, and, moreover, on equal terms with the men! Women pioneers such as Amy Johnson, Jean Batten and Amelia Earhart had already proved that it could be done. However, the most influential in securing a role for women in the ATA during the latter part of 1939, proved to be Pauline Gower. Not only was she a very competent pilot with an 'A', 'B' and navigator's licence, and some 2,000 flying hours to her credit, she was also the daughter of the solicitor and MP, Sir Robert Gower.

There is no doubt she had the advantage of some of her father's political clout behind her when she approached Francis Shelmerdine on 21 September, with a proposal for the formation of a women's section of the ATA. After a great deal of bureaucratic huffing and puffing, she was given approval to recruit eight women pilots to ferry open-cockpit Tiger Moths from the de Havilland factory into stored reserve in Scotland – a task that the RAF was only too pleased to shed. And so, on 1 January 1940, the first entirely civilian ferry pool was established at Hatfield.

Many must have wondered why Amy, who was at this time engaged on Army Co-operation flying duties with Portsmouth, Southsea & Isle of Wight Aviation Ltd, was not chosen to form the women's section of the ATA. After all, she was an internationally known pilot and on very good terms with the DGCA, Francis Shelmerdine, he having been the best man at her wedding to Jim in 1932. Maybe a clue for her not being chosen, is given in a minute from the DGCA to the Director of Civil Aviation Finance dated September 23rd 1939. After outlining the background to the proposed women's section, Shelmerdine goes on to commend Pauline Gower for the job and then adds: 'She has never been a stunt pilot with all the publicity which is attached to that role.'[143]

☆ ☆ ☆

335

Jim Mollison had 5,370 valuable flying hours in his log book when he drove through the gates of White Waltham to join the ATA on 1 October 1940. There is no doubt that the 'playboy airman' was an object of much curiosity and speculation amongst those he was about to work with, not least because Amy, who had joined the women's pool at Hatfield four months previously, was an almost daily visitor to the Berkshire station. Being in lodgings at Marlow, some thirty-five miles from No: 5 Ferry Pool at Hatfield, she had been given special permission from Gerard d'Erlanger to commute whenever she wished between the two airfields in the station's Fox Moth. In a letter to her mother around this time, she tells her how surprised she was to find out that Jim was at White Waltham, implying that it was an embarrassment for her. She went on to explain that he is constantly badgering her to go out with him again. Finally, she adds that he is a nuisance and that she finds him a complete bore.[144] Maybe it was a case of 'she protesteth too much', for in spite of her remarks they were seen together socially on more than one occasion. Many thought that she missed being married to Jim and were not surprised when a *Sunday Express* columnist reported their meetings and even hinted at a re-marriage. (One just wonders what Phyllis Hussey's reactions were when she read this, for she was living in London at the time). Amy had had a succession of boyfriends since leaving Jim, some in the service, but none, it seems, had ever been the right one for her.

On the Sunday afternoon that Amy died, JM was flying Hurricane Z2587 on a routine delivery flight from the factory at Langley in Buckinghamshire, to the west country airfield of Aston Down near Stroud. As he taxied in and switched off, he glanced at his wristwatch to note that it was precisely 14.45 on 5 January 1941. Little did he know that at that very moment his former wife was in a cold sweat as she sat alone in the cockpit of her Airspeed Oxford, lost and desperately looking for a break in the clouds somewhere over southern England.

Two days earlier, Pauline Gower had detailed First Officer A. Johnson to deliver an Airspeed Oxford from her home station to Prestwick. Amy set off, ran into bad weather in the Midlands and put down for the night at Ternhill, before continuing on the following day to Scotland. Upon arrival, she rang her boss for further instructions and was told that she could either return by the night train to London, if she was too tired for another flight, or fly another Oxford down to Kidlington. Not relishing the thought of sitting in the draughty corridor of a crowded wartime train for five hours, she decided to accept the delivery flight.

As she flew the twin-engined training machine down the Cumbrian coast, she rather suspected that the compass was reading incorrectly. Not badly, only a few degrees out, but enough to show that landmarks sighted were not tying up with the heading she had been following. To add to her troubles, the weather began to deteriorate and so she decided to break her journey and land at Squires Gate, Blackpool. It was convenient, for it would enable her to spend the night at her sister's home which was quite near to the airfield.

Molly and Trevor Jones arrived home early in the evening and were surprised to find Amy sitting in their lounge. She explained that the flight down from Scotland had been a 'sticky' one, and that she was having some trouble with the aircraft's compass. Trevor offered to telephone the duty crew at the aerodrome and ask them to have it fixed, but Amy dismissed the idea, saying that it was only a trivial fault anyway. She seemed in good spirits.

On the following morning, she arrived at the frost-laden aerodrome somewhere around 10.15 BST, only to be greeted with a message from the Duty Officer that weather conditions for her intended route were unfavourable. A thin band of stratus was covering the entire area to the south, with a cloud base varying from 800 to 2,000 feet, and with occasional slight sleet and snow falling beneath it. Ground visibility was poor. Amy decided to wait for an improvement in the weather, whilst in the meantime the aircraft's fuel tanks were topped up to give her some four hours thirty minutes' flying time at 120mph. She was anxious to get away, for she was keen to attend a party that Pauline Gower was organising for the next day. It was to celebrate the first year of operational flying by the women's pool at Hatfield. No mention was made of the compass.

At 11.49 BST Amy took off from Squires Gate, having told the ground crew that she would go 'over the top'. This meant that she would climb to a height above the cloud layer, where conditions were clear, and hope for a break in the clouds somewhere near her destination. In the absence of radio this practice was strictly forbidden to ATA pilots, who were instructed to maintain visual contact with the ground throughout their delivery flights. Nevertheless, it was a rule that was often ignored by ferry pilots, especially when aircraft were urgently needed.

Amy's ETA for Kidlington was approximately 13.00 hrs., but she failed to arrive. Her wisest action would have been to take a reciprocal heading and return to Blackpool. The reason she did not do so might well have been due to her pride. She had always boasted that she could 'smell' her way through. One can only conjecture on the probability of her movements over the next two hours or so, until she finally emerged from the clouds over the Thames estuary, more than eighty miles south-east of the Oxfordshire aerodrome.

She may have circled Kidlington for an hour or so looking for a hole in the clouds, or she may have made for the low ground of East Anglia and become lost there for some time. We shall never know. What is beyond doubt is that her aircraft crashed into the estuary sometime during the late afternoon. The exact time is uncertain, and as we shall see, its uncertainty is a factor that has a great bearing upon the reason for the disaster.

On the afternoon of her death, the convoy CE21, some two to three miles long, was proceeding into the mouth of the estuary and making for Sheerness. The convoy consisted of 15 merchant vessels being escorted by a further 17 ships giving cover, 9 of which formed a protective box around the merchant ships by flying low zone balloons at the customary operational height of 2,000 feet. These were designed to ward off low-level attacks by enemy aircraft. There is every possibility that Amy, whilst not seeing the convoy, might well have seen these balloons protruding above the layer of cloud. In which case she might well have supposed that she was still over land.

Many theories have been put forward on the cause of Amy's death, but they are too lengthy and complex to be dealt with fully here. However, suffice it to say that the most popularly accepted theory, that she ran out of fuel and baled out over the Thames, is highly unlikely. The times given by three different ships for her crash into the estuary, and the contention that these were given in GMT, are critical to the 'out of fuel' theory. The Commander of the *Fernie*, a Hunt-class destroyer, reported that it was 'about 15.00 hr'; the *Haselmere* reported it as 15.30hr; the Motor Launch Flotilla gives a precise time of 15.37 hr. If these times were in fact given in GMT, and it is far from certain that they were, then Amy would have been in the air for a period varying, according to these three reports, from 4hrs 11mins to 4hrs 48mins.

Several other factors militate against the above theory. Namely, it is unlikely that Amy, however lost, would not have known that she was over an area where it would have been safe to descend through the cloud layer. Therefore she would hardly have waited for the tanks to run dry before making such a descent. Moreover, she had always told colleagues that she would never jump but would always stay with the aircraft. The American journalist Drew Middleton[145] was with the convoy on that afternoon and he had first seen the Oxford descending at approximately 750 feet with engines idling. At 200 feet he saw something white flutter from the aircraft 'but not certainly, a parachute' (sic). Another member of the *Berkeley's* crew,[146] who was on duty in the forward control tower, sighted what he believed to be an Avro Anson descending, again with engines idling. At no time did he observe anyone leave the aircraft. In spite of a search from the *Berkeley's* whaler, which subsequently retrieved two pieces of Amy's luggage from the water, there was no sign of any parachute floating on the surface, neither was her body ever found.

Members of the crew of the *Haselmere* were the most closely involved in what they thought was a rescue attempt. Their Captain, Lt. Cdr. Walter Fletcher, dived in to swim towards a survivor, abandoned it for some unknown reason and swam towards a lifeboat that had been launched for the rescue. After ten minutes in the cold waters he was pulled unconscious into the boat and died later in hospital without regaining consciousness. Lt. Henry O'Dea, Leading Seaman Nicholas Roberts and Seaman Raymond Dean later testified that they had seen a woman in the water as they drew near her, and that she was heard by the seamen to cry: 'Hurry, please hurry' before she disappeared under the stern of the boat. O'Dea claimed he had seen two people in the water (most probably the two pieces of luggage) and Dean had seen a woman who 'appeared' to be wearing a life-jacket. However, the ATA did not issue life-jackets until after the invasion of France in June 1944, and members of the ground crew at Squires Gate testified that she was not wearing one when she left there. Furthermore, Lt. O'Dea admitted under close cross-questioning by Sir William Crocker,[147] solicitor conducting the inquiry at the request of the Johnson family, that on the question of identifying the sex of the person in the water, he was relying entirely upon his imagination.

Fifty years later, it seems more probable that Amy was shot down by the combined gunfire of the ships, gun-emplacements on the Martello towers in the estuary, and the coastal defence batteries. Gunner Richard Powell was a member of the Royal Artillery and at action stations with a Shoeburyness unit on that day. He recalls that her plane was circling round, its RAF markings being clearly visible, and that it was being fired upon by the ships.[148] If this is true, then Amy might well have been shot down whilst descending for any of the nearby aerodromes of Rochford, Manston, or even Gravesend (the latter one she was very familiar with).

In spite of the official reports of the ships that they opened fire on a Junkers 88 shortly *after* the time that Amy's plane crashed, at least one survivor of the *Berkeley's* crew is adamant that it was before. Leading Stoker Ernest Hannam is on record as saying: 'We were certainly not under attack after Amy Johnson's plane crashed, it came before.'[149]

Jim Mollison always believed to the end of his life that Amy was shot down by the Luftwaffe, but this can be discounted for Bundesarchiv do not support this. Their records show that *Luftflotte 2*, the Brussels' based wing which was responsible for covering the Thames estuary sector, did not report any aerial combat or aircraft lost on that day.

What is rather surprising is that two vital pieces of evidence were never kept. These being (a) A ten foot long portion of one of the Oxford's wings, clearly showing the serial number V3540, which was pulled from the water a few hours after the crash. And (b) Part of the tailplane's fin which was washed ashore on the mud flats near Shoeburyness. Both of these items, it seems, have disappeared without trace. When one compares this with the fact that parts of the Messerchmitt Bf 110 used by Rudolf Hess on his peace mission to Britain in 1941 are exhibited today in one of the country's leading aviation museums, one cannot but ask why the Oxford's wreckage was never thought important enough to keep. One must also ask why there was never a public inquiry into her death immediately after WW2. Could it be that the wreckage showed signs of gunfire penetration, and that it would have been demoralising for the nation to be told that we had shot down our own national heroine. At least one person was convinced that this was the case. Some fifteen years after the war, Police Constable Arundell Tucker, who was stationed at West Hampstead in January 1941, told his relatives that rumours were circulating in police quarters at that time that examination of parts of Amy's aircraft revealed damage by *anti-aircraft fire*.(150)

Amy had always told her friends that after her death she would soon be forgotten. Her usual remark being: 'A few headlines in the newspapers and then they forget you.' Remarkably, this has not proved to be the case, for the arguments concerning her untimely death continue even today. They are as powerful as those still surrounding Amelia Earhart's disappearance in the Pacific in 1937. Maybe the mystery could be solved if the main portion of the Oxford, that containing the cabin and the two Cheetah engines, were to be salvaged. Its approximate position is well known, showing that it lies on a sandy bed in only two to three metres of water on a low water spring tide. Its retrieval might well be expensive, but examination of the wreckage could possibly solve the riddle.

☆ ☆ ☆

The news of Amy's death was greeted by Jim Mollison with dismay, and those who knew him at the time tell how he became morose and withdrawn within himself. Whatever his feelings were for Amy, he kept them very much to himself. Even before her death he had become a very private person, with few close friends, and no doubt the refuge he sought in the gin-bottle gave some temporary respite from the pain of remorse he now felt. His well-known desire for privacy in the ATA did not mean that he was not popular amongst his colleagues, for there are a countless number today who recall that he was great company to be with, but only when perfectly sober. When he was on a bender, he could become quite aggressive. Sober, he was unusually modest, and had a reputation of being a highly amusing raconteur. Added to this, was his dry, laconic wit, which was usually spiced with his own brand of self-mocking humour. Joan Hughes, one of the wartime ferry pilots, recalls an occasion when she was sitting outside the Duty Office with a group of ATA pilots seriously discussing the sort of gadget that each would like to see fitted to modern aircraft. During a lull in the conversation, Joan turned to Jim and asked him what he thought. 'Well,' said Jim, in his rather fruity voice, 'There's only one thing I want in an aeroplane, and that's a button, that when I press it, I find myself back in bed.'[(151)]

The ATA, which came under the rules of the RAF where drinking was concerned, frowned upon the use of alcohol in anything other than its moderate use on social occasions. It meant that Mollison's drinking was necessarily done outside of the company of his colleagues. Even so it was an ill-kept secret. Through the constant imbibing of alcohol over the years he had developed a very florid complexion, and in order to disguise it he had taken to powdering his face. This was the cause of much merriment, especially to some of the younger men who regarded Jim, now in his late thirties, as being a bit over the hill. Several recall that even when visiting an out-station, one could always tell if Jim was on the premises by the trail of perfume left in his wake. Sniff, sniff. 'Yes, Jim's here,' and usually they were correct. Johnnie Jordan, a young ATA pilot at the time, remembers pulling the older man's leg mercilessly when he caught him in the toilets applying the talcum. 'Jim, you look like a b***** victoria plum!' To which the older man, in his rather polished accent, good humouredly replied: 'One must think of one's public, you know, my dear boy.'[(152)]

Towards the end of 1940, the newly appointed Minister of Aircraft Production, Lord Beaverbrook, was becoming increasingly concerned at the U-boat menace in the North Atlantic. American aircraft destined for Britain under Roosevelt's lease lend agreement were ending up at the bottom of the ocean instead of reaching the operational squadrons of the RAF. Beaverbrook was quick to recognise that what was needed was an Atlantic bridge in the form of an air ferry service. In spite of the difficulties of primitive weather forecasting, and wing icing during the winter months, an

Atlantic Ferry Organisation pilots at St. Hubert, Montreal, in 1941. From left: 'Tex' Adding, Al Torrey, Danny Dugan, 'Duke' Schiller, Jim Mollison, Bob Draper and Bill Vanderkloot.

Atlantic Ferry Organisation (ATFERO) was set up with Don Bennett appointed to act as the Superintendent of Flying.

Donald Bennett was an RAAF short service commission pilot, seconded to the RAF in Britain in the early Thirties, and a stickler for discipline. After flying Siskin and Bulldog fighters at North Weald with 29 Squadron, he was transferred to 210 Flying Boat Squadron at Calshot, from where he subsequently achieved a first class navigators licence. He had left the service in 1935 to join Imperial Airways and had since made a name for himself as an Atlantic pilot, principally on the Short-Mayo composite. This was a far-sighted 'pick-a-back' arrangement, whereby the parent aircraft, the flying boat *Maia*, took off with the smaller seaplane *Messenger* mounted above it. The configuration enabled the smaller seaplane, piloted by Bennett, to carry a far heavier fuel load than usual and thereby cover greater distances than would normally be possible. There is no doubt that it was subsequently the inspiration behind the idea of transporting the American Apollo space shuttle on the back of a Boeing 747, prior to it being launched from its Cape Canaveral site.

On 11 March 1941 Jim Mollison was officially posted to ATFERO, arriving in St Hubert, Montreal, for training under Don Bennett soon afterwards. One can only speculate that he was deemed a worthy candidate for the new service by virtue of his experience as a solo aviator over the same route. There is every likelihood that Lord Beaverbrook had something to do with the posting, for not only was JM a friend of the Canadian tycoon's son, Max Aitken, but it was possibly not overlooked that he had also boosted the sales of the *Daily Express* (Beaverbrook owned it) by his exploits during the economic depression of the Thirties.

If it was Beaverbrook's way of rewarding the Scot, it was certainly an ill-judged appointment and one doomed to failure. No two men could have been more dissimilar than Mollison and Bennett. Their relationship must have been fraught with danger right from the outset. Bennett was an abstemious man with a rather short fuse and a reputation for not suffering fools very gladly. He would certainly frown upon any form of drinking whilst on flying duties. He had surrounded himself with high calibre airline pilots to form the nucleus of ATFERO, men mainly recruited, like himself, from ex-Imperial Airways' staff. Amongst them were Gordon Store,* the legendary O. P. Jones, 'Taffy' Powell, A. L. 'Buddy' Messenger and the Dutch, ex-KLM pilot J. J. Moll. One must remember that JM had been a constant critic of Imperial Airways in those days, and to these pilots he would have been considered quite beneath the pale. Moreover, two of them, Bennett and Moll, had been Mollison's keen competitors in the Mildenhall Air race in 1934. One can imagine the talk in the St Hubert Mess when they heard that this raffish bohemian – suede shoes, perfume, et al – was being posted to them!

JM's log shows only four entries for his time in Montreal, all training sessions on Lockheed Hudsons, before it records his departure for the UK on 12 May aboard the four-engined Liberator AM913. Whilst JM's flying log gives the impression that he was in charge of the aircraft, Richard K. Smith reveals that Canadian records show that he was only acting as a 'supernumerary captain' to the ex-BOAC pilot Captain 'Buddy' Messenger when the bomber flew into Gander on that flight back to Prestwick.[153] Whether JM's hasty return from Canada was the result of some unacceptable behaviour, we shall probably never know. It seems highly unlikely that he would have dipped the flying tests, for he was far too competent a pilot to fail those. During his wartime service with the ATA he was not only to fly Hudsons and Liberators, but also to fly sixty-two other different types of aircraft. These ranged from four-engined Fortresses, Lancasters and Halifaxes, to single-engined Spitfires and Tempests. It might well have been that the days of ATFERO were numbered anyway, for in July of that year it ceased to be a civilian organisation. Air Chief Marshal Sir Frederick

*JM had broken the Salaman/Store Cape record in 1932.

Bowhill took over control of what was to become RAF Ferry Command, and Don Bennett departed to pastures new. From hereon, he was destined to earn fame as the leader of Bomber Command's newly created Pathfinder Force.

☆ ☆ ☆

Under Gerard d'Erlanger's fine leadership the pilots of the ATA soon became a vital part of the nation's war effort. Their leader had managed to weld, what were in effect, an elderly bunch of amateur pilots into a highly trained and effective force. By the summer of 1941 they were operating from twelve different Ferry Pools strategically placed around the the country and including Northern Ireland. Amongst their ranks were grocers, actors, farmers, stockbrokers, doctors, journalists, even an ex-TT rider and a conjurer! Most had been deemed unfit for military flying with the RAF by virtue of their age or physical fitness. Not surprisingly, these men soon earned the affectionate tag of being the nation's 'Ancient and Tattered Airmen'. In conjunction with their women counterparts, they were required, even after only a brief reading of an aircraft's handling notes, to fly and deliver a great diversity of unfamiliar aircraft at very short notice. Their workload could be as many as five deliveries in any one day.

Whilst discipline was not of the petty or nit-picking kind, it was nevertheless strictly enforced in the areas of safety and standards of behaviour. Philip Wills, the tall, bespectacled officer in charge of No: 1 Ferry Pool at White Waltham, had been a shipping director and amateur glider pilot of some repute before joining the ATA. He had a reputation for running a tight ship without being overbearing, but brooked no nonsense where necessary discipline was concerned.

Former ATA pilot Stanley Stephenson ('Stevie' the conjurer) recalls an incident that highlights Philip Wills' character. Stevie had just landed at an aerodrome in the Midlands when he noticed one of the Avro Anson's used for taxi purposes coming in on its landing approach. The pilot made a very poor fist of the landing, bouncing some ten feet into the air, and then six feet and so on, until he eventually put it down. The pilot went to the Flight Office to check in but made no mention of the heavy landing at all. Unfortunately for him, he had been observed by one of the ATA's more senior officers, who subsequently made a check to see if the pilot had reported the matter. By the book he should have admitted to his bad flying and asked for an undercarriage inspection to be carried out. The matter was reported by the observing officer to Philip Wills, who immediately asked to see the

miscreant at 09.00hrs sharp in his office the next morning. At 09.10 Stevie happened to bump into the chastened pilot in one of the corridors at the HQ. The man mumbled: 'I've just been sacked and told to pack my bags. I've to be off the station straight away.' In spite of the man's protestations of sorrow and remorse, Wills was adamant that the man must go. His senior officer's line of reasoning was that someone could have been killed on the the next flight of that Anson. In other words the pilot was sacked, not for his bad airmanship, but for failing to report a heavy landing.[154]

It was against this background of discipline that Jim Mollison returned to his duties at White Waltham after his period with ATFERO. Shortly afterwards, he was given leave and had spent a weekend in London. In one of the capital's nightclubs he had become the worse for drink and when refused more at the bar had become aggressive. When the staff could not calm him, the police were called and eventually he was thrown out of the premises.

The story quickly reached the ear of Gerard d'Erlanger and JM was summoned to his office. The Commander told him in no uncertain terms that not only was such behaviour bad for Mollison's reputation, it was also bad for the ATA's image. Mollison was trapped, he knew that d'Erlanger had the power to sack him on the spot. It was not a thought that he relished, for it would have meant the end of his wartime flying career. Quite coincidentally to Mollison's fracas with the police, d'Erlanger had recently received a request from the Ministry of Aircraft Production for one of his pilots to deliver a rather dicey prototype aeroplane, known as the 'Flying Wing', from Eastleigh to French West Equatorial Africa. He had pondered who, amongst his staff, should be sent on what was obviously a rather dangerous mission. With a rather submissive Flight Captain Mollison now standing before him, he was presented with the ideal opportunity for some rather judicious arm-twisting. 'Yes, Mollison, I could report this matter to higher authority, but I'll tell you what . . .' The deal was struck. Mollison would make the delivery to Africa.[155]

In November 1936 the well known long-distance aviator Clyde Pangborn had delivered the one and only version of the Burnelli UB-14B across the Atlantic to Britain. It was an unorthodox, twin-engined American design in which the fuselage formed part of the aerofoil of the main wing. In the wing was a cabin, which was designed to carry 15 to 20 people, depending upon its particular layout. Its conventional tailplane was supported by twin booms, and whilst the term was not truly descriptive, it became known as the 'Flying Wing'. The idea of a flying wing was not new in aviation history, for J. W. Dunne had been experimenting with tail-less aircaft since 1908. In

addition, Professor Hugo Junkers, the pioneer of all-metal aircraft, had produced drawings for his J1000 Flying Wing project in 1921, but it got no further than the drawing-board stage. The manufacturing rights of the Burnelli UB-14B had been purchased by the Scottish Aircraft & Engineering Company, who intended to produce a British version of it with RR Kestrel engines, and this was the reason for Pangborn's delivery. Early in 1937 Bill Courtenay suggested to Amy that she should fly the SAEC version of it in the Lindbergh Memorial Air Race. As it happened, the race was cancelled and the Scottish version of the aircraft never materialised. The Eastleigh based company Cunliffe-Owen Aircraft Co., took the project over shortly afterwards, and did in fact produce a prototype, OA-1, under licence. It was very similar to the UB-14B but used Bristol Perseus sleeve-valved engines. By the end of 1938 it was registered G-AFMB and made its first trial flight on 12 January 1939 in the hands of Clyde Pangborn. Its outstanding feature was its a ability to carry its own weight of 9,500lb in disposable load at a cruising speed of 195mph.

At the outbreak of war, G-AFMB was impressed by the Air Ministry along with all other civilian aircraft. No one knew what to do with the beast until early in 1941 a suggestion was made that it should be presented to General de Gaulle, who was at the time stationed in Brazzaville. Rumour has it that it was the only medium-sized transport plane in which the tall leader of the Free French Forces could stand up in without banging his head. Whatever the reason for its disposal might have been, James Mollison was the man chosen to captain it on its 5,000 mile journey.

At the end of May, JM disappeared from White Waltham without a word to anyone. The only clue to his departure being the cryptic words 'special mission' chalked against his name on the station's operations board. He had been allocated a crew consisting of a Free French co-pilot and RAF navigator, and on 1 June they began a series of familiarisation flights in the Flying Wing over Eastleigh.

The most direct route for the flight would have been down to Gibraltar and then across the Sahara to their destination at Bangui in Central Africa, but this was totally out of the question in 1941. There was no way in which refuelling stops could have been organised in time of war, and to have used the west coast of Africa route with Dakar still under the control of the French Vichy government was deemed too hazardous. The only alternative was to take the more circuitous route through the Middle East to Cairo. From here they would fly south to stop at Wadi Halfa on their way to Khartoum, before turning to fly westwards across Africa to Bangui, with stops at El Obeid, El Fasher, Geneina and Fort Archambault.

The unarmed Cunliffe-Owen OA-1 'Flying Wing' which Mollison ferried with two crew members (RAF and FFAF) from Eastleigh to Bangui in French Equatorial Africa in June 1941.

The flight was almost a disaster before it really got under way. The normal departure point to the ME for Allied aircrew was Portreath in Cornwall. However, JM and his crew were detailed to call in for a briefing at Kemble in Gloucestershire, the home of the Overseas Air Delivery Flight. Just before their departure, an RAF fitter[156] climbed into the cockpit to start the engines of G-AFMB. Unfortunately, whoever had last touched the controls had left the throttles wide open and the brakes off. This was overlooked by the fitter, who was unfamiliar with the throttle action on the Perseus engines. They were of an unconventional type, using a push-pull movement similar to the choke-control on most cars. Pilots would normally open the throttles after the engines had been switched off in order to clear the gases in the system and then immediately return them to the closed position. On this particular day the rigger had also failed to place chocks under the wheels before the engines were fired. As a consequence, as soon as the fitter started one of the engines the aircraft shot forward and careered across the hangar apron, only to be halted after it had slammed into a Bristol Bombay parked nearby. JM went ashen as he watched the incident actually take place and thought of its implications. No doubt the air was filled with more than a few choice expletives. Fortunately, the damage was only superficial, but bad enough to delay the flight for three days whilst repairs were carried out.

JM recalls that there were a few uneasy moments as they made a daylight flight across the northern part of German-occupied France in their unarmed aircraft. Apart from the possibility of falling prey to one of *Luftflotte 3's* Junkers 88s, which were at that time stationed around Cherbourg, there was more than a little apprehension in the mind of the French co-pilot at the prospect of baling out over his own country. Any member of the Free French Air Force falling into the hands of the Vichy government would have been considered guilty of treason and would possibly have faced execution. The Bay of Biscay crossing was also fraught with danger, inasmuch as it was an area in which the Flying Wing would have been easy meat for any of the four-engined FW 200 Condors that regularly plied their trade against Allied shipping in that region. One can only speculate on the reason why JM and his crew did not cover this leg of the journey by night. It probably had something to do with the hazard of landing on the notoriously short runway then existing at Gibraltar. Maybe he thought that it was better to chance being shot down, rather than suffer drowning by night in the Meditteranean harbour.

Similar apprehension prevailed on the second and third stages of the journey when they flew into and out of the aerodrome at Hal Far, Malta (the third stage from Malta to Cairo was flown at night). The small island was under almost constant aerial attack during this period. Not only by Mussolini's bombers but also by the Luftwaffe's Junkers 87 and 88s, which, since early in the spring, had been operating from the airfield at Catania in nearby Sicily. However, the rest of the flight passed uneventfully and they arrived at their destination on 28 June to deliver the aircraft in one piece. Former ATA pilot Diana Barnato Walker remembers that upon his return, Jim was always most proud of the gold cigarette case that was presented to him by De Gaulle.[157] Engraved on its side covers were maps of the route, together with the stopping places marked in rubies. It was all part of the entente cordiale!

☆ ☆ ☆

The 'African job', as it became known at White Waltham, must have ended any lingering suspicion amongst his ATA colleagues that JM was living on his laurels from the long-distance flying days of the past. The younger and more inexperienced members of the ATA were always fulsome in their praise of him, knowing that he was the first to help them during their settling in period at White Waltham. Joan Hughes, who was instructing at the station during the early part of 1941, recalls that 'he couldn't have been kinder to very junior pilots', and that 'he never pushed himself with them'. There was always the *mot juste* of course. On one occasion he was in the presence of a new pilot who had been detailed to fly a certain type of aeroplane for the very first time. The young man was working himself up into a bit of a frenzy with remarks such as: 'Oh gosh, I've forgotten what boost, revs and oil pressure, etc.' Jim looked up casually from his newspaper and said: 'Don't worry old boy. Just keep all the dials in about the middle.'[158]

In his book *I Couldn't Care Less*, former ATA pilot First Officer Anthony Phelps recalls how helpful Jim was to him when he first joined the unit at White Waltham. Not only in explaining procedures – colloquially known as the 'form' – but also in more practical ways in the air. It was the winter of 1941/42 and he had been detailed, along with Mollison and others, to collect some Hurricanes that were urgently needed up in Scotland. Most of the group got away in the morning, but JM and Phelps were delayed until the following afternoon. The older man had assured his young friend not to worry too much but to just tuck in behind and follow him. Phelps remembers how nervous he was when they struck out from the Cumbrian coast to cross the fifty miles or so across the Solway Firth. It was the younger man's first experience at flying over, what was for him, a lengthy expanse of open sea. As the weather deteriorated, he had all his work cut out just to keep JM within view. Eventually, in order to keep below the lowering cloud base, they were forced down to within only a few feet above the surface of the water. Phelps kept thinking: 'I wonder if he's as scared as I am.' As they finally scraped into the delivery airfield, the weather completely closed in on them. The palms of his hands were more than a trifle clammy as he realised how different the story might have been if his mentor had not been alongside.

Unfortunately, not all ATA pilots were as lucky as these two had been on this occasion. Captain F. A. White and co-pilot Captain F. D. Bradbrooke were crewing a Liberator on a return trip to Canada in 1941 with a number of ferry pilots on board, when it flew directly into a 2,800 ft peak on the Isle of Arran. Sadly, none of the 22 on board survived. Bad weather flying conditions claimed the lives of the majority of the 139 members of ATA aircrew who were killed in the wartime period. Representing as it did, a fatality rate of approximately 9.2% of their total number, it acts as a reminder of the dangers which these brave men and women faced almost daily.

Maybe it was inevitable that with such a diversity of aircraft being flown, risks were taken. After all, much like people, each aeroplane had its own peculiarities, some of which could be quite dangerous if they were not

Waiting to ferry Mosquito night-fighters from Hatfield on 12 February 1942. From left: Commander Frank Francis, Captain F. White, Commander T. H. N. 'Doc' Whitehurst, Flt. Captain K. Dlugaszewski, Flt. Captain Jim Mollison and Flt. Captain Bill Harben.

quickly mastered. Former ATA test-pilot, Captain J. A. V. Watson, recalls being in the HQ's flight office talking with the ATA's Chief Flying Instructor, Tommy Gale, when they were disturbed by the sound of a Douglas Boston circling low over the airfield. As they looked out of the window, they could see that it was now raining heavily. The rain had come after a long spell of hot dry weather, which had left the surface of the grass airfield hard-baked and unyielding. As a consequence, its surface was now as slippery as an ice-rink for any aircraft about to land on it.

Much to the consternation of the CFI, the twin-engined Boston bomber came in over the hedge at well over 100mph. The conversation in the flight office then went something like this: CFI, 'Who's flying this one? The damn fool's going to damage himself *and* the aircraft if he tries to land it here.' From the confident way the machine was being handled, Watson recognised who was flying the aeroplane, and he retorted: 'No, he'll be OK. It's Mollison.' Knowing that the aircraft had a tricycle undercarriage, his colleague was not so easily convinced. It meant that it landed in a low-drag attitude with an attendant high speed, quite unlike the more conventional tail-wheel type of aeroplane, such as the Mosquito, which lost its landing speed much more rapidly.

The two men watched in stunned silence as the Boston landed across the diagonal of the airfield, using its 1100 yard length to the full. However, when it was only a hundred yards or so from the far hedge, it was still travelling much too fast to pull up in time. They waited for the crunch. J.A.V. Watson then describes the nearest thing to the application of reverse thrust that he had ever seen in the age of propeller-driven aircraft. 'Mollison just opened the throttle on the starboard engine at the same time as he stamped on the brakes. The aircraft spun round through 180 degrees on its own axis, whereupon he opened the other throttle to taxy slowly back to the hangars.' 'What was more, the surface was so slippery that the undercarriage wasn't even damaged at all.'[159] Drink or no drink, JM had lost none of his old skills.

Whilst there is no known instance of ATA crews being shot down by enemy aircraft, it does not mean that none were ever fired upon by enemy machines. Mollison's flying log does in fact record a note alongside his entry for 10 February 1943, which reads, 'Anson regn: 4929, Aston Down to White Waltham, 16.10/16.40hr, Returning base (attacked).' Almost fifty years later, it is impossible to verify the incident from ex-ATA personnel, and unfortunately, the Bundesarchiv can neither confirm nor deny if an attack was made by any Luftwaffe aircraft on that day, in that particular area.[160] They simply state that their records for this period are partial and incomplete. However, since the entry is countersigned by the OC No: 1 Ferry Pilots Pool, Commander T. Whitehurst, the reported incident must have been taken seriously by the ATA's HQ at White Waltham. It is quite conceivable that some half-frozen German gunner, sitting alone in the *Sterbebett* under-belly gun position of a homeward bound Heinkel 111, might well have loosed off a few rounds at *der Englander* several thousand feet beneath him, just to relieve the boredom.

If the German crew had been more determined to press home an attack, then it might well have been a disastrous day for the ATA because the grey-green taxi Anson would have been carrying at least ten returning pilots on this occasion.

☆ ☆ ☆

The ATA's delivery activity increased rapidly just before the D-Day landings onto the beaches of Normandy on 6 June 1944. The skies of southern Britain were full of Allied aircraft, with their black and white underwing and fuselage identification markings, wending their way to the Continent as our ground forces slowly began to roll back a stubborn enemy.

The invasion plans had provided for the setting up of two RAF controlled Ground Support Units (GSU's), No: 83 at Redhill and No: 84 at Aston Down, in order to keep the 2nd Tactical Air Force in France topped up with fighters. At the same time the two ATA ferry pools, No: 1 at at White Waltham and No: 9 at Aston Down, were designated 'invasion' pools. Their job was to deliver the Spitfires, Mustangs and Tempests to the GSU's, whereupon RAF pilots would then ferry them across the Channel.

By 5 September GSU No: 84 had moved from Aston Down to Thruxton, and it was on this day that the procedure began to falter. It was found that aircraft were urgently needed in northern France and there were insufficient RAF pilots to deliver them. After some rapid telephone and written communication between Gerard d'Erlanger and Wing Cdr. Watkins, CO of No: 84 GSU, permission was given, by way of a concession, for the ATA to deliver two Spitfires on the following day. As a result, the honour of piloting them to the airstrip B31, situated between Dieppe and Abbeville, fell to Commander Hugh Bergel, CO of No: 9 Ferry Pool at Aston Down, and, appropriately enough, Flight Captain Maurice Harle, the first Frenchman to join the ATA.

With the fall of Paris to the Allied forces on 25 August, there was a scramble amongst ATA pilots to be the first into Le Bourget. Gerard d'Erlanger was anxious to be the first into the French capital for he had a sister living there throughout the German occupation. However, when the opportunity did suddenly arise on September 12th, the ATA's CO was unable to go because of the short notice given. Hugh Bergel was at Thruxton on that particular day and he describes the situation in his book, *Fly and Deliver*:

> Wing Commander Watkins didn't think he could lay on an Anson to go to Le Bourget, but by chance Jim Mollison, with one of White Waltham's Ansons, was actually on the aerodrome at Thruxton. Perhaps, fearful of letting Jim loose in Paris, D'Erlanger comandeered his Anson and instructed me to take it over. The last I saw of Jim that day was a sad figure with his tongue still hanging out.[161]

JM's first visit to the Continent after the invasion came quite early in October, when he was delegated to fly the taxi Anson to collect ferry pilots at Caen, Ypres and Brussels. It meant an overnight stay in the Belgian capital just four weeks after the Germans had made their hurried withdrawal. After four years of enemy occupation, ATA members were surprised to find that life in the city had soon returned, at least outwardly, to much of its pre-war normality. One pilot recalls that, 'the crowded yellow trams clanged along the Boulevard Adolphe Max much as usual', and that 'the cafés were filled with prosperous-looking people'.[162] Obviously there were food shortages for the general population, but no doubt, as in occupied France and elsewhere, the 'black market' provided for those who could afford it. According to JM, 'the word "British" was an open sesame to every Belgian home' at that time, and particularly so, it is said by some, when his parachute pack was stuffed with a generous supply of silk-stockings and cigarettes. He was never one to miss an opportunity!

One former member of the ATA who wishes to remain anonymous, recalls being told of JM's first visit to Paris, which fell on New Years Day 1945. It was termed a 'special duty' flight and on this occasion he was accompanied in the ubiquitous Anson by a rather youthful ATA Flight Engineer named Freddie Laker.* The normal stopover in Paris for ATA personnel was the Hotel de la Paix, on the Rue de la Paix, but Jim, being familiar with the pre-war capital, had other ideas. They eventually arrived at a small hotel which was run by a Scottish lady owner – it was probably less burdensome on their overnight allowance. Upon going upstairs to their room, the two men were highly amused to find German steel helmets under the beds for use as chamber-pots.

During the evening, Jim decided go off alone to explore the state of the liberated capital's night-spots, only to return in the early hours much the worse for wear. Freddie was awakened from his sleep by the sound of running water and upon going into the bathroom to investigate, found Jim lying submerged in the bath fully clothed. Not wishing to report the death of a colleague by drowning in a Parisian hotel, he quickly pulled him out.

Life was not all fun and frolic however, for with the advance of the American 3rd Army, together with the French 1st Army, into the area of the Belfort Gap in late November, replacement Spitfires were urgently needed by the FFAF Wing at Luxeuil. Its airfield, which was situated to the south-west of the Vosges Mountains, lay some 55 miles from the Swiss border and approximately 210 miles from Paris. JM had already made one flight to the airstrip from Reims on Christmas day, having ferried a Spitfire down from Brussels on the previous day. The weather deteriorated rapidly after this, into one of the severest winters that Europe had experienced for the past sixty years. However, although this hampered, it did not entirely stop ATA deliveries.

In January JM was detailed, along with eleven other pilots, to participate in one of the most hazardous of Spitfire deliveries undertaken during that winter of 1944/45. When they arrived at Hawkinge on the 16th the ground

---

*Later to become Sir Freddie Laker.

was already thick with snow, and temperatures were down below freezing. Three of the ATA pilots managed to get away by early afternoon, and made Luxeuil non-stop. The remaining nine aircraft were delayed for various reasons and their crews did not manage to get away until three days later. Even then, they were forced to put down at Le Bourget owing to the poor conditions. By 5pm of that afternoon the whole of France was covered by snow blizzards and they were forced to abandon their plans and wait. It meant an uncomfortable stay in Paris, which at that time was without coal and suffering from a severe curtailment of its electricity supplies. To make matters worse, owing to the small amount of space in the Spitfire's cockpit, the ATA pilots were without warm winter clothing, and for the most of their time in Paris they were forced to wander around in their flying suits.

On the 24th the 'Met' office reported a slight improvement in weather conditions in the Luxeuil area, and after scraping the snow and ice from their aircraft, five of the Spitfires managed to get away. Three of them returned shortly afterwards, after running into heavy snowstorms, and they rejoined the rest who were forced to continue their wait for a further nine days, by which time a thaw had set in.

At 2.30pm on the afternoon of February 1st, each Spitfire ploughed a bow wave down the slush-laden runway at Le Bourget before it finally clawed its way into the air. Their pilots drew small comfort from knowing that their radios were inoperative now that they were flying into the American sector ahead of them. As they scanned the bleak horizon, the rivers, roads and railway-tracks had all become obliterated by the snow into a featureless white landscape. It meant that their navigation was going to be difficult as they headed south-east to grope their way along valleys flanked by cloud-obscured mountains.

By late afternoon all had arrived at the FFAF air base except Jim, and by the time they were sitting down to a meal in the French Mess there was some concern for his safety. At 9pm he strode into the Mess, much to the surprise of his colleagues, and no doubt with much ribald leg-pulling as he explained that he had got lost among the snow-covered hills and forests. Quite by chance he had happened to sight a deserted airfield at Epinal, where fortunately he put down without damage. From here, he had hitch-hiked the 30 miles into Luxeuil.

☆ ☆ ☆

The war in Europe ended with the unconditional surrender of Germany on Luneberg Heath on 8 May 1945, whilst the fierce conflict in the Far East ended soon after on 15 August in the same year, accelerated no doubt by the dropping of atom bombs on Hiroshima and Nagasaki. The official closure of the ATA came on 30 November, by which time its pilots had made 308,567 deliveries over the six year period of its ferrying activity. JM had left sometime before then. The last entry in his wartime flying log shows that he delivered Dakota K9650 from Prestwick to Kemble, with an overnight stop at Squires Gate on 30 May.

In retrospect, one can see that the ATA pilots and their supporting staff were treated rather shabbily and given little formal recognition by the RAF, or their country. Former ATA pilot, Lettice Curtis, reminds us forcibly of this in her excellent book *Forgotten Pilots*, a definitive history of the ATA. Although there was a distribution of civilian honours in the form of CBE's to Gerard d'Erlanger and Philip Wills; OBE's to the Ferry Pool heads; and MBE's to selected Flight Captains, JM being amongst them, they hardly matched up to the military decorations and medals given by the Royal Navy to its Auxilaiary and Merchant Navy personnel. To rub salt in the wound, only twelve men and twelve women were asked to participate in the Victory parade through London on 8 June 1946. And even then, they were placed to march alongside transport workers, and not with the RAF!

As for Mollison, he now found himself without a job, and more importantly he found himself without a purpose in life. In a strange sort of way the war had been his salvation. It had provided him with self-esteem and a structure which, by virtue of its enforced discipline, had controlled his drinking. Now forty years of age, he was too old for a career in commercial aviation, and the Golden Age of record-breaking was gone forever.

Former ATA colleague Captain Charles Tutt recalls that JM probably missed his immediate postwar chances, when Frankie Francis, former CO of No: 1 Ferry Pool, millionaire and owner of much property in the West Indies, set up an air service in the Caribbean and would have been willing to offer the Scot a role in it. He comments: 'So when the war was over, Jim would be just the chap to fly the guests to any island or key they wished to see. When these opportunities occurred, he was missing! The whole atmosphere of mega-rich pleasure was his downfall. Very sad!'[163]

In a lighter vein, Stevie Stephenson remembers talking with Jim about their postwar prospects just before they left the ATA. Stevie had been a professional conjurer before joining the ATA, and, apart from being in great demand at ATA parties, had performed before members of the Royal family. In a moment of jocularity, Jim latched onto a bright idea for easy money. 'I'll tell you what Stevie. After the war we'll go to the States. I've got the freedom of the city of New York and we'll set up shop over there. You draw the customers in, and I'll skin them.'[164]

Chapter 20

'Steep Descent'

A slightly inebriated Jim Mollison was about to order another gin and tonic, when he spotted the balding head of the aircraft designer Edgar Percival sitting at the bar of the Royal Aero Club. The club was a favourite haunt of JM when he was in town, providing as it did somewhere where he could drink and at the same time be sure of enjoying the company of old friends. The last time the two men had met had been when they witnessed the departure of Beryl Markham on her transatlantic flight from Abingdon in September 1936, and now with a backlog of news to catch up on, they were soon deep into conversation.

During the war years the Australian's aircraft company at Luton had, in conjunction with their sub-contractors in Manchester, supplied almost a thousand Proctor three-seat communications aircraft of various marks to the RAF. The machine was the military version of the pre-war Vega Gull, so successfuly used by Beryl and many other long-distance solo aviators in the Thirties. With the cessation of hostilities the company, together with many other of its British fellow competitors, began to cast a judicious eye on the potential of overseas export markets.

Over drinks, Percival mentioned that he had received enquiries for his aircraft from Brazil and India, and that he intended shipping one demonstrator Proctor to each country. In spite of his alcoholic daze, Jim was not slow to see the possibility of a business opportunity, for at that time he was almost on his uppers and still without prospect of suitable employment. Discreetly, he enquired just how long their delivery would take on the sea-crossing and exactly how much the shipping costs were likely to be. As soon as Percival told him, JM, now well topped up, said: 'I'll fly them direct from your works, demonstrate them when I get there, *and* do it for less than the shipping costs.' The Australian, shrewd man that he was, knew a good deal when he saw one and took up the Scot's offer with a quick response of, 'You're on', and the matter was settled with a handshake.

Whenever JM subsequently told the story of this deal with Edgar Percival, something he did with great relish, a wry grin would spread across his face as he told how he remembered nothing of their meeting, until one day when he picked up a letter, along with his morning newspaper, from off the mat. The letter bore a Luton postmark and contained his contract to fly the first Proctor to Rio de Janeiro, whilst the newspaper told its readers that aircraft salesman, Jim Mollison, would be delivering the plane across the South Atlantic alone. There was no way he could duck the deal now, not even if he wanted to!

More than one of his former ATA colleagues told him he needed his head examining, to fly a single-engined aircraft across almost 2,000 miles of ocean. They were not slow to remind him that it was not unknown for a proven aero engine, not even a reliable Gipsy Queen II, to stop firing. They might just as well have saved their breath. He was going anyway.

☆ ☆ ☆

A chilling south-westerly off the Cornish coast combined with the Proctor's prop-wash to blow the last vestiges of sleep out of Mollison's eyes, as he climbed onto the wing of G-AGTA on the morning of 28 January 1946. Only the yellowish spurts of flame from the exhaust and the faint glow of the instrument panel relieved the darkness, as he squeezed himself in alongside the fifty-five gallon petrol tank that had been fitted in the space normally occupied by the co-pilot's seat. Ahead of him lay a 5,700 mile flight alone. How he must have longed for that imaginary button that would transport him back into the warmth of his bed! The journey was to be in four stages. The first from St Mawgan to Rabat in Morocco, a distance of 1,100 miles. And then a 1,600 mile stage from Rabat to Bathurst on the west coast of Africa. Then came the most hazardous part of the journey, the 1,940 mile ocean-crossing to Recife, Pernambuco, before making the final 1,075 miles down to Rio.

The aircraft's normal range of 500 miles had been extended to give it a four-fold increase by the use of additional fuel tanks, one of which was a 45 gallon drop-tank, positioned under the fuselage between the undercarriage. Unlike his earlier pre-war transatlantic crossings, JM now had the benefit of the Decca 'Navigator', an automatic navigational device which had been developed in wartime. Unfortunately, with its reliance upon ground-stations, it only worked over the first two stages of the journey.

In spite of it being Mollison's fourth solo transatlantic flight – a feat unparalleled in the history of aviation at that time – the attempted crossing barely warranted a few lines in Britain's newspapers. Since the war such flights were no longer front-page news, and Mollison's pioneering flights were now barely remembered. The nation's flying heroes were of a younger breed with DFC ribbons on their tunics to prove it. Jim hated it. It was something that he and others with his background found it hard to live with. C. W. A. Scott, Jim's old rival from the England-Australia days of record-breaking, met the same problem. In his case he solved it with a service revolver and a bullet to the head, soon after Jim returned from Brazil. At the time, Charles Scott was working for the UNRRA headquarters in Berlin and had been suffering from a bout of depression, something he usually coped with by turning to drink. In later years aviatrix Sheila Scott suffered similarly, when she could not come to terms with the lack of acknowledgement of her past successes (they included no less than 96 world records). On one occasion, she tried to commit suicide by slashing her wrists. History has shown that obscurity for the once famous is a hard pill to swallow.

Having delivered the Proctor to Rio in pristine condition, Edgar Percival now had every confidence in JM and had no hesitation in employing him to make a similar delivery to India. The Company had landed a lucrative order for twenty-six machines in that country and the first demonstrator was needed for a customer living in Bombay. On 18 April Jim set out from Lympne in G-AHBE, and when he failed to arrive on schedule in Karachi, the world's press reported him as missing. As it transpired he had merely been delayed for two days at Cairo and a further day at Habaniyah, without the Indian authorities being notified. It seemed to be all very reminiscent of his father's behaviour on the sea-voyage to Australia, and in retrospect one wonders if he was simply manipulating the media as he had done in the old days. It certainly gave him more press coverage than the earlier South American delivery had done, albeit it probably caused Edgar Percival a few sleepless nights into the bargain.

During his brief stay in India, he enjoyed the patronage of the Maharajahs of both Gwalior and Bhopal (he even gave the former his first flying lesson) whilst he demonstrated the aircraft. Having completed his assignment for Percival, he decided to take the opportunity to visit Australia and departed as a passenger in one of BOAC's Lancastrians* flying from the UK to Sydney. Mollison always had a soft spot for Australia and its people. It was most probably nostalgia that drew him there, and also the fact that he was more widely acclaimed in that country than in his own. Such was his popularity in Sydney that he was invited to broadcast whilst there, and, like the true

---

*The civilian version of the wartime Lancaster bomber.

Jim Mollison arrives at Bahrein in Percival Proctor, G-AHBE, whilst en route to India in April 1946. It was to be his last long-distance solo flight.

patriot that he was, made the most of the opportunity to plug the British aircraft industry.

In October he paid a brief visit to New Zealand, where Geoff Wells recalls that they spent an evening together in Auckland reminiscing about the old times with ANA. When Jim eventually spoke about Amy's death, he did so with obvious emotion saying, 'If ever a woman earned a permanent place in aviation history, she did.'

Jim Mollison was fully aware in 1946 that the future of air travel lay with the jet-engine, and that Britain held the lead in its development. What he and many others could not understand was the delay in putting aircraft such as the DH Comet 1 into service. Meanwhile, the postwar struggle to capture the world's market for civil airliners was rapidly being exploited by the United States, with derivatives of their successful piston-engined military aircraft. Modern American airliners such as the pressurised Boeing Stratocruiser, Lockheed Constellation and Douglas DC4 (a four-engined version of the well-proven DC3), were soon to dominate the scene. The best that Britain could offer in this field was the giant prototype Bristol Brabazon – a derivative of a proposed wartime 100 ton bomber with a wingspan of 225 feet – and the Saunders-Roe Princess flying boat, and although they were to be built and flown within a few years, sadly, they were never put into service.

☆ ☆ ☆

Although he was only twenty-five years of age, Meindert Kamphuys had already become a successsful businessman in his native Holland by the mid-Thirties. That was, until the cocoa processing factory at Zaandam, which he partly owned and ran under the name of Kamphuys Olie, burnt down. Such fires were not uncommon in an industry which supplied cocoa butter from the raw bean for the manufacture of chocolate, something for which the Dutch were particularly noted. The factory's wooden flooring, well-soaked in cocoa butter fat over the years, had readily ignited from some unknown source and caused a fire which now left only the empty shell of a building.

With the aid of a £10,000 loan from Egbert Bennick, the owner of a Dutch trading company going under the name of HVA, Meindert decided to move across the sea to establish a similar business venture in Hull, England. By May 1935 he had founded, along with colleagues Theodore Sloot, Bennick and others, a factory in Cleveland Street, which was to be eventually known as British Cocoa Mills (Hull) Ltd.

By August 1941 the Hull company and two other firms – Southern Cocoa Mills at Burghfield, near Reading, and Hook Mills, near Basingstoke – whilst still retaining their original names, had merged with Gill & Duffus to become the main supplier of raw material to the UK's chocolate manufacturers. As a result, the Dutchmen became major shareholders in the parent firm, and took temporary residence in the living accommodation for ex-patriate staff that was part of the registered offices in Portland Place, London.

Edward Spice was working as a clerk in Gill & Duffus' London offices soon after the war, and distinctly remembers Meindert Kamphuys coming to Eastcheap during those days. The Dutchman's visits caused something of a stir amongst the office staff, for they were more often than not made in an immaculately restored antique Rolls Royce. Of the man himself, he remembers that 'he usually wore a wide-brimmed trilby and struck me as being a rather dynamic young man. Ebullient, confident and sure of himself without being too cocky, I would say.'[165]

Business interests were interrupted with the outbreak of hostilities and with the fall of Holland in 1940, Meindert joined the exiled Dutch Air force in Britain. By the summer of 1943, he was a fully fledged pilot with the rank of Brevet Captain. Rapid promotion meant that by the time the war was nearing its close, he was the officer in command of the Dutch Communication Flight. As such he was a fairly frequent visitor at White Waltham and it must have been during this period that he met up with Jim Mollison. The two men quickly became good friends and JM was soon a regular visitor to the Kamphuys' luxurious home in Henley-on-Thames, where he met Meindert's wife, Maria, or Mary, as she was known in England.

Mary had that kind of vivacious charm which, allied to a very quick sense of humour, made her a very popular hostess and entertainer amongst her husband's friends. She was not what one would term outstandingly pretty, but she was distinctly attractive, with a warm smile never far from her lips. She was small in stature but hardly what one would describe as petite, being inclined to put on weight rather easily. Those who knew her most intimately describe her as being a highly intelligent woman, an intellectual, and particularly shrewd where business matters were concerned. There was, however, a strongly emotional side to her character, one which she kept carefully concealed from the outside world. When she met Jim Mollison it was a case of her heart ruling her head. She quickly fell for the charm and flattery that was part of his armoury, and was soon caught under his spell, much as Paula, Diana, Amy and Phyllis and many others had been before her.

☆ ☆ ☆

Towards the end of 1946, the directorship of British Cocoa Mills was extending its sphere of influence to include the setting up of an overseas operation. They intended to establish a cocoa-processing plant in Salvador, Bahia, and a factory at Takoradi, in Ghana. As an ex-pilot, Meindert Kamphuys was quick to see the benefit of BCM possessing its own executive aircraft, and he soon persuaded the Directors to purchase two aeroplanes to be based at White Waltham. The outcome was that the company purchased a Percival Proctor for UK and continental flights; and an Airspeed Consul – the civil version of the military Oxford – for longer trips to Africa and South America. The next step was to employ a pilot on a part-time basis, and this is where JM came into the saga. Soon after his return from delivering the Proctor to India, he was offered and accepted the post from BCM. There can be little doubt that Mary was the main attraction to the deal as far as JM was concerned.

Meindert Kamphuys and Theo Sloot visited South America later in the year to establish Joanes Industrial SA, in Salvador, but on this occasion it was by a chartered flight and not in the company's aircraft. How long they were

The Mollisons' residence at 'Lowlands', Hurley, Berkshire.

away is not known, but it appears that the liaison between Jim and Mary rapidly developed into a deep intimate relationship during this period. Upon her husband's return, JM was commissioned to fly the company's Consul to Amsterdam for a New Years Day celebration. On board were Meindert, Mary, Theo and Alice Sloot.

Sometime soon after the Amsterdam trip, Meindert discovered his wife's unfaithfulness, and after some heated discussion they decided to part. In settlement he made her an allowance of £500 a year, and she moved out of the Henley home to purchase a detached house in Hurley, one which she named 'Lowlands' for obvious reasons. Almost at once Jim Mollison moved in with her and they lived together as man and wife. As soon as his marriage foundered, Meindert changed his will, cutting Mary out and naming his younger brother Hans (also working for BCM as a pharmacologist) as the main benificiary.

From hereon a strange twist of events took place, beginning in July 1947 when Meindert decided to visit BCM's new factory at Takoradi in the company's Consul. Obviously his relationship with JM had soured after he found out that he had been cuckolded, and he looked around for another pilot to fly him to Africa. The man he chose was a former ATA Captain, the well-experienced fifty-four year old pilot Ralph Henderson, who happened to be doing some spare time flying at White Waltham. Henderson had been one of the party of twelve who had flown with Jim Mollison on the ATA's Spitfire delivery to Luxeuil in the winter of 1944, and he had a reputation for being a most meticulous and careful pilot. However, for some unknown reason, on the return journey he flew the company's Consul straight into one of the peaks of the Lumbreras mountains in Northern Spain, with Meindert and his younger brother Hans on board. Their bodies were recovered and all three were buried at Bilbao. It was rumoured that the height of the peaks was incorrectly marked on Henderson's flight map.[166] However, if there was ever an accident investigation, either in Spain, or in the UK, it is now no longer traceable. Needless to say it was a lucky escape for JM, because if the affair with Mary had not been discovered before the flight, he might well have been killed along with the two Dutchmen on that fateful day.

If Meindert had meant to make sure that Mary inherited none of his considerable wealth, then he signally failed to do so. It appears that the legal clauses necessary in his will to prevent his wife from inheriting, were not included in the document. With the unforseen death of Hans, coincident with that of Meindert's, it now meant that Mary, who was still the deceased's legal wife, was able to contest the will. At the time it was uncertain whether she would succeed if she pursued her claim through the Dutch courts. However, she had every incentive to do so, for Jim was virtually penniless and she, like him, had been accustomed to a luxurious lifestyle. Now left with only the small allowance given by her late husband, she was living far beneath the standard she had whilst married. Neither was she able to marry JM, for he was still legally married to Phyllis, who was at that time living in Curzon Street, Mayfair.

Jim continued to live with Mary at 'Lowlands' for a period it seems, until in December of that year when he either became restless or their relationship cooled. It was the same old Mollison. Never able to maintain a stable relationship with any woman for long, and having a complete inablity to remain in any one place for any length of time. On 18 December 1947 he arrived unobtrusively in Cape Town to book into the Mount Nelson Hotel. We learn something of his poor financial state at that time, by the fact that he had arrived as one of only four passsengers on board the cargo vessel, *Rochester Castle*.[167]

Jim's mother had by this time formed a warm relationship with Mary Kamphuys, whom she hoped would soon marry her son. Some who knew the old lady rather well, said, perhaps not without some justified cynicism, that she was always fond of people who had money. So maybe she sensed that Mary and the British Cocoa Mills inheritance from Meindert, would soon be in the Mollison family. One rather suspects this from the statement made to the South African press by JM, where he told them that he, and his mother, were co-Directors of a large business concern in England.[168] The comment was surely made more in a sense of anticipation than in any reality.*

There is no doubt that JM had a wonderful capacity where women were concerned to treat them indescribably badly, but still be able to go back to them and continue where he had left off. Charm, sheer gall, call it what one might, it worked. He had proved it with Amy, and even with Phyllis it seems that there was never any subsequent bitterness on her part towards him. None of his women it seems had the strength of will to cast him out completely, or if they did, it was always as a last resort and with the greatest reluctance. Maybe he drew out of them the same mothering instinct that they would have shown to a naughty but repentant offspring.

He returned to Mary at her Hurley home in the summer of 1948, where his log shows that he spent some of his time flying at White Waltham's West London Aero Club. Nothing serious, just one or two flights in the club's Fairchild, but enough to keep sufficient hours logged for the retention of his licence. However, by 16 September Canadian newspapers were reporting the arrival in Montreal of emigrant Jim Mollison on board a TCA airliner. He was, so he told reporters, to take up permanent residence in the country and to seek employment with the Canadian aircraft industry, whilst in his spare time he would pursue a career as a writer.[169] Whether he was serious or not, it is hard to tell, for apart from attending the Brantford Air Show at Toronto two days later, and a meeting of a group of pioneer Canadian airmen at the presentation of the McKee Trophy in Winnipeg early in October, history records little. By mid-November he was back in Britain. No doubt the major enticement for this trip had been the cheap air fare that he gained by filling in the necessary immigrant forms at Ontario House, London, less than a week before his departure. He admitted that a clipping from *Who's Who* appended to the application forms, had speeded things up considerably. Maybe it was just another variant on the old Mollison ploy of simply trading on his name.

☆ ☆ ☆

Mollie Jermey had left her native Norwich in the early 1920s to come to London in order to work for the wife of one of Kenya's ex-High Commissioners. The lady in question employed several women in a shop

---

*An apocryphal story has it that JM's family was related to a firm operating a chain of dry-cleaners under the Mollison name in Scotland, but this is denied by the remaining members of the family.

in Sloane Square, producing high quality hand-knitted garments for her rich clientile. Most of her customers were wealthy Americans, or members of Kenya's Happy Valley set, the majority of whom spent six months wintering in Nairobi and the rest of their time in London.

One evening in December 1948, Mollie Jermey had worked late on a dress, which she then needed to deliver urgently for despatch to New Zealand on the following morning. By the time she was ready to make her way home it was well past midnight, and the last bus along the particular route that would take her to her flat in Hertford Street had long since gone. She walked along the road, turning now and again to look for a taxi, until she came to a taxi rank. Others in a similar plight were waiting in a queue which dwindled until it left just her and one other person – a man. They exchanged small talk, such as, 'Have you far to go?' before deciding to give up on the taxis and walk together in the general direction of their destination.

Mollie's companion suddenly said: 'What's your name?' 'Names don't matter we're only walking to the next bus stop,' she replied. After a few hundred yards, her inquisitive companion said: 'My hotel's just over there. Won't you come in for a coffee?' 'No thank you, I don't go into strange men's rooms at 1.30am.' 'Then can I come home with you?' he enquired. 'No, the same thing applies, I'm afraid.' With that he said: 'Look, my name's Jim. Here's my card. Come and have a drink with me tomorrow. I'm in room number six.' Mollie considered the invitation, paused and said: 'For whom do I ask?' 'Oh, just ask for Jim Mollison.'[170]

And so began a clandestine love affair that was to last for the next eleven years.

To be fair to Mollison, he made no promises of marriage to Mollie. When he did tell her of his impending marriage to Mary he offered to break their relationship, but her attitude was very much a case of her being 'satisfied with the crumbs falling from the rich man's table'. She was infatuated with him. He had the key to her flat and would come and go as he pleased. Whenever he was in town, and most probably when Mary was away on business, he would spend the night with her. It suited Mollie and it suited him. Being six years older than Jim and knowing who he was, she was particularly flattered by their relationship.

According to Mollie Jermey, Mary, who by that time had established the legitimacy of her claim on her late husband's estate, would gain considerable tax advantages by marrying JM and becoming a British citizen. There was one fly in the ointment, Phyllis was reluctant to agree to divorcing JM, but after some financial persuasion by Mary, she consented. As a result, Mary became the third Mrs Mollison on 26 September 1949, when the wedding

Jim and Maria Clasina Kamphuis outside the Maidenhead registry office after their wedding on 26 September 1949.

took place at Maidenhead registry office. The best man was Jim's old friend Tommy Rose, and the other signatory as a witness to the ceremony was Joan Berker, second wife of Leslie Berker, the founder of the highly successful fashion house of *Berkertex*.

Mary's wealth had obviously been bruited about by the time of the wedding, for whilst on their honeymoon in Madeira, their home at 'Lowlands' was burgled. She lost a mink coat, a single string of pearls with a diamond clasp and a diamond pendant totalling over £2,000.[171] In 1949 this was a great deal of money, but knowing Mary's astuteness in financial matters, it is unlikely that she was uninsured.

Those who remember the Mollisons whilst they lived together at 'Lowlands', recall that they led a rather secluded and private existence. Both wanted to avoid the glare of publicity, for the climate of moral opinion was far less tolerant then, than it is today. They would be seen from time to time cycling into Hurley, but Mary, unlike Jim, rarely mixed with the locals. He became a regular visitor, not to the village inns, but to a small pub on the outskirts, where he would spend his time drinking and swapping yarns with the local farm labourers.

On the Saturday prior to the Henley regatta week, the Mollisons would regularly host a large garden party, with open-house for their ex-ATA flying friends based at White Waltham and other nearby aerodromes. Apart from this annual highlight, when Jim could really let himself go, there was little for him to do. Mary had bought him a small cabin-cruiser which he moored at Temple Island and occasionally they would make a trip together to a riverside hotel at Maidenhead for lunch. Other than that, he had no hobbies. It was a stultifying existence for a man who had lived for most of his life with danger as his companion. His wings had been well and truly clipped. Mary kept a tight hold on the purse strings where her husband's spending was concerned, for she knew him well enough to know that given half the chance he would be up and away globe-trotting. It caused a repression to build up inside of him like a poison. In some of his more embittered moments, he would pour his heart out to Mollie, bringing up the fact that Mary had promised him equal shares in her wealth when they married, to which his mistress would reply, 'You should have got that in writing.' On another occasion when she asked him why Mary had not made him a Director of BCM, he replied wistfully, 'Oh, she wouldn't even make me the office boy.'

For the first four years of his marriage he managed to retain his flying licence, and his log shows the occasional flight to Schipol, Jersey and the Isle of Wight, usually in one of the West London Aero Club's aircraft. It was during a visit that he made to the Isle of Wight early in April 1950, in a Fairchild Argus, that former ATA pilot and colleague, Peggy Eveleigh, records her impression of him on that day.

> The last time I saw Jim Mollison was after the war, when, having got a commercial licence and an instructor's endorsement, I was temporarily employed at Ryde airport. I had a drink(s?) with him at the bar there, and he took off having had, I think, too many, and went through the top of a hedge![172]

Stories such as the one above abound, and it is therefore little surprise that his heavy drinking came to the attention of the CAA's medical board, who finally revoked his flying licence at the end of 1953. It was a bitter pill for him to swallow and the agony was doubly compounded when, three years later, he was stopped in his car in Surbiton after making some rather dubious manoeuvres, and charged with dangerous driving. In spite of his solicitor pleading on his behalf that he was only travelling at 15mph, the court banned him from driving for twelve months.

With these two main avenues of freedom now denied to him, boredom and frustration began to engulf him with a vengeance. The only relief he could find was from the gin bottle, and the frequent visits to Hertford Street, where he would unburden himself on Mollie's friendly shoulder. There were several instances when he would arrive at her flat after quarelling with Mary over money matters, or after rows about his heavy drinking, telling Mollie that he had left his wife this time for good. She would calm him down and before the evening was out, urge him not to be so stupid, but to go back home, which he always did after sobering up.

It was during these visits to Mollie's flat that he would just lie on the floor and reminisce or chat. He often spoke about Amy and their times together on the Atlantic and India flights. His mistress always got the impression that whilst he had been fond of his first wife, he had never truly been in love with her. Of Phyllis, she had more first-hand knowledge, for there was one occasion when Jim was in London with Mollie and they happened to run into her, soon after her divorce from Jim. Mollie thought her a very elegant woman, beautifully dressed, handsome, but not particularly pretty. With some ill-concealed jealousy, Mollie described her as 'a social climber and not really Jim's type at all'. He had lived with her for only three months after the wedding before their lifestyles began to clash. He'd stuck it for a bit, but it really wasn't for him and he left her.'

On the day that Mollie first met Phyllis, they shared a taxi together with Jim through London, and it became evident during the ride that Phyllis was in a rather tetchy mood. She casually mentioned that she was on her way to see the dentist because she was having trouble with her plate. Jim immediately teased her good humouredly with, 'Oh Phyllis, and I thought that all those white teeth and flashing bosom were for real. Don't tell me you've deceived me all this time, my dear.' To which she tartly replied: 'Don't be so tiresome Jim.'(173)

Strangely enough, much like his relationship with Amy, the two estranged partners were to remain quite good friends right up until the end. Only two years before his death, Phyllis had written to him from Kenya, where she and her newly wed husband Patrick Kearney were managing a 4,000 acre farm for a large public company. In the letter she scolds him playfully for his meanness in not sending her a wedding present, and asks him if *Playboy of the Air* was still in print, because someone had borrowed her autographed copy and not returned it. After reminding him of the fun they had had on their honeymoon in Cuba and Miami, she ends with the greeting, 'From Your ex No: 2'. It is a telling piece of evidence of the way in which JM could treat all of his women so badly, and yet still remain on affectionate terms with them.

There was a serious side to Mollison however, one which still kept a keen interest in the world of aviation. Surprisingly, he also had a far-sighted

The John Alcock and Arthur Whitten-Brown Memorial between Terminals 2 and 3 at Heathrow Airport.

interest in those branches of science and technology which anticipated the feasibility of manned space flights. In February 1949, he had been invited to attend an informal gathering of scientists at the offices of the British Interplanetary Society in London. One who was privy to that meeting recalls that, '. . . they were discussing the pre-war BIS design and how it could be updated owing to the great developments with liquid propellants which had taken place during the war years with the V2 rocket'.[174] The talks hinged around the possibility of sending three astronauts to the moon, and the technical problems that would need to be solved before it could happen. Newspaper reports at the time stated that JM had met several scientists in Canada, with whom he had discussed the possibility of space travel, and that he was now offering his services as a volunteer on any proposed experimental flight to the moon.

On a more mundane level, JM was also the driving force behind the erection of the memorial to Sir John Alcock and Sir Arthur Whitten-Brown, one which today stands near Terminal 2 of Heathrow's airport. He felt strongly that these two airmen, the first to make a non-stop transatlantic flight in an aeroplane, should have national recognition. Mollison set about the task by instigating a series of letters which began to appear in the columns of the *Times*, agitating for a visible sign of that recognition. And so it was, with the help of Lord Brabazon, that the memorial – the work of William Macmillan, RA – was unveiled by the Minister of Transport and Civil Aviation, A. T. Lennox-Boyd, on 15 June 1954. Ironically, there is very little in the UK today, apart from a few streets being named after him in London, and a plaque on his birthplace, to remind anyone of Mollison's considerable pioneeering achievements in aviation. He seems destined to rest permanently under the shadow of the legendary Amy Johnson.

Just before the Easter of 1956, Jim and Mary flew to Holland to visit some of her relations. It was whilst they were in Amsterdam that a violent quarrel broke out between them. A week later, their relationship had deteriorated to the point where they agreed to separate. Understandably, Mary could take her husband's suicidal drinking habits no longer. She recognised that he was desperately ill, but there was little she, or anyone else for that matter, could do to help him. His wartime service in the ATA had been the moral glue that had held him together. It had given him a purpose to stay dry, something which he now lacked. He was to enter the De-toxification Unit of Bowden House Hospital, at Harrow-on-the-Hill, under Dr. Knapmann, on several occasions, where he was dried out, but he lacked the will to be completely cured. He would stay dry for a while and then with one drink he was 'gone', right back into the snake pit.

One wonders if the sheer recklessness of his drinking was in some way a repetitive cry for help, a sign of his inner loneliness, or even one of self-loathing. Whilst alcoholism was just beginning to be recognised by the medical world as an illness, to the public at large its victims were an object of ridicule. To them he was just a drunk. A pathetic figure. Someone to be mocked and despised.

After their separation, Mary decided that she would arrange for her solicitor to acquire a business for her husband, hoping that this would at least give him some interest in life. And so it was that the Carisbrooke Hotel in Surbiton was purchased and put into Jim's name, with the stipulation that it could never become a licensed premises. In addition, she also made him an allowance of £60 per week. Mollie always said that the pocket-money defeated the object of the the premises being dry, for Jim would merely press a £5 note into the hand of one of the maids, and tell her to nip out and buy him a bottle of Gilbey's.

Jim was able to appoint his own hotel staff at Surbiton, and as a result his mistress became the manageress. According to Mollie, at the time of her appointment Mary knew nothing of their eight year long intimate relationship. She may have suspected it, but if she did know, there was little she could do about it. At no time did she ever visit Jim at the hotel, and on the odd occasion when she did want to discuss their separation, they would meet over a lunch in the Hyde Park Hotel.

Mary had no doubt warned her mother-in-law, Thomasina, of the slide in her son's health, and it was not long after he had been installed in the hotel that his mother decided to visit him. From her angle, the visit was an attempt to straighten out her wayward son by simply talking sense into him. However, Jim saw things quite differently. On his part, he knew that his mother was quite wealthy, and saw her visit as an opportunity to get whatever money was due to him at her death, released now. According to Mollie, she spent the best part of the three weeks that his mother was there, keeping the two of them apart. As far as she could tell, it was case of every time Thomasina saw Jim, she saw red. She didn't see her son at all, she just saw his father, Hector.

Moreover, she took a firm dislike to Mollie. This came out in a letter she wrote to her son soon after her visit. Jim witheld the content of the letter for several months until one day, for some reason or other, he showed it to her. In it, Mollie read a description of herself as 'that frustrated woman of passion who manages your hotel'. Mollie looked up from reading the letter, paused a while, and then said: 'Your mother just doesn't know *you!* No woman would ever be frustrated with you around.' Jim was angry at first, smiled, and then they both burst out laughing.

By 1957 Mollison was having extreme difficulty in walking. The alcohol was poisoning his whole system to such an extent that it was destroying many of the peripheral nerves in his body. It was the first stage of alcoholic neuritis. Even the occasional trips up to London, usually made to meet up with old friends in the bar of the Royal Aero Club, were a pleasure denied him. The best that he could now manage, as a release from the four walls of the hotel, was to be navigated across the Victoria Road on the arm of Mollie, and into the 'Platform Bar' of the *Southampton* pub adjoining Surbiton's station. Locals would nudge one another and say: 'That's Jim Mollison, isn't it? Wasn't he the man who married Amy Johnson?'

A year later, he had a blackout whilst standing at the top of a flight of stairs in the hotel. In the fall, his head struck a row of glass jars that had been left there by one of the maids and he severed an artery. After being rushed to hospital and given blood transfusions, they wanted to notify Mary but he forbad them from doing so. Although he made a recovery and returned home, the doctors warned Mollie that if he continued drinking and not eating, he would be dead within a year. They were to be proved right.

Late in October 1959 he suffered a further blackout and was rushed into the Priory Hospital at Roehampton unconscious. He remained in a coma for

London roads at Enfield, Croydon and Edgware which are named after the aviator.

just over a week, with Mollie by his bedside for most of the time. On the Thursday, the day before he died, she sensed that the end was near, and during the evening telephoned Mary at 'Lowlands', telling her how seriously ill he was and urging her to visit him. Mary however declined, saying that if he specifically asked for her then she would come, otherwise no. At approximately 8am on the morning of the 30th, he went into convulsions and the doctors were called. He was immediately given an injection, but within a few hours he was dead. Although the death certificate merely stated that pneumonia was the cause of death, he had in fact succumbed to alcoholic epilepsy, the severest form of alcoholism.

He was cremated at the Brookwood Cemetery, St John's, Woking in Surrey, on the following Tuesday, when around twenty or so were present to pay their last respects. Mollie was amongst the mourners but neither Mary nor Thomasina were there. It is most likely that his mother, by now in her mid-eighties, was too frail to travel at such short notice.

Obituaries and tributes immediately went out in the *Times* and most of the other national daily newspapers. The one-time transatlantic aviator, John Grierson, was most fulsome in his praise with, 'In history, Jim Mollison must go down as the most courageous and accomplished long-distance flier of his era.' Whilst Sir Alan Cobham commented that, 'He certainly had plenty of courage. He was the most charming man I have ever met. He never did anybody a dirty trick.' His old friend Tommy Rose, one time holder of the England to Cape and return record, was quoted with, 'He may have made a fool of himself in his private life, but he had more guts than the rest of us put together.' The hacks from the tabloid press were equally generous in their way, but didn't pull back from describing his last days in mawkish detail. The shaking hands, the hunched shoulders, the inability to walk unaided, nothing was spared.

A thirty-minute memorial service was held in Christ Church, Mayfair, on Wednesday, 25 November, at which over two hundred people were gathered. Many of his old friends from the aircraft industry and others from the world of aviation were present. They included a large contingent of former ATA members, with eight of their number even managing to dust off and squeeze into their old dark blue uniforms as a sign of respect. Mary sat alongside Jim's mother, whilst in one of the pews discreetly opposite, sat the small trim figure of Mollie Jermey.

In his will, Jim Mollison left the Carisbrooke Hotel, at that time worth approximately £22,000, and all that he possessed to his mistress. Mollie feared that Mary might contest the will, but her suspicions were ill-founded and she never did. His ashes remained in the chapel of remembrance of the funeral-directors for almost eighteen months, long enough for Mollie to know that Mary was not interested in claiming them. Jim had always told his mistress that he would like to be buried in the ocean he had cheated so many times. In the Atlantic. So it was that Mollie travelled to Larne in Northern Ireland, where she chartered a small aeroplane and instructed the pilot to fly across to Galway, on the west coast of Eire. They circled the Clifden memorial, the spot marking where Alcock and Brown's twin-engined Vickers Vimy had touched down after the first Atlantic crossing in June 1919, and flew due west out over the Atlantic. Some seventeen miles from the coast, the tiny plane dipped in salute after she had scattered Jim's ashes out over the ocean.

☆ ☆ ☆

One is entitled to ask just what did Jim Mollison's life achieve? Did his pioneering flights really make all that difference to the development of air travel, particularly that of flying across the North Atlantic?

First let it be said that he was a visionary, inasmuch as he clearly saw that the airspace above the North Atlantic would become, as it has, the busiest and most lucrative of all the world's air routes. However, his most important

The commemorative plaque outside 33 Fotheringay Road, Pollokshields, Glasgow – the aviator's birthplace – was 'unveiled' on 19 April 1993 by the author.

contribution was to demonstrate that if he could fly the Atlantic in a light aircraft without radio, or sophisticated navigational equipment, then it was easily possible for multi-engined airliners to establish regular services across it. He capitalised on what Alcock & Brown, Lindbergh, Post and Earhart had done in the easterly direction, by putting down a vital marker for doing it in the more difficult direction. Of course there was a large element in the challenge of the westerly crossing, in being the first to fly it alone, but he believed passionately that the route would one day provide a commercial, mass air transit system. Air historian, Lesley Fordern, has summed up what Mollison and others pioneers like him achieved, with: 'Undoubtedly the greatest value of record flights over the usual Atlantic and Pacific routes was in the tremendous psychological impetus for others to follow, and in creating public acceptance and attracting investment capital for the airlines which would follow.'[175]

Well might we spare a thought for aviator James Allan Mollison, and others like him, for as we sit back to watch an in-flight movie somewhere over the Atlantic, in the comfort of our modern jet-airliner, we owe them much. These were the men and women who pioneered the air routes of today, and made it all possible for us to enjoy the benefit of modern air travel.

On a more personal note, Hugh Bergel, a former ATA ferry pilot and wartime colleague, had this to say of Jim Mollison:

> He was an infinitely nicer man than seemed possible after all the things that I had read and heard about him. As a man, Jim turned out to be delightful company. He was one of the very few people I have ever met who was completely honest about himself. He had no illusions at all about the way he had carried on and the sort of four-letter person he had been at the height of his notoriety. He became one of the ATA's most disciplined and reliable pilots . . .'[176]

Maybe the subject of this book should be allowed one small paragraph, for he once wrote, no doubt with such an occasion as this in mind: 'Be kind in your judgement of me . . . I am not wholly indifferent to what people think of me. Remember, I am kind to animals, I do not rob blind men, I have an immediate capacity for falling in love, I weep at music that appeals to me and I am indifferent to death.'[177]

Source Notes

In some cases it has not always been possible to trace the original source of an extract from a book or press-cutting, several having been sent to me unmarked. However, wherever possible, due acknowledgement has been given.

1. *Aberdeen & N E Scotland Family History Society Journal* No: 32, Autumn 1989.
2. Telephone interview with Janet Irving, December 1989.
3. Correspondence and telephone interview with Miss Kathleen Griffiths, January 1990.
4. Correspondence and telephone conversation with Mrs Betty Merton (name changed for requested anonymity), November 1989 & January 1990.
5. *Soho* by Judith Summers.
6. *The Age of Illusion* by Ronald Blythe.
7. *First in the Indian Skies* by Norman Franks.
8. *RAF Operations 1918-38* by Chaz Bowyer.
9. *First in the Indian Skies.*
10. *Death Cometh Soon or Late* by James Mollison.
11. *The Flowerdown Link* by Sqdn Ldr L. L. R. Burch.
12. *Playboy of the Air* by James Mollison.
13. *Flight*, 20 December 1957, 'Leaves from a Line Book' by 'Jaysee'.
14. *Tahiti* by David Howarth.
15. *POTA.*
16. *Wing Tips* - Circular No: 10, January 1929, - Australian Aero Club (South Australian Section)
17. *Flying Matilda* by Norman Ellison.
18. Correspondence with Graeme Frost during period, February 1991 - December 1992.
19. *Flying Matilda.*
20. *New York Times News Service*; Eric Weiner, 14 July 1990.
21. *Wingspan*, November 1991, 'The Southern Cross Replica.'
22. Letter from G. U. Allan, August 1990.
23. *The Sky Beyond* by Sir Gordon Taylor.
24. *The Aviators* by William Joy.
25. *Scott's Book* by C. W. A. Scott.
26. Ibid.
27. Letter from G. U. Allan, August 1990.
28. *Beyond the Blue Horizon* by Alexander Frater.
29. *Flying Matilda.*
30. Letter from G. U. Allan, August 1990.
31. *Immortal Era: The Birth of British Civil Aviation* by Lloyd C. Ifould.
32. *Sussex County Herald*, 7 August 1931.
33. *The Aeroplane*, 12 August 1931.
34. *The Story of the British Light Aeroplane* by Terence Boughton.
35. *The Old Bus* by Charles Kingsford Smith.
36. *The Glasgow Herald*, 15 August 1931.
37. *Double Harness* by Lord Drogheda.
38. Ibid.
39. *POTA.*
40. *Soho.*
41. *King Edward V111* by Philip Ziegler.
42. *Edward V111* by Frances Donaldson.
43. *Toronto Star*, 22 June 1937.
44. *The Adelaide Advertiser*, 19 February 1932.
45. *Scott's Book.*
46. *Airman Friday* by William Courtenay.
47. *The Flight of the Mew Gull* by Alex Henshaw.
48. *Sykroads of the World* by Amy Johnson.
49. *The Adelaide Advertiser*, 30 March 1932.
50. Ibid.
51. *SOTW.*
52. *POTA.*
53. *The Adelaide Advertiser*, 29 July 1932.
54. Letter from J. J. McCreadie, March 1990 (Former editor of the *Largs & Millport Weekly News*).
55. *RAF Operations 1918-38.*
56. Correspondence with Dr. Richard K. Smith, July 1990.
57. *Man's Fight to Fly* by J. P. V. Heinmuller.
58. *SOTW.*
59. *POTA.*
60. *The Aeroplane*, 8 June 1932.
61. Telephone interview with Miss Kathleen Griffiths, January 1990.
62. *POTA.*
63. Correspondence with Dr. Richard K. Smith, August 1990.
64. *The Last Hero* by Walter S. Ross.
65. Letter from Douglas Fairbanks, Jnr., dated 30 May 1990.
66. *POTA.*
67. *New York Herald Tribune*, 31 August 1932.
68. *New York Times*, 9 September 1932.
69. Correspondence with Max MacLeod, September 1990; and with Wilfred MacDonald, October 1990.
70. Letter from BBC Written Archives Centre dated 7 August 1990.

71. Telephone interview with James Mollison Steven (cousin of the aviator), 1 September 1989.
72. *Airman Friday.*
73. *Cape Argus,* 19 November 1932.
74. *Amy Johnson* by Constance Babington-Smith.
75. *Airman Friday.*
76. *Amy Johnson.*
77. *The Adelaide Advertiser,* 6 May 1933.
78. *Airman Friday.*
79. *POTA.*
80. *The Adelaide Advertiser,* 9 June 1933.
81. Correspondence with Sir Peter Masefield, August 1990.
82. Newspaper cutting supplied without source.
83. *Aeroplane Monthly,* July 1983, 'The Friendly Dragons' by Adam Smith.
84. Correspondence with Max MacLeod, September 1990.
85. *Aerospace,* February 1990, 'The Tired Pilot.'
86. *Man's Fight to Fly.*
87. *The Lighting Journal,* June 1990; 'Just a Smash at Twilight' by Donna Dawson.
88. Correspondence with Dr. Richard K. Smith, August 1990.
89. *The Sky's the Limit* by Wendy Boase.
90. *SOTW.*
91. Correspondence with George Blanchard, October 1990.
92. *Toronto Daily Star,* 16 September 1933.
93. Correspondence with Dr. Richard K. Smith, July 1990.
94. *Amy Johnson.*
95. *POTA.*
96. Telephone interview with James M. Steven, September 1989.
97. *Straight on Till Morning* by Mary Lovell.
98. *Blue is the Sky* by G. D. 'Flip' Fleming.
99. Air Ministry letter dated 30 June 1934 to H. Perrin of the Royal Aero Club.
100. *Jackie Cochran* by Jacqueline Cochran & Maryann B. Brinley.
101. Ibid.
102. *Sky Fever* by Sir Geoffrey de Havilland.
103. *SOTM.*
104. Ibid.
105. *Airman Friday.*
106. Correspondence with Jeffrey Quill, January 1990.
107. *The Great Air Race* by Arthur Swinson.
108. *Scott's Book.*
109. *The Great Air Race.*
110. Correspondence with Jehangir R. D. Tata, October 1989.
111. Telephone interview with Rex Pearson, January 1990.
112. Ibid.
113. *SOTW.*
114. Rex Pearson, January 1990.
115. Ibid.
116. Letter from JM to Royal Aero Club dated 21 November 1934.
117. Letter from Royal Aero Club to JM dated 26 November 1934.
118. *The Adelaide Advertiser,* 24 January 1935.
119. *White Mischief* by James Fox.
120. *Burbank Airport in the Thirties* by Dean Batchelor.
121. *Bring on the Empty Horses* by David Niven.
122. *Los Angeles Times,* 31 January 1936.
123. *Sydney Morning Herald,* 14 April 1936.
124. *POTA.*
125. *Amy Johnson.*
126. *West Lancashire Evening Gazette,* 12 January 1988 and subsequent telephone conversation with wife of W. H. Davies.
127. Telephone interview with Peter Glenville, November 1990.
128. Correspondence with William Parsons, September 1990.
129. 'The Bellanca Story and More' by Eric 'Jock' Bonar & Freddie Kent; tape-recording made at the Croydon Aiport Society meeting of 18 June 1986.
130. *POTA.*
131. *SOTM.*
132. 'The Bellanca Story and More.'
133. *Aircraft of the Spanish Civil War* by Gerald Howson.
134. Ibid.
135. Ibid.
136. Ibid.
137. Ibid.
138. Interview with Freddie Kent, September 1991.
139. 'Never a Dull Moment' by Peter. Q. Reiss, Lloyd's publication circa. mid-1970s.
140. Telephone conversation with Mrs Hermione Vickery, March 1990.
141. Correspondence with David Hussey, January 1990.
142. Ibid.
143. *The Forgotten Pilots* by Lettice Curtis.
144. *Amy Johnson.*
145. *Into the Blue* by Alexander McKee.

Source Notes

146. Correspondence with Dennis Turberfield, February 1989.
147. *Into the Blue.*
148. Telephone conversation with Richard Powell, September 1991; *Sunday Express*, 28 February 1988.
149. Interview with Ernest. L. Hannam, June 1988.
150. Telephone interview with Stuart V. Tucker, September 1991.
151. Telephone conversation with Joan Hughes, June 1990.
152. Telephone conversation with John Jordan, January 1990.
153. Correspondence with Dr. Richard K. Smith, July 1990.
154. Interview with Stanley Stephenson, November 1989.
155. Telephone interview with J. F. Zollner, December 1989.
156. Telephone conversation with John Woodward, November 1989.
157. Corresponence with Mrs Diana Barnato Walker, March 1990.
158. Joan Hughes, June 1990.
159. Telephone interview with J. A. V. Watson, June 1990.
160. Letter from the Bundesarchiv, June 1990.
161. *Fly and Deliver* by Hugh Bergel.
162. *Brief Glory* by E. C. Cheeseman.
163. Letter from Charles Tutt, January 1990.
164. Interview with Stanley Stephenson, November 1989.
165. Correspondence with Edward J. Spice, June 1990.
166. Telephone conversation with Joan Hughes, June 1990.
167. *Cape Times*, 18 December 1947.
168. Ibid.
169. *Toronto Telegram*, 16 September 1948.
170. Interview with Miss Mollie Jermey, July 1990.
171. *Maidenhead Advertiser*, 7 October 1949.
172. Correspondence with Mrs Peggy Stampfer, October 1991.
173. Mollie Jermey, July 1990.
174. Correspondence with Mr L. J. Carter of the British Interplanetary Society, July 1991.
175. Extract edited by Lesley Fordern - source not known.
176. *Fly and Deliver.*
177. *POTA.*

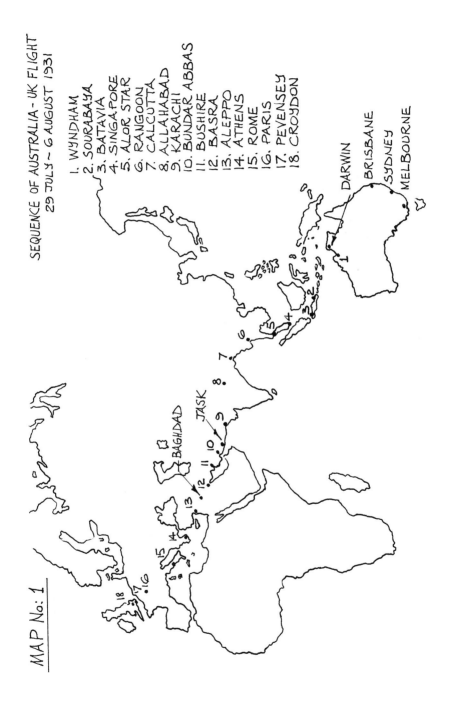

MAP No: 1

SEQUENCE OF AUSTRALIA - UK FLIGHT
29 JULY ~ 6 AUGUST 1931

1. WYNDHAM
2. SOURABAYA
3. BATAVIA
4. SINGAPORE
5. ALOR STAR
6. RANGOON
7. CALCUTTA
8. ALLAHABAD
9. KARACHI
10. BUNDAR ABBAS
11. BUSHIRE
12. BASRA
13. ALEPPO
14. ATHENS
15. ROME
16. PARIS
17. PEVENSEY
18. CROYDON

DARWIN
BRISBANE
SYDNEY
MELBOURNE

BAGHDAD
JASK

MAP No: 2

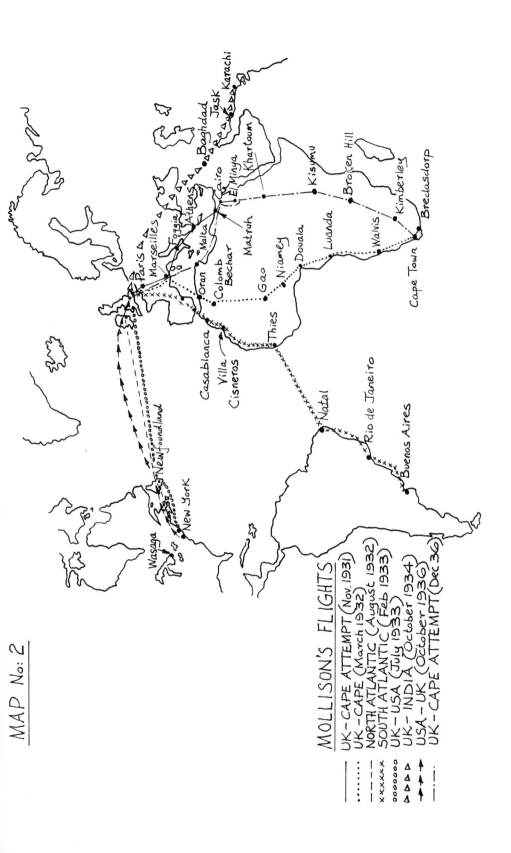

Wasaga

New York

Newfoundland

Paris
Marseilles
Foggia
Athens
Malta
Oran
Casablanca
Villa
Cisneros
Colomb
Bechar
Gao
Niamey
Thies

Baghdad
Jask
Karachi
Cairo
El Minya
Khartoum
Matruh

Dovala
Luanda
Kisymu
Broken Hill
Walvis
Kimberley
Bredasdorp
Cape Town

Natal
Rio de Janeiro
Buenos Aires

MOLLISON'S FLIGHTS

——— UK - CAPE ATTEMPT (Nov. 1931)
·········· UK - CAPE (March 1932)
- - - NORTH ATLANTIC (August 1932)
xxxxx SOUTH ATLANTIC (Feb 1933)
ooooooo UK-USA (July 1933)
△ △ △ UK-INDIA (October 1934)
↑↑↑ USA - UK (October 1936)
-·-·- UK - CAPE ATTEMPT (Dec 36)

Curriculum Vitae

1. Born 19 April 1905.
2. Entered RAF on a five year Short Service Commission, 1923-25.
3. Attempt on the Australia-England record; DH 60G Gipsy Moth, VH-UFT; machine struck telegraph wires on take-off at Darwin; 7 June 1931.
4. Australia-England record; 8 days 19 hours 25 minutes; DH 60G Gipsy Moth, VH-UFT; 29 July – 6 August 1931.
5. Attempt on the England-Cape Town record; DH 60G Gipsy Moth, VH-UFT; machine crashed at El Minya, Egypt, after petrol failure; 14 – 15 November 1931.
6. England-Cape Town record (first trans-Sahara flight to the Cape); 4 days 17 hours 30 minutes; DH 80A Puss Moth, G-ABKG; 24 - 28 March 1932.
7. First westward, non-stop solo flight across the North Atlantic; 30 hours 10 minutes; DH 80A Puss Moth, G-ABXY, 'The Hearts Content'; 18 – 19 August 1932.
8. First westward, non-stop solo flight across the South Atlantic and first flight from UK-South America; 3 days 10 hours 8 minutes (Atlantic crossing time 17 hours 40 minutes); 'The Hearts Content'; 6 – 9 February 1933.
9. Attempt on the world's long-distance record; DH 84 Dragon, G-ACCV, 'Seafarer'; machine's undercarriage collapsed in an attempted take-off at Croydon; 8 June 1933.
10. First flight direct from the UK-USA (co-pilot, Amy J. Mollison); 39 hours; DH 84 Dragon, G-ACCV, 'Seafarer'; 22 – 24 July 1933.
11. Attempt on the world's long-distance record (co-pilot, Amy J. Mollison); DH 84 Dragon, G-ACJM, 'Seafarer 11'; machine's undercarriage damaged in an attempted take-off at Wasaga Beach, Canada; 3 October 1933.
12. England-India record (co-pilot, Amy J. Mollison); 22 hours; DH 88 Comet, G-ACSP, 'Black Magic'; 20 October 1934.
13. First flight from New York-London (via Harbour Grace, Newfoundland); flying time 17 hours (Atlantic crossing time 13 hours 17 minutes; Bellanca Flash 28-70, G-AEPC, 'The Dorothy'; 28 – 30 October 1936.

14. Unofficial record for the England-Cape Town route (co-pilot, Edouard Corniglion-Molinier); 'The Dorothy'; diverted from Wing-field Airport by low cloud whilst within two hours of Amy Johnson's time of 3 days 6 hours 26 minutes. They were forced to land 100 miles to the south-east at Bredasdorp.

15. Transatlantic solo delivery flight in Percival Proctor V, G-AGTA, from St Mawgan to Rio de Janeiro; 28 January – 3 February 1946.

16. Solo delivery flight in Percival Proctor V, G-AHBE, from Luton to Bhopal, India; 18 – 26 April 1946.

17. Died 30 October 1959.

Selected Bibliography

BABINGTON SMITH, Constance, *Amy Johnson*; Patrick Stephens, 1988.

BEEDLE, J., *43 Squadron – The History of the Fighting Cocks*; Beaumont Aviation, 1966.

BENNETT, B., *Down Africa's Skyways*; Hutchinson, 1932.

BERGEL, Hugh, *Fly and Deliver*; Airlife, 1983.

BLYTHE, R., *The Age of Illusion*; Hamish Hamilton.

BOASE, Wendy, *The Sky's the Limit*; Osprey Publg., 1979.

BOWYER, Chaz., *RAF Operations 1918-38*; William Kimber, 1988.

Bristol F2B Fighter; Ian Allan, 1985.

B. A. C.; *Looking Forward 1919-69*; British Aircraft Corpn., 1969.

BURCH, L. L. R., *The Flowerdown Link*; Anglian Wessex Print, 1980.

CHEESEMAN, E. C., *Brief Glory*; Prescott Books.

CLARKE, Basil; *Atlantic Adventure*; Allan Wingate, 1958.

CLUETT, D; NASH, J, & LEARMOUTH, R., *Croydon Airport – The Great Days, 1928-39*; Borough of Sutton Libraries, 1980.

COCHRAN, Jacqueline, & BRINLEY, M. B., *Jackie Cochran*; Bantam Press, 1987.

COURTENAY, William, *Airman Friday*; Hutchinson, 1937.

CURTIS, Lettice, *The Forgotten Pilots*; Foulis, 1971.

de HAVILLAND, Sir Geoffrey, *Sky Fever*; Hamish Hamilton, 1961.

DESMOND, Florence, *Florence Desmond*; Clarke, Irwin, 1953.

DIXON, C., *Amy Johnson – Lone Girl Flyer*; Sampson Low, 1930.

DROGHEDA, Lord, *Double Harness*; Publr., N/K.

DUDGEON, A. G., *The Luck of the Devil*; Airlife, 1985.

ELLIS, E. & F. H., *Atlantic Air Conquest*; Publr., N/K.

ELLISON, Norman, *Flying Matilda*; Angus & Robertson.

FLEMING, G. D. 'Flip', *Blue is the Sky*; William Earl, 1945.

FOX, James, *White Mischief*; Penguin Books, 1984.

FRANKS Norman L. R., *First in the Indian Skies*; Life Publrs., 1981.

FRATER, Alexander, *Beyond the Blue Horizon*; Penguin Books, 1987.

GALLAGHER, D., *Shooting Suns and Things*; Kingford Press, 1986.

HARPER Harry, *Riders of the Sky*; Hodder & Stoughton, 1936. *My 50 Years in Flying*; Associated Newspapers, 1956.

HEINMULLER, J. P. V., *Man's Fight to Fly*; Funk & Wagnalls, 1944.

HMSO, *Atlantic Bridge – An Official Account of RAF Transport Command's Ocean Ferry*; 1945.

HOWARTH, D., *Tahiti*; Harvill Press, 1983.

HOWSON, Gerald, *Aircraft of the Spanish Civil War, 1936-39*; Putnam, 1990.

IFOULD, Lloyd C., *Immortal Era; The Birth of British Civil Aviation*; Adanar Press, Montreal, 1948.

JABLONSKI, E., *Atlantic Fever*; Macmillan, 1972.

JOHNSON, Amy, *Sky Roads of the World*; W & R Chambers, 1939.

JOY, William, *The Aviators*; Shakespeare Head Press.

KINGSFORD SMITH, Charles, *The Old Bus*; Herald Press, 1932.

LOVELL, Mary, *Straight on Till Morning*; Arrow Books, 1988. *Sound of Wings*; Hutchinson, 1989.

McDONOUGH, K., *Atlantic Wings*; Model Aeronautical Press, 1966.

McGEE, Alexander, *Into the Blue*; Publr., N/K.

McVICAR, Don, *Ferry Command*; Airlife, 1981.

MOLLISON, James A., *Death Cometh Soon or Late*; Hutchinson, 1932. *Playboy of the Air*; Michael Joseph, 1937.

NIVEN, David, *Bring on the Empty Horses*; Hamish Hamilton, 1975.

OGILVY, David, *DH 88 – The Story of de Havilland's Racing Comets*; Airlife, 1984.

OLLEY, Gordon, *A Million Miles in the Air*; Hodder & Stoughton, 1934.

Selected Bibliography

PARSONS, William, & BOWMAN, W., *The Challenge of the Atlantic*; Robinson – Blackmore, 1983.

PHELPS, A., *I Couldn't Care Less*; Publr., N/K., 1944.

PUTNAM, George P., *Soaring Wings*; G. C. Harrap (London), 1940.

RICH, Doris L., *Amelia Earhart*; Airlife, 1989.

RICHMAN, Harry, *A Hell of a Life*; Publr., N/K., 1966.

ROBERTSON, W., *History of 20 Squadron*; Private Publn., 1987.

ROWE, Percy, *The Great Atlantic Air Race*; Angus & Robertson, 1977.

SCOTT, Charles, W. A., *Scott's Book*; Hodder & Stoughton, 1934.

SHARP, C. Martin, *DH – A History of de Havilland*; Airlife, 1982.

SILVESTER, J., *Percival & Hunting Aircraft*; Midland Counties.

SUMMERS, J., *Soho*; Bloomsbury Publg., 1989.

SWINSON, A., *The Great Air Race*; Cassell & Co.

TAYLOR, Sir Gordon, *The Sky Beyond*; Cassell & Co., 1963.

TURNER, J. F. *Famous Flights*; Arthur Barker, 1978.

VINCENT, S. F., *Flying Fever*; Jarrolds, 1972.

VOLKERSZ, V., *The Sky and I*; W. H. Allen, 1956.

WATTEVILLE de H., *Waziristan, 1919-20*; Constable, 1925.

WELLS, Geoffrey N., *Head in the Clouds*; Hodder & Stoughton, 1973

WILLIAMS, Gareth, *Sands of Speed*; Christopher Davies, 1973.

WILSDON, Glynis, *The History of a Village Mill*; 1984.

WIXTED, E. P., *Lytton Flight Log*; Queensland Museum, 1989.

ZIEGLER, Philip, *King Edward V111*; Collins, 1990.

Extensive use was made of articles in the following newspapers, magazines and aviation journals;

ADELAIDE ADVERTISER; AUSTRALIAN ARGUS; BRANTFORD EXPOSITOR; CAPE ARGUS; CAPE TIMES; CARMARTHEN JOURNAL; DAILY EXPRESS; DAILY GLEANER; DUBLIN EVENING MAIL; EASTBOURNE CHRONICLE; EDINBURGH EVENING NEWS; FOLKESTONE HERALD; GLASGOW HERALD; HULL TIMES; HULL DAILY MAIL; ILLUSTRATED LONDON NEWS; IRISH TIMES; LEAMINGTON SPA COURIER; LOS ANGELES TIMES; MAIDENHEAD ADVERTISER; NEW YORK TIMES; NORTH BERKS HERALD; SEVENOAKS NEWS; SEVENOAKS CHRONICLE; SUNDAY SUN; SUSSEX COUNTY HERALD; SYDNEY MORNING HERALD; THE TATLER; THE TIMES; TORONTO GLOBE & MAIL; TORONTO DAILY STAR; TORONTO TELEGRAM; WINNIPEG TRIBUNE.

THE AEROPLANE; AEROPLANE MONTHLY; AVIATION IRELAND; CANADIAN AVIATION; CANADIAN AVIATION HISTORICAL SOCIETY'S JOURNAL ('What's in a Name?' by Revd. J. MacGillivray, Winter 1969); FLIGHT; POPULAR FLYING; SPORTSMAN PILOT; WESTERN FLYING; WING TIPS.

ABERDEEN & N. E. SCOTLAND FAMILY HISTORY SOCIETY; ARCHITECTURAL FORUM (Air Transportation Buildings, Terminals and Hangars; December 1930); CITY OF GLENDALE PLANNING DIVISION (Historic Preservation Element, 1977); GLENDALE HISTORICAL SOCIETY (Historic Sites in Glendale, Ca., 1989); NEW AIRTRAILS (Burbank Airport in the Thirties by D. Batchelor; Vol. 1, 1976); JOURNAL OF THE BRITISH PANTOMIME ASSOCN; ROYAL AIRCRAFT ESTABLISHMENT REPORTS.

Acknowledgements

The reader will no doubt be aware that a book such as this could never have been written without the help and co-operation from a multitude of people. Apart from Jim Mollison's memoirs, *Death Cometh Soon or Late*, and its later unexpurgated version, *Playboy of the Air*, upon which I have been forced to draw heavily, the aviator rarely put pen to paper. This has meant an extensive research period in order to obtain first-hand accounts from those who knew the man. I am deeply indebted to these people. Not only were they extremely helpful, but more often than not they went the second mile when I was obliged to go back to them on more than one occasion. My sincere thanks go to the following people and organisations:

Australia:
George 'Scotty' Allan; Corinne Collins (National Library of Australia); Grame Frost; David W. Gardner (RAAF Museum, Point Cook); Jenny Houghton; Charles Kingsford-Smith; Barbara Mayfield (The Mortlock Library of South Australiana); Graeme Powell (National Library of Australia); Greg Turner; John Ulm; Lexie Steel (Mitchell Library, Sydney); Nancy-Bird Walton, OBE; E. P. 'Ted' Wixted (Queensland Museum). The Australian Broadcasting Corporation and the Australian High Commission, London.

Canada:
George Blanchard; Bill Duck; John A. Garratt; Fred Hotson; T. R. Judge; Wilfrid MacDonald; Max MacLeod; Tom McGrath; Sybil Ogg; Douglas Ogle; William Parsons; Harry Proctor; Frank G. Warren; The Canadian Aviation Historical Society; National Science Library, Ottawa.

Great Britain:
A very special thanks must go to James Mollison Steven and Miss Kathleen Griffiths for covering certain aspects of the early period of the aviator's life; and to Miss Mollie Jermey who was Jim Mollison's ever faithful friend right up until the end of his life.
Peter Amos; William P. Anderson; Diana Barnato Walker, MBE; K. F. Bartlett; Marjorie Baxendale; Raymond Baxter; Norman Beech; Dr. G. Bennett; Edna Bianchi; Malcolm Bonar; Chaz. Bowyer; Dr. G. H. Bullmore; Charlie Chester; Michael J. Cobham; David G. Collyer; Lettice Curtis; Alan Davis; Peter Day; John P. Fielder; Elaine Finney; G. D. 'Flip' Fleming; Mona Forward; David George; Peter Glenville; Alan Hartley; Alex Henshaw; David J. Horner; Air Vice-Marshall P. Howard RAF (Ret'd); Joan Hughes; Ken Hunter and Gordon Leith of the Royal Air Force Museum; David Hussey; Philip Jarrett; Hugh Johnson; Nance

Acknowledgements

Johnstone; W. A. 'John' Jordan; Ewan G. Kennedy; Freddie Kent; Michael Kilgariff; John King; Mary S. Lovell; Maggie Macdonald; M. V. 'Mike' Marshall; Sir Peter Masefield; J. J. McCreadie; Robin McSkimming; Alan Mills; William Mollison; William Murray; Bert Nash; Ian Nicolson; Dr. Patrick J. O'Connor; Sheila Ogilvie; Ron Paine; Rex Pearson; Royston Powell; R. V. Primmer; Air Commodore H. A. Probert; Jeffrey Quill; J. A. Reiss; Frank Salt; Hugh Scanlan; Daniel Sharpe; Frank Soul; Edward J. Spice; Peggy Stampfer; G. A. Statham; Stevie Stephenson; Laurence Tait; R. R. T. Thomas; Steve Turnbull; C. Tutt; Hermione Vickery; Eric J. Viles, MBE; J. A. V. Watson; Dr. T. H. N. Whitehurst, OBE; R. P. 'Tim' Williams; Glynis Wilsdon; John F. Zollner.

Libraries:
A very special thanks to the dedicated staff at my local library, St. Annes-on-Sea; also to Brighton Central; Bury St. Edmunds; Canterbury; Cardiff Central; Carmarthen; Eastbourne Central; Edinburgh Central; Glasgow (Mitchell); Gravesend; Humberside; Leamington Spa; Leeds; Llandudno; Lytham; Maidenhead; Northampton Central; Oxford; Ramsgate; Rhyl; Southampton Central; Sutton Central; Winchester.

Air Accidents Investigation Branch; British Broadcasting Corporation; British Interplanetary Society; Civil Aviation Authority; Edinburgh Academy; Glasgow Academy; Planning Department, City of Glasgow; Inverclyde District Council; Kingston Heritage, Surrey; Scottish Tartan Society and the Suffolk Record Office.

Holland:
One of my most dogged helpers has been Major General D. L. Asjes, RMWO, ex-Royal Netherlands Air Force – thank you Dick for being so patient with me.
Jan Van Der Zeijden; Bevolkingsregister, Amsterdam; Royal Netherlands Aeronautical Association; Royal Netherlands Air Force Historical Branch;

South Africa:
Peter Bagshawe; Pam Barnes; A. Fanarof (Cape Town Library); John H. Hermann; Patsy Stephenson; Victor Smith; Johannesburg Public Library and the Natal Society.
USA:
A special word of thanks is due to Verville Fellow, Dr. Richard K. Smith,

Acknowledgements

who has been so generous in supplying research material, and who has been such an encouragement to me.

Richard S. Allen; Robert Factor; Douglas Fairbanks, Jnr.; Ken Freedman; Dr. Raymond E. Jankowich; Barbara Karpinski; Harvey H. Lippincott; Gerald Robinson; Mike Speciale; Robert H. Stepanek;

American Aviation Historical Society; Beech Aircraft Corporation; Burbank, Glendale, Pasadena Airport Authority; Bridgeport Public Library; Florida Aviation Historical Society; Margaret Herrick Library; New England Air Museum; Los Angeles Central Library, and the New York Public Library.

Elsewhere:
Greta S. Morris of Jamaica; David Sharpe and Geoff Wells of New Zealand; Jehangir R. D. Tata of Bombay; Archivo General del Aire, Madrid; Bundesarchiv; National Library of Jamaica;

Extract Rights:
Permission has been given from the following:
Airman Friday – Hutchinson; *Blue is the Sky* – G. D. 'Flip' Fleming; *First in the Indian Skies* – Norman L. R. Franks; *Fly and Deliver* – Airlife; *Flying Matilda* – Angus & Robertson; *Immortal Era* – London Borough of Sutton Libraries & Arts Services; *Pinks Poem* – Chaz. Bowyer; *Playboy of the Air* – Miss Mollie Jermey (sole beneficiary of the James A. Mollison estate); *RAF Operations, 1918-38* – Chaz. Bowyer; *Scott's Book* – Hodder & Stoughton; *The Sky Beyond* – Macmillan Publishing Company; *Straight on Till Morning* – Hutchinson & Mary S. Lovell;

Illustrations:
John Adkings, p. 313; G. U. Allan p. 85 bottom left: Richard S.Allen, p. 216 top; Blackpool Evening Gazette, p. 282; Chaz. Bowyer, p. 40 British Library p. 308; David G. Collyer, pp. 155 & 360; Croydon Airport Society Archives, p. 206; Alan Davis (The Squadron, North Weald), p. 277; Alan Davis, p. 363; Kareen Diniz, p. 370 ; Glasgow District Council, p. 375; Glasgow Herald, pp. 141, 159, 161, 323, 328, 367 & rear cover; Miss Kathleen Griffiths, p. 14 top & bottom; Alan Hartley, p. 271; Hawker Siddeley via Chaz. Bowyer, p. 350; Fred Hotson, pp. 176 & 342; Philip Jarrett, pp. 248, 347 & front cover;; Hugh Johnson, p. 286; Gerald Lambert via Suffolk Record Office (Bury St. Edmunds Branch), p. 253; Harvey H. Lippincott, pp. 216 bottom & 296; Mary Lovell, p. 234; Max MacLeod,

Acknowledgements

p. 237; Peter Maurice Music Ltd., p. 193; Alan Mills, p. 94; Sybil Ogg, p. 179; J. A. Reiss, p. 326; RAF Museum, p. 4; Shell Archive Photo via Hugh Scanlan, p. 227; Sporting Pilot, Inc., frontispiece; State Library of New South Wales (General Reference Library), p. 90: James Mollison Steven, p. 9; Sutton Libraries & Arts Services, p. 305; Times Newspapers Ltd., pp. 204 & 256; Greg Turner from the collection of the late George Robert Turner, p. 107; Mrs Hermione Vickery, p. 330; Geoffrey Wells, p. 262; R. P. 'Tim' Williams, p. 139; Edward Wixted of the Queensland Museum, p. 85 top right, top left & bottom right.

Every effort has been made to trace the sources of extracts and illustrations used throughout this book. However, apologies are given if there has been any infringement of rights.

Index

Index

Index

Index

Index

Index

Index

Index

Index